W9-CXL-109

Dog Tales

Dog Tales

*Timeless and Compelling Stories about Man's
and Woman's Best Friend and Companion*

Edited and with an Introduction
by Lamar Underwood

LP

**LYONS
PRESS**

Essex, Connecticut

An imprint of Globe Pequot, the trade division of
The Rowman & Littlefield Publishing Group, Inc.
4501 Forbes Blvd., Ste. 200
Lanham, MD 20706
www.rowman.com

Distributed by NATIONAL BOOK NETWORK

British Library Cataloguing in Publication Information available

Library of Congress Cataloging-in-Publication Data
Names: Underwood, Lamar, editor.
Title: Dog tales : timeless and compelling stories about man's and woman's best
    friend and companion / Lamar Underwood.
Description: Essex, Connecticut : Lyons Press, [2023]
Identifiers: LCCN 2022017633 (print) | LCCN 2022017634 (ebook) |
    ISBN 9781493066988 (cloth) | ISBN 9781493066995 (epub)
Subjects: LCSH: Dogs. | Dogs—Anecdotes.
Classification: LCC SF426.2 .D6462 2023 (print) | LCC SF426.2 (ebook) |
    DDC 636.7—dc23/eng/20220601
LC record available at https://lccn.loc.gov/2022017633
LC ebook record available at https://lccn.loc.gov/2022017634

♾️™ The paper used in this publication meets the minimum requirements of American
National Standard for Information Sciences—Permanence of Paper for Printed Library
Materials, ANSI/NISO Z39.48-1992.

CONTENTS

Introduction

by Lamar Underwood

LIKE COUNTLESS OTHERS, I AM A WOUNDED DOG LOVER.

Crumpet, a pug, a miracle gift to our family and with us for fifteen years, is gone. My wife and two daughters have emerged from the heartbreak of our pet's passing with an awareness of loss that I doubt will ever be completely extinguished by the passing years. The tiny bundle of energy and affection that leaped into our laps rather than lie on the floor lives only in memory now.

As a professional editor and writer, I am not unusual in creating a large personal library. Dog novels and stories are well represented there. I never seem to tire of them. And I can tell you why.

I keep looking for expressions of the same love and joy dogs have given me over the years. No, the dogs and their owners in print do not send my heartbeat and emotions soaring, as Crumpet once did. But they often awaken old and valuable feelings I treasure and always will. Dogs do that to us. And sometimes, when the prose is good enough and the story has drama, the pages I am reading become close friends.

As I mentioned in my introduction to another Globe Pequot book, *Hunting Dog Stories*, most of my dog ownership experiences have come from two pointers and a springer spaniel. Hunting dogs can become proper family pets given the right handling, as Tom Hennessey points out in these pages in the story "Homebodies." Alas, while I have found that to be true in many respects, for sheer affection and delight my years with a pug cannot be equaled by life with my hunting companions.

There is a great movie expression from films about spies and war when the heavily accented official demands, "Show me your papers." Compared to my other dogs, pug Crumpet's pedigree suggested canine royalty. She was very expensive, even some time ago. I never regretted a single cent.

Dog stories in a book such as this suggest tales cuddly and warm. We have plenty of those, but in these pages you'll also find hard-headed rascals and underachievers. Some with "papers," some without. Whether breeding or training is the fault, some dogs just don't get the message.

A good friend who once worked at the J. Walter Thompson advertising agency in New York told me one of the copywriters there had a sign in his office that read: "It's not what you said that counts. It's what they heard!" The late Dick Wolters of dog-training-book fame was a strong advocate of that concept. In his many books on retrievers, family pets, and others, he goes to great lengths with photographs and text to advance a "show-and-tell" idea in dog training. To Dick, it's all about the dog getting the message. The right message!

To an editor like myself, launching an anthology like this makes me feel like I do when I push a canoe or small boat into a river with a friend aboard. I can only stand and watch as the current takes you downstream, out of sight—through whatever awaits you there. I have tried to give you a good idea of what to expect. But there will be some surprises, perhaps even some disappointments.

As one reader and dog lover to another, I hope your journey will be pleasant and memorable.

Editor's note: You'll find in this volume some story selections and introductions previously made by Nancy Butler in her book Great American Dog Stories *(Lyons Press, 2020). Some of the story introductions are also by Nancy.*

The Power of the Dog

by Rudyard Kipling

The novels, short stories, and poems of Rudyard Kipling fill many, many volumes of literature. Sometimes lost in the mix is this powerful statement attesting to his love of dogs.

There is sorrow enough in the natural way
From men and women to fill our day;
But when we are certain of sorrow in store,
Why do we always arrange for more?
*Brothers and sisters, I bid you beware
Of giving your heart to a dog to tear.*

Buy a pup and your money will buy
Love unflinching that cannot lie—
Perfect passion and worship fed
By a kick in the ribs or a pat on the head.
*Nevertheless it is hardly fair
To risk your heart for a dog to tear.*

When the fourteen years which Nature permits
Are closing in asthma, or tumour, or fits,
And the vet's unspoken prescription runs
To lethal chambers or loaded guns,
*Then you will find—it's your own affair—
But . . . you've given your heart to a dog to tear.*

When the body that lived at your single will,
When the whimper of welcome is stilled (how still!),
When the spirit that answered your every mood
Is gone—wherever it goes—for good,
You will discover how much you care,
And will give your heart to a dog to tear!

We've sorrow enough in the natural way,
When it comes to burying Christian clay.
Our loves are not given, but only lent,
At compound interest of cent per cent.
Though it is not always the case, I believe,
That the longer we've kept 'em, the more do we grieve:
For, when debts are payable, right or wrong,
A short-time loan is as bad as a long—
So why in Heaven (before we are there!)
Should we give our hearts to a dog to tear?

Lad—A Dog

by Albert Payson Terhune

Albert Payson Terhune was an American author, dog breeder, and journalist. He was popular for his novels relating the adventures of his beloved collies and as a breeder of collies at his Sunnybank Kennels. His novel Lad: A Dog *is a wonderful statement of his collie love. This excerpt begins where that book ends, in the last chapter.*

FOR MORE YEARS THAN HE COULD REMEMBER, LAD HAD BEEN KING. HE had ruled at The Place, from boundary-fence to boundary-fence, from highway to Lake. He had had, as subjects, many a thoroughbred collie; and many a lesser animal and bird among the Little Folk of The Place. His rule of them all had been lofty and beneficent.

The other dogs at The Place recognized Lad's rulership—recognized it without demur. It would no more have occurred to any of them, for example, to pass in or out through a doorway ahead of Lad than it would occur to a courtier to shoulder his way into the throne-room ahead of his sovereign. Nor would one of them intrude on the "cave" under the living-room piano which for more than a decade had been Lad's favorite resting-place.

Great was Lad. And now he was old—very old.

He was thirteen—which is equivalent to the human age of seventy. His long, clean lines had become blurred with flesh. He was undeniably stout. When he ran fast, he rolled slightly in his stride. Nor could he run as rapidly or as long as of yore. While he was not wheezy or asthmatic, yet a brisk five-mile walk would make him strangely anxious for an hour's rest.

He would not confess, even to himself, that age was beginning to hamper him so cruelly. And he sought to do all the things he had once done—if the Mistress or the Master were looking. But when he was alone, or with the other dogs, he spared himself every needless step. And he slept a great deal.

Withal, Lad's was a hale old age. His spirit and his almost uncanny intelligence had not faltered. Save for the silvered muzzle—first outward sign of age in a dog—his face and head were as classically young as ever. So were the absurdly small fore-paws—his one gross vanity—on which he spent hours of care each day, to keep them clean and snowy.

He would still dash out of the house as of old—with the wild trumpeting bark which he reserved as greeting to his two deities alone—when the Mistress or the Master returned home after an absence. He would still frisk excitedly around either of them at hint of a romp. But the exertion was an exertion. And despite Lad's valiant efforts at youthfulness, everyone could see it was.

No longer did he lead the other dogs in their headlong rushes through the forest in quest of rabbits. Since he could not now keep the pace, he let the others go on these breath-and-strength-taking excursions without him; and he contented himself with an occasional lone and stately walk through the woods where once he had led the run—strolling along in leisurely fashion, with the benign dignity of some plump and ruddy old squire inspecting his estate.

There had been many dogs at The Place during the thirteen years of Lad's reign—dogs of all sorts and conditions, including Lad's worshipped collie mate, the dainty gold-and-white "Lady." But in this later day there were but three dogs beside himself.

One of them was Wolf, the only surviving son of Lad and Lady—a slender, powerful young collie, with some of his sire's brain and much of his mother's appealing grace—an ideal play-dog. Between Lad and Wolf there had always been a bond of warmest affection. Lad had trained this son of his and had taught him all he knew. He unbent from his lofty dignity with Wolf as with none of the others.

The second of the remaining dogs was Bruce ("Sunnybank Goldsmith"), tawny as Lad himself, descendant of eleven international champions and winner of many a ribbon and medal and cup. Bruce was—and is—flawless in physical perfection and in obedience and intelligence.

The third was Rex—a giant, a freak, a dog oddly out of place among a group of thoroughbreds. On his father's side Rex was pure collie; on his mother's, pure bull-terrier. That is an accidental blending of two breeds which cannot blend. He looked more like a fawn-colored Great Dane than anything else. He was short-haired, full two inches taller and ten pounds heavier than Lad, and had the bunch-muscled jaws of a killer.

There was not an outlander dog for two miles in either direction that Rex had not at one time or another met and vanquished. The bull-terrier strain, which blended so ill with collie blood, made its possessor a terrific fighter. He was swift as a deer, strong as a puma.

In many ways he was a lovable and affectionate pet; slavishly devoted to the Master and grievously jealous of the latter's love for Lad. Rex was five years old—in his fullest prime—and, like the rest, he had ever taken Lad's rulership for granted.

I have written at perhaps prosy length, introducing these characters of my war-story. The rest is action.

March, that last year, was a month of drearily recurrent snows. In the forests beyond The Place, the snow lay light and fluffy at a depth of sixteen inches.

On a snowy, blowy, bitter cold Sunday—one of those days nobody wants—Rex and Wolf elected to go rabbit-hunting.

Bruce was not in the hunt, sensibly preferring to lie in front of the living-room fire on so vile a day rather than to flounder through dust-fine drifts in search of game that was not worth chasing under such conditions. Wolf, too, was monstrous comfortable on the old fur rug by the fire, at the Mistress' feet.

But Rex, who had waxed oddly restless of late, was bored by the indoor afternoon. The Mistress was reading; the Master was asleep. There seemed no chance that either would go for a walk or otherwise amuse their four-footed friends. The winter forests were calling. The powerful crossbred dog would find the snow a scant obstacle to his hunting. And the warmly quivering body of a new-caught rabbit was a tremendous lure.

Rex got to his feet, slouched across the living-room to Bruce and touched his nose. The drowsing collie paid no heed. Next Rex moved over to where Wolf lay. The two dogs' noses touched.

Now, this is no *Mowgli* tale, but a true narrative. I do not pretend to say whether or not dogs have a language of their own. (Personally, I think they have, and a very comprehensive one, too. But I cannot prove it.) No dog-student, however, will deny that two dogs communicate their wishes to each other in some way by (or during) the swift contact of noses.

By that touch Wolf understood Rex's hint to join in the foray. Wolf was not yet four years old—at an age when excitement still outweighs lazy comfort. Moreover, he admired and aped Rex, as much as ever the school's littlest boy models himself on the class bully. He was up at once and ready to start.

A maid was bringing in an armful of wood from the veranda. The two dogs slipped out through the half-open door. As they went, Wolf cast a sidelong glance at Lad, who was snoozing under the piano. Lad noted the careless invitation. He also noted that Wolf did not hesitate when his father refused to join the outing but trotted gayly off in Rex's wake.

Perhaps this defection hurt Lad's abnormally sensitive feelings. For of old he had always led such forest-runnings. Perhaps the two dogs' departure merely woke in him the memory of the chase's joys and stirred a longing for the snow-clogged woods.

For a minute or two the big living-room was quiet, except for the scratch of dry snow against the panes, the slow breathing of Bruce and the turning of a page in the book the Mistress was reading. Then Lad got up heavily and walked forth from his piano-cave.

He stretched himself and crossed to the Mistress' chair. There he sat down on the rug very close beside her and laid one of his ridiculously tiny white fore-paws in her lap. Absent-mindedly, still absorbed in her book, she put out a hand and patted the soft fur of his ruff and ears.

Often, Lad came to her or to the Master for some such caress; and, receiving it, would return to his resting-place. But to-day he was seeking to attract her notice for something much more important. It had occurred to him that it would be jolly to go with her for a tramp in the snow. And his mere presence failing to convey the hint, he began to "talk."

To the Mistress and the Master alone did Lad condescend to "talk"— and then only in moments of stress or appeal. No one hearing him at such a time could doubt the dog was trying to frame human speech. His vocal efforts ran the gamut of the entire scale. Wordless, but decidedly eloquent, this "talking" would continue sometimes for several minutes without ceasing; its tones carried whatever emotion the old dog sought to convey—whether of joy, of grief, of request, or of complaint.

To-day there was merely playful entreaty in the speechless "speech." The Mistress looked up.

"What is it, Laddie?" she asked. "What do you want?"

For answer Lad glanced at the door, then at the Mistress; then he solemnly went out into the hall—whence presently he returned with one of her fur gloves in his mouth.

"No, no," she laughed. "Not to-day, Lad. Not in this storm. We'll take a good, long walk to-morrow."

The dog sighed and returned sadly to his lair beneath the piano. But the vision of the forests was evidently hard to erase from his mind. And a little later, when the front door was open again by one of the servants, he stalked out.

The snow was driving hard, and there was a sting in it. The thermometer was little above zero; but the snow had been a familiar bedfellow for centuries to Lad's Scottish forefathers; and the cold was harmless against the woven thickness of his tawny coat. Picking his way in stately fashion along the ill-broken track of the driveway, he strolled toward the woods. To humans there was nothing in the outdoor day but snow and chill and bluster and bitter loneliness. To the trained eye and the miraculous scent-power of a collie it contained a million things of dramatic interest.

Here a rabbit had crossed the trail—not with leisurely bounds or mincing hops, but stomach to earth, in flight for very life. Here, close at the terrified bunny's heels, had darted a red fox. Yonder, where the piling snow covered a swirl of tracks, the chase had ended.

The little ridge of snow-heaped furrow, to the right, held a basketful of cowering quail—who heard Lad's slow step and did not reckon on his flawless gift of smell. On the hemlock tree just ahead a hawk had lately torn a blue-jay asunder. A fluff of gray feathers still stuck to a bough, and the scent of blood had not been blown out of the air. Underneath, a field-mouse was plowing its way into the frozen earth, its tiny paw-scrapes wholly audible to the ears of the dog above it.

Here, through the stark and drifted undergrowth, Rex and Wolf had recently swept along in pursuit of a half-grown rabbit. Even a human eye could not have missed their partly-covered tracks; but Lad knew whose track was whose and which dog had been in the lead.

Yes, to humans, the forest would have seemed a deserted white waste. Lad knew it was thick-populated with the Little People of the woodland, and that all day and all night the seemingly empty and placid groves were a blend of battlefield, slaughterhouse and restaurant. Here, as much as in the cities or in the trenches, abode strenuous life, violent death, struggle, greed and terror.

A partridge rocketed upward through a clump of evergreen, while a weasel, jaws a-quiver, glared after it, baffled. A shaggy owl crouched at a tree-limb hole and blinked sulkily about in search of prey and in hope of dusk. A crow, its black feet red with a slain snowbird's blood, flapped clumsily overhead. A poet would have vowed that the still and white-shrouded wilderness was a shrine sacred to solitude and severe peace. Lad could have told him better. Nature (beneath the surface) is never solitary and never at peace.

When a dog is very old and very heavy and a little unwieldy, it is hard to walk through sixteen-inch snow, even if one moves slowly and sedately. Hence Lad was well pleased to come upon a narrow wood-land track, made by a laborer who had passed and repassed through that same strip of forest during the last few hours. To follow in that trampled rut made walking much easier; it was a rut barely wide enough for one wayfarer.

More and more like an elderly squire patrolling his acres, Lad rambled along, and presently his ears and his nose told him that his two loving friends Rex and Wolf were coming toward him on their homebound way. His plumy tail wagged expectantly. He was growing a bit lonely on this Sunday afternoon walk of his, and a little tired. It would be a pleasure to have company—especially Wolf's.

Rex and Wolf had fared ill on their hunt. They had put up two rabbits. One had doubled and completely escaped them; and in the chase Rex had cut his foot nastily on a strip of unseen barbed wire. The sand-like snow had gotten into the jagged cut in a most irritating way.

The second rabbit had dived under a log. Rex had thrust his head fiercely through a snowbank in quest of the vanished prey; and a long briar-thorn, hidden there, had plunged its needle point deep into the inside of his left nostril. The inner nostril is a hundred-fold the most agonizingly sensitive part of a dog's body, and the pain wrung a yell of rage and hurt from the big dog.

With a nostril and a foot both hurt, there was no more fun in hunting, and—angry, cross, savagely in pain—Rex loped homeward, Wolf pattering along behind him. Like Lad, they came upon the laborer's trampled path and took advantage of the easier going.

Thus it was, at a turn in the track, that they came face-to-face with Lad. Wolf had already smelled him, and his brush began to quiver in welcome. Rex, his nose in anguish, could smell nothing; not until that turn did he know of Lad's presence. He halted, sulky, and ill-tempered. The queer restlessness, the pre-springtime savagery that had obsessed him of late had been brought to a head by his hurts. He was not himself. His mind was sick.

There was not room for two large dogs to pass each other in that narrow trail. One or the other must flounder out into the deep snow to the side. Ordinarily, there would be no question about any other dog on The Place turning out for Lad. It would have been a matter of course, and so, today, Lad expected it to be. Onward he moved, at that same dignified walk, until he was not a yard away from Rex.

The latter, his brain fevered and his hurts torturing him, suddenly flamed into rebellion. Even as a younger buck sooner or later assails for mastery the leader of the herd, so the brain-sick Rex went back, all at once, to primal instincts, a maniac rage mastered him—the rage of the angry underling, the primitive lust for mastery.

With not so much as a growl or warning, he launched himself upon Lad. Straight at the tired old dog's throat he flew. Lad, all unprepared for such unheard-of mutiny, was caught clean off his guard. He had not even time enough to lower his head to protect his throat or to rear and meet his erstwhile subject's attack halfway. At one moment he had been plodding gravely toward his two supposedly loyal friends; the next, Rex's ninety pounds of whale-bone muscle had smitten him violently to earth, and Rex's fearsome jaws—capable of cracking a beef-bone as a man cracks a filbert—had found a vise-grip in the soft fur of his throat.

Down amid a flurry of high-tossed snow, crashed Lad, his snarling enemy upon him, pinning him to the ground, the huge jaws tearing and rending at his ruff—the silken ruff that the Mistress daily combed with such loving care to keep it fluffy and beautiful.

It was a grip and a leverage that would have made the average opponent helpless. With a short-haired dog it would have meant the end, but the providence that gave collies a mattress of fur—to stave off the cold in their herding work amid the snowy moors—has made that fur thickest about the lower neck.

Rex had struck in crazy rage and had not gauged his mark as truly as though he had been cooler. He had missed the jugular and found himself grinding at an enormous mouthful of matted hair—and at very little else; and Lad belonged to the breed that is never to be taken wholly by surprise and that acts by the swiftest instinct or reason known to dogdom. Even as he fell, he instinctively threw his body sideways to avoid the full jar of Rex's impact—and gathered his feet under him.

With a heave that wrenched his every unaccustomed muscle, Lad shook off the living weight and scrambled upright. To prevent this, Rex threw his entire body forward to reinforce his throat-grip. As a result, a double handful of ruff-hair and a patch of skin came away in his jaws. And Lad was free.

He was free—to turn tail and run for his life from the unequal combat—and that his hero-heart would not let him do. He was free, also, to stand his ground and fight there in the snowbound forest until he should be slain by his younger and larger and stronger foe, and this folly his almost-human intelligence would not permit.

There was one chance and only one—one compromise alone between sanity and honor. And this chance Lad took.

He *would* not run. He *could* not save his life by fighting where he stood. His only hope was to keep his face to his enemy, battling as best he could, and all the time keep backing toward home. If he could last until he came within sight or sound of the folk at the house, he knew he would be saved. Home was a full half-mile away and the snow was almost chest-deep. Yet, on the instant, he laid out his plan of campaign and put it into action.

Rex cleared his mouth of the impeding hair and flew at Lad once more—before the old dog had fairly gotten to his feet, but not before the line of defense had been thought out. Lad half wheeled, dodging the snapping jaws by an inch and taking the impact of the charge on his left shoulder, at the same time burying his teeth in the right side of Rex's face.

At the same time Lad gave ground, moving backward three or four yards, helped along by the impetus of his opponent. Home was a half-mile behind him, in an oblique line, and he could not turn to gauge his direction. Yet he moved in precisely the correct angle.

(Indeed, a passer-by who witnessed the fight, and the Master, who went carefully over the ground afterward, proved that at no point in the battle did Lad swerve or mistake his exact direction. Yet not once could he have been able to look around to judge it, and his foot-prints showed that not once had he turned his back on the foe.)

The hold Lad secured on Rex's cheek was good, but it was not good enough. At thirteen, a dog's "biting teeth" are worn short and dull, and his yellowed fangs are blunted; nor is the jaw by any means as powerful as once it was. Rex writhed and pitched in the fierce grip, and presently tore free from it and to the attack again, seeking now to lunge over the top of Lad's lowered head to the vital spot at the nape of the neck, where sharp teeth may pierce through to the spinal cord.

Thrice Rex lunged, and thrice Lad reared on his hind legs, meeting the shock with his deep, shaggy breast, snapping and slashing at his enemy and every time receding a few steps between charges. They had left the path now, and were plowing a course through deep snow. The snow was scant barrier to Rex's full strength, but it terribly impeded the steadily backing Lad. Lad's extra flesh, too, was a bad handicap; his wind was not at all what it should have been, and the unwonted exertion began to tell sharply on him.

Under the lead-hued skies and the drive of the snow, the fight swirled and eddied. The great dogs reared, clashed, tore, battered against tree-trunks, lost footing and rolled, staggered up again and renewed the on-slaught. Ever Lad maneuvered his way backward, waging a desperate "rear-guard action." In the battle's wake was an irregular but mathematically straight line of trampled and blood-spattered snow.

Oh, but it was slow going, this ever-fighting retreat of Lad's, through the deep drifts, with his mightier foe pressing him and rending at his throat and shoulders at every backward step! The old dog's wind was gone; his once-superb strength was going, but he fought on with blazing fury—the fury of a dying king who *will* not be deposed.

In sheer skill and brain-work and generalship, Lad was wholly Rex's superior, but these served him ill in a death-grapple. With dogs, as with human pugilists, mere science and strategy avail little against superior size and strength and youth. Again and again Lad found or made an opening. Again and again his weakening jaws secured the right grip only to be shaken off with more and more ease by the younger combatant.

Again and again Lad "slashed" as do his wolf cousins and as does almost no civilized dog but the collie. But the slashes had lost their one-time lightning speed and prowess. And the blunt "rending fangs" scored only superficial furrows in Rex's fawn-colored hide.

There was meager hope of reaching home alive. Lad must have known that. His strength was gone. It was his heart and his glorious ancestry now that were doing his fighting—not his fat and age-depleted body. From Lad's mental vocabulary the word *quit* had ever been absent. Wherefore—dizzy, gasping, feebler every minute—he battled fearlessly on in the dying day; never losing his sense of direction, never turning tail, never dreaming of surrender, taking dire wounds, inflicting light ones.

There are many forms of dog-fight. Two strange dogs, meeting, will fly at each other because their wild forebears used to do so. Jealous dogs will battle even more fiercely. But the deadliest of all canine conflicts is the "murder-fight." This is a struggle wherein one or both contestants have decided to give no quarter, where the victor will fight on until his antagonist is dead and will then tear his body to pieces. It is a recognized form of canine mania.

And it was a murder-fight that Rex was waging, for he had gone quite insane. (This is wholly different, by the way, from "going mad.")

Down went Lad, for perhaps the tenth time, and once more—though now with an effort that was all but too much for him—he writhed to his feet, gaining three yards of ground by the move. Rex was upon him with one leap, the frothing and bloody jaws striking for his mangled throat. Lad reared to block the attack. Then suddenly, overbalanced, he crashed backward into the snowdrift.

Rex had not reached him, but young Wolf had.

Wolf had watched the battle with a growing excitement that at last had broken all bounds. The instinct, which makes a fluff-headed college-boy mix into a scrimmage that is no concern of his, had suddenly possessed Lad's dearly loved son.

Now, if this were a fiction yarn, it would be edifying to tell how Wolf sprang to the aid of his grand old sire and how he thereby saved Lad's life. But the shameful truth is that Wolf did nothing of the sort. Rex was his model, the bully he had so long and so enthusiastically imitated. And now Rex was fighting a most entertaining bout, fighting it with a maniac fury that infected his young disciple and made him yearn to share in the glory.

Wherefore, as Lad reared to meet Rex's lunge, Wolf hurled himself like a furry whirlwind upon the old dog's flank, burying his white teeth in the muscles of the lower leg.

The flank attack bowled Lad completely over. There was no chance now for such a fall as would enable him to spring up again unscathed. He was thrown heavily upon his back, and both his murderers plunged at his unguarded throat and lower body.

But a collie thrown is not a collie beaten, as perhaps I have said once before. For thirty seconds or more the three thrashed about in the snow in a growling, snarling, right unloving embrace. Then, by some miracle, Lad was on his feet again.

His throat had a new and deep wound, perilously close to the jugular. His stomach and left side were slashed as with razor-blades. But he was up. And even in that moment of dire stress—with both dogs flinging themselves upon him afresh—he gained another yard or two in his line of retreat.

He might have gained still more ground. For his assailants, leaping at the same instant, collided and impeded each other's charge. But, for the first time the wise old brain clouded, and the hero-heart went sick as Lad saw his own loved and spoiled son ranged against him in the murder-fray. He could not understand. Loyalty was as much a part of himself as were his sorrowful brown eyes or his tiny white fore-paws. And Wolf's amazing treachery seemed to numb the old warrior, body and mind.

But the second of dumfounded wonder passed quickly—too quickly for either of the other dogs to take advantage of it. In its place surged a righteous wrath that, for the instant, brought back youth and strength to the aged fighter.

With a yell that echoed far through the forest's sinister silence, Lad whizzed forward at the advancing Rex. Wolf, who was nearer, struck for his father's throat—missed and rolled in the snow from the force of his own momentum. Lad did not heed him. Straight for Rex he leaped. Rex, bounding at him, was already in midair. The two met, and under the berserk onset Rex fell back into the snow.

Lad was upon him at once. The worn-down teeth found their goal above the jugular. Deep and raggedly they drove, impelled by the brief flash of power that upbore their owner.

Almost did that grip end the fight and leave Rex gasping out his life in the drift. But the access of false strength faded. Rex, roaring like a hurt tiger, twisted and tore himself free. Lad realizing his own bolt was shot, gave ground, backing away from two assailants instead of one.

It was easier now to retreat. For Wolf, unskilled in practical warfare, at first hindered Rex almost as much as he helped him, again and again getting in the bigger dog's way and marring a rush. Had Wolf understood "teamwork," Lad must have been pulled down and slaughtered in less than a minute.

But soon Wolf grasped the fact that he could do worse damage by keeping out of his ally's way and attacking from a different quarter, and thereafter he fought to more deadly purpose. His favorite ruse was to dive for Lad's forelegs and attempt to break one of them. That is a collie maneuver inherited direct from Wolf's namesake ancestors.

Several times his jaws reached the slender white forelegs, cutting and slashing them and throwing Lad off his balance. Once he found a hold on the left haunch and held it until his victim shook loose by rolling.

Lad defended himself from this new foe as well as he might, by dodging or by brushing him to one side, but never once did he attack Wolf, or so much as snap at him. (Rex after the encounter was plentifully scarred. Wolf had not so much as a scratch.)

Backward, with ever-increasing difficulty, the old dog fought his way, often borne down to earth and always staggering up more feebly than before. But ever he was warring with the same fierce courage; despite an ache and bewilderment in his honest heart at his son's treason.

The forest lay behind the fighters. The deserted highroad was passed. Under Lad's clawing and reeling feet was the dear ground of The Place—The Place where for thirteen happy years he had reigned as king, where he had benevolently ruled his kind and had given worshipful service to his gods.

But the house was still nearly a furlong off, and Lad was well-nigh dead. His body was one mass of wounds. His strength was turned to water. His breath was gone. His bloodshot eyes were dim. His brain was dizzy and refused its office. Loss of blood had weakened him full as much as had the tremendous exertion of the battle.

Yet—uselessly now—he continued to fight. It was a grotesquely futile resistance. The other dogs were all over him—tearing, slashing, gripping, at will—unhindered by his puny effort to fend them off. The slaughter-time had come. Drunk with blood and fury, the assailants plunged at him for the last time.

Down went Lad, helpless beneath the murderous avalanche that overwhelmed him. And this time his body flatly refused to obey the grim command of his will. The fight was over—the good, good fight of a white-souled paladin against hopeless odds.

The living-room fire crackled cheerily. The snow hissed and slithered against the glass. A sheet of frost on every pane shut out the stormy twilit world. The screech of the wind was music to the comfortable shut-ins.

The Mistress drowsed over her book by the fire. Bruce snored snugly in front of the blaze. The Master had awakened from his nap and was in the adjoining study, sorting fishing-tackle and scouring a rusted hunting-knife.

Then came a second's lull in the gale, and all at once Bruce was wide awake. Growling, he ran to the front door and scratched imperatively at the panel. This is not the way a well-bred dog makes known his desire to leave the house. And Bruce was decidedly a well-bred dog.

The Mistress, thinking some guest might be arriving whose scent or tread displeased the collie, called to the Master to shut Bruce in the study, lest he insult the supposed visitor by barking. Reluctantly—very reluctantly—Bruce obeyed the order. The Master shut the study door behind him and came into the living-room, still carrying the half-cleaned knife.

As no summons at bell or knocker followed Bruce's announcement, the Mistress opened the front door and looked out. The dusk was falling, but it was not too dark for her to have seen the approach of anyone, nor was it too dark for the Mistress to see two dogs tearing at something that lay hidden from her view in the deep snow a hundred yards away. She recognized Rex and Wolf at once and amusedly wondered with what they were playing.

Then from the depth of snow beneath them she saw a feeble head rear itself—a glorious head, though torn and bleeding—a head that waveringly lunged toward Rex's throat.

"They're—they're killing—*Lad!*" she cried in stark, unbelieving horror. Forgetful of thin dress and thinner slippers, she ran toward the trio. Halfway to the battlefield the Master passed by her, running and lurching through the knee-high snow at something like record speed.

She heard his shout. And at sound of it she saw Wolf slink away from the slaughter like a scared schoolboy. But Rex was too far gone in murder-lust to heed the shout. The Master seized him by the studded collar and tossed him ten feet or more to one side. Rage-blind, Rex came flying back to the kill. The Master stood astride his prey, and in his blind mania the cross-breed sprang at the man.

The Master's hunting-knife caught him squarely behind the left fore-leg. And with a grunt like the sound of an exhausted soda-siphon, the huge dog passed out of this story and out of life as well.

There would be ample time, later, for the Master to mourn his enforced slaying of the pet dog that had loved and served him so long. At present he had eyes only for the torn and senseless body of Lad lying huddled in the red-blotched snow.

In his arms he lifted Lad and carried him tenderly into the house. There the Mistress' light fingers dressed his hideous injuries. Not less than thirty-six deep wounds scored the worn-out old body. Several of these were past the skill of home treatment.

A grumbling veterinary was summoned on the telephone and was lured by pledge of a triple fee to chug through ten miles of storm in a balky car to the rescue.

Lad was lying with his head in the Mistress' lap. The vet' looked the unconscious dog over and then said tersely:

"I wish I'd stayed at home. He's as good as dead."

"He's a million times better than dead," denied the Master. "I know Lad. You don't. He's got into the habit of living, and he's not going to break that habit, not if the best nursing and surgery in the State can keep him from doing it. Get busy!"

"There's nothing to keep me here," objected the vet'. "He's—"

"There's everything to keep you here," gently contradicted the Master. "You'll stay here till Lad's out of danger—if I have to steal your trousers and your car. You're going to cure him. And if you do, you can write your bill on a Liberty Bond."

Two hours later Lad opened his eyes. He was swathed in smelly bandages and he was soaked in liniments. Patches of hair had been shaved away from his worst wounds. Digitalis was reinforcing his faint heart-action.

He looked up at the Mistress with his only available eye. By a herculean struggle he wagged his tail—just once. And he essayed the trumpeting bark wherewith he always welcomed her return after an absence. The bark was a total failure.

After which Lad tried to tell the Mistress the story of the battle. Very weakly, but very persistently he "talked." His tones dropped now and then to the shadow of a ferocious growl as he related his exploits and then scaled again to a puppy-like whimper.

He had done a grand day's work, had Lad, and he wanted applause. He had suffered much and he was still in racking pain, and he wanted sympathy and petting. Presently he fell asleep.

It was two weeks before Lad could stand upright, and two more before he could go out of doors unhelped. Then on a warm, early spring morning, the vet' declared him out of all danger.

Very thin was the invalid, very shaky, snow-white of muzzle and with the air of an old, old man whose too-fragile body is sustained only by a regal dignity. But he was *alive*.

Slowly he marched from his piano cave toward the open front door. Wolf—in black disgrace for the past month—chanced to be crossing the living-room toward the veranda at the same time. The two dogs reached the door-way simultaneously.

Very respectfully, almost cringingly, Wolf stood aside for Lad to pass out.

His sire walked by with never a look. But his step was all at once stronger and springier, and he held his splendid head high.

For Lad knew he was still king!

AFTERWORD

The stories of Lad, in various magazines, found unexpectedly kind welcome. Letters came to me from soldiers and sailors in Europe, from hosts of children; from men and women, everywhere.

Few of the letter-writers bothered to praise the stories themselves. But all of them praised Lad, which pleased me far better. And more than a hundred of them wanted to know if he were a real dog; and if the tales of his exploits were true.

Perhaps those of you who have followed Lad's adventures, through these pages, may also be a little interested to know more about him.

Yes, Lad was a "real" dog—the greatest dog by far I have known or shall know. And the chief happenings in nearly all of my Lad stories are absolutely true. This accounts for such measure of success as the stories may have won.

After his "Day of Battle," Lad lived for more than two years—still gallant of spirit, loyally mighty of heart, uncanny of wisdom—still the undisputed king of The Place's "Little People."

Then, on a warm September morning in 1918, he stretched himself to sleep in the coolest and shadiest corner of the veranda. And, while he slept, his great heart very quietly stopped beating. He had no pain, no illness, none of the distressing features of extreme age. He had lived out a full span of sixteen years—years rich in life and happiness and love.

Surely, there was nothing in such a death to warrant the silly grief that was ours, nor the heartsick gloom that overhung The Place! It was wholly illogical, not to say maudlin. I admit that without argument. The cleric-author of "The Mansion Yard" must have known the same miserable sense of loss, I think, when he wrote:

> Stretched on the hearthrug in a deep content,
> Fond of the fire as I.
> Oh, there was something with the old dog
> went I had not thought could die!

We buried Lad in a sunlit nook that had been his favorite lounging place, close to the house he had guarded so long and so gallantly. With him we buried his honorary Red Cross and Blue Cross—awards for money raised in his name. Above his head we set a low granite block, with a carven line or two thereon.

The Mistress wanted the block inscribed: "The Dearest Dog!" I suggested: "The Dog God Made." But we decided against both epitaphs. We did not care to risk making our dear old friend's memory ridiculous by words at which saner folk might one day sneer. So on the granite is engraved:

Lad
Thoroughbred In Body And Soul

Some people are wise enough to know that a dog has no soul. These will find ample theme for mirth in our foolish inscription. But no one who knew Lad will laugh at it.

3

The Road to Tinkhamtown

by Corey Ford

If you own a copy of the June 1970 issue of Field & Stream *magazine, consider yourself lucky. That was the seventy-fifth anniversary
issue, a fine thing. But that's not the reason that issue was so precious.
Illustrated with a painting by Howard Terpning, Corey Ford's story
"The Road to Tinkhamtown" makes that issue a classic. The editors
prefaced it with this blurb: "This story by the late Corey Ford, here
published for the first time anywhere, is a moving tale which will not
soon be forgotten. It is for all those who mourned his death that we
present this farewell from the creator of 'The Lower Forty.'" A few
months after he wrote this story, Ford passed away. He never saw
"Tinkhamtown" in print. Ford's stories and his "Lower Forty" column
were* Field & Stream *favorites. His setters provided the background
of many of his tales. "Tinkhamtown" was his masterpiece, written
in the evening of his life, with skill and love, a dog story unlike any
other. More than any story I know, this one brings to mind the great
William Faulkner quote: "The past is never dead. It's not even past."*

IT WAS A LONG WAY, BUT HE KNEW WHERE HE WAS GOING. HE WOULD
follow the road through the woods and over the crest of a hill and down
the hill to the stream, and cross the sagging timbers of the bridge, and
on the other side would be the place called Tinkhamtown. He was going
back to Tinkhamtown.

He walked slowly at first, his legs dragging with each step. He had not walked for almost a year, and his flanks had shriveled and wasted away from lying in bed so long; he could fit his fingers around his thigh. Doc Towle had said he would never walk again, but that was Doc for you, always on the pessimistic side. Why, now he was walking quite easily, once he had started. The strength was coming back into his legs, and he did not have to stop for breath so often. He tried jogging a few steps, just to show he could, but he slowed again because he had a long way to go.

It was hard to make out the old road, choked with alders and covered by matted leaves, and he shut his eyes so he could see it better. He could always see it when he shut his eyes. Yes, here was the beaver dam on the right, just as he remembered it, and the flooded stretch where he had picked his way from hummock to hummock while the dog splashed unconcernedly in front of him. The water had been over his boot tops in one place, and sure enough, as he waded it now his left boot filled with water again, the same warm squidgy feeling. Everything was the way it had been that afternoon, nothing had changed in ten years. Here was the blowdown across the road that he had clambered over, and here on a knoll was the clump of thorn apples where a grouse had flushed as they passed. Shad had wanted to look for it, but he had whistled him back. They were looking for Tinkhamtown.

He had come across the name on a map in the town library. He used to study the old maps and survey charts of the state; sometimes they showed where a farming community had flourished, a century ago, and around the abandoned pastures and in the orchards grown up to pine the birds would be feeding undisturbed. Some of his best grouse covers had been located that way. The map had been rolled up in a cardboard cylinder; it crackled with age as he spread it out. The date was 1857. It was the sector between Cardigan and Kearsarge Mountains, a wasteland of slash and second-growth timber without habitation today, but evidently it had supported a number of families before the Civil War. A road was marked on the map, dotted with X's for homesteads, and the names of the owners were lettered beside them: Nason J. Tinkham, Allard R. Tinkham. Half the names were Tinkham. In the center of the map—the paper was so yellow that he could barely make it out—was the word "Tinkhamtown."

He had drawn a rough sketch on the back of an envelope, noting where the road left the highway and ran north to a fork and then turned east and crossed a stream that was not even named; and the next morning he and Shad had set out together to find the place. They could not drive very far in the jeep because washouts had gutted the roadbed and laid bare the ledges and boulders. He had stuffed the sketch in his hunting-coat pocket, and hung his shotgun over his forearm and started walking, the setter trotting ahead with the bell on his collar tinkling. It was an old-fashioned sleigh bell, and it had a thin silvery note that echoed through the woods like peepers in the spring. He could follow the sound in the thickest cover, and when it stopped he would go to where he heard it last and Shad would be on point. After Shad's death, he had put the bell away. He'd never had another dog.

It was silent in the woods without the bell, and the way was longer than he remembered. He should have come to the big hill by now. Maybe he'd taken the wrong turn back at the fork. He thrust a hand into his hunting coat; the envelope with the sketch was still in the pocket. He sat down on a flat rock to get his bearings, and then he realized, with a surge of excitement, that he had stopped on this very rock for lunch ten years ago. Here was the waxed paper from his sandwich, tucked in a crevice, and here was the hollow in the leaves where Shad had stretched out beside him, the dog's soft muzzle flattened on his thigh. He looked up, and through the trees he could see the hill.

He rose and started walking again, carrying his shotgun. He had left the gun standing in its rack in the kitchen when he had been taken to the state hospital, but now it was hooked over his arm by the trigger guard; he could feel the solid heft of it. The woods grew more dense as he climbed, but here and there a shaft of sunlight slanted through the trees. "And there were forests ancient as the hills," he thought, "enfolding sunny spots of greenery." Funny that should come back to him now; he hadn't read it since he was a boy. Other things were coming back to him: the smell of dank leaves and sweet fern and frosted apples, the sharp contrast of sun and cool shade, the November stillness before snow. He walked faster, feeling the excitement swell within him.

He paused on the crest of the hill, straining his ears for the faint mutter of the stream below him, but he could not hear it because of the voices. He wished they would stop talking so he could hear the stream. Someone was saying his name over and over, "Frank, Frank," and he opened his eyes reluctantly and worried, and there was nothing to worry about. He tried to tell her where he was going, but when he moved his lips the words would not form. "What did you say, Frank?" she asked, bending her head lower. "I don't understand." He couldn't make the words any clearer, and she straightened and said to Doc Towle: "It sounded like Tinkhamtown."

"Tinkhamtown?" Doc shook his head. "Never heard him mention any place by that name."

He smiled to himself. Of course he'd never mentioned it to Doc. Things like a secret grouse cover you didn't mention to anyone, not even to as close a friend as Doc was. No, he and Shad were the only ones who knew. They found it together, that long ago afternoon, and it was their secret.

They had come to the stream—he shut his eyes so he could see it again—and Shad had trotted across the bridge. He had followed more cautiously, avoiding the loose planks and walking along a beam with his shotgun held out to balance himself. On the other side of the stream the road mounted steeply to a clearing in the woods, and he halted before the split-stone foundation of a house, the first of the series of farms shown on the map. It must have been a long time since the building had fallen in; the cottonwoods growing in the cellar hole were twenty, maybe thirty years old. His boot overturned a rusted axe blade, and the handle of a china cup in the grass; that was all. Beside the doorstep was a lilac bush, almost as tall as the cottonwoods. He thought of the wife who had set it out, a little shrub then, and the husband who had chided her for wasting time on such frivolous things with all the farmwork to be done. But the work had come to nothing, and still the lilac bloomed each spring, the one thing that had survived.

Shad's bell was moving along the stone wall at the edge of the clearing, and he strolled after him, not hunting, wondering about the people who had gone away and left their walls to crumble and their buildings to collapse under the winter snows. Had they ever come back to Tinkhamtown? Were they here now, watching him unseen? His toe stubbed against a block of hewn granite hidden by briers, part of the sill of the old barn. Once it had been a tight barn, warm with cattle steaming in their stalls, rich with the blend of hay and manure and harness leather. He liked to think of it the way it was; it was more real than this bare rectangle of blocks and the emptiness inside. He'd always felt that way about the past. Doc used to argue that what's over is over, but he would insist Doc was wrong. Everything is the way it was, he'd tell Doc. The past never changes. You leave it and go on to the present, but it is still there, waiting for you to come back to it.

He had been so wrapped in his thoughts that he had not realized Shad's bell had stopped. He hurried across the clearing holding his gun ready. In a corner of the stone wall an ancient apple tree had littered the ground with fallen fruit, and beneath it Shad was standing motionless. The white fan of his tail was lifted a little and his backline was level, the neck craned forward, one foreleg cocked. His flanks were trembling with the nearness of grouse, and a thin skein of drool hung from his jowls. The dog did not move as he approached, but the brown eyes rolled back until their whites showed, looking for him. "Steady, boy," he called. His throat was tight, the way it always got when Shad was on point, and he had to swallow hard. "Steady, I'm coming."

"I think his lips moved just now," his sister's voice said. He did not open his eyes because he was waiting for the grouse to get up in front of Shad, but he knew Doc Towle was looking at him. "He's sleeping," Doc said after a moment. "Maybe you better get some sleep yourself, Mrs. Duncombe." He heard Doc's heavy footsteps cross the room. "Call me if there's any change," Doc said, and closed the door, and in the silence he could hear his sister's chair creaking beside him, her silk dress rustling regularly as she breathed.

What was she doing here, he wondered. Why had she come all the way from California to see him? It was the first time they had seen each other since she had married and moved out West. She was his only relative, but they had never been very close; they had nothing in common, really. He heard from her now and then, but it was always the same letter: Why didn't he sell the old place, it was too big for him now that the folks had passed on; why didn't he take a small apartment in town where he wouldn't be alone? But he liked the big house, and he wasn't alone, not with Shad. He had closed off all the other rooms and moved into the kitchen so everything would be handy. His sister didn't approve of his bachelor ways, but it was very comfortable with his cot by the stove and Shad curled on the floor near him at night, whinnying and scratching the linoleum with his claws as he chased a bird in a dream. He wasn't alone when he heard that.

He had never married. He had looked after the folks as long as they lived; maybe that was why. Shad was his family. They were always together—Shad was short for Shadow—and there was a closeness between them that he did not feel for anyone else, not his sister or Doc even. He and Shad used to talk without words, each knowing what the other was thinking, and they could always find one another in the woods. He still remembered the little things about him: the possessive thrust of his jaw, the way he false-yawned when he was vexed, the setter stubbornness sometimes, the clownish grin when they were going hunting, the kind eyes. That was it: Shad was the kindest person he had ever known.

They had not hunted again after Tinkhamtown. The old dog had stumbled several times, walking back to the jeep, and he had to carry him in his arms the last hundred yards. It was hard to realize he was gone. He liked to think of him the way he was; it was like the barn, it was more real than the emptiness. Sometimes at night, lying awake with the pain in his legs, he would hear the scratch of claws on the linoleum, and he would turn on the light and the hospital room would be empty. But when he turned the light off he would hear the scratching again, and he would be content and drop off to sleep, or what passed for sleep in these days and nights that ran together without dusk or dawn.

Once he asked Doc point-blank if he would ever get well. Doc was giving him something for the pain, and he hesitated a moment and finished what he was doing and cleaned the needle and then looked at him and said: "I'm afraid not, Frank." They had grown up in the town together, and Doc knew him too well to lie. "I'm afraid there's nothing to do." Nothing to do but lie there and wait till it was over. "Tell me, Doc," he whispered, for his voice wasn't very strong, "what happens when it's over?" And Doc fumbled with the catch of his black bag and closed it and said well he supposed you went on to someplace else called the Hereafter. But he shook his head: He always argued with Doc. "No, it isn't someplace else," he told him, "it's someplace you've been where you want to be again." Doc didn't understand, and he couldn't explain it any better. He knew what he meant, but the shot was taking effect and he was tired.

He was tired now, and his legs ached a little as he started down the hill, trying to find the stream. It was too dark under the trees to see the sketch he had drawn, and he could not tell direction by the moss on the north side of the trunks. The moss grew all around them, swelling them out of size, and huge blowdowns blocked his way. Their upended roots were black and misshapen, and now instead of excitement he felt a surge of panic. He floundered through a pile of slash, his legs throbbing with pain as the sharp points stabbed him, but he did not have the strength to get to the other side and he had to back out again and circle. He did not know where he was going. It was getting late, and he had lost the way.

There was no sound in the woods, nothing to guide him, nothing but his sister's chair creaking and her breath catching now and then in a dry sob. She wanted him to turn back, and Doc wanted him to, they all wanted him to turn back. He thought of the big house; if he left it alone it would fall in with the winter snows and cottonwoods would grow in the cellar hole. And there were all the other doubts, but most of all there was the fear. He was afraid of the darkness, and being alone, and not knowing where he was going. It would be better to turn around and go back. He knew the way back.

And then he heard it, echoing through the woods like peepers in the spring, the thin silvery tinkle of a sleigh bell. He started running toward it, following the sound down the hill. His legs were strong again, and he hurdled the blowdowns, he leapt over fallen logs, he put one fingertip on a pile of slash and sailed over it like a grouse skimming. He was getting nearer and the sound filled his ears, louder than a thousand church bells ringing, louder than all the choirs in the sky, as loud as the pounding of his heart. The fear was gone; he was not lost. He had the bell to guide him now.

He came to the stream, and paused for a moment at the bridge. He wanted to tell them he was happy, if they only knew how happy he was, but when he opened his eyes he could not see them anymore. Everything else was bright, but the room was dark.

The bell had stopped and he looked across the stream. The other side was bathed in sunshine, and he could see the road mounting steeply, and the clearing in the woods, and the apple tree in a corner of the stone wall. Shad was standing motionless beneath it, the white fan of his tail lifted, his neck craned forward and one foreleg cocked. The whites of his eyes showed as he looked back. waiting for him.

"Steady," he called, "steady, boy." He started across the bridge. "I'm coming."

4

The Call of the Wild

by Jack London

The numerous novels and short stories of Jack London seem to always bring readers back to one title, The Call of the Wild. *The story of Buck, a mixed-breed dog whose fate carries him to the Klondike and a life of adventure, is a classic in every way. This excerpt begins with a short section from the first pages of the novel, then carries you to the last two chapters and an ending that lives on in literature today.*

The story has been edited for clarity and removal of unnecessary and archaic language in certain instances. Misspelled words have not been corrected.

BUCK DID NOT READ THE NEWSPAPERS, OR HE WOULD HAVE KNOWN THAT trouble was brewing, not alone for himself, but for every tide-water dog, strong of muscle and with warm, long hair, from Puget Sound to San Diego. Because men, groping in the Arctic darkness, had found a yellow metal, and because steamship and transportation companies were booming the find, thousands of men were rushing into the Northland. These men wanted dogs, and the dogs they wanted were heavy dogs, with strong muscles by which to toil, and furry coats to protect them from the frost.

Buck lived at a big house in the sun-kissed Santa Clara Valley. Judge Miller's place, it was called. It stood back from the road, half hidden among the trees, through which glimpses could be caught of the wide cool veranda that ran around its four sides ...

And over this great demesne Buck ruled. Here he was born, and here he had lived the four years of his life. It was true, there were other dogs.

There could not but be other dogs on so vast a place, but they did not count. They came and went, resided in the populous kennels, or lived obscurely in the recesses of the house after the fashion of Toots, the Japanese pug, or Ysabel, the Mexican hairless—strange creatures that rarely put nose out of doors or set foot to ground. On the other hand, there were the fox terriers, a score of them at least, who yelped fearful promises at Toots and Ysabel looking out of the windows at them and protected by a legion of housemaids armed with brooms and mops.

But Buck was neither house-dog nor kennel-dog. The whole realm was his. He plunged into the swimming tank or went hunting with the Judge's sons; he escorted Mollie and Alice, the Judge's daughters, on long twilight or early morning rambles; on wintry nights he lay at the Judge's feet before the roaring library fire; he carried the Judge's grandsons on his back, or rolled them in the grass, and guarded their footsteps through wild adventures down to the fountain in the stable yard, and even beyond, where the paddocks were, and the berry patches. Among the terriers he stalked imperiously, and Toots and Ysabel he utterly ignored, for he was king—king over all creeping, crawling, flying things of Judge Miller's place, humans included.

His father, Elmo, a huge St. Bernard, had been the Judge's inseparable companion, and Buck bid fair to follow in the way of his father. He was not so large—he weighed only one hundred and forty pounds—for his mother, Shep, had been a Scotch shepherd dog. Nevertheless, one hundred and forty pounds, to which was added the dignity that comes of good living and universal respect, enabled him to carry himself in right royal fashion. During the four years since his puppyhood he had lived the life of a sated aristocrat; he had a fine pride in himself, was even a trifle egotistical, as country gentlemen sometimes become because of their insular situation. But he had saved himself by not becoming a mere pampered house-dog. Hunting and kindred outdoor delights had kept down the fat and hardened his muscles; and to him, as to the cold-tubbing races, the love of water had been a tonic and a health preserver.

And this was the manner of dog Buck was in the fall of 1897, when the Klondike strike dragged men from all the world into the frozen

North. But Buck did not read the newspapers, and he did not know that Manuel, one of the gardener's helpers, was an undesirable acquaintance. Manuel had one besetting sin. He loved to play Chinese lottery. Also, in his gambling, he had one besetting weakness—faith in a system; and this made his damnation certain. For to play a system requires money, while the wages of a gardener's helper do not lap over the needs of a wife and numerous progeny.

The Judge was at a meeting of the Raisin Growers' Association, and the boys were busy organizing an athletic club, on the memorable night of Manuel's treachery. No one saw him and Buck go off through the orchard on what Buck imagined was merely a stroll. And with the exception of a solitary man, no one saw them arrive at the little flag station known as College Park. This man talked with Manuel, and money chinked between them.

"You might wrap up the goods before you deliver 'm," the stranger said gruffly, and Manuel doubled a piece of stout rope around Buck's neck under the collar.

"Twist it, an' you'll choke 'm plentee," said Manuel, and the stranger grunted a ready affirmative.

Buck had accepted the rope with quiet dignity. To be sure, it was an unwonted performance: but he had learned to trust in men he knew, and to give them credit for a wisdom that outreached his own. But when the ends of the rope were placed in the stranger's hands, he growled menacingly. He had merely intimated his displeasure, in his pride believing that to intimate was to command. But to his surprise the rope tightened around his neck, shutting off his breath. In quick rage he sprang at the man, who met him halfway, grappled him close by the throat, and with a deft twist threw him over on his back. Then the rope tightened mercilessly, while Buck struggled in a fury, his tongue lolling out of his mouth and his great chest panting futilely. Never in all his life had he been so vilely treated, and never in all his life had he been so angry. But his strength ebbed, his eyes glazed, and he knew nothing when the train was flagged and the two men threw him into the baggage car.

The next he knew, he was dimly aware that his tongue was hurting and that he was being jolted along in some kind of a conveyance. The hoarse shriek of a locomotive whistling a crossing told him where he was. He had travelled too often with the Judge not to know the sensation of riding in a baggage car. He opened his eyes, and into them came the unbridled anger of a kidnapped king. The man sprang for his throat, but Buck was too quick for him. His jaws closed on the hand, nor did they relax till his senses were choked out of him once more.

"Yep, has fits," the man said, hiding his mangled hand from the baggageman, who had been attracted by the sounds of struggle. "I'm takin' 'm up for the boss to 'Frisco. A crack dog-doctor there thinks that he can cure 'm."

[Editor's note: Buck not only survived the trip, but after reaching the Klondike, he survived life with wicked men and with the powerful and vicious sled dogs he was forced to work among. We begin here at the end chapters of the novel, when Buck is owned by a man named John Thornton, who appreciated this powerful dog now in his care.]

When John Thornton froze his feet in the previous December, his partners had made him comfortable and left him to get well, going on themselves up the river to get out a raft of saw-logs for Dawson. He was still limping slightly at the time he rescued Buck, but with the continued warm weather even the slight limp left him. And here, lying by the river bank through the long spring days, watching the running water, listening lazily to the songs of birds and the hum of nature, Buck slowly won back his strength.

A rest comes very good after one has travelled three thousand miles, and it must be confessed that Buck waxed lazy as his wounds healed, his muscles swelled out, and the flesh came back to cover his bones. For that matter, they were all loafing—Buck, John Thornton, and Skeet waiting for the raft to come that was to carry them down to Dawson. Skeet was a little Irish setter who early made friends with Buck, who, in a dying condition, was unable to resent her first advances. She had the doctor trait which some dogs possess; and as a mother cat washes her kittens, so she washed and cleansed Buck's wounds. Regularly, each morning after he had finished his breakfast, she performed her self-appointed task.

To Buck's surprise these dogs manifested no jealousy toward him. They seemed to share the kindliness and largeness of John Thornton. As Buck grew stronger they enticed him into all sorts of ridiculous games, in which Thornton himself could not forbear to join; and in this fashion Buck romped through his convalescence and into a new existence. Love, genuine passionate love, was his for the first time. This he had never experienced at Judge Miller's down in the sun-kissed Santa Clara Valley. With the Judge's sons, hunting and tramping, it had been a working partnership; with the Judge's grandsons, a sort of pompous guardianship; and with the Judge himself, a stately and dignified friendship. But love that was feverish and burning, that was adoration, that was madness, it had taken John Thornton to arouse.

This man had saved his life, which was something; but, further, he was the ideal master. Other men saw to the welfare of their dogs from a sense of duty and business expediency; he saw to the welfare of his as if they were his own children, because he could not help it. And he saw further. He never forgot a kindly greeting or a cheering word, and to sit down for a long talk with them ("gas" he called it) was as much his delight as theirs. He had a way of taking Buck's head roughly between his hands, and resting his own head upon Buck's, of shaking him back and forth, the while calling him ill names that to Buck were love names. Buck knew no greater joy than that rough embrace and the sound of murmured oaths, and at each jerk back and forth it seemed that his heart would be shaken out of his body so great was its ecstasy. And when, released, he sprang to his feet, his mouth laughing, his eyes eloquent, his throat vibrant with unuttered sound, and in that fashion remained without movement, John Thornton would reverently exclaim, "God! You can all but speak!"

Buck had a trick of love expression that was akin to hurt. He would often seize Thornton's hand in his mouth and close so fiercely that the flesh bore the impress of his teeth for some time afterward. And as Buck understood the oaths to be love words, so the man understood this feigned bite for a caress.

For the most part, however, Buck's love was expressed in adoration. While he went wild with happiness when Thornton touched him or spoke to him, he did not seek these tokens. Unlike Skeet, who was wont to shove her nose under Thornton's hand and nudge and nudge till petted, Buck was content to adore at a distance. He would lie by the hour, eager, alert, at Thornton's feet, looking up into his face, dwelling upon it, studying it, following with keenest interest each fleeting expression, every movement or change of feature. Or, as chance might have it, he would lie farther away, to the side or rear, watching the outlines of the man and the occasional movements of his body. And often, such was the communion in which they lived, the strength of Buck's gaze would draw John Thornton's head around, and he would return the gaze, without speech, his heart shining out of his eyes as Buck's heart shone out.

For a long time after his rescue, Buck did not like Thornton to get out of his sight. From the moment he left the tent to when he entered it again, Buck would follow at his heels. His transient masters since he had come into the Northland had bred in him a fear that no master could be permanent. He was afraid that Thornton would pass out of his life as Perrault and François and the Scotch half-breed had passed out. Even in the night, in his dreams, he was haunted by this fear. At such times he would shake off sleep and creep through the chill to the flap of the tent, where he would stand and listen to the sound of his master's breathing.

But in spite of this great love he bore John Thornton, which seemed to bespeak the soft civilizing influence, the strain of the primitive, which the Northland had aroused in him, remained alive and active. Faithfulness and devotion, things born of fire and roof, were his; yet he retained his wildness and wiliness. He was a thing of the wild, come in from the wild to sit by John Thornton's fire, rather than a dog of the soft Southland stamped with the marks of generations of civilization. Because of his very great love, he could not steal from this man, but from any other man, in any other camp, he did not hesitate an instant; while the cunning with which he stole enabled him to escape detection.

His face and body were scored by the teeth of many dogs, and he fought as fiercely as ever and more shrewdly. Skeet was too good-natured for quarrelling—besides, she belonged to John Thornton; but the strange dog, no matter what the breed or valor, swiftly acknowledged Buck's supremacy or found himself struggling for life with a terrible antagonist. And Buck was merciless. He had learned well the law of club and fang, and he never forewent an advantage or drew back from a foe he had started on the way to Death. He had lessoned from Spitz, and from the chief fighting dogs of the police and mail, and knew there was no middle course. He must master or be mastered; while to show mercy was a weakness. Mercy did not exist in the primordial life. It was misunderstood for fear, and such misunderstandings made for death. Kill or be killed, eat or be eaten, was the law; and this mandate, down out of the depths of Time, he obeyed.

He was older than the days he had seen and the breaths he had drawn. He linked the past with the present, and the eternity behind him throbbed through him in a mighty rhythm to which he swayed as the tides and seasons swayed. He sat by John Thornton's fire, a broad-breasted dog, white-fanged and long-furred; but behind him were the shades of all manner of dogs, half-wolves and wild wolves, urgent and prompting, tasting the savor of the meat he ate, thirsting for the water he drank, scenting the wind with him, listening with him and telling him the sounds made by the wild life in the forest, dictating his moods, directing his actions, lying down to sleep with him when he lay down, and dreaming with him and beyond him and becoming themselves the stuff of his dreams.

So peremptorily did these shades beckon him, that each day mankind and the claims of mankind slipped farther from him. Deep in the forest a call was sounding, and as often as he heard this call, mysteriously thrilling and luring, he felt compelled to turn his back upon the fire and the beaten earth around it, and to plunge into the forest, and on and on, he knew not where or why; nor did he wonder where or why, the call sounding imperiously, deep in the forest. But as often as he gained the soft unbroken earth and the green shade, the love for John Thornton drew him back to the fire again.

Thornton alone held him. The rest of mankind was as nothing. Chance travellers might praise or pet him; but he was cold under it all, and from a too demonstrative man he would get up and walk away. When Thornton's partners, Hans and Pete, arrived on the long-expected raft, Buck refused to notice them till he learned they were close to Thornton; after that he tolerated them in a passive sort of way, accepting favors from them as though he favored them by accepting. They were of the same large type as Thornton, living close to the earth, thinking simply and seeing clearly; and ere they swung the raft into the big eddy by the saw-mill at Dawson, they understood Buck and his ways, and did not insist upon an intimacy such as obtained with Skeet.

For Thornton, however, his love seemed to grow and grow. He, alone among men, could put a pack upon Buck's back in the summer travelling. Nothing was too great for Buck to do, when Thornton commanded. One day (they had grub-staked themselves from the proceeds of the raft and left Dawson for the head-waters of the Tanana) the men and dogs were sitting on the crest of a cliff which fell away, straight down, to naked bedrock three hundred feet below. John Thornton was sitting near the edge, Buck at his shoulder. A thoughtless whim seized Thornton, and he drew the attention of Hans and Pete to the experiment he had in mind. "Jump, Buck!" he commanded, sweeping his arm out and over the chasm. The next instant he was grappling with Buck on the extreme edge, while Hans and Pete were dragging them back into safety.

"It's uncanny," Pete said, after it was over and they had caught their speech.

Thornton shook his head. "No, it is splendid, and it is terrible, too. Do you know, it sometimes makes me afraid."

"I'm not hankering to be the man that lays hands on you while he's around," Pete announced conclusively, nodding his head toward Buck.

"Py Jingo!" was Hans's contribution. "Not mineself either."

It was at Circle City, ere the year was out, that Pete's apprehensions were realized. "Black" Burton, a man evil-tempered and malicious, had been picking a quarrel with a tenderfoot at the bar, when Thornton stepped good-naturedly between. Buck, as was his custom, was lying in a corner, head on paws, watching his master's every action. Burton struck out, without warning, straight from the shoulder. Thornton was sent spinning, and saved himself from falling only by clutching the rail of the bar.

Those who were looking on heard what was neither bark nor yelp, but a something which is best described as a roar, and they saw Buck's body rise up in the air as he left the floor for Burton's throat. The man saved his life by instinctively throwing out his arm, but was hurled backward to the floor with Buck on top of him. Buck loosed his teeth from the flesh of the arm and drove in again for the throat. This time the man succeeded only in partly blocking, and his throat was torn open. Then the crowd was upon Buck, and he was driven off; but while a surgeon checked the bleeding, he prowled up and down, growling furiously, attempting to rush in, and being forced back by an array of hostile clubs. A "miners' meeting," called on the spot, decided that the dog had sufficient provocation, and Buck was discharged. But his reputation was made, and from that day his name spread through every camp in Alaska.

Later on, in the fall of the year, he saved John Thornton's life in quite another fashion. The three partners were lining a long and narrow poling-boat down a bad stretch of rapids on the Forty-Mile Creek. Hans and Pete moved along the bank, snubbing with a thin Manila rope from tree to tree, while Thornton remained in the boat, helping its descent by means of a pole, and shouting directions to the shore. Buck, on the bank, worried and anxious, kept abreast of the boat, his eyes never off his master.

At a particularly bad spot, where a ledge of barely submerged rocks jutted out into the river, Hans cast off the rope, and, while Thornton poled the boat out into the stream, ran down the bank with the end in his hand to snub the boat when it had cleared the ledge. This it did, and was flying down-stream in a current as swift as a mill-race, when Hans checked it with the rope and checked too suddenly. The boat flirted over and snubbed in to the bank bottom up, while Thornton, flung sheer out of it, was carried down-stream toward the worst part of the rapids, a stretch of wild water in which no swimmer could live.

Buck had sprung in on the instant; and at the end of three hundred yards, amid a mad swirl of water, he overhauled Thornton. When he felt him grasp his tail, Buck headed for the bank, swimming with all his splendid strength. But the progress shoreward was slow; the progress down-stream amazingly rapid. From below came the fatal roaring where the wild current went wilder and was rent in shreds and spray by the rocks which thrust through like the teeth of an enormous comb. The suck of the water as it took the beginning of the last steep pitch was frightful, and Thornton knew that the shore was impossible. He scraped furiously over a rock, bruised across a second, and struck a third with crushing force. He clutched its slippery top with both hands, releasing Buck, and above the roar of the churning water shouted: "Go, Buck! Go!"

Buck could not hold his own, and swept on down-stream, struggling desperately, but unable to win back. When he heard Thornton's command repeated, he partly reared out of the water, throwing his head high, as though for a last look, then turned obediently toward the bank. He swam powerfully and was dragged ashore by Pete and Hans at the very point where swimming ceased to be possible and destruction began.

They knew that the time a man could cling to a slippery rock in the face of that driving current was a matter of minutes, and they ran as fast as they could up the bank to a point far above where Thornton was hanging on. They attached the line with which they had been snubbing the boat to Buck's neck and shoulders, being careful that it should neither strangle him nor impede his swimming, and launched him into the stream. He struck out boldly, but not straight enough into the stream. He discovered the mistake too late, when Thornton was abreast of him and a bare half-dozen strokes away while he was being carried helplessly past.

Hans promptly snubbed with the rope, as though Buck were a boat. The rope thus tightening on him in the sweep of the current, he was jerked under the surface, and under the surface he remained till his body struck against the bank and he was hauled out. He was half drowned, and Hans and Pete threw themselves upon him, pounding the breath into him and the water out of him. He staggered to his feet and fell down. The faint sound of Thornton's voice came to them, and though they could not make out the words of it, they knew that he was in his extremity. His master's voice acted on Buck like an electric shock. He sprang to his feet and ran up the bank ahead of the men to the point of his previous departure.

Again the rope was attached and he was launched, and again he struck out, but this time straight into the stream. He had miscalculated once, but he would not be guilty of it a second time. Hans paid out the rope, permitting no slack, while Pete kept it clear of coils. Buck held on till he was on a line straight above Thornton; then he turned, and with the speed of an express train headed down upon him. Thornton saw him coming, and, as Buck struck him like a battering ram, with the whole force of the current behind him, he reached up and closed with both arms around the shaggy neck. Hans snubbed the rope around the tree, and Buck and Thornton were jerked under the water. Strangling, suffocating, sometimes one uppermost and sometimes the other, dragging over the jagged bottom, smashing against rocks and snags, they veered in to the bank.

Thornton came to, belly downward and being violently propelled back and forth across a drift log by Hans and Pete. His first glance was for Buck, over whose limp and apparently lifeless body Skeet was licking the wet face and closed eyes. Thornton was himself bruised and battered, and he went carefully over Buck's body, when he had been brought around, finding three broken ribs.

"That settles it," he announced. "We camp right here." And camp they did, till Buck's ribs knitted and he was able to travel.

That winter, at Dawson, Buck performed another exploit, not so heroic, perhaps, but one that put his name many notches higher on the totem-pole of Alaskan fame. This exploit was particularly gratifying to the three men; for they stood in need of the outfit which it furnished, and were enabled to make a long-desired trip into the virgin East, where miners had not yet appeared. It was brought about by a conversation in the Eldorado Saloon, in which men waxed boastful of their favorite dogs. Buck, because of his record, was the target for these men, and Thornton was driven stoutly to defend him. At the end of half an hour one man stated that his dog could start a sled with five hundred pounds and walk off with it; a second bragged six hundred for his dog; and a third, seven hundred.

"Pooh! pooh!" said John Thornton; "Buck can start a thousand pounds."

"And break it out? and walk off with it for a hundred yards?" demanded Matthewson, a Bonanza King, he of the seven hundred vaunt.

"And break it out, and walk off with it for a hundred yards," John Thornton said coolly.

"Well," Matthewson said, slowly and deliberately, so that all could hear, "I've got a thousand dollars that says he can't. And there it is." So saying, he slammed a sack of gold dust of the size of a bologna sausage down upon the bar.

Nobody spoke. Thornton's bluff, if bluff it was, had been called. He could feel a flush of warm blood creeping up his face. His tongue had tricked him. He did not know whether Buck could start a thousand pounds. Half a ton! The enormousness of it appalled him. He had great faith in Buck's strength and had often thought him capable of starting such a load; but never, as now, had he faced the possibility of it, the eyes of a dozen men fixed upon him, silent and waiting. Further, he had no thousand dollars; nor had Hans or Pete.

"I've got a sled standing outside now, with twenty fifty-pound sacks of flour on it," Matthewson went on with brutal directness; "so don't let that hinder you."

Thornton did not reply. He did not know what to say. He glanced from face to face in the absent way of a man who has lost the power of thought and is seeking somewhere to find the thing that will start it going again. The face of Jim O'Brien, a Mastodon King and old-time comrade, caught his eyes. It was as a cue to him, seeming to rouse him to do what he would never have dreamed of doing.

"Can you lend me a thousand?" he asked, almost in a whisper.

"Sure," answered O'Brien, thumping down a plethoric sack by the side of Matthewson's. "Though it's little faith I'm having, John, that the beast can do the trick."

The Eldorado emptied its occupants into the street to see the test. The tables were deserted, and the dealers and gamekeepers came forth to see the outcome of the wager and to lay odds. Several hundred men, furred and mittened, banked around the sled within easy distance. Matthewson's sled, loaded with a thousand pounds of flour, had been standing for a couple of hours, and in the intense cold (it was sixty below zero) the runners had frozen fast to the hard-packed snow. Men offered odds of two to one that Buck could not budge the sled. A quibble arose concerning the phrase "break out." O'Brien contended it was Thornton's privilege to knock the runners loose, leaving Buck to "break it out" from a dead standstill. Matthewson insisted that the phrase included breaking the runners from the frozen grip of the snow. A majority of the men who had witnessed the making of the bet decided in his favor, whereat the odds went up to three to one against Buck.

There were no takers. Not a man believed him capable of the feat. Thornton had been hurried into the wager, heavy with doubt; and now that he looked at the sled itself, the concrete fact, with the regular team of ten dogs curled up in the snow before it, the more impossible the task appeared. Matthewson waxed jubilant.

"Three to one!" he proclaimed. "I'll lay you another thousand at that figure, Thornton. What d'ye say?"

Thornton's doubt was strong in his face, but his fighting spirit was aroused—the fighting spirit that soars above odds, fails to recognize the impossible, and is deaf to all save the clamor for battle. He called Hans and Pete to him. Their sacks were slim, and with his own the three partners could rake together only two hundred dollars. In the ebb of their fortunes, this sum was their total capital; yet they laid it unhesitatingly against Matthewson's six hundred.

The team of ten dogs was unhitched, and Buck, with his own harness, was put into the sled. He had caught the contagion of the excitement, and he felt that in some way he must do a great thing for John Thornton. Murmurs of admiration at his splendid appearance went up. He was in perfect condition, without an ounce of superfluous flesh, and the one hundred and fifty pounds that he weighed were so many pounds of grit and virility. His furry coat shone with the sheen of silk. Down the neck and across the shoulders, his mane, in repose as it was, half bristled and seemed to lift with every movement, as though excess of vigor made each particular hair alive and active. The great breast and heavy fore legs were no more than in proportion with the rest of the body, where the muscles showed in tight rolls underneath the skin. Men felt these muscles and proclaimed them hard as iron, and the odds went down to two to one.

"Gad, sir! Gad, sir!" stuttered a member of the latest dynasty, a king of the Skookum Benches. "I offer you eight hundred for him, sir, before the test, sir; eight hundred just as he stands."

Thornton shook his head and stepped to Buck's side.

"You must stand off from him," Matthewson protested. "Free play and plenty of room."

The crowd fell silent; only could be heard the voices of the gamblers vainly offering two to one. Everybody acknowledged Buck a magnificent animal, but twenty fifty-pound sacks of flour bulked too large in their eyes for them to loosen their pouch-strings.

Thornton knelt down by Buck's side. He took his head in his two hands and rested cheek on cheek. He did not playfully shake him, as was his wont, or murmur soft love curses; but he whispered in his ear. "As you love me, Buck. As you love me," was what he whispered. Buck whined with suppressed eagerness.

The crowd was watching curiously. The affair was growing mysterious. It seemed like a conjuration. As Thornton got to his feet, Buck seized his mittened hand between his jaws, pressing in with his teeth and releasing slowly, half-reluctantly. It was the answer, in terms, not of speech, but of love. Thornton stepped well back.

"Now, Buck," he said.

Buck tightened the traces, then slacked them for a matter of several inches. It was the way he had learned.

"Gee!" Thornton's voice rang out, sharp in the tense silence.

Buck swung to the right, ending the movement in a plunge that took up the slack and with a sudden jerk arrested his one hundred and fifty pounds. The load quivered, and from under the runners arose a crisp crackling.

"Haw!" Thornton commanded.

Buck duplicated the manœuvre, this time to the left. The crackling turned into a snapping, the sled pivoting and the runners slipping and grating several inches to the side. The sled was broken out. Men were holding their breaths, intensely unconscious of the fact.

"Now, MUSH!"

Thornton's command cracked out like a pistol-shot. Buck threw himself forward, tightening the traces with a jarring lunge. His whole body was gathered compactly together in the tremendous effort, the muscles writhing and knotting like live things under the silky fur. His great chest was low to the ground, his head forward and down, while his feet were flying like mad, the claws scarring the hard-packed snow in parallel grooves. The sled swayed and trembled, half-started forward. One of his feet slipped, and one man groaned aloud. Then the sled lurched ahead in what appeared a rapid succession of jerks, though it never really came to a dead stop again . . . half an inch . . . an inch . . . two inches . . . The jerks perceptibly diminished; as the sled gained momentum, he caught them up, till it was moving steadily along.

Men gasped and began to breathe again, unaware that for a moment they had ceased to breathe. Thornton was running behind, encouraging Buck with short, cheery words. The distance had been measured off, and as he neared the pile of firewood which marked the end of the hundred yards, a cheer began to grow and grow, which burst into a roar as he passed the firewood and halted at command. Every man was tearing himself loose, even Matthewson. Hats and mittens were flying in the air. Men were shaking hands, it did not matter with whom, and bubbling over in a general incoherent babel.

But Thornton fell on his knees beside Buck. Head was against head, and he was shaking him back and forth. Those who hurried up heard him cursing Buck, and he cursed him long and fervently, and softly and lovingly.

"Gad, sir! Gad, sir!" spluttered the Skookum Bench king. "I'll give you a thousand for him, sir, a thousand, sir—twelve hundred, sir."

Thornton rose to his feet. His eyes were wet. The tears were streaming frankly down his cheeks. "Sir," he said to the Skookum Bench king, "no, sir. You can go to hell, sir. It's the best I can do for you, sir."

Buck seized Thornton's hand in his teeth. Thornton shook him back and forth. As though animated by a common impulse, the onlookers drew back to a respectful distance; nor were they again indiscreet enough to interrupt.

When Buck earned sixteen hundred dollars in five minutes for John Thornton, he made it possible for his master to pay off certain debts and to journey with his partners into the East after a fabled lost mine, the history of which was as old as the history of the country. Many men had sought it; few had found it; and more than a few there were who had never returned from the quest. This lost mine was steeped in tragedy and shrouded in mystery. No one knew of the first man. The oldest tradition stopped before it got back to him. From the beginning there had been an ancient and ramshackle cabin. Dying men had sworn to it, and to the mine the site of which it marked, clinching their testimony with nuggets that were unlike any known grade of gold in the Northland.

But no living man had looted this treasure house, and the dead were dead; wherefore John Thornton and Pete and Hans, with Buck and half a dozen other dogs, faced into the East on an unknown trail to achieve where men and dogs as good as themselves had failed. They sledded seventy miles up the Yukon, swung to the left into the Stewart River, passed the Mayo and the McQuestion, and held on until the Stewart itself became a streamlet, threading the upstanding peaks which marked the backbone of the continent.

John Thornton asked little of man or nature. He was unafraid of the wild. With a handful of salt and a rifle he could plunge into the wilderness and fare wherever he pleased and as long as he pleased. Being in no haste, Indian fashion, he hunted his dinner in the course of the day's travel; and if he failed to find it, like the Indian, he kept on travelling, secure in the knowledge that sooner or later he would come to it. So, on this great journey into the East, straight meat was the bill of fare, ammunition and tools principally made up the load on the sled, and the time-card was drawn upon the limitless future.

To Buck it was boundless delight, this hunting, fishing, and indefinite wandering through strange places. For weeks at a time they would hold on steadily, day after day; and for weeks upon end they would camp, here and there, the dogs loafing and the men burning holes through frozen muck and gravel and washing countless pans of dirt by the heat of the fire. Sometimes they went hungry, sometimes they feasted riotously, all according to the abundance of game and the fortune of hunting. Summer arrived, and dogs and men packed on their backs, rafted across blue mountain lakes, and descended or ascended unknown rivers in slender boats whipsawed from the standing forest.

The months came and went, and back and forth they twisted through the uncharted vastness, where no men were and yet where men had been if the Lost Cabin were true. They went across divides in summer blizzards, shivered under the midnight sun on naked mountains between the timber line and the eternal snows, dropped into summer valleys amid swarming gnats and flies, and in the shadows of glaciers picked strawberries and flowers as ripe and fair as any the Southland could boast. In the fall of the year they penetrated a weird lake country, sad and silent, where wildfowl had been, but where then there was no life nor sign of life—only the blowing of chill winds, the forming of ice in sheltered places, and the melancholy rippling of waves on lonely beaches.

And through another winter they wandered on the obliterated trails of men who had gone before. Once, they came upon a path blazed through the forest, an ancient path, and the Lost Cabin seemed very near. But the path began nowhere and ended nowhere, and it remained mystery, as the man who made it and the reason he made it remained mystery. Another time they chanced upon the time-graven wreckage of a hunting lodge, and amid the shreds of rotted blankets John Thornton found a long-barrelled flint-lock. He knew it for a Hudson Bay Company gun of the young days in the Northwest, when such a gun was worth its height in beaver skins packed flat. And that was all—no hint as to the man who in an early day had reared the lodge and left the gun among the blankets.

Spring came on once more, and at the end of all their wandering they found, not the Lost Cabin, but a shallow placer in a broad valley where the gold showed like yellow butter across the bottom of the washing-pan. They sought no farther. Each day they worked earned them thousands of dollars in clean dust and nuggets, and they worked every day. The gold was sacked in moose-hide bags, fifty pounds to the bag, and piled like so much firewood outside the spruce-bough lodge. Like giants they toiled, days flashing on the heels of days like dreams as they heaped the treasure up.

There was nothing for the dogs to do, save the hauling in of meat now and again that Thornton killed, and Buck spent long hours musing by the fire. The vision of the short-legged hairy man came to him more frequently, now that there was little work to be done; and often, blinking by the fire, Buck wandered with him in that other world which he remembered.

The salient thing of this other world seemed fear. When he watched the hairy man sleeping by the fire, head between his knees and hands clasped above, Buck saw that he slept restlessly, with many starts and awakenings, at which times he would peer fearfully into the darkness and fling more wood upon the fire. Did they walk by the beach of a sea, where the hairy man gathered shellfish and ate them as he gathered, it was with eyes that roved everywhere for hidden danger and with legs prepared to run like the wind at its first appearance. Through the forest they crept noiselessly, Buck at the hairy man's heels; and they were alert and vigilant, the pair of them, ears twitching and moving and nostrils quivering, for the man heard and smelled as keenly as Buck. The hairy man could spring up into the trees and travel ahead as fast as on the ground, swinging by the arms from limb to limb, sometimes a dozen feet apart, letting go and catching, never falling, never missing his grip. In fact, he seemed as much at home among the trees as on the ground; and Buck had memories of nights of vigil spent beneath trees wherein the hairy man roosted, holding on tightly as he slept.

And closely akin to the visions of the hairy man was the call still sounding in the depths of the forest. It filled him with a great unrest and strange desires. It caused him to feel a vague, sweet gladness, and he was aware of wild yearnings and stirrings for he knew not what. Sometimes he pursued the call into the forest, looking for it as though it were a tangible thing, barking softly or defiantly, as the mood might dictate. He would thrust his nose into the cool wood moss, or into the black soil where long grasses grew, and snort with joy at the fat earth smells; or he would crouch for hours, as if in concealment, behind fungus-covered trunks of fallen trees, wide-eyed and wide-eared to all that moved and sounded about him. It might be, lying thus, that he hoped to surprise this call he could not understand. But he did not know why he did these various things. He was impelled to do them, and did not reason about them at all.

Irresistible impulses seized him. He would be lying in camp, dozing lazily in the heat of the day, when suddenly his head would lift and his ears cock up, intent and listening, and he would spring to his feet and dash away, and on and on, for hours, through the forest aisles and across the open spaces where the grass bunched. He loved to run down dry watercourses, and to creep and spy upon the bird life in the woods. For a day at a time he would lie in the underbrush where he could watch the partridges drumming and strutting up and down. But especially he loved to run in the dim twilight of the summer midnights, listening to the subdued and sleepy murmurs of the forest, reading signs and sounds as man may read a book, and seeking for the mysterious something that called—called, waking or sleeping, at all times, for him to come.

One night he sprang from sleep with a start, eager-eyed, nostrils quivering and scenting, his mane bristling in recurrent waves. From the forest came the call (or one note of it, for the call was many noted), distinct and definite as never before—a long-drawn howl, like, yet unlike, any noise made by husky dog. And he knew it, in the old familiar way, as a sound heard before. He sprang through the sleeping camp and in swift silence dashed through the woods. As he drew closer to the cry he went more slowly, with caution in every movement, till he came to an open place among the trees, and looking out saw, erect on haunches, with nose pointed to the sky, a long, lean timber wolf.

He had made no noise, yet it ceased from its howling and tried to sense his presence. Buck stalked into the open, half crouching, body gathered compactly together, tail straight and stiff, feet falling with unwonted care. Every movement advertised commingled threatening and overture of friendliness. It was the menacing truce that marks the meeting of wild beasts that prey. But the wolf fled at sight of him. He followed, with wild leapings, in a frenzy to overtake. He ran him into a blind channel, in the bed of the creek where a timber jam barred the way. The wolf whirled about, pivoting on his hind legs after the fashion of Joe and of all cornered husky dogs, snarling and bristling, clipping his teeth together in a continuous and rapid succession of snaps.

Buck did not attack, but circled him about and hedged him in with friendly advances. The wolf was suspicious and afraid; for Buck made three of him in weight, while his head barely reached Buck's shoulder. Watching his chance, he darted away, and the chase was resumed. Time and again he was cornered, and the thing repeated, though he was in poor condition, or Buck could not so easily have overtaken him. He would run till Buck's head was even with his flank, when he would whirl around at bay, only to dash away again at the first opportunity.

But in the end Buck's pertinacity was rewarded; for the wolf, finding that no harm was intended, finally sniffed noses with him. Then they became friendly, and played about in the nervous, half-coy way with which fierce beasts belie their fierceness. After some time of this the wolf started off at an easy lope in a manner that plainly showed he was going somewhere. He made it clear to Buck that he was to come, and they ran side by side through the sombre twilight, straight up the creek bed, into the gorge from which it issued, and across the bleak divide where it took its rise.

On the opposite slope of the watershed they came down into a level country where were great stretches of forest and many streams, and through these great stretches they ran steadily, hour after hour, the sun rising higher and the day growing warmer. Buck was wildly glad. He knew he was at last answering the call, running by the side of his wood brother toward the place from where the call surely came. Old memories were coming upon him fast, and he was stirring to them as of old he stirred to the realities of which they were the shadows. He had done this thing before, somewhere in that other and dimly remembered world, and he was doing it again, now, running free in the open, the unpacked earth underfoot, the wide sky overhead.

They stopped by a running stream to drink, and, stopping, Buck remembered John Thornton. He sat down. The wolf started on toward the place from where the call surely came, then returned to him, sniffing noses and making actions as though to encourage him. But Buck turned about and started slowly on the back track. For the better part of an hour the wild brother ran by his side, whining softly. Then he sat down, pointed his nose upward, and howled. It was a mournful howl, and as Buck held steadily on his way, he heard it grow faint and fainter until it was lost in the distance.

John Thornton was eating dinner when Buck dashed into camp and sprang upon him in a frenzy of affection, overturning him, scrambling upon him, licking his face, biting his hand—"playing the general tom-fool," as John Thornton characterized it, the while he shook Buck back and forth and cursed him lovingly.

For two days and nights Buck never left camp, never let Thornton out of his sight. He followed him about at his work, watched him while he ate, saw him into his blankets at night and out of them in the morning. But after two days the call in the forest began to sound more imperiously than ever. Buck's restlessness came back on him, and he was haunted by recollections of the wild brother, and of the smiling land beyond the divide and the run side by side through the wide forest stretches. Once again he took to wandering in the woods, but the wild brother came no more; and though he listened through long vigils, the mournful howl was never raised.

He began to sleep out at night, staying away from camp for days at a time; and once he crossed the divide at the head of the creek and went down into the land of timber and streams. There he wandered for a week, seeking vainly for fresh sign of the wild brother, killing his meat as he travelled and travelling with the long, easy lope that seems never to tire. He fished for salmon in a broad stream that emptied somewhere into the sea, and by this stream he killed a large black bear, blinded by the mosquitoes while likewise fishing, and raging through the forest helpless and terrible. Even so, it was a hard fight, and it aroused the last latent remnants of Buck's ferocity. And two days later, when he returned to his kill and found a dozen wolverenes quarrelling over the spoil, he scattered them like chaff; and those that fled left two behind who would quarrel no more.

The blood-longing became stronger than ever before. He was a killer, a thing that preyed, living on the things that lived, unaided, alone, by virtue of his own strength and prowess, surviving triumphantly in a hostile environment where only the strong survived. Because of all this he became possessed of a great pride in himself, which communicated itself like a contagion to his physical being. It advertised itself in all his movements, was apparent in the play of every muscle, spoke plainly as speech in the way he carried himself, and made his glorious furry coat if anything more glorious. But for the stray brown on his muzzle and above his eyes, and for the splash of white hair that ran midmost down his chest, he might well have been mistaken for a gigantic wolf, larger than the largest of the breed. From his St. Bernard father he had inherited size and weight, but it was his shepherd mother who had given shape to that size and weight. His muzzle was the long wolf muzzle, save that it was larger than the muzzle of any wolf; and his head, somewhat broader, was the wolf head on a massive scale.

His cunning was wolf cunning, and wild cunning; his intelligence, shepherd intelligence and St. Bernard intelligence; and all this, plus an experience gained in the fiercest of schools, made him as formidable a creature as any that roamed the wild. A carnivorous animal living on a straight meat diet, he was in full flower, at the high tide of his life, overspilling with vigor and virility. When Thornton passed a caressing hand along his back, a snapping and crackling followed the hand, each hair discharging its pent magnetism at the contact. Every part, brain and body, nerve tissue and fibre, was keyed to the most exquisite pitch; and between all the parts there was a perfect equilibrium or adjustment. To sights and sounds and events which required action, he responded with lightning-like rapidity. Quickly as a husky dog could leap to defend from attack or to attack, he could leap twice as quickly. He saw the movement, or heard sound, and responded in less time than another dog required to compass the mere seeing or hearing. He perceived and determined and responded in the same instant. In point of fact the three actions of perceiving, determining, and responding were sequential; but so infinitesimal were the intervals of time between them that they appeared simultaneous. His muscles were surcharged with vitality, and snapped into play sharply, like steel springs. Life streamed through him in splendid flood, glad and rampant, until it seemed that it would burst him asunder in sheer ecstasy and pour forth generously over the world.

"Never was there such a dog," said John Thornton one day, as the partners watched Buck marching out of camp.

"When he was made, the mould was broke," said Pete.

"Py jingo! I t'ink so mineself," Hans affirmed.

They saw him marching out of camp, but they did not see the instant and terrible transformation which took place as soon as he was within the secrecy of the forest. He no longer marched. At once he became a thing of the wild, stealing along softly, cat-footed, a passing shadow that appeared and disappeared among the shadows. He knew how to take advantage of every cover, to crawl on his belly like a snake, and like a snake to leap and strike. He could take a ptarmigan from its nest, kill a rabbit as it slept, and snap in mid air the little chipmunks fleeing a second too late for the trees. Fish, in open pools, were not too quick for him; nor were beaver, mending their dams, too wary. He killed to eat, not from wantonness; but he preferred to eat what he killed himself. So a lurking humor ran through his deeds, and it was his delight to steal upon the squirrels, and, when he all but had them, to let them go, chattering in mortal fear to the treetops.

As the fall of the year came on, the moose appeared in greater abundance, moving slowly down to meet the winter in the lower and less rigorous valleys. Buck had already dragged down a stray part-grown calf; but he wished strongly for larger and more formidable quarry, and he came upon it one day on the divide at the head of the creek. A band of twenty moose had crossed over from the land of streams and timber, and chief among them was a great bull. He was in a savage temper, and, standing over six feet from the ground, was as formidable an antagonist as even Buck could desire. Back and forth the bull tossed his great palmated antlers, branching to fourteen points and embracing seven feet within the tips. His small eyes burned with a vicious and bitter light, while he roared with fury at sight of Buck.

From the bull's side, just forward of the flank, protruded a feathered arrow-end, which accounted for his savageness. Guided by that instinct which came from the old hunting days of the primordial world, Buck proceeded to cut the bull out from the herd. It was no slight task. He would bark and dance about in front of the bull, just out of reach of the great antlers and of the terrible splay hoofs which could have stamped his life out with a single blow. Unable to turn his back on the fanged danger and go on, the bull would be driven into paroxysms of rage. At such moments he charged Buck, who retreated craftily, luring him on by a simulated inability to escape. But when he was thus separated from his fellows, two or three of the younger bulls would charge back upon Buck and enable the wounded bull to rejoin the herd.

There is a patience of the wild—dogged, tireless, persistent as life itself—that holds motionless for endless hours the spider in its web, the snake in its coils, the panther in its ambuscade; this patience belongs peculiarly to life when it hunts its living food; and it belonged to Buck as he clung to the flank of the herd, retarding its march, irritating the young bulls, worrying the cows with their half-grown calves, and driving the wounded bull mad with helpless rage. For half a day this continued. Buck multiplied himself, attacking from all sides, enveloping the herd in a whirlwind of menace, cutting out his victim as fast as it could rejoin its mates, wearing out the patience of creatures preyed upon, which is a lesser patience than that of creatures preying.

As the day wore along and the sun dropped to its bed in the northwest (the darkness had come back and the fall nights were six hours long), the young bulls retraced their steps more and more reluctantly to the aid of their beset leader. The down-coming winter was harrying them on to the lower levels, and it seemed they could never shake off this tireless creature that held them back. Besides, it was not the life of the herd, or of the young bulls, that was threatened. The life of only one member was demanded, which was a remoter interest than their lives, and in the end they were content to pay the toll.

As twilight fell the old bull stood with lowered head, watching his mates—the cows he had known, the calves he had fathered, the bulls he had mastered—as they shambled on at a rapid pace through the fading light. He could not follow, for before his nose leaped the merciless fanged terror that would not let him go. Three hundredweight more than half a ton he weighed; he had lived a long, strong life, full of fight and struggle, and at the end he faced death at the teeth of a creature whose head did not reach beyond his great knuckled knees.

From then on, night and day, Buck never left his prey, never gave it a moment's rest, never permitted it to browse the leaves of trees or the shoots of young birch and willow. Nor did he give the wounded bull opportunity to slake his burning thirst in the slender trickling streams they crossed. Often, in desperation, he burst into long stretches of flight. At such times Buck did not attempt to stay him, but loped easily at his heels, satisfied with the way the game was played, lying down when the moose stood still, attacking him fiercely when he strove to eat or drink.

The great head drooped more and more under its tree of horns, and the shambling trot grew weak and weaker. He took to standing for long periods, with nose to the ground and dejected ears dropped limply; and Buck found more time in which to get water for himself and in which to rest. At such moments, panting with red lolling tongue and with eyes fixed upon the big bull, it appeared to Buck that a change was coming over the face of things. He could feel a new stir in the land. As the moose were coming into the land, other kinds of life were coming in. Forest and stream and air seemed palpitant with their presence. The news of it was borne in upon him, not by sight, or sound, or smell, but by some other and subtler sense. He heard nothing, saw nothing, yet knew that the land was somehow different; that through it strange things were afoot and ranging; and he resolved to investigate after he had finished the business in hand.

At last, at the end of the fourth day, he pulled the great moose down. For a day and a night he remained by the kill, eating and sleeping, turn and turn about. Then, rested, refreshed and strong, he turned his face toward camp and John Thornton. He broke into the long easy lope, and went on, hour after hour, never at loss for the tangled way, heading straight home through strange country with a certitude of direction that put man and his magnetic needle to shame.

As he held on he became more and more conscious of the new stir in the land. There was life abroad in it different from the life which had been there throughout the summer. No longer was this fact borne in upon him in some subtle, mysterious way. The birds talked of it, the squirrels chattered about it, the very breeze whispered of it. Several times he stopped and drew in the fresh morning air in great sniffs, reading a message which made him leap on with greater speed. He was oppressed with a sense of calamity happening, if it were not calamity already happened; and as he crossed the last watershed and dropped down into the valley toward camp, he proceeded with greater caution.

Three miles away he came upon a fresh trail that sent his neck hair rippling and bristling, It led straight toward camp and John Thornton. Buck hurried on, swiftly and stealthily, every nerve straining and tense, alert to the multitudinous details which told a story—all but the end. His nose gave him a varying description of the passage of the life on the heels of which he was travelling. He remarked the pregnant silence of the forest. The bird life had flitted. The squirrels were in hiding. One only he saw—a sleek gray fellow, flattened against a gray dead limb so that he seemed a part of it, a woody excrescence upon the wood itself.

As Buck slid along with the obscureness of a gliding shadow, his nose was jerked suddenly to the side as though a positive force had gripped and pulled it. He followed the new scent into a thicket and found a dog. He was lying on his side, dead where he had dragged himself, an arrow protruding, head and feathers, from either side of his body.

A hundred yards farther on, Buck came upon one of the sled-dogs Thornton had bought in Dawson. This dog was thrashing about in a death-struggle, directly on the trail, and Buck passed around him without stopping. From the camp came the faint sound of many voices, rising and falling in a sing-song chant. Bellying forward to the edge of the clearing, he found Hans, lying on his face, feathered with arrows like a porcupine. At the same instant Buck peered out where the spruce-bough lodge had been and saw what made his hair leap straight up on his neck and shoulders. A gust of overpowering rage swept over him. He did not know that he growled, but he growled aloud with a terrible ferocity. For the last time in his life he allowed passion to usurp cunning and reason, and it was because of his great love for John Thornton that he lost his head.

The Yeehats were dancing about the wreckage of the spruce-bough lodge when they heard a fearful roaring and saw rushing upon them an animal the like of which they had never seen before. It was Buck, a live hurricane of fury, hurling himself upon them in a frenzy to destroy. He sprang at the foremost man (it was the chief of the Yeehats), ripping the throat wide open till the rent jugular spouted a fountain of blood. He did not pause to worry the victim, but ripped in passing, with the next bound tearing wide the throat of a second man. There was no withstanding him. He plunged about in their very midst, tearing, rending, destroying, in constant and terrific motion which defied the arrows they discharged at him. In fact, so inconceivably rapid were his movements, and so closely were the Indians tangled together, that they shot one another with the arrows; and one young hunter, hurling a spear at Buck in mid air, drove it through the chest of another hunter with such force that the point broke through the skin of the back and stood out beyond. Then a panic seized the Yeehats, and they fled in terror to the woods, proclaiming as they fled the advent of the Evil Spirit.

And truly Buck was the Fiend incarnate, raging at their heels and dragging them down like deer as they raced through the trees. It was a fateful day for the Yeehats. They scattered far and wide over the country, and it was not till a week later that the last of the survivors gathered together in a lower valley and counted their losses. As for Buck, wearying of the pursuit, he returned to the desolated camp. He found Pete where he had been killed in his blankets in the first moment of surprise. Thornton's desperate struggle was fresh-written on the earth, and Buck scented every detail of it down to the edge of a deep pool. By the edge, head and fore feet in the water, lay Skeet, faithful to the last. The pool itself, muddy and discolored from the sluice boxes, effectually hid what it contained, and it contained John Thornton; for Buck followed his trace into the water, from which no trace led away.

All day Buck brooded by the pool or roamed restlessly about the camp. Death, as a cessation of movement, as a passing out and away from the lives of the living, he knew, and he knew John Thornton was dead. It left a great void in him, somewhat akin to hunger, but a void which ached and ached, and which food could not fill. At times, when he paused to contemplate the carcasses of the Yeehats, he forgot the pain of it; and at such times he was aware of a great pride in himself, a pride greater than any he had yet experienced. He had killed man, the noblest game of all, and he had killed in the face of the law of club and fang. He sniffed the bodies curiously. They had died so easily. It was harder to kill a husky dog than them. They were no match at all, were it not for their arrows and spears and clubs. Thenceforward he would be unafraid of them except when they bore in their hands their arrows, spears, and clubs.

Night came on, and a full moon rose high over the trees into the sky, lighting the land till it lay bathed in ghostly day. And with the coming of the night, brooding and mourning by the pool, Buck became alive to a stirring of the new life in the forest other than that which the Yeehats had made. He stood up, listening and scenting. From far away drifted a faint, sharp yelp, followed by a chorus of similar sharp yelps. As the moments passed the yelps grew closer and louder. Again Buck knew them as things heard in that other world which persisted in his memory. He walked to the centre of the open space and listened. It was the call, the many-noted call, sounding more luringly and compellingly than ever before. And as never before, he was ready to obey. John Thornton was dead. The last tie was broken. Man and the claims of man no longer bound him.

Hunting their living meat, as the Yeehats were hunting it, on the flanks of the migrating moose, the wolf pack had at last crossed over from the land of streams and timber and invaded Buck's valley. Into the clearing where the moonlight streamed, they poured in a silvery flood; and in the centre of the clearing stood Buck, motionless as a statue, waiting their coming. They were awed, so still and large he stood, and a moment's pause fell, till the boldest one leaped straight for him. Like a flash Buck struck, breaking the neck. Then he stood, without movement, as before, the stricken wolf rolling in agony behind him. Three others tried it in sharp succession; and one after the other they drew back, streaming blood from slashed throats or shoulders.

This was sufficient to fling the whole pack forward, pell-mell, crowded together, blocked and confused by its eagerness to pull down the prey. Buck's marvellous quickness and agility stood him in good stead. Pivoting on his hind legs, and snapping and gashing, he was everywhere at once, presenting a front which was apparently unbroken so swiftly did he whirl and guard from side to side. But to prevent them from getting behind him, he was forced back, down past the pool and into the creek bed, till he brought up against a high gravel bank. He worked along to a right angle in the bank which the men had made in the course of mining, and in this angle he came to bay, protected on three sides and with nothing to do but face the front.

And so well did he face it, that at the end of half an hour the wolves drew back discomfited. The tongues of all were out and lolling, the white fangs showing cruelly white in the moonlight. Some were lying down with heads raised and ears pricked forward; others stood on their feet, watching him; and still others were lapping water from the pool. One wolf, long and lean and gray, advanced cautiously, in a friendly manner, and Buck recognized the wild brother with whom he had run for a night and a day. He was whining softly, and, as Buck whined, they touched noses.

Then an old wolf, gaunt and battle-scarred, came forward. Buck writhed his lips into the preliminary of a snarl, but sniffed noses with him, Whereupon the old wolf sat down, pointed nose at the moon, and broke out the long wolf howl. The others sat down and howled. And now the call came to Buck in unmistakable accents. He, too, sat down and howled. This over, he came out of his angle and the pack crowded around him, sniffing in half-friendly, half-savage manner. The leaders lifted the yelp of the pack and sprang away into the woods. The wolves swung in behind, yelping in chorus. And Buck ran with them, side by side with the wild brother, yelping as he ran.

And here may well end the story of Buck. The years were not many when the Yeehats noted a change in the breed of timber wolves; for some were seen with splashes of brown on head and muzzle, and with a rift of white centering down the chest. But more remarkable than this, the Yeehats tell of a Ghost Dog that runs at the head of the pack. They are afraid of this Ghost Dog, for it has cunning greater than they, stealing from their camps in fierce winters, robbing their traps, slaying their dogs, and defying their bravest hunters.

Nay, the tale grows worse. Hunters there are who fail to return to the camp, and hunters there have been whom their tribesmen found with throats slashed cruelly open and with wolf prints about them in the snow greater than the prints of any wolf. Each fall, when the Yeehats follow the movement of the moose, there is a certain valley which they never enter. And women there are who become sad when the word goes over the fire of how the Evil Spirit came to select that valley for an abiding-place.

In the summers there is one visitor, however, to that valley, of which the Yeehats do not know. It is a great, gloriously coated wolf, like, and yet unlike, all other wolves. He crosses alone from the smiling timber land and comes down into an open space among the trees. Here a yellow stream flows from rotted moose-hide sacks and sinks into the ground, with long grasses growing through it and vegetable mould overrunning it and hiding its yellow from the sun; and here he muses for a time, howling once, long and mournfully, ere he departs.

But he is not always alone. When the long winter nights come on and the wolves follow their meat into the lower valleys, he may be seen running at the head of the pack through the pale moonlight or glimmering borealis, leaping gigantic above his fellows, his great throat a-bellow as he sings a song of the younger world, which is the song of the pack.

5

A Dark-Brown Dog

by Stephen Crane

Best known for his amazing novel The Red Badge of Courage—
*amazing because it is so good, yet Crane had never served in the Civil
War—this is one of Crane's short stories that illustrates his storytelling
skill and his love of dogs.*

A CHILD WAS STANDING ON A STREET-CORNER. HE LEANED WITH ONE
shoulder against a high board fence and swayed the other to and fro, the
while kicking carelessly at the gravel.

Sunshine beat upon the cobbles, and a lazy summer wind raised yellow
dust which trailed in clouds down the avenue. Clattering trucks moved
with indistinctness through it. The child stood dreamily gazing. After a
time, a little dark-brown dog came trotting with an intent air down the
sidewalk. A short rope was dragging from his neck. Occasionally he trod
upon the end of it and stumbled.

He stopped opposite the child, and the two regarded each other. The
dog hesitated for a moment, but presently he made some little advances
with his tail. The child put out his hand and called him. In an apologetic
manner the dog came close, and the two had an interchange of friendly
pattings and waggles. The dog became more enthusiastic with each moment of the interview, until with his gleeful caperings he threatened to
overturn the child. Whereupon the child lifted his hand and struck the
dog a blow upon the head.

This thing seemed to overpower and astonish the little dark-brown dog, and wounded him to the heart. He sank down in despair at the child's feet. When the blow was repeated, together with an admonition in childish sentences, he turned over upon his back, and held his paws in a peculiar manner. At the same time with his ears and his eyes he offered a small prayer to the child.

He looked so comical on his back, and holding his paws peculiarly, that the child was greatly amused and gave him little taps repeatedly, to keep him so. But the little dark-brown dog took this chastisement in the most serious way, and no doubt considered that he had committed some grave crime, for he wriggled contritely and showed his repentance in every way that was in his power. He pleaded with the child and petitioned him, and offered more prayers.

At last the child grew weary of this amusement and turned toward home. The dog was praying at the time. He lay on his back and turned his eyes upon the retreating form.

Presently he struggled to his feet and started after the child. The latter wandered in a perfunctory way toward his home, stopping at times to investigate various matters. During one of these pauses he discovered the little dark-brown dog who was following him with the air of a footpad.

The child beat his pursuer with a small stick he had found. The dog lay down and prayed until the child had finished, and resumed his journey. Then he scrambled erect and took up the pursuit again.

On the way to his home the child turned many times and beat the dog, proclaiming with childish gestures that he held him in contempt as an unimportant dog, with no value save for a moment. For being this quality of animal the dog apologized and eloquently expressed regret, but he continued stealthily to follow the child. His manner grew so very guilty that he slunk like an assassin.

When the child reached his doorstep, the dog was industriously ambling a few yards in the rear. He became so agitated with shame when he again confronted the child that he forgot the dragging rope. He tripped upon it and fell forward.

The child sat down on the step and the two had another interview. During it the dog greatly exerted himself to please the child. He performed a few gambols with such abandon that the child suddenly saw him to be a valuable thing. He made a swift, avaricious charge and seized the rope.

He dragged his captive into a hall and up many long stairways in a dark tenement. The dog made willing efforts, but he could not hobble very skillfully up the stairs because he was very small and soft, and at last the pace of the engrossed child grew so energetic that the dog became panic-stricken. In his mind he was being dragged toward a grim unknown. His eyes grew wild with the terror of it. He began to wiggle his head frantically and to brace his legs.

The child redoubled his exertions. They had a battle on the stairs. The child was victorious because he was completely absorbed in his purpose, and because the dog was very small. He dragged his acquirement to the door of his home, and finally with triumph across the threshold.

No one was in. The child sat down on the floor and made overtures to the dog. These the dog instantly accepted. He beamed with affection upon his new friend. In a short time they were firm and abiding comrades.

When the child's family appeared, they made a great row. The dog was examined and commented upon and called names. Scorn was leveled at him from all eyes, so that he became much embarrassed and drooped like a scorched plant. But the child went sturdily to the center of the floor, and, at the top of his voice, championed the dog. It happened that he was roaring protestations, with his arms clasped about the dog's neck, when the father of the family came in from work.

The parent demanded to know what the blazes they were making the kid howl for. It was explained in many words that the infernal kid wanted to introduce a disreputable dog into the family.

A family council was held. On this depended the dog's fate, but he in no way heeded, being busily engaged in chewing the end of the child's dress.

The affair was quickly ended. The father of the family, it appears, was in a particularly savage temper that evening, and when he perceived that it would amaze and anger everybody if such a dog were allowed to remain, he decided that it should be so. The child, crying softly, took his friend off to a retired part of the room to hobnob with him, while the father quelled a fierce rebellion of his wife. So it came to pass that the dog was a member of the household.

He and the child were associated together at all times save when the child slept. The child became a guardian and a friend. If the large folk kicked the dog and threw things at him, the child made loud and violent objections. Once when the child had run, protesting loudly, with tears raining down his face and his arms outstretched, to protect his friend, he had been struck in the head with a very large saucepan from the hand of his father, enraged at some seeming lack of courtesy in the dog. Ever after, the family were careful how they threw things at the dog. Moreover, the latter grew very skillful in avoiding missiles and feet. In a small room containing a stove, a table, a bureau and some chairs, he would display strategic ability of a high order, dodging, feinting and scuttling about among the furniture. He could force three or four people armed with brooms, sticks and handfuls of coal, to use all their ingenuity to get in a blow. And even when they did, it was seldom that they could do him a serious injury or leave any imprint.

But when the child was present these scenes did not occur. It came to be recognized that if the dog was molested, the child would burst into sobs, and as the child, when started, was very riotous and practically unquenchable, the dog had therein a safeguard.

However, the child could not always be near. At night, when he was asleep, his dark-brown friend would raise from some black corner a wild, wailful cry, a song of infinite loneliness and despair, that would go shuddering and sobbing among the buildings of the block and cause people to swear. At these times the singer would often be chased all over the kitchen and hit with a great variety of articles.

Sometimes, too, the child himself used to beat the dog, although it is not known that he ever had what truly could be called a just cause. The dog always accepted these thrashings with an air of admitted guilt. He was too much of a dog to try to look to be a martyr or to plot revenge.

He received the blows with deep humility, and furthermore he forgave his friend the moment the child had finished, and was ready to caress the child's hand with his little red tongue.

When misfortune came upon the child, and his troubles overwhelmed him, he would often crawl under the table and lay his small distressed head on the dog's back. The dog was ever sympathetic. It is not to be supposed that at such times he took occasion to refer to the unjust beatings his friend, when provoked, had administered to him.

He did not achieve any notable degree of intimacy with the other members of the family. He had no confidence in them, and the fear that he would express at their casual approach often exasperated them exceedingly. They used to gain a certain satisfaction in underfeeding him, but finally his friend the child grew to watch the matter with some care, and when he forgot it, the dog was often successful in secret for himself.

So the dog prospered. He developed a large bark, which came wondrously from such a small rug of a dog. He ceased to howl persistently at night. Sometimes, indeed, in his sleep, he would utter little yells, as from pain, but that occurred, no doubt, when in his dreams he encountered huge flaming dogs who threatened him direfully.

His devotion to the child grew until it was a sublime thing. He wagged at his approach; he sank down in despair at his departure. He could detect the sound of the child's step among all the noises of the neighborhood. It was like a calling voice to him.

The scene of their companionship was a kingdom governed by this terrible potentate, the child; but neither criticism nor rebellion ever lived for an instant in the heart of the one subject. Down in the mystic, hidden fields of his little dog-soul bloomed flowers of love and fidelity and perfect faith.

The child was in the habit of going on many expeditions to observe strange things in the vicinity. On these occasions his friend usually jogged aimfully along behind. Perhaps, though, he went ahead. This necessitated his turning around every quarter-minute to make sure the child was coming. He was filled with a large idea of the importance of these journeys. He would carry himself with such an air! He was proud to be the retainer of so great a monarch.

One day, however, the father of the family got quite exceptionally drunk. He came home and held carnival with the cooking utensils, the furniture and his wife. He was in the midst of this recreation when the child, followed by the dark-brown dog, entered the room. They were returning from their voyages.

The child's practiced eye instantly noted his father's state. He dived under the table, where experience had taught him was a rather safe place. The dog, lacking skill in such matters, was, of course, unaware of the true condition of affairs. He looked with interested eyes at his friend's sudden dive. He interpreted it to mean: Joyous gambol. He started to patter across the floor to join him. He was the picture of a little dark-brown dog en route to a friend.

The head of the family saw him at this moment. He gave a huge howl of joy, and knocked the dog down with a heavy coffee-pot. The dog, yelling in supreme astonishment and fear, writhed to his feet and ran for cover. The man kicked out with a ponderous foot. It caused the dog to swerve as if caught in a tide. A second blow of the coffee-pot laid him upon the floor.

Here, the child, uttering loud cries, came valiantly forth like a knight. The father of the family paid no attention to these calls of the child, but advanced with glee upon the dog. Upon being knocked down twice in swift succession, the latter apparently gave up all hope of escape. He rolled over on his back and held his paws in a peculiar manner. At the same time with his eyes and his ears he offered up a small prayer.

But the father was in a mood for having fun, and it occurred to him that it would be a fine thing to throw the dog out of the window. So he reached down and, grabbing the animal by a leg, lifted him, squirming, up. He swung him two or three times hilariously about his head, and then flung him with great accuracy through the window.

The soaring dog created a surprise in the block. A woman watering plants in an opposite window gave an involuntary shout and dropped a flower-pot. A man in another window leaned perilously out to watch the flight of the dog. A woman who had been hanging out clothes in a yard began to caper wildly. Her mouth was filled with clothes-pins, but her arms gave vent to a sort of exclamation. In appearance she was like a gagged prisoner. Children ran whooping.

The dark-brown body crashed in a heap on the roof of a shed five stories below. From thence it rolled to the pavement of an alleyway.

The child in the room far above burst into a long, dirge-like cry, and toddled hastily out of the room. It took him a long time to reach the alley, because his size compelled him to go downstairs backward, one step at a time, and holding with both hands to the step above.

When they came for him later, they found him seated, by the body of his dark-brown friend.

6

Bingo

by Ernest Thompson Seton

*From the prolific pen of Ernest Thompson Seton, who numbered among
his achievements author, naturalist, illustrator, and cofounder of the
Boy Scouts of America, comes the tale of Bingo, a dog of the West that
has just a little too much adventure in his soul. Run-ins with wolves
and poisoned horse carcasses don't deter Bingo from roaming free on
the Plains. Though he and his master share an uneasy partnership, in
the end he is a dog who comes through for those he loves.*

IT WAS EARLY IN NOVEMBER 1882, AND THE MANITOBA WINTER HAD
just set in. I was tilting back in my chair for a few lazy moments after
breakfast, idly alternating my gaze from the one window-pane of our
shanty, through which was framed a bit of the prairie and the end of our
cowshed, to the old rhyme of the "Franckelyn's dogge" pinned on the logs
nearby. But the dreamy mixture of rhyme and view was quickly dispelled
by the sight of a large gray animal dashing across the prairie into the cowshed, with a smaller black and white animal in hot pursuit.

"A wolf," I exclaimed, and seizing a rifle dashed out to help the dog.
But before I could get there they had left the stable, and after a short run
over the snow the wolf again turned at bay, and the dog, our neighbor's
collie, circled about watching his chance to snap.

I fired a couple of long shots, which had the effect only of setting
them off again over the prairie. After another run this matchless dog
closed and seized the wolf by the haunch, but again retreated to avoid the

fierce return chop. Then there was another stand at bay, and again a race over the snow. Every few hundred yards this scene was repeated, the dog managing so that each fresh rush should be toward the settlement, while the wolf vainly tried to break back toward the dark belt of trees in the east. At last after a mile of this fighting and running I overtook them, and the dog, seeing that he now had good backing, closed in for the finish.

After a few seconds the whirl of struggling animals resolved itself into a wolf, on his back, with a bleeding collie gripping his throat, and it was now easy for me to step up and end the fight by putting a ball through the wolf's head.

Then, when this dog of marvelous wind saw that his foe was dead, he gave him no second glance, but set out at a lope for a farm four miles across the snow where he had left his master when first the wolf was started. He was a wonderful dog, and even if I had not come he undoubtedly would have killed the wolf alone, as I learned he had already done with others of the kind, in spite of the fact that the wolf, though of the smaller or prairie race, was much larger than himself. I was filled with admiration for the dog's prowess and at once sought to buy him at any price. The scornful reply of his owner was, "Why don't you try to buy one of the children?"

Since Frank was not in the market I was obliged to content myself with the next best thing, one of his alleged progeny. That is, a son of his wife. This probable offspring of an illustrious sire was a roly-poly ball of black fur that looked more like a long-tailed bear cub than a puppy. But he had some tan markings like those on Frank's coat, that were, I hoped, guarantees of future greatness, and also a very characteristic ring of white that he always wore on his muzzle.

Having got possession of his person, the next thing was to find him a name. Surely this puzzle was already solved. The rhyme of the "Franckelyn's dogge" was in-built with the foundation of our acquaintance, so with adequate pomp we "yclept him little Bingo."

The rest of that winter Bingo spent in our shanty, living the life of a blubbery, fat, well-meaning, ill-doing puppy; gorging himself with food and growing bigger and clumsier each day. Even sad experience failed to teach him that he must keep his nose out of the rattrap. His most friendly overtures to the cat were wholly misunderstood and resulted only in an armed neutrality that varied by occasional reigns of terror, continued to the end; which came when Bingo, who early showed a mind of his own, got a notion for sleeping at the barn and avoiding the shanty altogether.

When the spring came I set about his serious education. After much pains on my behalf and many pains on his, he learned to go at the word in quest of our old yellow cow, that pastured at will on the unfenced prairie.

Once he had learned his business, he became very fond of it and nothing pleased him more than an order to go and fetch the cow. Away he would dash, barking with pleasure and leaping high in the air that he might better scan the plain for his victim. In a short time he would return driving her at full gallop before him, and gave her no peace until, puffing and blowing, she was safely driven into the farthest corner of her stable.

Less energy on his part would have been more satisfactory, but we bore with him until he grew so fond of this semi-daily hunt that he began to bring "old Dunne" without being told. And at length not once or twice but a dozen times a day this energetic cowherd would sally forth on his own responsibility and drive the cow home to the stable.

At last things came to such a pass that whenever he felt like taking a little exercise, or had a few minutes of spare time, or even happened to think of it, Bingo would sally forth at racing speed over the plain and a few minutes later return, driving the unhappy yellow cow at full gallop before him.

At first this did not seem very bad, as it kept the cow from straying too far; but soon it was seen that it hindered her feeding. She became thin and gave less milk; it seemed to weigh on her mind too, as she was always watching nervously for that hateful dog, and in the mornings would hang around the stable as though afraid to venture off and subject herself at once to an onset.

This was going too far. All attempts to make Bingo more moderate in his pleasure were failures, so he was compelled to give it up altogether. After this, though he dared not bring her home, he continued to show his interest by lying at her stable door while she was being milked.

As the summer came on the mosquitoes became a dreadful plague, and the consequent vicious switching of Dunne's tail at milking-time was even more annoying than the mosquitoes.

Fred, the brother who did the milking, was of an inventive as well as an impatient turn of mind, and he devised a simple plan to stop the switching. He fastened a brick to the cow's tail, then set blithely about his work assured of unusual comfort while the rest of us looked on in doubt.

Suddenly through the mist of mosquitoes came a dull whack and an outburst of "language." The cow went on placidly chewing till Fred got on his feet and furiously attacked her with the milking-stool. It was bad enough to be whacked on the ear with a brick by a stupid old cow, but the uproarious enjoyment and ridicule of the bystanders made it unendurable. Bingo, hearing the uproar, and divining that he was needed, rushed in and attacked Dunne on the other side. Before the affair quieted down the milk was spilt, the pail and stool were broken, and the cow and the dog severely beaten.

Poor Bingo could not understand it at all. He had long ago learned to despise that cow, and now in utter disgust he decided to forsake even her stable door, and from that time he attached himself exclusively to the horses and their stable.

The cattle were mine, the horses were my brother's, and in transferring his allegiance from the cow-stable to the horse-stable Bingo seemed to give me up too, and anything like daily companionship ceased, and yet, whenever any emergency arose Bingo turned to me and I to him, and both seemed to feel that the bond between man and dog is one that lasts as long as life.

The only other occasion on which Bingo acted as cowherd was in the autumn of the same year at the annual Carberry Fair. Among the dazzling inducements to enter one's stock there was, in addition to a prospect of glory, a cash prize of "two dollars" for the "best collie in training."

Misled by a false friend, I entered Bingo, and early on the day fixed, the cow was driven to the prairie just outside of the village. When the time came she was pointed out to Bingo and the word given—"Go fetch the cow." It was the intention, of course, that he should bring her to me at the judge's stand.

But the animals knew better. They hadn't rehearsed all summer for nothing. When Dunne saw Bingo's careering form she knew that her only hope for safety was to get into her stable, and Bingo was equally sure that his sole mission in life was to quicken her pace in that direction. So off they raced over the prairie, like a wolf after a deer, and heading straight toward their home two miles away, they disappeared from view.

That was the last that judge or jury ever saw of dog or cow. The prize was awarded to the only other entry.

Bingo's loyalty to the horses was quite remarkable; by day he trotted beside them, and by night he slept at the stable door. Where the team went Bingo went, and nothing kept him away from them. This interesting assumption of ownership lent the greater significance to the following circumstance.

I was not superstitious, and up to this time had had no faith in omens, but was now deeply impressed by a strange occurrence in which Bingo took a leading part. There were but two of us now living on the De Winton Farm. One morning my brother set out for Boggy Creek for a load of hay. It was a long day's journey there and back, and he made an early start. Strange to tell, Bingo for once in his life did not follow the team. My brother called to him, but still he stood at a safe distance, and eyeing the team askance, refused to stir. Suddenly he raised his nose in the air and gave vent to a long, melancholy howl. He watched the wagon out of sight, and even followed for a hundred yards or so, raising his voice from time to time in the most doleful howlings.

All that day he stayed about the barn, the only time that he was willingly separated from the horses, and at intervals howled a very death dirge. I was alone, and the dog's behavior inspired me with an awful foreboding of calamity, that weighed upon us more and more as the hours passed away.

About six o'clock Bingo's howlings became unbearable, so that for lack of a better thought I threw something at him, and ordered him away. But oh, the feeling of horror that filled me. Why did I let my brother go away alone? Should I ever again see him alive? I might have known from the dog's actions that something dreadful was about to happen.

At length the hour for his return arrived, and there was John on his load. I took charge of the horses, vastly relieved, and with an air of assumed unconcern, asked, "All right?"

"Right," was the laconic answer.

Who now can say that there is nothing in omens.

And yet when, long afterward, I told this to one skilled in the occult, he looked grave, and said, "Bingo always turned to you in a crisis?"

"Yes."

"Then do not smile. It was you that were in danger that day; he stayed and saved your life, though you never knew from what."

Early in the spring I had begun Bingo's education. Very shortly afterward he began mine.

Midway on the two-mile stretch of prairie that lay between our shanty and the village of Carberry was the corner-stake of the farm; it was a stout post in a low mound of earth, and was visible from afar.

I soon noticed that Bingo never passed without minutely examining this mysterious post. Next I learned that it was also visited by the prairie wolves as well as by all the dogs in the neighborhood, and at length, with the aid of a telescope, I made a number of observations that helped me to an understanding of the matter and enabled me to enter more fully into Bingo's private life.

The post was by common agreement a registry of the canine tribes. Their exquisite sense of smell enabled each individual to tell at once by the track and trace what other had recently been at the post. When the snow came much more was revealed. I then discovered that this post was but one of a system that covered the country; that, in short, the entire region was laid out in signal stations at convenient intervals. These were marked by any conspicuous post, stone, buffalo skull, or other object that chanced to be in the desired locality, and extensive observation showed that it was a very complete system for getting and giving the news.

Each dog or wolf makes a point of calling at those stations that are near his line of travel to learn who has recently been there, just as a man calls at his club on returning to town and looks up the register.

I have seen Bingo approach the post, sniff, examine the ground about, then growl, and with bristling mane and glowing eyes, scratch fiercely and contemptuously with his hind feet, finally walking off very stiffly, glancing back from time to time. All of which, being interpreted, said:

"*Grrrh! woof!* There's that dirty cur of McCarthy's. *Woof!* I'll 'tend to him tonight. *Woof! woof!*"

On another occasion, after the preliminaries, he became keenly interested and studied a coyote's track that came and went, saying to himself, as I afterward learned:

"A coyote track coming from the north, smelling of dead cow. Indeed? Pollworth's old Brindle must be dead at last. This is worth looking into."

At other times he would wag his tail, trot about the vicinity and come again and again to make his own visit more evident, perhaps for the benefit of his brother Bill just back from Brandon! So that it was not by chance that one night Bill turned up at Bingo's home and was taken to the hills, where a delicious dead horse afforded a chance to suitably celebrate the reunion.

At other times he would be suddenly aroused by the news, take up the trail, and race to the next station for later information.

Sometimes his inspection produced only an air of grave attention, as though he said to himself, "Dear me, who the deuce is this?" or "It seems to me I met that fellow at the Portage last summer."

One morning on approaching the post Bingo's every hair stood on end, his tail dropped and quivered, and he gave proof that he was suddenly sick at the stomach, sure signs of terror. He showed no desire to follow up or know more of the matter, but returned to the house, and half an hour afterward his mane was still bristling and his expression one of hate or fear.

I studied the dreaded track and learned that in Bingo's language the half-terrified, deep-gurgled *grr-wff* means "timber wolf."

These were among the things that Bingo taught me. And in the after time when I might chance to see him arouse from his frosty nest by the stable door, and after stretching himself and shaking the snow from his shaggy coat, disappear into the gloom at a steady trot, trot, trot, I used to think:

"Ahh! old dog, I know where you are off to, and why you eschew the shelter of the shanty. Now I know why your nightly trips over the country are so well timed, and how you know just where to go for what you want, and when and how to seek it."

In the autumn of 1884, the shanty at De Winton farm was closed and Bingo changed his home to the establishment—that is, to the stable, not the house—of Gordon Wright, our most intimate neighbor.

Since the winter of his puppyhood he had declined to enter a house at any time excepting during a thunderstorm. Of thunder and guns he had a deep dread—no doubt the fear of the first originated in the second, and that arose from some unpleasant shotgun experiences, the cause of which will be seen. His nightly couch was outside the stable, even during the coldest weather, and it was easy to see he enjoyed to the full the complete nocturnal liberty entailed. Bingo's midnight wanderings extended across the plains for miles. There was plenty of proof of this. Some farmers at very remote points sent word to old Gordon that if he did not keep his dog home nights, they would use the shotgun, and Bingo's terror of fire-arms would indicate that the threats were not idle. A man living as far away as Petrel said he saw a large black wolf kill a coyote on the snow one winter evening, but afterward he changed his opinion and "reckoned it must 'a' been Wright's dog." Whenever the body of a winter-killed ox or horse was exposed, Bingo was sure to repair to it nightly, and driving away the prairie wolves, feast to repletion.

Sometimes the object of a night foray was merely to maul some distant neighbor's dog, and notwithstanding vengeful threats, there seemed no reason to fear that the Bingo breed would die out. One man even avowed that he had seen a prairie wolf accompanied by three young ones which resembled the mother, excepting that they were very large and black and had a ring of white around the muzzle. True or not as that may be, I know that late in March, while we were out in the sleigh with Bingo trotting behind, a prairie wolf was started from a hollow. Away it went with Bingo in full chase, but the wolf did not greatly exert itself to escape, and within a short distance Bingo was close up, yet strange to tell, there was no grappling, no fight!

Bingo trotted amiably alongside and licked the wolf's nose.

We were astounded, and shouted to urge Bingo on. Our shouting and approach several times started the wolf off at speed and Bingo again pursued until he had overtaken it, but his gentleness was too obvious.

"It is a she-wolf, he won't harm her," I exclaimed as the truth dawned on me. And Gordon said: "Well, I be darned."

So we called our unwilling dog and drove on.

For weeks after this we were annoyed by the depredations of a prairie wolf who killed our chickens, stole pieces of pork from the end of the house, and several times terrified the children by looking into the window of the shanty while the men were away.

Against this animal Bingo seemed to be no safeguard. At length the wolf, a female, was killed, and then Bingo plainly showed his hand by his lasting enmity toward Oliver, the man who did the deed.

It is wonderful and beautiful how a man and his dog will stick to one another, through thick and thin. Butler tells of an undivided Indian tribe in the Far North which was all but exterminated by an internecine feud over a dog that belonged to one man and was killed by his neighbor; and among ourselves we have lawsuits, fights, and deadly feuds, all pointing the same old moral, "Love me, love my dog."

One of our neighbors had a very fine hound that he thought the best and dearest dog in the world. I loved him, so I loved his dog, and when one day poor Tan crawled home terribly mangled and died by the door, I joined my threats of vengeance with those of his master and thenceforth lost no opportunity of tracing the miscreant, both by offering rewards and by collecting scraps of evidence. At length it was clear that one of three men to the southward had had a hand in the cruel affair. The scent was warming up, and soon we should have been in a position to exact rigorous justice, at least, from the wretch who had murdered poor old Tan.

Then something took place which at once changed my mind and led me to believe that the mangling of the old hound was not by any means an unpardonable crime, but indeed on second thoughts was rather commendable than otherwise.

Gordon Wright's farm lay to the south of us, and while there one day, Gordon Jr., knowing that I was tracking the murderer, took me aside and looking about furtively, he whispered, in tragic tones:

"It was Bing done it."

And the matter dropped right there. For I confess that from that moment I did all in my power to baffle the justice I had previously striven so hard to further. I had given Bingo away long before, but the feeling of ownership did not die; and of this indissoluble fellowship of dog and man he was soon to take part in another important illustration.

Old Gordon and Oliver were close neighbors and friends; they joined in a contract to cut wood, and worked together harmoniously till late on in winter. Then Oliver's old horse died, and he, determining to profit as far as possible, dragged it out on the plain and laid poison baits for wolves around it. Alas for poor Bingo! He would lead a wolfish life, though again and again it brought him into wolfish misfortunes.

He was as fond of dead horse as any of his wild kindred. That very night, with Wright's own dog Curley, he visited the carcass. It seemed as though Bing had busied himself chiefly keeping off the wolves, but Curley feasted immoderately. The tracks in the snow told the story of the banquet; the interruption as the poison began to work, and of the dreadful spasms of pain during the erratic course back home where Curley, falling in convulsions at Gordon's feet, died in the greatest agony.

"Love me, love my dog." No explanations or apology were acceptable; it was useless to urge that it was accidental; the long-standing feud between Bingo and Oliver was now remembered as an important sidelight. The wood-contract was thrown up, all friendly relations ceased, and to this day there is no county big enough to hold the rival factions which were called at once into existence and to arms by Curley's dying yell.

It was months before Bingo really recovered from the poison. We believed indeed that he never again would be the sturdy old-time Bingo. But when the spring came he began to gain strength, and bettering as the grass grew, he was within a few weeks once more in full health and vigor to be a pride to his friends and a nuisance to his neighbors.

Changes took me far away from Manitoba, and on my return in 1886 Bingo was still a member of Wright's household. I thought he would have forgotten me after two years' absence, but not so. One day early in the winter, after having been lost for forty-eight hours, he crawled home to Wright's with a wolf-trap and a heavy log fast to one foot, and the foot frozen to stony hardness. No one had been able to approach to help him, he was so savage, when I, the stranger now, stooped down and laid hold of the trap with one hand and his leg with the other. Instantly he seized my wrist in his teeth.

Without stirring I said, "Bing, don't you know me?"

He had not broken the skin and at once released his hold and offered no further resistance, although he whined a good deal during the removal of the trap. He still acknowledged me his master in spite of his change of residence and my long absence, and notwithstanding my surrender of ownership I still felt that he was my dog.

Bing was carried into the house much against his will and his frozen foot thawed out. During the rest of the winter he went lame and two of his toes eventually dropped off. But before the return of warm weather his health and strength were fully restored, and to a casual glance he bore no mark of his dreadful experience in the steel trap.

During that same winter I caught many wolves and foxes who did not have Bingo's good luck in escaping the traps, which I kept out right into the spring, for bounties are good even when fur is not.

Kennedy's Plain was always a good trapping ground because it was unfrequented by man and yet lay between the heavy woods and the settlement. I had been fortunate with the fur here, and late in April rode in on one of my regular rounds.

The wolf-traps are made of heavy steel and have two springs, each of one hundred pounds power. They are set in fours around a buried bait, and after being strongly fastened to concealed logs are carefully covered in cotton and in fine sand so as to be quite invisible. A prairie wolf was caught in one of these. I killed him with a club and throwing him aside proceeded to reset the trap as I had done so many hundred times before.

All was quickly done. I threw the trap-wrench over toward the pony, and seeing some fine sand nearby, I reached out for a handful of it to add a good finish to the setting.

Oh, unlucky thought! Oh, mad heedlessness born of long immunity! That fine sand was on the next wolf trap and in an instant I was a prisoner. Although not wounded, for the traps have no teeth, and my thick trapping gloves deadened the snap, I was firmly caught across the hand above the knuckles. Not greatly alarmed at this, I tried to reach the trap-wrench with my right foot. Stretching out at full length, face downward, I worked myself toward it, making my imprisoned arm as long and straight as possible. I could not see and reach at the same time, but counted on my toe telling me when I touched the little iron key to my fetters. My first effort was a failure; strain as I might at the chain my toe struck no metal. I swung slowly around my anchor, but still failed. Then a painfully taken observation showed I was much too far to the west. I set about working around, tapping blindly with my toe to discover the key. Thus wildly groping with my right foot I forgot about the other till there was a sharp clank and the iron jaws of trap No. 5 closed tight on my left foot.

The terrors of the situation did not, at first, impress me, but I soon found that all my struggles were in vain. I could not get free from either trap or move the traps together, and there I lay stretched out and firmly staked to the ground.

What would become of me now? There was not much danger of freezing for the cold weather was over, but Kennedy's Plain was never visited by the winter woodcutters. No one knew where I had gone, and unless I could manage to free myself there was no prospect ahead but to be devoured by wolves, or else die of cold and starvation.

As I lay there the red sun went down over the spruce swamp west of the plain, and a shorelark on a gopher mound a few yards off twittered his evening song, just as one had done the night before at our shanty door, and though the numb pains were creeping up my arm, and a deadly chill possessed me, I noticed how long his little ear-tufts were. Then my thoughts went to the comfortable supper-table at Wright's shanty, and I thought, now they are frying the pork for supper, or just sitting down.

My pony still stood as I left him with his bridle on the ground patiently waiting to take me home. He did not understand the long delay, and when I called, he ceased nibbling the grass and looked at me in dumb, helpless inquiry. If he would only go home the empty saddle might tell the tale and bring help. But his very faithfulness kept him waiting hour after hour while I was perishing of cold and hunger.

Then I remembered how old Girou the trapper had been lost, and in the following spring his comrades found his skeleton held by the leg in a bear-trap. I wondered which part of my clothing would show my identity. Then a new thought came to me. This is how a wolf feels when he is trapped. Oh! What misery have I been responsible for! Now I'm to pay for it.

Night came slowly on. A prairie wolf howled, the pony pricked up his ears and, walking nearer to me, stood with his head down. Then another prairie wolf howled and another, and I could make out that they were gathering in the neighborhood. There I lay prone and helpless, wondering if it would not be strictly just that they should come and tear me to pieces. I heard them calling for a long time before I realized that dim, shadowy forms were sneaking near. The horse saw them first, and his terrified snort drove them back at first, but they came nearer next time and sat around me on the prairie. Soon one bolder than the others crawled up and tugged at the body of his dead relative. I shouted and he retreated growling. The pony ran to a distance in terror. Presently the wolf returned, and after two or three of these retreats and returns, the body was dragged off and devoured by the rest in a few minutes.

After this they gathered nearer and sat on their haunches to look at me, and the boldest one smelt the rifle and scratched dirt on it. He retreated when I kicked at him with my free foot and shouted, but growing bolder as I grew weaker he came and snarled right in my face. At this several others snarled and came up closer, and I realized that I was to be devoured by the foe that I most despised; when suddenly out of the gloom with a guttural roar sprang a great black wolf. The prairie wolves scattered like chaff except the bold one, which, seized by the black newcomer, was in a few moments a draggled corpse, and then, oh horrors!

this mighty brute bounded at me and—Bingo—noble Bingo, rubbed his shaggy, panting sides against me and licked my cold face.

"Bingo—Bing—old—boy—Fetch me the trap wrench!" Away he went and returned dragging the rifle, for he knew only that I wanted something.

"No—Bing—the trap-wrench." This time it was my sash, but at last he brought the wrench and wagged his tail in joy that it was right. Reaching out with my free hand, after much difficulty I unscrewed the pillar-nut. The trap fell apart and my hand was released, and a minute later I was free. Bing brought the pony up, and after slowly walking to restore the circulation I was able to mount. Then slowly at first but soon at a gallop, with Bingo as herald careering and barking ahead, we set out for home, there to learn that the night before, though never taken on the trapping rounds, the brave dog had acted strangely, whimpering and watching the timber-trail; and at last when night came on, in spite of attempts to detain him he had set out in the gloom and guided by a knowledge that is beyond us had reached the spot in time to avenge me as well as set me free.

Staunch old Bing—he was a strange dog. Though his heart was with me, he passed me next day with scarcely a look, but responded with alacrity when little Gordon called him to a gopher-hunt. And it was so to the end; and to the end also he lived the wolfish life that he loved, and never failed to seek the winter-killed horses and found one again with a poisoned bait, and wolfishly bolted that; then feeling the pang, set out, not for Wright's but to find me, and reached the door of my shanty where I should have been. Next day on returning I found him dead in the snow with his head on the sill of the door—the door of his puppyhood's days; my dog to the last in his heart of hearts—it was my help he sought, and vainly sought, in the hour of his bitter extremity.

7

A Dog's Tale

by Mark Twain

While most dog stories are told from the viewpoint of the dog's owner and trainers, Mark Twain creates amazing atmosphere and feeling by telling his story from the viewpoint of the dog itself. "A Dog's Tale" is exactly that, and displays the talent that makes Twain an icon of American literature. Twain was a campaigner against cruelty to animals, particularly during the last few years of his life. His greatest weapon was his pen, and his 1904 book A Dog's Tale *told a popular and sentimental story that made the point to a wide audience. In 1907 he followed that book with* A Horse's Tale, *which was supposed to do the same thing for horses. It was less successful than the dog book, possibly because of an excess of narrators and possibly because of an equal excess of melodrama.*

MY FATHER WAS A ST. BERNARD, MY MOTHER WAS A COLLIE, BUT I AM A Presbyterian. This is what my mother told me, I do not know these nice distinctions myself. To me they are only fine large words meaning nothing. My mother had a fondness for such; she liked to say them, and see other dogs look surprised and envious, as wondering how she got so much education. But, indeed, it was not real education; it was only show: she got the words by listening in the dining-room and drawing-room when there was company, and by going with the children to Sunday-school and listening there; and whenever she heard a large word she said it over to herself many times, and so was able to keep it until there was a dogmatic gathering in the neighborhood, then she would get it off, and surprise and distress them all, from pocket-pup to mastiff, which rewarded her for all her trouble. If there was a stranger he was nearly sure to be suspicious, and when he got his breath again he would ask her what it meant. And she always told him. He was never expecting this but thought he would catch her; so when she told him, he was the one that looked ashamed, whereas he had thought it was going to be she. The others were always waiting for this, and glad of it and proud of her, for they knew what was going to happen, because they had had experience. When she told the meaning of a big word they were all so taken up with admiration that it never occurred to any dog to doubt if it was the right one; and that was natural, because, for one thing, she answered up so promptly that it seemed like a dictionary speaking, and for another thing, where could they find out whether it was right or not? For she was the only cultivated dog there was. By and by, when I was older, she brought home the word Unintellectual, one time, and worked it pretty hard all the week at different gatherings, making much unhappiness and despondency; and it was at this time that I noticed that during that week she was asked for the meaning at eight different assemblages, and flashed out a fresh definition every time, which showed me that she had more presence of mind than culture, though I said nothing, of course. She had one word which she always kept on hand, and ready, like a life-preserver, a kind of emergency word to strap on when she was likely to get washed overboard in a sudden way—that was the word Synonymous. When she happened to fetch out a long word which had had its day weeks before and its prepared meanings gone to her dump-pile, if there was a stranger there of course it knocked him groggy for a couple of minutes, then he would come to, and by that time she would be away down wind on another tack, and not expecting anything; so when he'd hail and ask her to cash in, I (the only dog on the inside of her game) could see her canvas flicker a moment—but only just a moment—then it would belly out taut and full, and she would say, as calm as a summer's day, "It's synonymous with supererogation," or some godless long reptile of a word like that, and go placidly about and skim away on the next tack, perfectly comfortable, you know, and leave that stranger looking profane and embarrassed, and the initiated slapping the floor with their tails in unison and their faces transfigured with a holy joy.

And it was the same with phrases. She would drag home a whole phrase, if it had a grand sound, and play it six nights and two matinees, and explain it a new way every time—which she had to, for all she cared for was the phrase; she wasn't interested in what it meant, and knew those dogs hadn't wit enough to catch her, anyway. Yes, she was a daisy! She got so she wasn't afraid of anything, she had such confidence in the ignorance of those creatures. She even brought anecdotes that she had heard the family and the dinner-guests laugh and shout over; and as a rule she got the nub of one chestnut hitched onto another chestnut, where, of course, it didn't fit and hadn't any point; and when she delivered the nub she fell over and rolled on the floor and laughed and barked in the most insane way, while I could see that she was wondering to herself why it didn't seem as funny as it did when she first heard it. But no harm was done; the others rolled and barked too, privately ashamed of themselves for not seeing the point, and never suspecting that the fault was not with them and there wasn't any to see.

You can see by these things that she was of a rather vain and frivolous character; still, she had virtues, and enough to make up, I think. She had a kind heart and gentle ways, and never harbored resentments for injuries done her, but put them easily out of her mind and forgot them; and she taught her children her kindly way, and from her we learned also to be brave and prompt in time of danger, and not to run away, but face the peril that threatened friend or stranger, and help him the best we could without stopping to think what the cost might be to us. And she taught us not by words only, but by example, and that is the best way and the surest and the most lasting. Why, the brave things she did, the splendid things! She was just a soldier; and so modest about it—well, you couldn't help admiring her, and you couldn't help imitating her; not even a King Charles spaniel could remain entirely despicable in her society. So, as you see, there was more to her than her education.

When I was well grown, at last, I was sold and taken away, and I never saw her again. She was broken-hearted, and so was I, and we cried; but she comforted me as well as she could, and said we were sent into this world for a wise and good purpose, and must do our duties without repining, take our life as we might find it, live it for the best good of others, and never mind about the results; they were not our affair. She said men who did like this would have a noble and beautiful reward by and by in another world, and although we animals would not go there, to do well and right without reward would give to our brief lives a worthiness and dignity which in itself would be a reward. She had gathered these things from time to time when she had gone to the Sunday-school with the children, and had laid them up in her memory more carefully than she had done with those other words and phrases; and she had studied them deeply, for her good and ours. One may see by this that she had a wise and thoughtful head, for all there was so much lightness and vanity in it.

So we said our farewells, and looked our last upon each other through our tears; and the last thing she said—keeping it for the last to make me remember it the better, I think—was, "In memory of me, when there is a time of danger to another do not think of yourself, think of your mother, and do as she would do."

Do you think I could forget that? No.

It was such a charming home!—my new one; a fine great house, with pictures, and delicate decorations, and rich furniture, and no gloom anywhere, but all the wilderness of dainty colors lit up with flooding sunshine; and the spacious grounds around it, and the great garden—oh, greensward, and noble trees, and flowers, no end! And I was the same as a member of the family; and they loved me, and petted me, and did not give me a new name, but called me by my old one that was dear to me because my mother had given it me—Aileen Mavourneen. She got it out of a song; and the Grays knew that song, and said it was a beautiful name.

Mrs. Gray was thirty, and so sweet and so lovely, you cannot imagine it; and Sadie was ten, and just like her mother, just a darling slender little copy of her, with auburn tails down her back, and short frocks; and the baby was a year old, and plump and dimpled, and fond of me, and never could get enough of hauling on my tail, and hugging me, and laughing out its innocent happiness; and Mr. Gray was thirty-eight, and tall and slender and handsome, a little bald in front, alert, quick in his movements, business-like, prompt, decided, unsentimental, and with that kind of trim-chiseled face that just seems to glint and sparkle with frosty intellectuality! He was a renowned scientist. I do not know what the word means, but my mother would know how to use it and get effects. She would know how to depress a rat-terrier with it and make a lap-dog look sorry he came. But that is not the best one; the best one was Laboratory. My mother could organize a Trust on that one that would skin the tax-collars off the whole herd. The laboratory was not a book, or a picture, or a place to wash your hands in, as the college president's dog said—no, that is the lavatory; the laboratory is quite different, and is filled with jars, and bottles, and electrics, and wires, and strange machines; and every week other scientists came there and sat in the place, and used the machines, and discussed, and made what they called experiments and discoveries; and often I came, too, and stood around and listened, and tried to learn, for the sake of my mother, and in loving memory of her, although it was a pain to me, as realizing what she was losing out of her life and I gaining nothing at all; for try as I might, I was never able to make anything out of it at all.

Other times I lay on the floor in the mistress's work-room and slept, she gently using me for a foot-stool, knowing it pleased me, for it was a caress; other times I spent an hour in the nursery, and got well tousled and made happy; other times I watched by the crib there, when the baby was asleep and the nurse out for a few minutes on the baby's affairs; other times I romped and raced through the grounds and the garden with Sadie till we were tired out, then slumbered on the grass in the shade of a tree while she read her book; other times I went visiting among the neighbor dogs—for there were some most pleasant ones not far away, and one very handsome and courteous and graceful one, a curly-haired Irish setter by the name of Robin Adair, who was a Presbyterian like me, and belonged to the Scotch minister. The servants in our house were all kind to me and were fond of me, and so, as you see, mine was a pleasant life. There could not be a happier dog that I was, nor a gratefuller one. I will say this for myself, for it is only the truth: I tried in all ways to do well and right, and honor my mother's memory and her teachings, and earn the happiness that had come to me, as best I could.

By and by came my little puppy, and then my cup was full, my happiness was perfect. It was the dearest little waddling thing, and so smooth and soft and velvety, and had such cunning little awkward paws, and such affectionate eyes, and such a sweet and innocent face; and it made me so proud to see how the children and their mother adored it, and fondled it, and exclaimed over every little wonderful thing it did. It did seem to me that life was just too lovely to . . .

Then came the winter. One day I was standing a watch in the nursery. That is to say, I was asleep on the bed. The baby was asleep in the crib, which was alongside the bed, on the side next the fireplace. It was the kind of crib that has a lofty tent over it made of gauzy stuff that you can see through. The nurse was out, and we two sleepers were alone. A spark from the wood-fire was shot out, and it lit on the slope of the tent. I suppose a quiet interval followed, then a scream from the baby awoke me, and there was that tent flaming up toward the ceiling! Before I could think, I sprang to the floor in my fright, and in a second was half-way to the door; but in the next half-second my mother's farewell was sounding in my ears, and I was back on the bed again. I reached my head through the flames and dragged the baby out by the waist-band, and tugged it along, and we fell to the floor together in a cloud of smoke; I snatched a new hold, and dragged the screaming little creature along and out at the door and around the bend of the hall, and was still tugging away, all excited and happy and proud, when the master's voice shouted:

"Begone you cursed beast!" and I jumped to save myself; but he was furiously quick, and chased me up, striking furiously at me with his cane, I dodging this way and that, in terror, and at last a strong blow fell upon my left foreleg, which made me shriek and fall, for the moment, helpless; the cane went up for another blow, but never descended, for the nurse's voice rang wildly out, "The nursery's on fire!" and the master rushed away in that direction, and my other bones were saved.

The pain was cruel, but, no matter, I must not lose any time; he might come back at any moment; so I limped on three legs to the other end of the hall, where there was a dark little stairway leading up into a garret where old boxes and such things were kept, as I had heard say, and where people seldom went. I managed to climb up there, then I searched my way through the dark among the piles of things, and hid in the secretest place I could find. It was foolish to be afraid there, yet still I was; so afraid that I held in and hardly even whimpered, though it would have been such a comfort to whimper, because that eases the pain, you know. But I could lick my leg, and that did some good.

For half an hour there was a commotion downstairs, and shoutings, and rushing footsteps, and then there was quiet again. Quiet for some minutes, and that was grateful to my spirit, for then my fears began to go down; and fears are worse than pains—oh, much worse. Then came a sound that froze me. They were calling me—calling me by name—hunting for me!

It was muffled by distance, but that could not take the terror out of it, and it was the most dreadful sound to me that I had ever heard. It went all about, everywhere, down there: along the halls, through all the rooms, in both stories, and in the basement and the cellar; then outside, and farther and farther away—then back, and all about the house again, and I thought it would never, never stop. But at last it did, hours and hours after the vague twilight of the garret had long ago been blotted out by black darkness.

Then in that blessed stillness my terrors fell little by little away, and I was at peace and slept. It was a good rest I had, but I woke before the twilight had come again. I was feeling fairly comfortable, and I could think out a plan now. I made a very good one; which was, to creep down, all the way down the back stairs, and hide behind the cellar door, and slip out and escape when the iceman came at dawn, while he was inside filling the refrigerator; then I would hide all day, and start on my journey when night came; my journey to—well, anywhere where they would not know me and betray me to the master. I was feeling almost cheerful now; then suddenly I thought: Why, what would life be without my puppy!

That was despair. There was no plan for me; I saw that; I must stay where I was; stay, and wait, and take what might come—it was not my affair; that was what life is—my mother had said it. Then—well, then the calling began again! All my sorrows came back. I said to myself, the master will never forgive. I did not know what I had done to make him so bitter and so unforgiving, yet I judged it was something a dog could not understand, but which was clear to a man and dreadful.

They called and called—days and nights, it seemed to me. So long that the hunger and thirst near drove me mad, and I recognized that I was getting very weak. When you are this way you sleep a great deal, and I did. Once I woke in an awful fright—it seemed to me that the calling was right there in the garret! And so it was: it was Sadie's voice, and she was crying; my name was falling from her lips all broken, poor thing, and I could not believe my ears for the joy of it when I heard her say:

"Come back to us—oh, come back to us, and forgive—it is all so sad without our—"

I broke in with SUCH a grateful little yelp, and the next moment Sadie was plunging and stumbling through the darkness and the lumber and shouting for the family to hear, "She's found, she's found!"

The days that followed—well, they were wonderful. The mother and Sadie and the servants—why, they just seemed to worship me. They couldn't seem to make me a bed that was fine enough; and as for food, they couldn't be satisfied with anything but game and delicacies that were out of season; and every day the friends and neighbors flocked in to hear about my heroism—that was the name they called it by, and it means agriculture. I remember my mother pulling it on a kennel once, and explaining it in that way, but didn't say what agriculture was, except that it was synonymous with intramural incandescence; and a dozen times a day Mrs. Gray and Sadie would tell the tale to new-comers, and say I risked my life to save the baby's, and both of us had burns to prove it, and then the company would pass me around and pet me and exclaim about me, and you could see the pride in the eyes of Sadie and her mother; and when the people wanted to know what made me limp, they looked ashamed and changed the subject, and sometimes when people hunted them this way and that way with questions about it, it looked to me as if they were going to cry.

And this was not all the glory; no, the master's friends came, a whole twenty of the most distinguished people, and had me in the laboratory, and discussed me as if I was a kind of discovery; and some of them said it was wonderful in a dumb beast, the finest exhibition of instinct they could call to mind; but the master said, with vehemence, "It's far above instinct; it's REASON, and many a man, privileged to be saved and go with you and me to a better world by right of its possession, has less of it than this poor silly quadruped that's foreordained to perish"; and then he laughed, and said: "Why, look at me—I'm a sarcasm! Bless you, with all my grand intelligence, the only thing I inferred was that the dog had gone mad and was destroying the child, whereas but for the beast's intelligence—it's REASON, I tell you!—the child would have perished!"

They disputed and disputed, and I was the very center of subject of it all, and I wished my mother could know that this grand honor had come to me; it would have made her proud.

Then they discussed optics, as they called it, and whether a certain injury to the brain would produce blindness or not, but they could not agree about it, and said they must test it by experiment by and by; and next they discussed plants, and that interested me, because in the summer Sadie and I had planted seeds—I helped her dig the holes, you know—and after days and days a little shrub or a flower came up there, and it was a wonder how that could happen; but it did, and I wished I could talk—I would have told those people about it and shown then how much I knew, and been all alive with the subject; but I didn't care for the optics; it was dull, and when they came back to it again it bored me, and I went to sleep.

Pretty soon it was spring, and sunny and pleasant and lovely, and the sweet mother and the children patted me and the puppy good-by, and went away on a journey and a visit to their kin, and the master wasn't any company for us, but we played together and had good times, and the servants were kind and friendly, so we got along quite happily and counted the days and waited for the family.

And one day those men came again, and said, now for the test, and they took the puppy to the laboratory, and I limped three-leggedly along, too, feeling proud, for any attention shown to the puppy was a pleasure to me, of course. They discussed and experimented, and then suddenly the puppy shrieked, and they set him on the floor, and he went staggering around, with his head all bloody, and the master clapped his hands and shouted:

"There, I've won—confess it! He's as blind as a bat!" And they all said: "It's so—you've proved your theory, and suffering humanity owes you a great debt from henceforth," and they crowded around him, and wrung his hand cordially and thankfully, and praised him.

But I hardly saw or heard these things, for I ran at once to my little darling, and snuggled close to it where it lay, and licked the blood, and it put its head against mine, whimpering softly, and I knew in my heart it was a comfort to it in its pain and trouble to feel its mother's touch, though it could not see me. Then it dropped down, presently, and its little velvet nose rested upon the floor, and it was still, and did not move any more.

Soon the master stopped discussing a moment, and rang in the footman, and said, "Bury it in the far corner of the garden," and then went on with the discussion, and I trotted after the footman, very happy and grateful, for I knew the puppy was out of its pain now, because it was asleep. We went far down the garden to the farthest end, where the children and the nurse and the puppy and I used to play in the summer in the shade of a great elm, and there the footman dug a hole, and I saw he was going to plant the puppy, and I was glad, because it would grow and come up a fine handsome dog, like Robin Adair, and be a beautiful surprise for the family when they came home; so I tried to help him dig, but my lame leg was no good, being stiff, you know, and you have to have two, or it is no use. When the footman had finished and covered little Robin up, he patted my head, and there were tears in his eyes, and he said: "Poor little doggie, you saved HIS child!"

I have watched two whole weeks, and he doesn't come up! This last week a fright has been stealing upon me. I think there is something terrible about this. I do not know what it is, but the fear makes me sick, and I cannot eat, though the servants bring me the best of food; and they pet me so, and even come in the night, and cry, and say, "Poor doggie—do give it up and come home; don't break our hearts!" and all this terrifies me the more, and makes me sure something has happened. And I am so weak; since yesterday I cannot stand on my feet anymore. And within this hour the servants, looking toward the sun where it was sinking out of sight and the night chill coming on, said things I could not understand, but they carried something cold to my heart.

"Those poor creatures! They do not suspect. They will come home in the morning, and eagerly ask for the little doggie that did the brave deed, and who of us will be strong enough to say the truth to them: 'The humble little friend is gone where go the beasts that perish.'"

8

Beautiful Joe

by Marshall Saunders

Focusing on the sometimes precarious relationship between human and dog, this is an excerpt from Beautiful Joe *by Marshall Saunders. This is the beloved tale of an ugly, misfit mongrel who suffers at the hands of his first owner until at last he finds a loving home. The book was written as a response to* Black Beauty, *which told a similar tale of a horse's odyssey through life, withstanding ignorance and harsh treatment until he, too, finds his own green pastures. Beautiful Joe was an attempt to make readers aware of the casual mistreatment of dogs.*

My name is Beautiful Joe, and I am a brown dog of medium size. I am not called Beautiful Joe because I am a beauty. Mr. Morris, the clergyman, in whose family I have lived for the last twelve years, says that he thinks I must be called Beautiful Joe for the same reason that his grandfather, down South, called a very ugly lad Cupid and his mother Venus.

I do not know what he means by that, but when he says it people always look at me and smile. I know that I am not beautiful, and I know that I am not a thoroughbred. I am only a cur.

When my mistress went every year to register me and pay my tax, and the man in the office asked what breed I was, she said part fox-terrier and part bull-terrier; but he always put me down a cur. I don't think she liked having him call me a cur; still, I have heard her say that she preferred curs, for they have more character than well-bred dogs. Her father said that she liked ugly dogs for the same reason that a nobleman at the court of a certain king did—namely, that no one else would.

I am an old dog now, and am writing, or rather getting a friend to write, the story of my life. I have seen my mistress laughing and crying over a little book that she says is a story of a horse's life, and sometimes she puts the book down close to my nose to let me see the pictures.

I love my dear mistress; I can say no more than that; I love her better than any one else in the world; and I think it will please her if I write the story of a dog's life. She loves dumb animals, and it always grieves her to see them treated cruelly.

I have heard her say that if all the boys and girls in the world were to rise up and say that there should be no more cruelty to animals, they could put a stop to it. Perhaps it will help a little if I tell a story. I am fond of boys and girls, and though I have seen many cruel men and women, I have seen few cruel children. I think the more stories there are written about dumb animals, the better it will be for us.

In telling my story, I think I had better begin at the first and come right on to the end. I was born in a stable on the outskirts of a small town in Maine called Fairport. The first thing I remember was lying close to my mother and being very snug and warm. The next thing I remember was being always hungry. I had a number of brothers and sisters—six in all—and my mother never had enough milk for us. She was always half starved herself, so she could not feed us properly.

I am very unwilling to say much about my early life, I have lived so long in a family where there is never a harsh word spoken, and where no one thinks of ill-treating anybody or anything, that it seems almost wrong even to think or speak of such a matter as hurting a poor dumb beast.

The man that owned my mother was a milkman. He kept one horse and three cows, and he had a shaky old cart that he used to put his milk cans in. I don't think there can be a worse man in the world than that milkman. It makes me shudder now to think of him. His name was Jenkins, and I am glad to think that he is getting punished now for his cruelty to poor dumb animals and to human beings. If you think it is wrong that I am glad, you must remember that I am only a dog.

The first notice that he took of me when I was a little puppy, just able to stagger about, was to give me a kick that sent me into a corner of the stable. He used to beat and starve my mother. I have seen him use his heavy whip to punish her till her body was covered with blood. When I got older I asked her why she did not run away. She said she did not wish to; but I soon found out that the reason she did not run away was because she loved Jenkins. Cruel and savage as he was, she yet loved him, and I believe she would have laid down her life for him. Now that I am old, I know that there are more men in the world like Jenkins. They are not crazy, they are not drunkards; they simply seem to be possessed with a spirit of wickedness. There are well-to-do people, yes, and rich people, who will treat animals, and even little children, with such terrible cruelty that one cannot even mention the things that they are guilty of.

One reason for Jenkins' cruelty was his idleness. After he went his rounds in the morning with his milk cans, he had nothing to do till late in the afternoon but take care of his stable and yard. If he had kept them neat, and groomed his horse, and cleaned the cows, and dug up the garden, it would have taken up all his time; but he never tidied the place at all, till his yard and stable got so littered up with things he threw down that he could not make his way about.

His house and stable stood in the middle of a large field, and they were at some distance from the road. Passers-by could not see how untidy the place was. Occasionally, a man came to look at the premises, and see that they were in good order, but Jenkins always knew when to expect him, and had things cleaned up a little.

I used to wish that some of the people that took milk from him would come and look at his cows. In the spring and summer he drove them out to pasture, but during the winter they stood all the time in the dirty, dark stable, where the chinks in the wall were so big that the snow swept through almost in drifts. The ground was always muddy and wet; there was only one small window on the north side, where the sun only shone in for a short time in the afternoon.

They were very unhappy cows, but they stood patiently and never complained, though sometimes I know they must have nearly frozen in the bitter winds that blew through the stable on winter nights. They were lean and poor, and were never in good health. Besides being cold they were fed on very poor food.

Jenkins used to come home nearly every afternoon with a great tub in the back of his cart that was full of what he called "peelings." It was kitchen stuff that he asked the cooks at the different houses where he delivered milk, to save for him. They threw rotten vegetables, fruit parings, and scraps from the table into a tub, and gave them to him at the end of a few days. A sour, nasty mess it always was, and not fit to give any creature.

Sometimes, when he had not many "peelings," he would go to town and get a load of decayed vegetables that grocers were glad to have him take off their hands.

This food, together with poor hay, made the cows give very poor milk, and Jenkins used to put some white powder in it, to give it "body," as he said.

Once a very sad thing happened about the milk that no one knew about but Jenkins and his wife. She was a poor, unhappy creature, very frightened of her husband, and not daring to speak much to him. She was not a clean woman, and I never saw a worse-looking house than she kept.

She used to do very queer things that I know now no housekeeper should do. I have seen her catch up the broom to pound potatoes in the pot. She pounded with the handle, and the broom would fly up and down in the air, dropping dust into the pot where the potatoes were. Her pan of soft-mixed bread she often left uncovered in the kitchen, and sometimes the hens walked in and sat in it.

The children used to play in mud puddles about the door. It was the youngest of them that sickened with some kind of fever early in the spring, before Jenkins began driving the cows out to pasture. The child was very ill, and Mrs. Jenkins wanted to send for a doctor, but her husband would not let her. They made a bed in the kitchen, close to the stove, and Mrs. Jenkins nursed the child as best she could. She did all her work near by, and I saw her several times wiping the child's face with the cloth that she used for washing her milk pans.

Nobody knew outside the family that the little girl was ill. Jenkins had such a bad name that none of the neighbors would visit them. By-and-by the child got well, and a week or two later Jenkins came home with quite a frightened face and told his wife that the husband of one of his customers was very ill with typhoid fever.

After a time the gentleman died, and the cook told Jenkins that the doctor wondered how he could have taken the fever, for there was not a case in town.

There was a widow left with three orphans, and they never knew that they had to blame a dirty, careless milkman for taking a kind husband and father from them . . .

I have said that Jenkins spent most of his days in idleness. He had to start out very early in the morning in order to supply his customers with milk for breakfast. Oh, how ugly he used to be when he came into the stable on cold winter mornings, before the sun was up.

He would hang his lantern on a hook, and get his milking stool, and if the cows did not step aside just to suit him, he would seize a broom or fork, and beat them cruelly.

My mother and I slept on a heap of straw in the corner of the stable, and when she heard his step in the morning she always roused me so that we could run out-doors as soon as he opened the stable door. He always aimed a kick at us as we passed, but my mother taught me how to dodge him.

After he finished milking, he took the pails of milk up to the house for Mrs. Jenkins to strain and put in the cans, and he came back and harnessed his horse to the cart. His horse was called Toby, and a poor, miserable, broken-down creature he was. He was weak in the knees, and weak in the back, and weak all over, and Jenkins had to beat him all the time to make him go. He had been a cab horse, and his mouth had been jerked, and twisted, and sawed at, till one would think there could be no feeling left in it; still I have seen him wince and curl up his lip when Jenkins thrust in the frosty bit on a winter's morning.

Poor old Toby! I used to lie on my straw sometimes and wonder he did not cry out with pain. Cold and half starved he always was in the winter time, and often with raw sores on his body that Jenkins would try to hide by putting bits of cloth under the harness. But Toby never murmured, and he never tried to kick and bite, and he minded the least word from Jenkins, and if he swore at him, Toby would start back, or step up quickly, he was so anxious to please him.

After Jenkins put him in the cart, and took in the cans, he set out on his rounds. My mother, whose name was Jess, always went with him. I used to ask her why she followed such a brute of a man, and she would hang her head, and say that sometimes she got a bone from the different houses they stopped at. But that was not the whole reason. She liked Jenkins so much that she wanted to be with him.

I had not her sweet and patient disposition, and I would not go with her. I watched her out of sight, and then ran up to the house to see if Mrs. Jenkins had any scraps for me. I nearly always got something, for she pitied me, and often gave me a kind word or look with the bits of food that she threw to me.

When Jenkins came home, I often coaxed mother to run about and see some of the neighbors' dogs with me. But she never would, and I would not leave her. So, from morning to night we had to sneak about, keeping out of Jenkins' way as much as we could, and yet trying to keep him in sight. He always sauntered about with a pipe in his mouth, and his hands in his pockets, growling first at his wife and children, and then at his dumb creatures.

I have not told what became of my brothers and sisters. One rainy day, when we were eight weeks old, Jenkins, followed by two or three of his ragged, dirty children, came into the stable and looked at us. Then he began to swear because we were so ugly, and said if we had been good-looking, he might have sold some of us. Mother watched him anxiously, and fearing some danger to her puppies, ran and jumped in the middle of us, and looked pleadingly up at him.

It only made him swear the more. He took one pup after another, and right there, before his children and my poor distracted mother, put an end to their lives. Some of them he seized by the legs and knocked against the stalls till their brains were dashed out; others he killed with a fork. It was very terrible. My mother ran up and down the stable, screaming with pain, and I lay weak and trembling, and expecting every instant that my turn would come next. I don't know why he spared me. I was the only one left.

His children cried, and he sent them out of the stable and went out himself. Mother picked up all the puppies and brought them to our nest in the straw and licked them, and tried to bring them back to life; but it was of no use; they were quite dead. We had them in our corner of the stable for some days till Jenkins discovered them, and swearing horribly at us, he took his stable fork and threw them out in the yard and put some earth over them.

My mother never seemed the same after this. She was weak and miserable, and though she was only four years old, she seemed like an old dog. This was on account of the poor food she had been fed on. She could not run after Jenkins, and she lay on our heap of straw, only turning over with her nose the scraps of food I brought her to eat. One day she licked me gently, wagged her tail, and died.

As I sat by her, feeling lonely and miserable, Jenkins came into the stable. I could not bear to look at him. He had killed my mother. There she lay, a little, gaunt, scarred creature, starved and worried to death by him. Her mouth was half open, her eyes were staring. She would never again look kindly at me, or curl up to me at night to keep me warm. Oh, how I hated her murderer! But I sat quietly, even when he went up and turned her over with his foot to see if she was really dead. I think he was a little sorry, for he turned scornfully toward me and said, "She was worth two of you; why didn't you go instead?"

Still I kept quiet till he walked up to me and kicked at me. My heart was nearly broken, and I could stand no more. I flew at him and gave him a savage bite on the ankle.

"Oho," he said, "so you are going to be a fighter, are you? I'll fix you for that." His face was red and furious. He seized me by the back of the neck and carried me out to the yard where a log lay on the ground. "Bill," he called to one of his children, "bring me the hatchet."

He laid my head on the log and pressed one hand on my struggling body. I was now a year old and a full-sized dog. There was a quick, dreadful pain, and he had cut off my ear, not in the way they cut puppies' ears, but close to my head, so close that he cut off some of the skin beyond it. Then he cut off the other ear, and, turning me swiftly round, cut off my tail close to my body.

Then he let me go and stood looking at me as I rolled on the ground and yelped in agony. He was in such a passion that he did not think that people passing by on the road might hear me.

There was a young man going by on a bicycle. He heard my screams and, springing off his bicycle, came hurrying up the path and stood among us before Jenkins caught sight of him.

In the midst of my pain, I heard him in say fiercely, "What have you been doing to that dog?"

"I've been cuttin' his ears for fightin', my young gentleman," said Jenkins. "There is no law to prevent that, is there?"

"And there is no law to prevent my giving you a beating," said the young man, angrily. In a trice he had seized Jenkins by the throat and was pounding him with all his might. Mrs. Jenkins came and stood at the house door, crying, but making no effort to help her husband.

"Bring me a towel," the young man cried to her, after he had stretched Jenkins, bruised and frightened, on the ground. She snatched off her apron and ran down with it, and the young man wrapped me in it, and taking me carefully in his arms, walked down the path to the gate. There were some little boys standing there, watching him, their mouths wide open with astonishment. "Sonny," he said to the largest of them, "if you will come behind and carry this dog, I will give you a quarter."

The boy took me, and we set out. I was all smothered up in a cloth, and moaning with pain, but still I looked out occasionally to see which way we were going. We took the road to the town and stopped in front of a house on Washington Street. The young man leaned his bicycle up against the house, took a quarter from his pocket and put it in the boy's hand, and lifting me gently in his arms, went up a lane leading to the back of the house.

There was a small stable there. He went into it, put me down on the floor, and uncovered my body. Some boys were playing about the stable, and I heard them say, in horrified tones, "Oh, Cousin Harry, what is the matter with that dog?"

"Hush," he said. "Don't make a fuss. You, Jack, go down to the kitchen and ask Mary for a basin of warm water and a sponge, and don't let your mother or Laura hear you."

A few minutes later, the young man had bathed my bleeding ears and tail, and had rubbed something on them that was cool and pleasant, and had bandaged them firmly with strips of cotton. I felt much better and was able to look about me.

I was in a small stable that was evidently not used for a stable, but more for a play-room. There were various kinds of toys scattered about and a swing and bar, such as boys love to twist about on, in two different corners. In a box against the wall was a guinea pig, looking at me in an interested way. This guinea pig's name was Jeff, and he and I became good friends. A long-haired French rabbit was hopping about, and a tame white rat was perched on the shoulder of one of the boys and kept his foothold there, no matter how suddenly the boy moved. There were so many boys, and the stable was so small, that I suppose he was afraid he would get stepped on if he went on the floor. He stared hard at me with his little, red eyes, and never even glanced at a queer-looking, gray cat that was watching me, too, from her bed in the back of the vacant horse stall. Out in the sunny yard, some pigeons were pecking at grain, and a spaniel lay asleep in a corner.

I had never seen anything like this before, and my wonder at it almost drove the pain away. Mother and I always chased rats and birds, and once we killed a kitten. While I was puzzling over it, one of the boys cried out, "Here is Laura!"

"Take that rag out of the way," said Mr. Harry, kicking aside the old apron I had been wrapped in, and that was stained with my blood. One of the boys stuffed it into a barrel, and then they all looked toward the house.

A young girl, holding up one hand to shade her eyes from the sun, was coming up the walk that led from the house to the stable. I thought then that I never had seen such a beautiful girl, and I think so still. She was tall and slender, and had lovely brown eyes and brown hair, and a sweet smile, and just to look at her was enough to make one love her. I stood in the stable door, staring at her with all my might.

"Why, what a funny dog," she said, and stopped short to looked at me. Up to this, I had not thought what a queer-looking sight I must be. Now I twisted round my head, saw the white bandage on my tail, and knowing I was not a fit spectacle for a pretty young lady like that, I slunk into a corner.

"Poor doggie, have I hurt your feelings?" she said, and with a sweet smile at the boys, she passed by them and came up to the guinea pig's box, behind which I had taken refuge. "What is the matter with your head, good dog?" she said, curiously, as she stooped over me.

"He has a cold in it," said one of the boys with a laugh; "so we put a nightcap on." She drew back, and turned very pale. "Cousin Harry, there are drops of blood on this cotton. Who has hurt this dog?"

"Dear Laura," and the young man, coming up, laid his hand on her shoulder, "he got hurt, and I have been bandaging him."

"Who hurt him?"

"I had rather not tell you."

"But I wish to know." Her voice was as gentle as ever, but she spoke so decidedly that the young man was obliged to tell her everything. All the time he was speaking, she kept touching me gently with her fingers. When he had finished his account of rescuing me from Jenkins, she said, quietly:

"You will have the man punished?"

"What is the use? That won't stop him from being cruel." "It will put a check on his cruelty."

"I don't think it would do any good," said the young man, doggedly. "Cousin Harry!" and the young girl stood up very straight and tall, her brown eyes flashing, and one hand pointing at me: "Will you let that pass? That animal has been wronged, it looks to you to right it. The coward who has maimed it for life should be punished. A child has a voice to tell its wrong—a poor, dumb creature must suffer in silence; in bitter, bitter silence. And," eagerly, as the young man tried to interrupt her, "you are doing the man himself an injustice. If he is bad enough to ill-treat his dog, he will ill-treat his wife and children. If he is checked and punished now for his cruelty, he may reform. And even if his wicked heart is not changed, he will be obliged to treat them with outward kindness, through fear of punishment."

The young man looked convinced, and almost as ashamed as if he had been the one to crop my ears. "What do you want me to do?" he said, slowly, and looking sheepishly at the boys who were staring openmouthed at him and the young girl.

The girl pulled a little watch from her belt. "I want you to report that man immediately. It is now five o'clock. I will go down to the police station with you, if you like."

"Very well," he said, his face brightening, and together they went off to the house.

The boys watched them out of sight, then one of them, whose name I afterward learned was Jack, and who came next to Miss Laura in age, gave a low whistle and said, "Doesn't the old lady come out strong when anyone or anything gets abused? I'll never forget the day she found me setting Jim on that black cat of the Wilsons. She scolded me, and then she cried, till I didn't know where to look. Plague on it, how was I going to know he'd kill the old cat? I only wanted to drive it out of the yard. Come on, let's look at the dog."

They all came and bent over me as I lay on the floor in my corner. I wasn't much used to boys, and I didn't know how they would treat me. But I soon found by the way they handled me and talked to me, that they knew a good deal about dogs, and were accustomed to treat them kindly. It seemed very strange to have them pat me, and call me "good dog." No one had ever said that to me before today.

"He's not much of a beauty, is he?" said one of the boys, whom they called Tom.

"Not by a long shot," said Jack Morris, with a laugh. "Not any nearer the beauty mark than yourself, Tom."

Tom flew at him, and they had a scuffle. The other boys paid no attention to them, but went on looking at me. One of them, a little boy with eyes like Miss Laura's, said, "What did Cousin Harry say the dog's name was?"

"Joe," answered another boy. "The little chap that carried him home told him."

"We might call him 'Ugly Joe' then," said a lad with a round, fat face and laughing eyes. I wondered very much who this boy was, and, later on, I found out that he was another of Miss Laura's brothers, and his name was Ned. There seemed to be no end to the Morris boys.

"I don't think Laura would like that," said Jack Morris, suddenly coming up behind him. He was very hot, and was breathing fast, but his manner was as cool as if he had never left the group about me. He had beaten Tom, who was sitting on a box, ruefully surveying a hole in his jacket. "You see," he went on, gaspingly, "if you call him 'Ugly Joe,' her ladyship will say that you are wounding the dear dog's feelings. 'Beautiful Joe,' would be more to her liking."

A shout went up from the boys. I didn't wonder that they laughed. Plain-looking I naturally was; but I must have been hideous in those bandages.

"'Beautiful Joe,' then let it be!" they cried. "Let us go and tell mother, and ask her to give us something for our beauty to eat."

They all trooped out of the stable, and I was very sorry, for when they were with me, I did not mind so much the tingling in my ears, and the terrible pain in my back. They soon brought me some nice food, but I could not touch it; so they went away to their play, and I lay in the box they put me in, trembling with pain, and wishing that the pretty young lady was there to stroke me with her gentle fingers. By-and-by it got dark. The boys finished their play and went into the house, and I saw lights twinkling in the windows. I felt lonely and miserable in this strange place. I would not have gone back to Jenkins' for the world; still it was the only home I had known, and though I felt that I should be happy here, I had not yet gotten used to the change. Then the pain all through my body was dreadful. My head seemed to be on fire, and there were sharp, darting pains up and down my backbone. I did not dare to howl, lest I should make the big dog, Jim, angry.

He was sleeping in a kennel, out in the yard.

The stable was very quiet. Up in the loft above, some rabbits that I had heard running about had now gone to sleep. The guinea pig was nestling in the corner of his box, and the cat and the tame rat had scampered into the house long ago.

At last I could bear the pain no longer, I sat up in my box and looked about me. I felt as if I was going to die, and, though I was very weak, there was something inside me that made me feel as if I wanted to crawl away somewhere out of sight. I slunk out into the yard and along the stable wall, where there was a thick clump of raspberry bushes. I crept in among them and lay down in the damp earth. I tried to scratch off my bandages, but they were fastened on too firmly, and I could not do it. I thought about my poor mother, and wished she was here to lick my sore ears. Though she was so unhappy herself, she never wanted to see me suffer. If I had not disobeyed her, I would not now be suffering so much pain. She had told me again and again not to snap at Jenkins, for it made him worse.

In the midst of my trouble I heard a soft voice calling, "Joe! Joe!" It was Miss Laura's voice, but I felt as if there were weights on my paws, and I could not go to her.

"Joe! Joe!" she said, again. She was going up the walk to the stable, holding up a lighted lamp in her hand. She had on a white dress, and I watched her till she disappeared in the stable. She did not stay long in there. She came out and stood on the gravel. "Joe, Joe, Beautiful Joe, where are you? You are hiding somewhere, but I shall find you." Then she came right to the spot where I was. "Poor doggie," she said, stooping down and patting me. "Are you very miserable, and did you crawl away to die? I have had dogs do that before, but I am not going to let you die, Joe." And she set her lamp on the ground, and took me in her arms.

I was very thin then, not nearly so fat as I am now; still I was quite an armful for her. But she did not seem to find me heavy. She took me right into the house, through the back door, and down a long flight of steps, across a hall, and into a snug kitchen.

"For the land sakes, Miss Laura," said a woman who was bending over a stove, "what have you got there?"

"A poor sick dog, Mary," said Miss Laura, seating herself on a chair. "Will you please warm a little milk for him? And have you a box or a basket down here that he can lie in?"

"I guess so," said the woman; "but he's awful dirty; you're not going to let him sleep in the house, are you?"

"Only for to-night. He is very ill. A dreadful thing happened to him, Mary." And Miss Laura went on to tell her how my ears had been cut off.

"Oh, that's the dog the boys were talking about," said the woman. "Poor creature, he's welcome to all I can do for him." She opened a closet door, and brought out a box, and folded a piece of blanket for me to lie on. Then she heated some milk in a saucepan, and poured it in a saucer, and watched me while Miss Laura went upstairs to get a little bottle of something that would make me sleep. They poured a few drops of this medicine into the milk and offered it to me.

I lapped a little, but I could not finish it, even though Miss Laura coaxed me very gently to do so. She dipped her finger in the milk and held it out to me, and though I did not want it, I could not be ungrateful enough to refuse to lick her finger as often as she offered it to me. After the milk was gone, Mary lifted up my box and carried me into the wash-room that was off the kitchen.

I soon fell sound asleep, and could not rouse myself through the night, even though I both smelled and heard some one coming near me several times. The next morning I found out that it was Miss Laura. Whenever there was a sick animal in the house, no matter if it was only the tame rat, she would get up two or three times in the night to see if there was anything she could do to make it more comfortable.

9

Stickeen

by John Muir

John Muir's prose is remembered in several books as some of the best in natural history experiences. Here he turns his considerable talent to the tale of the dog Stickeen. Muir takes us to Alaska for this one, and the atmosphere and setting provide the perfect background for the heroics of a faithful dog.

IN THE SUMMER OF 1880 I SET OUT FROM FORT WRANGEL IN A CANOE to continue the exploration of the icy region of southeastern Alaska, begun in the fall of 1879. After the necessary provisions, blankets, etc., had been collected and stowed away, and my Indian crew were in their places ready to start, while a crowd of their relatives and friends on the wharf were bidding them good-by and good-luck, my companion, the Rev. S. H. Young, for whom we were waiting, at last came aboard, followed by a little black dog that immediately made himself at home by curling up in a hollow among the baggage. I like dogs, but this one seemed so small and worthless that I objected to his going, and asked the missionary why he was taking him.

"Such a little helpless creature will only be in the way," I said; "you had better pass him up to the Indian boys on the wharf, to be taken home to play with the children. This trip is not likely to be good for toy-dogs. The poor silly thing will be in rain and snow for weeks or months and will require care like a baby."

But his master assured me that he would be no trouble at all; that he was a perfect wonder of a dog, could endure cold and hunger like a bear, swim like a seal, and was wondrous wise and cunning, etc., making out a list of virtues to show he might be the most interesting member of the party.

Nobody could hope to unravel the lines of his ancestry. In all the wonderfully mixed and varied dog-tribe I never saw any creature very much like him, though in some of his sly, soft, gliding motions and gestures he brought the fox to mind. He was short-legged and bunchy-bodied, and his hair, though smooth, was long and silky and slightly waved, so that when the wind was at his back it ruffled, making him look shaggy. At first sight his only noticeable feature was his fine tail, which was about as airy and shady as a squirrel's, and was carried curling forward almost to his nose. On closer inspection you might notice his thin sensitive ears, and sharp eyes with cunning tan-spots above them. Mr. Young told me that when the little fellow was a pup about the size of a woodrat he was presented to his wife by an Irish prospector at Sitka, and that on his arrival at Fort Wrangel he was adopted with enthusiasm by the Stickeen Indians as a sort of new good-luck totem, was named "Stickeen" for the tribe, and became a universal favorite; petted, protected, and admired wherever he went, and regarded as a mysterious fountain of wisdom.

On our trip he soon proved himself a queer character—odd, concealed, independent, keeping invincibly quiet, and doing many little puzzling things that piqued my curiosity. As we sailed week after week through the long intricate channels and inlets among the innumerable islands and mountains of the coast, he spent most of the dull days in sluggish ease, motionless, and apparently as unobserving as if in deep sleep. But I discovered that somehow he always knew what was going on. When the Indians were about to shoot at ducks or seals, or when anything along the shore was exciting our attention, he would rest his chin on the edge of the canoe and calmly look out like a dreamy-eyed tourist. And when he heard us talking about making a landing, he immediately roused himself to see what sort of a place we were coming to, and made ready to jump overboard and swim ashore as soon as the canoe neared the beach. Then, with a vigorous shake to get rid of the brine in his hair, he ran into the woods to hunt small game. But though always the first out of the canoe, he was always the last to get into it. When we were ready to start he could never be found, and refused to come to our call. We soon found out, however, that though we could not see him at such times, he saw us, and from the cover of the briers and huckleberry bushes in the fringe of the woods was watching the canoe with wary eye. For as soon as we were fairly off he came trotting down the beach, plunged into the surf, and swam after us, knowing well that we would cease rowing and take him in. When the contrary little vagabond came alongside, he was lifted by the neck, held at arm's length a moment to drip, and dropped aboard. We tried to cure him of this trick by compelling him to swim a long way, as if we had a mind to abandon him; but this did no good: the longer the swim the better he seemed to like it.

Though capable of great idleness, he never failed to be ready for all sorts of adventures and excursions. One pitch-dark rainy night we landed about ten o'clock at the mouth of a salmon stream when the water was phosphorescent. The salmon were running, and the myriad fins of the on-rushing multitude were churning all the stream into a silvery glow, wonderfully beautiful and impressive in the ebon darkness. To get a good view of the show I set out with one of the Indians and sailed up through the midst of it to the foot of a rapid about half a mile from camp, where the swift current dashing over rocks made the luminous glow most glorious. Happening to look back down the stream, while the Indian was catching a few of the struggling fish, I saw a long spreading fan of light like the tail of a comet, which we thought must be made by some big strange animal that was pursuing us. On it came with its magnificent train, until we imagined we could see the monster's head and eyes; but it was only Stickeen, who, finding I had left the camp, came swimming after me to see what was up.

When we camped early, the best hunter of the crew usually went to the woods for a deer, and Stickeen was sure to be at his heels, provided I had not gone out. For, strange to say, though I never carried a gun, he always followed me, forsaking the hunter and even his master to share my wanderings. The days that were too stormy for sailing I spent in the woods, or on the adjacent mountains, wherever my studies called me; and Stickeen always insisted on going with me, however wild the weather, gliding like a fox through dripping huckleberry bushes and thorny tangles of panax and rubus, scarce stirring their rain-laden leaves; wading and wallowing through snow, swimming icy streams, skipping over logs and rocks and the crevasses of glaciers with the patience and endurance of a determined mountaineer, never tiring or getting discouraged. Once he followed me over a glacier the surface of which was so crusty and rough that it cut his feet until every step was marked with blood; but he trotted on with Indian fortitude until I noticed his red track, and, taking pity on him, made him a set of moccasins out of a handkerchief. However great his troubles he never asked help or made any complaint, as if, like a philosopher, he had learned that without hard work and suffering there could be no pleasure worth having.

Yet none of us was able to make out what Stickeen was really good for. He seemed to meet danger and hardships without anything like reason, insisted on having his own way, never obeyed an order, and the hunter could never set him on anything, or make him fetch the birds he shot. His equanimity was so steady it seemed due to want of feeling; ordinary storms were pleasures to him, and as for mere rain, he flourished in it like a vegetable. No matter what advances you might make, scarce a glance or a tail-wag would you get for your pains. But though he was apparently as cold as a glacier and about as impervious to fun, I tried hard to make his acquaintance, guessing there must be something worth while hidden beneath so much courage, endurance, and love of wild-weather adventure. No superannuated mastiff or bulldog grown old in office surpassed this fluffy midget in stoic dignity. He sometimes reminded me of a small, squat, unshakable desert cactus. For he never displayed a single trace of the merry, tricksy, elfish fun of the terriers and collies that we all know, nor of their touching affection and devotion. Like children, most small dogs beg to be loved and allowed to love; but Stickeen seemed a very Diogenes, asking only to be let alone: a true child of the wilderness, holding the even tenor of his hidden life with the silence and serenity of nature. His strength of character lay in his eyes. They looked as old as the hills, and as young, and as wild. I never tired of looking into them: it was like looking into a landscape; but they were small and rather deep-set, and had no explaining lines around them to give out particulars. I was accustomed to look into the faces of plants and animals, and I watched the little sphinx more and more keenly as an interesting study. But there is no estimating the wit and wisdom concealed and latent in our lower fellow mortals until made manifest by profound experiences; for it is through suffering that dogs as well as saints are developed and made perfect.

After exploring the Sumdum and Tahkoo fiords and their glaciers, we sailed through Stephen's Passage into Lynn Canal and thence through Icy Strait into Cross Sound, searching for unexplored inlets leading toward the great fountain ice-fields of the Fairweather Range. Here, while the tide was in our favor, we were accompanied by a fleet of icebergs drifting out to the ocean from Glacier Bay. Slowly we paddled around Vancouver's Point, Wimbledon, our frail canoe tossed like a feather on the massive heaving swells coming in past Cape Spenser. For miles the sound is bounded by precipitous mural cliffs, which, lashed with wave-spray and their heads hidden in clouds, looked terribly threatening and stern. Had our canoe been crushed or upset we could have made no landing here, for the cliffs, as high as those of Yosemite, sink sheer into deep water. Eagerly we scanned the wall on the north side for the first sign of an opening fiord or harbor, all of us anxious except Stickeen, who dozed in peace or gazed dreamily at the tremendous precipices when he heard us talking about them. At length we made the joyful discovery of the mouth of the inlet now called "Taylor Bay," and about five o'clock reached the head of it and encamped in a spruce grove near the front of a large glacier.

While camp was being made, Joe the hunter climbed the mountain wall on the east side of the fiord in pursuit of wild goats, while Mr. Young and I went to the glacier. We found that it is separated from the waters of the inlet by a tide-washed moraine, and extends, an abrupt barrier, all the way across from wall to wall of the inlet, a distance of about three miles. But our most interesting discovery was that it had recently advanced, though again slightly receding. A portion of the terminal moraine had been plowed up and shoved forward, uprooting and overwhelming the woods on the east side. Many of the trees were down and buried, or nearly so, others were leaning away from the ice-cliffs, ready to fall, and some stood erect, with the bottom of the ice plow still beneath their roots and its lofty crystal spires towering high above their tops. The spectacle presented by these century-old trees standing close beside a spiry wall of ice, with their branches almost touching it, was most novel and striking. And when I climbed around the front, and a little way up the west side of the glacier, I found that it had swelled and increased in height and width in accordance with its advance, and carried away the outer ranks of trees on its bank.

On our way back to camp after these first observations, I planned a far-and-wide excursion for the morrow. I awoke early, called not only by the glacier, which had been on my mind all night, but by a grand flood-storm. The wind was blowing a gale from the north and the rain was flying with the clouds in a wide passionate horizontal flood, as if it were all passing over the country instead of falling on it. The main perennial streams were booming high above their banks, and hundreds of new ones, roaring like the sea, almost covered the lofty gray walls of the inlet with white cascades and falls. I had intended making a cup of coffee and getting something like a breakfast before starting, but when I heard the storm and looked out I made haste to join it; for many of Nature's finest lessons are to be found in her storms, and if careful to keep in right relations with them, we may go safely abroad with them, rejoicing in the grandeur and beauty of their works and ways, and chanting with the old Norsemen, "The blast of the tempest aids our oars, the hurricane is our servant and drives us whither we wish to go." So, omitting breakfast, I put a piece of bread in my pocket and hurried away.

Mr. Young and the Indians were asleep, and so, I hoped, was Stickeen; but I had not gone a dozen rods before he left his bed in the tent and came boring through the blast after me. That a man should welcome storms for their exhilarating music and motion, and go forth to see God making landscapes, is reasonable enough; but what fascination could there be in such tremendous weather for a dog? Surely nothing akin to human enthusiasm for scenery or geology. Anyhow, on he came, breakfastless, through the choking blast. I stopped and did my best to turn him back. "Now don't," I said, shouting to make myself heard in the storm, "now don't, Stickeen. What has got into your queer noddle now? You must be daft. This wild day has nothing for you. There is no game abroad, nothing but weather. Go back to camp and keep warm, get a good breakfast with your master, and be sensible for once. I can't carry you all day or feed you, and this storm will kill you."

But Nature, it seems, was at the bottom of the affair, and she gains her ends with dogs as well as with men, making us do as she likes, shoving and pulling us along her ways, however rough, all but killing us at times in getting her lessons driven hard home. After I had stopped again and again, shouting good warning advice, I saw that he was not to be shaken off; as well might the earth try to shake off the moon. I had once led his master into trouble, when he fell on one of the topmost jags of a mountain and dislocated his arm; now the turn of his humble companion was coming. The pitiful little wanderer just stood there in the wind, drenched and blinking, saying doggedly, "Where thou goest I will go." So at last I told him to come on if he must, and gave him a piece of the bread I had in my pocket; then we struggled on together, and thus began the most memorable of all my wild days.

The level flood, driving hard in our faces, thrashed and washed us wildly until we got into the shelter of a grove on the east side of the glacier near the front, where we stopped awhile for breath and to listen and look out. The exploration of the glacier was my main object, but the wind was too high to allow excursions over its open surface, where one might be dangerously shoved while balancing for a jump on the brink of a crevasse. In the mean time the storm was a fine study. Here the end of the glacier, descending an abrupt swell of resisting rock about five hundred feet high, leans forward and falls in ice cascades. And as the storm came down the glacier from the north, Stickeen and I were beneath the main current of the blast, while favorably located to see and hear it. What a psalm the storm was singing, and how fresh the smell of the washed earth and leaves, and how sweet the still small voices of the storm! Detached wafts and swirls were coming through the woods, with music from the leaves and branches and furrowed boles, and even from the splintered rocks and ice-crags overhead, many of the tones soft and low and flute-like, as if each leaf and tree, crag and spire were a tuned reed. A broad torrent, draining the side of the glacier, now swollen by scores of new streams from the mountains, was rolling boulders along its rocky channel, with thudding, bumping, muffled sounds, rushing towards the bay with tremendous energy, as if in haste to get out of the mountains; the waters above and beneath calling to each other, and all to the ocean, their home.

Looking southward from our shelter, we had this great torrent and the forested mountain wall above it on our left, the spiry ice-crags on our right, and smooth gray gloom ahead. I tried to draw the marvelous scene in my note-book, but the rain blurred the page in spite of all my pains to shelter it, and the sketch was almost worthless. When the wind began to abate, I traced the east side of the glacier. All the trees standing on the edge of the woods were barked and bruised, showing high-ice mark in a very telling way, while tens of thousands of those that had stood for centuries on the bank of the glacier farther out lay crushed and being crushed. In many places I could see down fifty feet or so beneath the margin of the glacier-mill, where trunks from one to two feet in diameter were being ground to pulp against outstanding rock-ribs and bosses of the bank.

About three miles above the front of the glacier I climbed to the surface of it by means of axe-steps made easy for Stickeen. As far as the eye could reach, the level, or nearly level, glacier stretched away indefinitely beneath the gray sky, a seemingly boundless prairie of ice. The rain continued, and grew colder, which I did not mind, but a dim snowy look in the drooping clouds made me hesitate about venturing far from land. No trace of the west shore was visible, and in case the clouds should settle and give snow, or the wind again become violent, I feared getting caught in a tangle of crevasses. Snow-crystals, the flowers of the mountain clouds, are frail, beautiful things, but terrible when flying on storm-winds in darkening, benumbing swarms or when welded together into glaciers full of deadly crevasses. Watching the weather, I sauntered about on the crystal sea. For a mile or two out I found the ice remarkably safe. The marginal crevasses were mostly narrow, while the few wider ones were easily avoided by passing around them, and the clouds began to open here and there.

Thus encouraged, I at last pushed out for the other side; for Nature can make us do anything she likes. At first we made rapid progress, and the sky was not very threatening, while I took bearings occasionally with a pocket compass to enable me to find my way back more surely in case the storm should become blinding; but the structure lines of the glacier were my main guide. Toward the west side we came to a closely crevassed section in which we had to make long, narrow tacks and doublings, tracing the edges of tremendous transverse and longitudinal crevasses, many of which were from twenty to thirty feet wide, and perhaps a thousand feet deep—beautiful and awful. In working a way through them I was severely cautious, but Stickeen came on as unhesitating as the flying clouds. The widest crevasse that I could jump he would leap without so much as halting to take a look at it. The weather was now making quick changes, scattering bits of dazzling brightness through the wintry gloom; at rare intervals, when the sun broke forth wholly free, the glacier was seen from shore to shore with a bright array of encompassing mountains partly revealed, wearing the clouds as garments, while the prairie bloomed and sparkled with irised light from myriads of washed crystals. Then suddenly all the glorious show would be darkened and blotted out.

Stickeen seemed to care for none of these things, bright or dark, nor for the crevasses, wells, moulins, or swift flashing streams into which he might fall. The little adventurer was only about two years old, yet nothing seemed novel to him, nothing daunted him. He showed neither caution nor curiosity, wonder nor fear, but bravely trotted on as if glaciers were playgrounds. His stout, muffled body seemed all one skipping muscle, and it was truly wonderful to see how swiftly and to all appearance heedlessly he flashed across nerve-trying chasms six or eight feet wide. His courage was so unwavering that it seemed to be due to dullness of perception, as if he were only blindly bold; and I kept warning him to be careful. For we had been close companions on so many wilderness trips that I had formed the habit of talking to him as if he were a boy and understood every word.

We gained the west shore in about three hours; the width of the glacier here being about seven miles. Then I pushed northward in order to see as far back as possible into the fountains of the Fairweather Mountains, in case the clouds should rise. The walking was easy along the margin of the forest, which, of course, like that on the other side, had been invaded and crushed by the swollen, overflowing glacier. In an hour or so, after passing a massive headland, we came suddenly on a branch of the glacier, which, in the form of a magnificent ice-cascade two miles wide, was pouring over the rim of the main basin in a westerly direction, its surface broken into wave-shaped blades and shattered blocks, suggesting the wildest updashing, heaving, plunging motion of a great river cataract. Tracing it down three or four miles, I found that it discharged into a lake, filling it with icebergs.

I would gladly have followed the lake outlet to tide-water, but the day was already far spent, and the threatening sky called for haste on the return trip to get off the ice before dark. I decided therefore to go no farther, and, after taking a general view of the wonderful region, turned back, hoping to see it again under more favorable auspices. We made good speed up the cañon of the great ice-torrent, and out on the main glacier until we had left the west shore about two miles behind us. Here we got into a difficult network of crevasses, the gathering clouds began to drop misty fringes, and soon the dreaded snow came flying thick and fast. I now began to feel anxious about finding a way in the blurring storm. Stickeen showed no trace of fear. He was still the same silent, able little hero. I noticed, however, that after the storm-darkness came on he kept close up behind me. The snow urged us to make still greater haste, but at the same time hid our way. I pushed on as best I could, jumping innumerable crevasses, and for every hundred rods or so of direct advance traveling a mile in doubling up and down in the turmoil of chasms and dislocated ice-blocks. After an hour or two of this work we came to a series of longitudinal crevasses of appalling width, and almost straight and regular in trend, like immense furrows. These I traced with firm nerve, excited and strengthened by the danger, making wide jumps, poising cautiously on their dizzy edges after cutting hollows for my feet before making the spring, to avoid possible slipping or any uncertainty on the farther sides, where only one trial is granted—exercise at once frightful and inspiring. Stickeen followed seemingly without effort.

Many a mile we thus traveled, mostly up and down, making but little real headway in crossing, running instead of walking most of the time as the danger of being compelled to spend the night on the glacier became threatening. Stickeen seemed able for anything. Doubtless we could have weathered the storm for one night, dancing on a flat spot to keep from freezing, and I faced the threat without feeling anything like despair; but we were hungry and wet, and the wind from the mountains was still thick with snow and bitterly cold, so of course that night would have seemed a very long one. I could not see far enough through the blurring snow to judge in which general direction the least dangerous route lay, while the few dim, momentary glimpses I caught of mountains through rifts in the flying clouds were far from encouraging either as weather signs or as guides. I had simply to grope my way from crevasse to crevasse, holding a general direction by the ice-structure, which was not to be seen everywhere, and partly by the wind. Again and again I was put to my mettle, but Stickeen followed easily, his nerve apparently growing more unflinching as the danger increased. So it always is with mountaineers when hard beset. Running hard and jumping, holding every minute of the remaining daylight, poor as it was, precious, we doggedly persevered and tried to hope that every difficult crevasse we overcame would prove to be the last of its kind. But on the contrary, as we advanced they became more deadly trying.

At length our way was barred by a very wide and straight crevasse, which I traced rapidly northward a mile or so without finding a crossing or hope of one; then down the glacier about as far, to where it united with another uncrossable crevasse. In all this distance of perhaps two miles there was only one place where I could possibly jump it, but the width of this jump was the utmost I dared attempt, while the danger of slipping on the farther side was so great that I was loath to try it. Furthermore, the side I was on was about a foot higher than the other, and even with this advantage the crevasse seemed dangerously wide. One is liable to underestimate the width of crevasses where the magnitudes in general are great. I therefore stared at this one mighty keenly, estimating its width and the shape of the edge on the farther side, until I thought that I could jump it if necessary, but that in case I should be compelled to jump back from the lower side I might fail. Now, a cautious mountaineer seldom takes a step on unknown ground which seems at all dangerous that he cannot retrace in case he should be stopped by unseen obstacles ahead. This is the rule of mountaineers who live long, and, though in haste, I compelled myself to sit down and calmly deliberate before I broke it.

Retracing my devious path in imagination as if it were drawn on a chart, I saw that I was recrossing the glacier a mile or two farther up stream than the course pursued in the morning, and that I was now entangled in a section I had not before seen. Should I risk this dangerous jump, or try to regain the woods on the west shore, make a fire, and have only hunger to endure while waiting for a new day? I had already crossed so broad a stretch of dangerous ice that I saw it would be difficult to get back to the woods through the storm, before dark, and the attempt would most likely result in a dismal night-dance on the glacier; while just beyond the present barrier the surface seemed more promising, and the east shore was now perhaps about as near as the west. I was therefore eager to go on. But this wide jump was a dreadful obstacle.

At length, because of the dangers already behind me, I determined to venture against those that might be ahead, jumped and landed well, but with so little to spare that I more than ever dreaded being compelled to take that jump back from the lower side. Stickeen followed, making nothing of it, and we ran eagerly forward, hoping we were leaving all our troubles behind. But within the distance of a few hundred yards we were stopped by the widest crevasse yet encountered. Of course I made haste to explore it, hoping all might yet be remedied by finding a bridge or a way around either end. About three-fourths of a mile upstream I found that it united with the one we had just crossed, as I feared it would. Then, tracing it down, I found it joined the same crevasse at the lower end also, maintaining throughout its whole course a width of forty to fifty feet. Thus to my dismay I discovered that we were on a narrow island about two miles long, with two barely possible ways of escape: one back by the way we came, the other ahead by an almost inaccessible sliver-bridge that crossed the great crevasse from near the middle of it!

After this nerve-trying discovery I ran back to the sliver-bridge and cautiously examined it. Crevasses, caused by strains from variations in the rate of motion of different parts of the glacier and convexities in the channel, are mere cracks when they first open, so narrow as hardly to admit the blade of a pocket-knife, and gradually widen according to the extent of the strain and the depth of the glacier. Now some of these cracks are interrupted, like the cracks in wood, and in opening, the strip of ice between overlapping ends is dragged out, and may maintain a continuous connection between the sides, just as the two sides of a slivered crack in wood that is being split are connected. Some crevasses remain open for months or even years, and by the melting of their sides continue to increase in width long after the opening strain has ceased; while the sliver-bridges, level on top at first and perfectly safe, are at length melted to thin, vertical, knife-edged blades, the upper portion being most exposed to the weather; and since the exposure is greatest in the middle, they at length curve downward like the cables of suspension bridges. This one was evidently very old, for it had been weathered and wasted until it was the most dangerous and inaccessible that ever lay in my way. The width of the crevasse was here about fifty feet, and the sliver crossing diagonally was about seventy feet long; its thin knife-edge near the middle was depressed twenty-five or thirty feet below the level of the glacier, and the upcurving ends were attached to the sides eight or ten feet below the brink. Getting down the nearly vertical wall to the end of the sliver and up the other side were the main difficulties, and they seemed all but insurmountable. Of the many perils encountered in my years of wandering on mountains and glaciers, none seemed so plain and stern and merciless as this. And it was presented when we were wet to the skin and hungry, the sky dark with quick driving snow, and the night near. But we were forced to face it. It was a tremendous necessity.

Beginning, not immediately above the sunken end of the bridge, but a little to one side, I cut a deep hollow on the brink for my knees to rest in. Then, leaning over, with my short-handled axe I cut a step sixteen or eighteen inches below, which on account of the sheerness of the wall was necessarily shallow. That step, however, was well made; its floor sloped slightly inward and formed a good hold for my heels. Then, slipping cautiously upon it, and crouching as low as possible, with my left side toward the wall, I steadied myself against the wind with my left hand in a slight notch, while with the right I cut other similar steps and notches in succession, guarding against losing balance by glinting of the axe, or by wind-gusts, for life and death were in every stroke and in the niceness of finish of every foothold.

After the end of the bridge was reached I chipped it down until I had made a level platform six or eight inches wide, and it was a trying thing to poise on this little slippery platform while bending over to get safely astride of the sliver. Crossing was then comparatively easy by chipping off the sharp edge with short, careful strokes, and hitching forward an inch or two at a time, keeping my balance with my knees pressed against the sides. The tremendous abyss on either hand I studiously ignored. To me the edge of that blue sliver was then all the world. But the most trying part of the adventure, after working my way across inch by inch and chipping another small platform, was to rise from the safe position astride and to cut a stepladder in the nearly vertical face of the wall—chipping, climbing, holding on with feet and fingers in mere notches. At such times one's whole body is eye, and common skill and fortitude are replaced by power beyond our call or knowledge. Never before had I been so long under deadly strain. How I got up that cliff I never could tell. The thing seemed to have been done by somebody else. I never have held death in contempt, though in the course of my explorations I have oftentimes felt that to meet one's fate on a noble mountain, or in the heart of a glacier, would be blessed as compared with death from disease, or from some shabby lowland accident. But the best death, quick and crystal-pure, set so glaringly open before us, is hard enough to face, even though we feel gratefully sure that we have already had happiness enough for a dozen lives.

But poor Stickeen, the wee, hairy, sleekit beastie, think of him! When I had decided to dare the bridge, and while I was on my knees chipping a hollow on the rounded brow above it, he came behind me, pushed his head past my shoulder, looked down and across, scanned the sliver and its approaches with his mysterious eyes, then looked me in the face with a startled air of surprise and concern, and began to mutter and whine; saying as plainly as if speaking with words, "Surely, you are not going into that awful place." This was the first time I had seen him gaze deliberately into a crevasse, or into my face with an eager, speaking, troubled look. That he should have recognized and appreciated the danger at the first glance showed wonderful sagacity. Never before had the daring midget seemed to know that ice was slippery or that there was any such thing as danger anywhere. His looks and tones of voice when he began to complain and speak his fears were so human that I unconsciously talked to him in sympathy as I would to a frightened boy, and in trying to calm his fears perhaps in some measure moderated my own. "Hush your fears, my boy," I said, "we will get across safe, though it is not going to be easy. No right way is easy in this rough world. We must risk our lives to save them. At the worst we can only slip, and then how grand a grave we will have, and by and by our nice bones will do good in the terminal moraine."

But my sermon was far from reassuring him: he began to cry, and after taking another piercing look at the tremendous gulf, ran away in desperate excitement, seeking some other crossing. By the time he got back, baffled of course, I had made a step or two. I dared not look back, but he made himself heard; and when he saw that I was certainly bent on crossing he cried aloud in despair. The danger was enough to daunt anybody, but it seems wonderful that he should have been able to weigh and appreciate it so justly. No mountaineer could have seen it more quickly or judged it more wisely, discriminating between real and apparent peril.

When I gained the other side, he screamed louder than ever, and after running back and forth in vain search for a way of escape, he would return to the brink of the crevasse above the bridge, moaning and wailing as if in the bitterness of death. Could this be the silent, philosophic Stickeen? I shouted encouragement, telling him the bridge was not so bad as it looked, that I had left it flat and safe for his feet, and he could walk it easily. But he was afraid to try. Strange so small an animal should be capable of such big, wise fears. I called again and again in a reassuring tone to come on and fear nothing; that he could come if he would only try. He would hush for a moment, look down again at the bridge, and shout his unshakable conviction that he could never, never come that way; then lie back in despair, as if howling, "O-o-oh! what a place! No-o-o, I can never go-o-o down there!" His natural composure and courage had vanished utterly in a tumultuous storm of fear. Had the danger been less, his distress would have seemed ridiculous. But in this dismal, merciless abyss lay the shadow of death, and his heartrending cries might well have called Heaven to his help. Perhaps they did. So hidden before, he was now transparent, and one could see the workings of his heart and mind like the movements of a clock out of its case. His voice and gestures, hopes and fears, were so perfectly human that none could mistake them; while he seemed to understand every word of mine. I was troubled at the thought of having to leave him out all night, and of the danger of not finding him in the morning. It seemed impossible to get him to venture. To compel him to try through fear of being abandoned, I started off as if leaving him to his fate, and disappeared back of a hummock; but this did no good; he only lay down and moaned in utter hopeless misery. So, after hiding a few minutes, I went back to the brink of the crevasse and in a severe tone of voice shouted across to him that now I must certainly leave him, I could wait no longer, and that, if he would not come, all I could promise was that I would return to seek him next day. I warned him that if he went back to the woods the wolves would kill him, and finished by urging him once more by words and gestures to come on, come on.

He knew very well what I meant, and at last, with the courage of despair, hushed and breathless, he crouched down on the brink in the hollow I had made for my knees, pressed his body against the ice as if trying to get the advantage of the friction of every hair, gazed into the first step, put his little feet together and slid them slowly, slowly over the edge and down into it, bunching all four in it and almost standing on his head. Then, without lifting his feet, as well as I could see through the snow, he slowly worked them over the edge of the step and down into the next and the next in succession in the same way, and gained the end of the bridge. Then, lifting his feet with the regularity and slowness of the vibrations of a seconds pendulum, as if counting and measuring one-two-three, holding himself steady against the gusty wind, and giving separate attention to each little step, he gained the foot of the cliff, while I was on my knees leaning over to give him a lift should he succeed in getting within reach of my arm. Here he halted in dead silence, and it was here I feared he might fail, for dogs are poor climbers. I had no cord. If I had had one, I would have dropped a noose over his head and hauled him up. But while I was thinking whether an available cord might be made out of clothing, he was looking keenly into the series of notched steps and finger-holds I had made, as if counting them, and fixing the position of each one of them in his mind. Then suddenly up he came in a springy rush, hooking his paws into the steps and notches so quickly that I could not see how it was done, and whizzed past my head, safe at last!

And now came a scene! "Well done, well done, little boy! Brave boy!" I cried, trying to catch and caress him; but he would not be caught. Never before or since have I seen anything like so passionate a revulsion from the depths of despair to exultant, triumphant, uncontrollable joy. He flashed and darted hither and thither as if fairly demented, screaming and shouting, swirling round and round in giddy loops and circles like a leaf in a whirlwind, lying down, and rolling over and over, sidewise and heels over head, and pouring forth a tumultuous flood of hysterical cries and sobs and gasping mutterings. When I ran up to him to shake him, fearing he might die of joy, he flashed off two or three hundred yards, his feet in a mist of motion; then, turning suddenly, came back in a wild rush and launched himself at my face, almost knocking me down, all the time screeching and screaming and shouting as if saying, "Saved! saved! saved!" Then away again, dropping suddenly at times with his feet in the air, trembling and fairly sobbing. Such passionate emotion was enough to kill him. Moses' stately song of triumph after escaping the Egyptians and the Red Sea was nothing to it. Who could have guessed the capacity of the dull, enduring little fellow for all that most stirs this mortal frame? Nobody could have helped crying with him!

But there is nothing like work for toning down excessive fear or joy. So I ran ahead, calling him in as gruff a voice as I could command to come on and stop his nonsense, for we had far to go and it would soon be dark. Neither of us feared another trial like this. Heaven would surely count one enough for a lifetime. The ice ahead was gashed by thousands of crevasses, but they were common ones. The joy of deliverance burned in us like fire, and we ran without fatigue, every muscle with immense rebound glorying in its strength. Stickeen flew across everything in his way, and not till dark did he settle into his normal fox-like trot. At last the cloudy mountains came in sight, and we soon felt the solid rock beneath our feet, and were safe. Then came weakness. Danger had vanished, and so had our strength. We tottered down the lateral moraine in the dark, over boulders and tree trunks, through the bushes and devil-club thickets of the grove where we had sheltered ourselves in the morning, and across the level mud-slope of the terminal moraine. We reached camp about ten o'clock, and found a big fire and a big supper. A party of Hoona Indians had visited Mr. Young, bringing a gift of porpoise meat and wild strawberries, and Hunter Joe had brought in a wild goat. But we lay down, too tired to eat much, and soon fell into a troubled sleep. The man who said, "The harder the toil, the sweeter the rest," never was profoundly tired. Stickeen kept springing up and muttering in his sleep, no doubt dreaming that he was still on the brink of the crevasse; and so did I, that night and many others long afterward, when I was overtired.

Thereafter Stickeen was a changed dog. During the rest of the trip, instead of holding aloof, he always lay by my side, tried to keep me constantly in sight, and would hardly accept a morsel of food, however tempting, from any hand but mine. At night, when all was quiet about the camp-fire, he would come to me and rest his head on my knee with a look of devotion as if I were his god. And often as he caught my eye he seemed to be trying to say, "Wasn't that an awful time we had together on the glacier?"

Nothing in after years has dimmed that Alaska storm-day. As I write it all comes rushing and roaring to mind as if I were again in the heart of it. Again I see the gray flying clouds with their rain-floods and snow, the ice-cliffs towering above the shrinking forest, the majestic ice-cascade, the vast glacier outspread before its white mountain fountains, and in the heart of it the tremendous crevasse—emblem of the valley of the shadow of death—low clouds trailing over it, the snow falling into it; and on its brink I see little Stickeen, and I hear his cries for help and his shouts of joy. I have known many dogs, and many a story I could tell of their wisdom and devotion; but to none do I owe so much as to Stickeen. At first the least promising and least known of my dog-friends, he suddenly became the best known of them all. Our storm-battle for life brought him to light, and through him as through a window I have ever since been looking with deeper sympathy into all my fellow mortals.

None of Stickeen's friends knows what finally became of him. After my work for the season was done, I departed for California, and I never saw the dear little fellow again. In reply to anxious inquiries his master wrote me that in the summer of 1883 he was stolen by a tourist at Fort Wrangel and taken away on a steamer. His fate is wrapped in mystery. Doubtless he has left this world—crossed the last crevasse—and gone to another. But he will not be forgotten. To me Stickeen is immortal.

Homebodies

by Tom Hennessey

For an old geezer like myself in his mid-eighties, the loss of dear friends is inevitable. That does not make it any easier, and when Tom Hennessey passed in 2018 my heart fell to the ground. A skilled writer and artist, and outdoor editor of the Bangor (Maine) Daily News, *Tom always seemed indestructible to me. He was of the essence of Maine: strong-willed, capable in all weather, and as Maine as birch bark, rock-rimmed mountains, ruffed grouse, brook trout, black bears, and salty ocean ledges. He was a dog man supreme, never without one, Labrador retrievers and pointing dogs. Tom was a master of capturing powerful emotions in a few words. This piece is one of my favorites, excerpted from his book* Feathers 'n Fins (1989). *Here, Tom takes on one of the consistent and major questions in gun dog hunting: Can a dog be excellent in the field and a great companion at home?*

I'D BET THAT BY NOW SOMEONE WHO CAUGHT HIS FIRST AND ONLY salmon three years ago has gone out of his way to inform you that a salmon won't take a fly when the river is shrouded with mist. Don't believe it. I'd also wager that some sage observer who has never been behind a bird dog has made a point of telling you that a woodcock, when flushed, always pauses at the top of its rise. I've always had a sneaking suspicion that this information was passed down by a woodcock. Here's another that could just as well have gone unsaid: You can't keep a hunting dog in the house because it will lose its sense of smell.

I've had the pleasure and privilege of owning a few hunting dogs. Some were kenneled, some took up residence in the house. Without hesitation I can say that my "house dogs" could hunt alongside my "kennel dogs" any day of the week. Misty, a Brittany spaniel who lived in my house and was as good a bird dog as I've seen, would tear the rugs off the floors whenever I put on my hunting hat or picked up a gun. On the same note, Sam and Jake, two birdy characters who occupied my kennel, turned themselves inside out whenever I appeared in hunting togs, or made the mistake of picking up a dog's bell.

Again, I have never been aware of a dog's physical hunting abilities being affected by its abode. If a pup's natural instincts are honed by training and hunting experience, the result is usually a dog stuffed full of desire to hunt. As long as the dog is well cared for, it wouldn't make any difference if it curled up to sleep in a kennel or the Waldorf Towers. Once instilled, that desire is there for the duration.

It is, of course, difficult to have several dogs living in a house. Packs of hounds obviously are kept in kennels. Reference here is to the bird dog, retriever, or, perhaps, the rabbit hound whose owner prefers to make it a part of the family. Those who vacuum the floors and rugs will tell you that a dog in the house creates a lot of work. No question. At present I keep two hunting partners in the house and have to admit that life would often be easier if they were kenneled.

You're probably well aware that a hunting dog who shares your dwelling soon becomes a person disguised as a Brittany spaniel, English setter, beagle, or Labrador retriever. Directly, you'll discover that Duke has established his own schedule, which he must strictly adhere and attend to regardless of your plans or commitments.

Daylight is his signal to stop sleeping. And it won't make any difference if you're plastered into a body cast and have both legs in traction, he'll sit by the bed staring at you and making noises until, mumbling and grumbling, you arise and start the day shift. And try to explain to him, when daylight saving time rolls around, that even though it's light outside, it's only 5 a.m. Doesn't mean a thing. You might as well get up. Sooner war, sooner peace.

A creature of habit, Duke's schedule dictates that he must "turn in" not too long after the supper dishes are dry. Don't, however, think that having a few friends in for the evening will change things. No, siree, bub. No way. Pretty soon you'll notice him pacing and casting you sidelong looks. When that fails, he'll sit in the hallway leading to the bedrooms and run through his repertoire of grunts, groans, whimpers, and whines, which he punctuates with a bark.

Barking. Now there's a subject you would never have become well versed in if ol' Duke were kenneled. There is a bark—"yip"—that, translated, means water. Another—usually a sharp "yap" often preceded by an attention-getting growl—that means food. An indignant "woof" means he wants the scraps on the sideboard, and a high-pitched "yelp" indicates that his ball is under the couch and you'd better get the hell over there and get it out.

The roaring bark that rattles windows, however, he reserves for the paperboy, trash man, UPS driver, Girl Scouts selling cookies, and things that go bump in the night. As you know, that midnight warning can be hazardous to your health. It will hit you straight up out of a sound sleep. Straighten your hair, stop your breathing, and leave you with palpitations of the heart. Not to mention that you'll have to break loose from your wife's headlock.

If you have a live-in Labrador retriever, it's no secret to you that this breed just naturally loves to lug things around. Seldom does a Lab go from one room to another without bringing a "present." Consequently, you spend a lot of time looking for the mates to shoes, boots, socks, slippers, and gloves. Exasperating as it is, it can also become embarrassing. Take, for instance, the time a few of my hunting pals and I were batting the breeze in my kitchen. Coke, my chocolate Lab, seized the opportunity to visit the laundry room and then sashay onto center stage dragging certain of my wife's unmentionables. Nancy, of course, was present. See what you miss by keeping your dogs kenneled?

A hunting dog that lives in the house learns quickly. Because Jill is in close contact with you she becomes sensitive to the inflections of your voice, your facial expressions, and reads, unerringly, your every change of attitude. Make no mistake about it, she knows your mood and mindset just by the way you pull on your pants. And I'm sure you've noticed that she quietly leaves the room whenever you begin spouting exclamations beginning with "son-of . . ." and ending with names found in the Bible.

I regret that I had to keep some of my dogs in the kennel. For that reason I never got to fully know and understand them. Nor was I able to recognize many of their traits and characteristics. Sure, I had a great rapport with them, especially during hunting season. But other than that, I spent time with them only when I fed them or took them for a run each day. They never got to ride down to the post office or the hardware store, or up to the salmon club to listen to the fireside stories like Coke does. And it bothers me that there must have been nights when, after a day's hunting, my kenneled dogs were sore or lame. Often, I wouldn't become aware of it until the following day.

Can a hunting dog live in the house? You bet. Will ol' feather-finder "lose his nose"? You can't prove it by me. Again, the dogs that have slept curled on my den couch, and who got a portion of my pancakes in the morning, hunted just as hard and performed every bit as well as any dog I had quartered in the kennel. And all of them, insiders and outsiders, lived and hunted into their thirteenth and fourteenth years.

The only drawback of keeping a hunting a dog in the house is that you become ridiculously attached to it. So much, in fact, that you'll feel guilty when you tell your setter or retriever, "Stay!" as you leave the house to go deer hunting. It gets worse, especially if your wife is also addicted to dogs. Nancy has always admonished me for hunting alone. One morning, as Coke and I were getting into my pickup, she leaned out the back door and asked, "Who are you going hunting with?"

"I'm going alone," I answered.

Her pause and reply were as chilling as the pre-dawn darkness: "If something happens to you, how will that dog get home?"

11

A Yellow Dog

by Bret Harte

Short-story author Bret Harte was known for his picaresque evoca-
tions of the denizens of the Old West. His "Yellow Dog" is a raffish
canine who is the local miscreant in the mining camp called Rattlers
Ridge. The locals simultaneously revile him and brag about his ex-
ploits. When a "good woman" visits the camp, she wins over the entire
male population, but are her sweet words enough to turn that "yaller"
dog from his wicked ways?

I NEVER KNEW WHY IN THE WESTERN STATES OF AMERICA A YELLOW
dog should be proverbially considered the acme of canine degradation
and incompetency, nor why the possession of one should seriously affect
the social standing of its possessor. But the fact being established, I think
we accepted it at Rattlers Ridge without question. The matter of ownership was more difficult to settle; and although the dog I have in my
mind at the present writing attached himself impartially and equally to
everyone in camp, no one ventured to exclusively claim him; while, after
the perpetration of any canine atrocity, everybody repudiated him with
indecent haste.

"Well, I can swear he hasn't been near our shanty for weeks," or the
retort, "He was last seen comin' out of YOUR cabin," expressed the eagerness with which Rattlers Ridge washed its hands of any responsibility.
Yet he was by no means a common dog, nor even an unhandsome dog;
and it was a singular fact that his severest critics vied with each other in

narrating instances of his sagacity, insight, and agility which they themselves had witnessed.

He had been seen crossing the "flume" that spanned Grizzly Canyon at a height of nine hundred feet, on a plank six inches wide. He had tumbled down the "shoot" to the South Fork, a thousand feet below, and was found sitting on the riverbank "without a scratch, 'cept that he was lazily givin' himself with his off hind paw." He had been forgotten in a snowdrift on a Sierran shelf, and had come home in the early spring with the conceited complacency of an Alpine traveler and a plumpness alleged to have been the result of an exclusive diet of buried mail bags and their contents. He was generally believed to read the advance election posters, and disappear a day or two before the candidates and the brass band—which he hated—came to the Ridge. He was suspected of having overlooked Colonel Johnson's hand at poker, and of having conveyed to the Colonel's adversary, by a succession of barks, the danger of betting against four kings.

While these statements were supplied by wholly unsupported witnesses, it was a very human weakness of Rattlers Ridge that the responsibility of corroboration was passed to the dog himself, and HE was looked upon as a consummate liar.

"Snoopin' round yere, and CALLIN' yourself a poker sharp, are ye! Scoot, you yaller pizin!" was a common adjuration whenever the unfortunate animal intruded upon a card party. "Ef thar was a spark, an ATOM of truth in THAT DOG, I'd believe my own eyes that I saw him sittin' up and trying to magnetize a jay bird off a tree. But wot are ye goin' to do with a yaller equivocator like that?"

I have said that he was yellow—or, to use the ordinary expression, "yaller." Indeed, I am inclined to believe that much of the ignominy attached to the epithet lay in this favorite pronunciation. Men who habitually spoke of a "YELLOW bird," a "YELLOW-hammer," a "YELLOW leaf," always alluded to him as a "YALLER dog."

He certainly WAS yellow. After a bath—usually compulsory—he presented a decided gamboge streak down his back, from the top of his forehead to the stump of his tail, fading in his sides and flank to a delicate straw color. His breast, legs, and feet—when not reddened by "slumgullion," in which he was fond of wading—were white. A few attempts at ornamental decoration from the India-ink pot of the storekeeper failed, partly through the yellow dog's excessive agility, which would never give the paint time to dry on him, and partly through his success in transferring his markings to the trousers and blankets of the camp.

The size and shape of his tail—which had been cut off before his introduction to Rattlers Ridge—were favorite sources of speculation to the miners, as determining both his breed and his moral responsibility in coming into camp in that defective condition. There was a general opinion that he couldn't have looked worse with a tail, and its removal was therefore a gratuitous effrontery.

His best feature was his eyes, which were a lustrous Vandyke brown, and sparkling with intelligence; but here again he suffered from evolution through environment, and their original trustful openness was marred by the experience of watching for flying stones, sods, and passing kicks from the rear, so that the pupils were continually reverting to the outer angle of the eyelid.

Nevertheless, none of these characteristics decided the vexed question of his BREED. His speed and scent pointed to a "hound," and it is related that on one occasion he was laid on the trail of a wildcat with such success that he followed it apparently out of the State, returning at the end of two weeks footsore, but blandly contented.

Attaching himself to a prospecting party, he was sent under the same belief, "into the brush" to drive off a bear, who was supposed to be haunting the campfire. He returned in a few minutes WITH the bear, DRIVING IT INTO the unarmed circle and scattering the whole party. After this the theory of his being a hunting dog was abandoned. Yet it was said—on the usual uncorroborated evidence—that he had "put up" a quail; and his qualities as a retriever were for a long time accepted, until, during a shooting expedition for wild ducks, it was discovered that the one he had brought back had never been shot, and the party were obliged to compound damages with an adjacent settler.

His fondness for paddling in the ditches and "slumgullion" at one time suggested a water spaniel. He could swim, and would occasionally bring out of the river sticks and pieces of bark that had been thrown in; but as HE always had to be thrown in with them, and was a good-sized dog, his aquatic reputation faded also. He remained simply "a yaller dog." What more could be said? His actual name was "Bones"—given to him, no doubt, through the provincial custom of confounding the occupation of the individual with his quality, for which it was pointed out precedent could be found in some old English family names.

But if Bones generally exhibited no preference for any particular individual in camp, he always made an exception in favor of drunkards. Even an ordinary roistering bacchanalian party brought him out from under a tree or a shed in the keenest satisfaction. He would accompany them through the long straggling street of the settlement, barking his delight at every step or misstep of the revelers, and exhibiting none of that mistrust of eye which marked his attendance upon the sane and the respectable. He accepted even their uncouth play without a snarl or a yelp, hypocritically pretending even to like it; and I conscientiously believe would have allowed a tin can to be attached to his tail if the hand that tied it on were only unsteady, and the voice that bade him "lie still" were husky with liquor. He would "see" the party cheerfully into a saloon, wait outside the door—his tongue fairly lolling from his mouth in enjoyment—until they reappeared, permit them even to tumble over him with pleasure, and then gambol away before them, heedless of awkwardly projected stones and epithets. He would afterward accompany them separately home, or lie with them at crossroads until they were assisted to their cabins. Then he would trot rakishly to his own haunt by the saloon stove, with the slightly conscious air of having been a bad dog, yet of having had a good time.

We never could satisfy ourselves whether his enjoyment arose from some merely selfish conviction that he was more SECURE with the physically and mentally incompetent, from some active sympathy with active wickedness, or from a grim sense of his own mental superiority at such moments. But the general belief leant toward his kindred sympathy as a "yaller dog" with all that was disreputable. And this was supported by another very singular canine manifestation—the "sincere flattery" of simulation or imitation.

"Uncle Billy" Riley for a short time enjoyed the position of being the camp drunkard, and at once became an object of Bones' greatest solicitude. He not only accompanied him everywhere, curled at his feet or head according to Uncle Billy's attitude at the moment, but, it was noticed, began presently to undergo a singular alteration in his own habits and appearance. From being an active, tireless scout and forager, a bold and un-overtakable marauder, he became lazy and apathetic; allowed gophers to burrow under him without endeavoring to undermine the settlement in his frantic endeavors to dig them out, permitted squirrels to flash their tails at him a hundred yards away, forgot his usual caches, and left his favorite bones unburied and bleaching in the sun. His eyes grew dull, his coat lusterless, in proportion as his companion became blear-eyed and ragged; in running, his usual arrowlike directness began to deviate, and it was not unusual to meet the pair together, zigzagging up the hill. Indeed, Uncle Billy's condition could be predetermined by Bones' appearance at times when his temporary master was invisible. "The old man must have an awful jag on today," was casually remarked when an extra fluffiness and imbecility was noticeable in the passing Bones. At first it was believed that he drank also, but when careful investigation proved this hypothesis untenable, he was freely called a "derned time-servin', yaller hypocrite." Not a few advanced the opinion that if Bones did not actually lead Uncle Billy astray, he at least "slavered him over and coddled him until the old man got conceited in his wickedness." This undoubtedly led to a compulsory divorce between them, and Uncle Billy was happily dispatched to a neighboring town and a doctor.

Bones seemed to miss him greatly, ran away for two days, and was supposed to have visited him, to have been shocked at his convalescence, and to have been "cut" by Uncle Billy in his reformed character; and he returned to his old active life again, and buried his past with his forgotten bones. It was said that he was afterward detected in trying to lead an intoxicated tramp into camp after the methods employed by a blind man's dog, but was discovered in time by the—of course—uncorroborated narrator.

I should be tempted to leave him thus in his original and picturesque sin, but the same veracity which compelled me to transcribe his faults and iniquities obliges me to describe his ultimate and somewhat monotonous reformation, which came from no fault of his own.

It was a joyous day at Rattlers Ridge that was equally the advent of his change of heart and the first stagecoach that had been induced to diverge from the high road and stop regularly at our settlement. Flags were flying from the post office and Polka saloon, and Bones was flying before the brass band that he detested, when the sweetest girl in the county—Pinkey Preston—daughter of the county judge and hopelessly beloved by all Rattlers Ridge, stepped from the coach which she had glorified by occupying as an invited guest.

"What makes him run away?" she asked quickly, opening her lovely eyes in a possibly innocent wonder that anything could be found to run away from her.

"He don't like the brass band," we explained eagerly.

"How funny," murmured the girl; "is it as out of tune as all that?"

This irresistible witticism alone would have been enough to satisfy us—we did nothing but repeat it to each other all the next day—but we were positively transported when we saw her suddenly gather her dainty skirts in one hand and trip off through the red dust toward Bones, who, with his eyes over his yellow shoulder, had halted in the road, and half-turned in mingled disgust and rage at the spectacle of the descending trombone. We held our breath as she approached him. Would Bones evade her as he did us at such moments, or would he save our reputation, and consent, for the moment, to accept her as a new kind of inebriate? She came nearer; he saw her; he began to slowly quiver with excitement—his stump of a tail vibrating with such rapidity that the loss of the missing portion was scarcely noticeable. Suddenly she stopped before him, took his yellow head between her little hands, lifted it, and looked down in his handsome brown eyes with her two lovely blue ones. What passed between them in that magnetic glance no one ever knew. She returned with him; said to him casually: "We're not afraid of brass bands, are we?" to which he apparently acquiesced, at least stifling his disgust of them while he was near her—which was nearly all the time.

During the speechmaking her gloved hand and his yellow head were always near together, and at the crowning ceremony—her public checking of Yuba Bill's "waybill" on behalf of the township, with a gold pencil presented to her by the Stage Company—Bones' joy, far from knowing no bounds, seemed to know nothing but them, and he witnessed it apparently in the air. No one dared to interfere. For the first time a local pride in Bones sprang up in our hearts—and we lied to each other in his praises openly and shamelessly.

Then the time came for parting. We were standing by the door of the coach, hats in hand, as Miss Pinkey was about to step into it; Bones was waiting by her side, confidently looking into the interior, and apparently selecting his own seat on the lap of Judge Preston in the corner, when Miss Pinkey held up the sweetest of admonitory fingers. Then, taking his head between her two hands, she again looked into his brimming eyes, and said, simply, "GOOD dog," with the gentlest of emphasis on the adjective, and popped into the coach.

The six bay horses started as one, the gorgeous green and gold vehicle bounded forward, the red dust rose behind, and the yellow dog danced in and out of it to the very outskirts of the settlement. And then he soberly returned.

A day or two later he was missed—but the fact was afterward known that he was at Spring Valley, the county town where Miss Preston lived, and he was forgiven. A week afterward he was missed again, but this time for a longer period, and then a pathetic letter arrived from Sacramento for the storekeeper's wife.

"Would you mind," wrote Miss Pinkey Preston, "asking some of your boys to come over here to Sacramento and bring back Bones? I don't mind having the dear dog walk out with me at Spring Valley, where everyone knows me; but here he DOES make one so noticeable, on account of HIS COLOR. I've got scarcely a frock that he agrees with. He don't go with my pink muslin, and that lovely buff tint he makes three shades lighter. You know yellow is SO trying."

A consultation was quickly held by the whole settlement, and a deputation sent to Sacramento to relieve the unfortunate girl. We were all quite indignant with Bones—but, oddly enough, I think it was greatly tempered with our new pride in him. While he was with us alone, his peculiarities had been scarcely appreciated, but the recurrent phrase "that yellow dog that they keep at the Rattlers" gave us a mysterious importance along the countryside, as if we had secured a "mascot" in some zoological curiosity.

This was further indicated by a singular occurrence. A new church had been built at the crossroads, and an eminent divine had come from San Francisco to preach the opening sermon. After a careful examination of the camp's wardrobe, and some felicitous exchange of apparel, a few of us were deputed to represent "Rattlers" at the Sunday service. In our white ducks, straw hats, and flannel blouses, we were sufficiently picturesque and distinctive as "honest miners" to be shown off in one of the front pews.

Seated near the prettiest girls, who offered us their hymn books—in the cleanly odor of fresh pine shavings, and ironed muslin, and blown over by the spices of our own woods through the open windows, a deep sense of the abiding peace of Christian communion settled upon us. At this supreme moment someone murmured in an awe-stricken whisper:

"WILL you look at Bones?"

We looked. Bones had entered the church and gone up in the gallery through a pardonable ignorance and modesty; but, perceiving his mistake, was now calmly walking along the gallery rail before the astounded worshipers. Reaching the end, he paused for a moment, and carelessly looked down. It was about fifteen feet to the floor below—the simplest jump in the world for the mountain-bred Bones. Daintily, gingerly, lazily, and yet with a conceited airiness of manner, as if, humanly speaking, he had one leg in his pocket and were doing it on three, he cleared the distance, dropping just in front of the chancel, without a sound, turned himself around three times, and then lay comfortably down.

Three deacons were instantly in the aisle, coming up before the eminent divine, who, we fancied, wore a restrained smile. We heard the hurried whispers: "Belongs to them." "Quite a local institution here, you know." "Don't like to offend sensibilities"; and the minister's prompt "By no means," as he went on with his service.

A short month ago we would have repudiated Bones; today we sat there in slightly supercilious attitudes, as if to indicate that any affront offered to Bones would be an insult to ourselves, and followed by our instantaneous withdrawal in a body.

All went well, however, until the minister, lifting the large Bible from the communion table and holding it in both hands before him, walked toward a reading stand by the altar rails. Bones uttered a distinct growl. The minister stopped.

We, and we alone, comprehended in a flash the whole situation. The Bible was nearly the size and shape of one of those soft clods of sod which we were in the playful habit of launching at Bones when he lay half-asleep in the sun, in order to see him cleverly evade it.

We held our breath. What was to be done? But the opportunity belonged to our leader, Jeff Briggs—a confoundedly good-looking fellow, with the golden mustache of a northern Viking and the curls of an Apollo. Secure in his beauty and bland in his self-conceit, he rose from the pew and stepped before the chancel rails.

"I would wait a moment, if I were you, sir," he said, respectfully, "and you will see that he will go out quietly."

"What is wrong?" whispered the minister in some concern.

"He thinks you are going to heave that book at him, sir, without giving him a fair show, as we do."

The minister looked perplexed, but remained motionless, with the book in his hands. Bones arose, walked halfway down the aisle, and vanished like a yellow flash!

With this justification of his reputation, Bones disappeared for a week. At the end of that time we received a polite note from Judge Preston, saying that the dog had become quite domiciled in their house, and begged that the camp, without yielding up their valuable PROPERTY in him, would allow him to remain at Spring Valley for an indefinite time; that both the judge and his daughter—with whom Bones was already an old friend—would be glad if the members of the camp would visit their old favorite whenever they desired, to assure themselves that he was well cared for.

I am afraid that the bait thus ingenuously thrown out had a good deal to do with our ultimate yielding. However, the reports of those who visited Bones were wonderful and marvelous. He was residing there in state, lying on rugs in the drawing-room, coiled up under the judicial desk in the judge's study, sleeping regularly on the mat outside Miss Pinkey's bedroom door, or lazily snapping at flies on the judge's lawn.

"He's as yaller as ever," said one of our informants, "but it don't somehow seem to be the same back that we used to break clods over in the old time, just to see him scoot out of the dust."

And now I must record a fact which I am aware all lovers of dogs will indignantly deny, and which will be furiously bayed at by every faithful hound since the days of Ulysses. Bones not only FORGOT, but absolutely CUT US! Those who called upon the judge in "store clothes" he would perhaps casually notice, but he would sniff at them as if detecting and resenting them under their superficial exterior. The rest he simply paid no attention to. The more familiar term of "Bonesy"—formerly applied to him, as in our rare moments of endearment—produced no response. This pained, I think, some of the more youthful of us; but, through some strange human weakness, it also increased the camp's respect for him. Nevertheless, we spoke of him familiarly to strangers at the very moment he ignored us. I am afraid that we also took some pains to point out that he was getting fat and unwieldy, and losing his elasticity, implying covertly that his choice was a mistake and his life a failure.

A year after, he died, in the odor of sanctity and respectability, being found one morning coiled up and stiff on the mat outside Miss Pinkey's door. When the news was conveyed to us, we asked permission, the camp being in a prosperous condition, to erect a stone over his grave. But when it came to the inscription we could only think of the two words murmured to him by Miss Pinkey, which we always believe effected his conversion: "GOOD Dog!"

12

My Most Memorable Dog

by Archibald Rutledge

This editor has always looked upon the works of Archibald Rutledge with great awe: His prose and poetry set in the South Carolina Lowcountry call out the life I spent as a youth in southeast Georgia. My days afield could not match the great Archibald Rutledge's adventures from Hampton and the Santee River area, but I found much reading that bonded me with him. Poet laureate of South Carolina and author of numerous stories and books, Rutledge was a man who led two lives. In one life he grew up on Hampton Plantation and returned there for lengthy Christmas vacations every year. His other life was as an English professor at Mercersburg Academy in Pennsylvania. His years of hunting experience were as diverse as bobwhite quail and ruffed grouse. This Rutledge classic was presented in my friend Jim Casada's book Bird Dog Days, Wingshooting Ways *(2016), a bountiful collection of Rutledge upland hunting stories. It includes the best short biography of Archibald Rutledge I've ever seen.*

DURING THE YEARS OF MY YOUNG MANHOOD, WHEN I WAS A TEACHER IN the beautiful Cumberland Valley of Pennsylvania, I hunted quail and grouse a great deal, and I raised and trained a good many bird dogs.

Animals can occasionally be as memorable as human beings; among dogs I give the first place to Mike. Although he was no beauty, he was a joy forever. There was a pathos about him as if he were aware of his unpromising looks.

In those early years I inevitably hunted quail but finally gave it up, for I love the birds too much. One year I went quite overboard in buying a registered pointer with the proud name of Savannah Count. He arrived in a crate that looked like a palace. He was huge, handsome, and supercilious. For some reason, he seemed especially oblivious to me.

On the first day of the season I took His Majesty into the fields. At the first shot he vanished over the rolling countryside. The lordly Count was gun-shy. I did not retrieve him for days.

I was reminded of a dog I took to old Galboa to correct the same fault. Galboa was a native African who had a way with animals. Telling the old man my troubles, I left the dog with him for two weeks. When I returned, he gestured with contempt toward the dog lying in the grass. "You must learn," he said, "that nothing can be done about a fool."

There are few plights worse for a quail hunter than to have no bird dog when the season opens. When Count defected, I at once called up a Pennsylvania Game protector, a good friend of mine, to ask him if he could relieve my emergency. He raised bird dogs "on the side," and I had bought several good ones from him. But his report was disappointing. "I did have two dandies," he said, "but I sold both last week. I haven't got a thing now but Mike, and I don't like to sell him to you. You and I have been good friends."

Although this seemed like a sinister introduction, I said, "Ship him to me." As if to sink Mike even lower in my estimation, my friend said, "I could not change you more than $15.00 for this mutt." (I had paid $100.00 for my airborne Savannah Count.)

When Mike arrived, I found him, in appearance, no "hound of heaven." Undersized, angular, with bristly red and yellow hair, for a bird dog he appeared to be put together wrong. His ears were small and peaked; someone had cut off more than half his tail. No one had lately taken him to a beauty parlor. But, as a judge once said to me, about the possible verdict of a jury, "Brother, you never know."

As if he had everything else against him, Mike's feet were too large, so that he walked as if he had snowshoes on. Despite all these adverse factors, Mike had qualities to admire, and, for me, a human and lovable nature. He had a good head, which should presage wisdom and a keen nose. Mike had, too, like some people, a certain air about him; an ugly air, but unique and unforgettable.

Of course, Mike had not any social background. To gracious living, he was alien. Yet already I could feel his loyalty to me. He was also courageous. As I led him up to my home, which was near the express office, we met a big dog that I knew to be a mean one. The big dog, bristling, made some invidious remarks about Mike's mother. Mike bristled also, took a step forward, growling. He was ready for a fight.

I never learned anything of Mike's ancestry; but somewhere in it a blooded pointer probably could be found. He looked to be all cur; but there was something about him that made me know that he wasn't. He had ways and wiles about him.

I have owned many good dogs, but Mike was a character. He was always surprising me with the things he did, which he had thought out all by himself, things that endeared him to me. For example, one afternoon we were crossing a field when we came to a rather cold dark stream with steep banks. Mike did not like the looks of it; but his heart must have kept saying, "Whither thou goest, I will go." I managed to slip down the bank, cross the water with the aid of some limbs, and literally crawled up the farther bank. I then looked for Mike and called him.

Having estimated the problem, and disliking cold water, he had calmly walked away from the creek in a straight line, just as a high jumper or a pole vaulter would, in order to afford himself a speedy run for his takeoff. He went about thirty yards, turned, and came running full speed for the creek. There was a break in the trees so that I could watch him land safely. I was surprised how high he went.

A wild white-tailed deer has been known to jump forty-two feet; a horse, thirty-six feet; a man, twenty-eight feet. I am sure that Mike jumped between twenty and twenty-five feet, and he did so with certainty and grace.

The same week I took a friend hunting quail. Every time he shot, he missed. Meanwhile Mike disappeared. I was not surprised, as his russet coloring blended perfectly with those of the autumn. When I found him he was lying flat in a ditch, his head on his outstretched paws. He looked at me with eyes that seemed to express disappointment, chagrin, and even disgust. He was not able to take any more strong doses of missing! It made him sick; besides, all his work was going for nothing. Of course, I may have misinterpreted his expression; but it looked like humiliating regret to me. Indeed, Mike's expression was so forlorn it would not have surprised me if big dash tears had rolled down his cheeks.

As we approached an old rail fence one day, Mike sprang up to the top rail. It must have been at that moment that one of the top rails began to swing at right angles to the line of the fence. Just at that moment the hot and heavy scent of a covey of quail, almost beneath him, assailed Mike's nostrils. He crept forward a step to make certain, and found himself with all four feet on the swaying fence rail. Mike's game was to keep his balance and also not to frighten the covey. I can still see him, the picture of shrewd loyalty and devotion, holding his balance until I could come up. He was rocking perfectly.

On another occasion I missed him. After a few minutes he came creeping and crawling back to me. On reaching me, he whined, turned around and started back the way he had come. He paused, looking back to make sure I understood his message and was following. His gait was very peculiar. He was walking as if he were stepping on eggs. He led me to a big covey of quail. He must have known that I could not see him; so he came and got me!

One day Mike and I were out on a sandy road when a big crowd of frolicking young people came by. Purely in jest, one of them threw a pine cone at Mike. It did not hit him; but even if it had, it could not have hurt him. But it wounded his dignity; and he never forgot it.

Except for the one who threw the cone, all the others could enter my yard in perfect safety. But the one who threw the cone would stop outside the gate and call for someone please to "tie Mike up." Really gentle by disposition, Mike would not let anyone take liberties with him.

When I hunted in Pennsylvania, there were some ringneck pheasants there. We were allowed to kill only the cock birds, which are easily distinguished by their gaudy colors and their long tails. It is characteristic of these birds that they will often run long distances on the ground before taking flight. One afternoon, in a wild valley, Mike struck a trail. I knew at once it must be a pheasant because of the distance he was going. At last he came to a stand. I walked carefully to flush the bird. After all our long walk, it was a hen! Of course, I did not shoot. As I stood idly there, Mike, apparently in anger, whirled on me and barked in the most disgusted fashion! There was no mistaking what he meant: "After all my careful work, what in the world is the matter with you?" Some dogs are certainly capable of rebuking their masters—if the provocation is great.

Once when Mike and I were hunting in a field of wheat stubble near a thicket of blackberry canes, he came back to me whining, and he seemed to be cringing. Something had scared him, and he was not a dog easily scared. I was wearing my corduroy trousers; and he took hold of the cuff of one leg, to pull me back, or at least to delay me. But feeling I should investigate, I literally dragged Mike through the stubble. As we drew near the briar patch, I heard what had frightened Mike; then I saw the snake, that ashen heap of death. I have lost dogs that have been struck by rattlers, and have located these lethal serpents by dogs which barked at them— being wary enough to keep their distance. I looked at Mike. In his eyes was a distinct warning. I had dealt with dogs all my life, but what kind of a dog was this? I have had a good dog "take on" a wild boar that had personal designs on me. Yet I doubt if that brave dog was really defending me. With Mike it was different. He cautiously warned me against what he knew was deadly danger. Is it any wonder that I love and honor his memory?

Early in our acquaintance he gave me a good idea of his unusualness. Early one damp morning, I drove out in a buggy (I had no car) to hunt quail. Mike lay in the bottom of the buggy and a robe covered him and my knees. About a mile from town a heavy Osage orange hedge stood on the left of the road. As we were passing this, something happened— something for which I could not at first account. The robe had risen off my knees. Mike was standing up. As soon as I saw the trance-like look in his eyes, I knew that he had winded quail, and had pointed them from the buggy! For precaution's sake, I drove forward a few paces, where I got out of the buggy. But as he was still pointing, I had to lift him down to the roadway. He was still pointing, and as stiff as a board.

When his feet touched the ground he began a curious stiff-legged walk back down the road. Then he came to a perfect point. As the grass was rather thin, I saw the quail on the ground, a beautiful covey of about sixteen birds. When they rose and whirled over the hedge, I did not shoot—partly, I think, because of the strange magic of Mike's behavior.

On another occasion I took a friend duck hunting. Flight shooting was then permitted after sundown. I put my friend on a good stand and he blazed away for an hour. I shot only twice. But when dark came, and I started down the old bank on which we had been standing, I almost fell over a big pile of wild ducks. That was Mike's work. He had brought all my friend's ducks to me! He had original ideas about loyalty.

When the Great Depression came, I had three sons in college. I had already sold some heirloom furniture. Was there anything else that might bring in some money? There was Mike. Unfortunately a man of means had seen him work. He had several times approached me to buy him. Meanwhile the university treasurer kept bearing down on me. On a disastrous day I decided to let my dear Mike go. I felt worse than a sinner. While I was making the crate, Mike watched me curiously. When I put him in and nailed it shut, he must have had an inkling of what was coming. He lay flat on the bottom of the box, and looked at me with big misty eyes. I set the crate in the wheelbarrow, and rolled it down to the express office. I heard some subdued whimpering, but I really believe that Mike was weeping. Nor was he the only one. I left him at the office to be shipped out.

But I had hardly reached home when the enormity of my crime overcame me. I rushed back to the express office (although no train was due for several hours). "It's a mistake!" I exclaimed to the express agent. "I'm not going to sell him."

Not long after that I decided to stop quail shooting. By then Mike was getting old. The aspect of the approach of age is always sad with a dog as active and intelligent as Mike. While he was still strong, I could expect him always to meet me halfway down the avenue that led to my home.

He apparently timed my arrival; but was usually an hour or so early, just lying there waiting. At other times, he would pull at my corduroy trousers, trying to get me started on a hunt, or would run down the avenue, barking, and looking expectantly toward the house for me to join him. But then came days when he did not meet me. And sometimes when I would seem to be getting ready to go for a hunt, he would lie in the sun by the steps, thump the ground with his tail, and look at me with a nameless wistfulness. He seemed to be acknowledging his own weakness, and doing so with tragic regret. His eyes spoke for him. Like King Lear, he was saying, "I am old now."

Then, too, Mike began to make mistakes in the field. One day he was holding a point on the briared bank of a ditch. I was sure he had a quail or a pheasant. But as I got near him he gave up the point, and turned back to me, his expression registering shame and apology. He crawled up to me whining, and rubbed against my boots, as if imploring forgiveness. He was abashed that he had been pointing an old land turtle! Yet the finest part of his life was yet to come. He had always loved children, and had been a great favorite with them. One of my grandsons was crazy about Mike; when, therefore, the boy's mother told me that another child was expected, I let them take him. "He might make a nurse for the baby," I said, never dreaming of the real import of my words.

In a pretty room on the second floor of my son's house all was made ready for the new baby. In the center of the room was the immaculate crib, all lacy and frilly. There was a mahogany footboard around the base. One day when the mother came into the room she was greeted by a low growl. Mike had taken possession of the little square box beneath the bassinet. Please don't ask me how he knew a baby was coming there. Perhaps he had dealt with a baby before, in another family. True, there was an unwonted air of suppressed excitement and expectancy, and he may have interpreted these. Do some animals, at certain times, have the eerie clairvoyance of premonition? At any rate, Mike planted himself under the bassinet, and would not leave. He had to be fed and watered there.

The mother was at the hospital two weeks. When she brought the tiny daughter home, Mike barked delightedly. And he took charge. Except for the mother, he would let no one else enter the room. When the baby cried, or even fretted, Mike barked. After some months had passed, and the baby began to crawl about the room, Mike would come close and lie down so that tiny Bonnie could sleep with him for a pillow. My daughter-in-law said, "I feel much safer with Mike than with a nurse."

When Bonnie was a year and a half old, she was allowed to run up and down the pavement in front of her house—but only if Mike went with her. He was not by then keeping up with the baby very well. He always stayed between her and the street. One day she threw a little rubber ball out into the road, and at once, like a fairy, ran after it. Mike was old then and not nearly so fast as he had once been. Two cars were coming from opposite directions. Mike, making the effort of his life, dashed between Bonnie and one car. She was saved, but he was struck and killed.

Mike was a dog that looked all wrong, but was all right. Ugly, he was loyal and smart. Many redeeming faults were his—those same human qualities that make people lovable. It is not hard for me to forget Savannah Count; but I shall always remember Mike.

13

That Spot

by Jack London

One Jack London tale, The Call of the Wild, already provides reader reward in this book, but we've added a second Jack London story, "That Spot." Set in familiar ground for London, the Klondike, this adventure follows a dog that could not be trained, or broken, or left behind.

The story has been edited for clarity and removal of archaic and unnecessary language in certain instances.

I DON'T THINK MUCH OF STEPHEN MACKAYE ANYMORE, THOUGH I USED to swear by him. I know that in those days I loved him more than my own brother. If ever I meet Stephen Mackaye again, I shall not be responsible for my actions. It passes beyond me that a man with whom I shared food and blanket, and with whom I mushed over the Chilcoot Trail, should turn out the way he did. I always sized Steve up as a square man, a kindly comrade, without an iota of anything vindictive or malicious in his nature. I shall never trust my judgment in men again. Why, I nursed that man through typhoid fever; we starved together on the headwaters of the Stewart; and he saved my life on the Little Salmon. And now, after the years we were together, all I can say of Stephen Mackaye is that he is the meanest man I ever knew.

We started for the Klondike in the fall rush of 1897, and we started too late to get over Chilcoot Pass before the freeze-up. We packed our outfit on our backs part way over, when the snow began to fly, and then we had to buy dogs in order to sled it the rest of the way. That was how we came to get that Spot. Dogs were high, and we paid one hundred and ten dollars for him. He looked worth it. I say looked, because he was one of the finest-appearing dogs I ever saw. He weighed sixty pounds, and he had all the lines of a good sled animal. We never could make out his breed. He wasn't husky, nor Malemute, nor Hudson Bay; he looked like all of them and he didn't look like any of them; and on top of it all he had some of the white man's dog in him, for on one side, in the thick of the mixed yellow-brown-red-and-dirty-white that was his prevailing colour, there was a spot of coal-black as big as a water-bucket. That was why we called him Spot.

He was a good looker all right. When he was in condition his muscles stood out in bunches all over him. And he was the strongest-looking brute I ever saw in Alaska, also the most intelligent-looking. To run your eyes over him, you'd think he could outpull three dogs of his own weight. Maybe he could, but I never saw it. His intelligence didn't run that way. He could steal and forage to perfection; he had an instinct that was positively gruesome for divining when work was to be done and for making a sneak accordingly; and for getting lost and not staying lost he was nothing short of inspired. But when it came to work, the way that intelligence dribbled out of him and left him a mere clot of wobbling, stupid jelly would make your heart bleed.

There are times when I think it wasn't stupidity. Maybe, like some men I know, he was too wise to work. I shouldn't wonder if he put it all over us with that intelligence of his. Maybe he figured it all out and decided that a licking now and again and no work was a whole lot better than work all the time and no licking. He was intelligent enough for such a computation. I tell you, I've sat and looked into that dog's eyes till the shivers ran up and down my spine and the marrow crawled like yeast, what of the intelligence I saw shining out. I can't express myself about that intelligence. It is beyond mere words. I saw it, that's all. At times it was like gazing into a human soul, to look into his eyes; and what I saw there frightened me and started all sorts of ideas in my own mind of reincarnation and all the rest. I tell you I sensed something big in that brute's eyes; there was a message there, but I wasn't big enough myself to catch it. Whatever it was (I know I'm making a fool of myself)—whatever it was, it baffled me. I can't give an inkling of what I saw in that brute's eyes; it wasn't light, it wasn't colour; it was something that moved, away back, when the eyes themselves weren't moving. And I guess I didn't see it move either; I only sensed that it moved. It was an expression—that's what it was—and I got an impression of it. No; it was different from a mere expression; it was more than that. I don't know what it was, but it gave me a feeling of kinship just the same. Oh, no, not sentimental kinship. It was, rather, a kinship of equality. Those eyes never pleaded like a deer's eyes. They challenged. No, it wasn't defiance. It was just a calm assumption of equality. And I don't think it was deliberate. My belief is that it was unconscious on his part. It was there because it was there, and it couldn't help shining out. No, I don't mean shine. It didn't shine; it moved. I know I'm talking rot, but if you'd looked into that animal's eyes the way I have, you'd understand. Steve was affected the same way I was. Why, I tried to kill that Spot once—he was no good for anything; and I fell down on it. I led him out into the brush, and he came along slow and unwilling. He knew what was going on. I stopped in a likely place, put my foot on the rope, and pulled my big Colt's. And that dog sat down and looked at me. I tell you he didn't plead. He just looked. And I saw all kinds of incomprehensible things moving, yes, moving, in those eyes of his. I didn't really see them move; I thought I saw them, for, as I said before, I guess I only sensed them. And I want to tell you right now that it got beyond me. It was like killing a man, a conscious, brave man, who looked calmly into your gun as much as to say, "Who's afraid?"

Then, too, the message seemed so near that, instead of pulling the trigger quick, I stopped to see if I could catch the message. There it was, right before me, glimmering all around in those eyes of his. And then it was too late. I got scared. I was trembly all over, and my stomach generated a nervous palpitation that made me seasick. I just sat down and looked at the dog, and he looked at me, till I thought I was going crazy. Do you want to know what I did? I threw down the gun and ran back to camp with the fear of God in my heart. Steve laughed at me. But I notice that Steve led Spot into the woods, a week later, for the same purpose, and that Steve came back alone, and a little later Spot drifted back, too.

At any rate, Spot wouldn't work. We paid a hundred and ten dollars for him from the bottom of our sack, and he wouldn't work. He wouldn't even tighten the traces. Steve spoke to him the first time we put him in harness, and he sort of shivered, that was all. Not an ounce on the traces. He just stood still and wobbled, like so much jelly. Steve touched him with the whip. He yelped, but not an ounce. Steve touched him again, a bit harder, and he howled—the regular long wolf howl. Then Steve got mad and gave him half a dozen, and I came on the run from the tent.

I told Steve he was brutal with the animal, and we had some words— the first we'd ever had. He threw the whip down in the snow and walked away mad. I picked it up and went to it. That Spot trembled and wobbled and cowered before ever I swung the lash, and with the first bite of it he howled like a lost soul. Next he lay down in the snow. I started the rest of the dogs, and they dragged him along while I threw the whip into him. He rolled over on his back and bumped along, his four legs waving in the air, himself howling as though he was going through a sausage machine. Steve came back and laughed at me, and I apologized for what I'd said.

There was no getting any work out of that Spot; and to make up for it, he was the biggest pig-glutton of a dog I ever saw. On top of that, he was the cleverest thief. There was no circumventing him. Many a breakfast we went without our bacon because Spot had been there first. And it was because of him that we nearly starved to death up the Stewart. He figured out the way to break into our meat-cache, and what he didn't eat, the rest of the team did. But he was impartial. He stole from everybody. He was a restless dog, always very busy snooping around or going somewhere. And there was never a camp within five miles that he didn't raid. The worst of it was that they always came back on us to pay his board bill, which was just, being the law of the land; but it was mighty hard on us, especially that first winter on the Chilcoot, when we were busted, paying for whole hams and sides of bacon that we never ate. He could fight, too, that Spot. He could do everything but work. He never pulled a pound, but he was the boss of the whole team. The way he made those dogs stand around was an education. He bullied them, and there was always one or more of them fresh-marked with his fangs. But he was more than a bully. He wasn't afraid of anything that walked on four legs; and I've seen him march, single-handed into a strange team, without any provocation whatever, and put the kibosh on the whole outfit. Did I say he could eat? I caught him eating the whip once. That's straight. He started in at the lash, and when I caught him he was down to the handle, and still going.

But he was a good looker. At the end of the first week we sold him for seventy-five dollars to the Mounted Police. They had experienced dog-drivers, and we knew that by the time he'd covered the six hundred miles to Dawson he'd be a good sled-dog. I say we knew, for we were just getting acquainted with that Spot. A little later we were not brash enough to know anything where he was concerned. A week later we woke up in the morning to the dangdest dog-fight we'd ever heard. It was that Spot come back and knocking the team into shape. We ate a pretty depressing breakfast, I can tell you; but cheered up two hours afterward when we sold him to an official courier, bound in to Dawson with government despatches. That Spot was only three days in coming back, and, as usual, celebrated his arrival with a rough house.

We spent the winter and spring, after our own outfit was across the pass, freighting other people's outfits; and we made a fat stake. Also, we made money out of Spot. If we sold him once, we sold him twenty times. He always came back, and no one asked for their money. We didn't want the money. We'd have paid handsomely for any one to take him off our hands for keeps. We had to get rid of him, and we couldn't give him away, for that would have been suspicious. But he was such a fine looker that we never had any difficulty in selling him. "Unbroke," we'd say, and they'd pay any old price for him. We sold him as low as twenty-five dollars, and once we got a hundred and fifty for him. That particular party returned him in person, refused to take his money back, and the way he abused us was something awful. He said it was cheap at the price to tell us what he thought of us; and we felt he was so justified that we never talked back. But to this day I've never quite regained all the old self-respect that was mine before that man talked to me.

When the ice cleared out of the lakes and river, we put our outfit in a Lake Bennett boat and started for Dawson. We had a good team of dogs, and of course we piled them on top the outfit. That Spot was along—there was no losing him; and a dozen times, the first day, he knocked one or another of the dogs overboard in the course of fighting with them. It was close quarters, and he didn't like being crowded. "What that dog needs is space," Steve said the second day. "Let's maroon him."

We did, running the boat in at Caribou Crossing for him to jump ashore. Two of the other dogs, good dogs, followed him; and we lost two whole days trying to find them. We never saw those two dogs again; but the quietness and relief we enjoyed made us decide, like the man who refused his hundred and fifty, that it was cheap at the price. For the first time in months Steve and I laughed and whistled and sang. We were as happy as clams. The dark days were over. The nightmare had been lifted. That Spot was gone.

Three weeks later, one morning, Steve and I were standing on the river-bank at Dawson. A small boat was just arriving from Lake Bennett. I saw Steve give a start, and heard him say something that was not nice and that was not under his breath. Then I looked; and there, in the bow of the boat, with ears pricked up, sat Spot. Steve and I sneaked immediately, like beaten curs, like cowards, like absconders from justice. It was this last that the lieutenant of police thought when he saw us sneaking. He surmised that there were law-officers in the boat who were after us. He didn't wait to find out, but kept us in sight, and in the M. & M. saloon got us in a corner. We had a merry time explaining, for we refused to go back to the boat and meet Spot; and finally he held us under guard of another policeman while he went to the boat. After we got clear of him, we started for the cabin, and when we arrived, there was that Spot sitting on the stoop waiting for us. Now how did he know we lived there? There were forty thousand people in Dawson that summer, and how did he savvy our cabin out of all the cabins? How did he know we were in Dawson, anyway? I leave it to you. But don't forget what I said about his intelligence and that immortal something I have seen glimmering in his eyes.

There was no getting rid of him any more. There were too many people in Dawson who had bought him up on Chilcoot, and the story got around. Half a dozen times we put him on board steamboats going down the Yukon; but he merely went ashore at the first landing and trotted back up the bank. We couldn't sell him, we couldn't kill him (both Steve and I had tried), and nobody else was able to kill him. He bore a charmed life. I've seen him go down in a dogfight on the main street with fifty dogs on top of him, and when they were separated, he'd appear on all his four legs, unharmed, while two of the dogs that had been on top of him would be lying dead.

I saw him steal a chunk of moose-meat from Major Dinwiddie's cache so heavy that he could just keep one jump ahead of Mrs. Dinwiddie's cook, who was after him with an axe. As he went up the hill, after the cook gave up, Major Dinwiddie himself came out and pumped his Winchester into the landscape. He emptied his magazine twice, and never touched that Spot. Then a policeman came along and arrested him for discharging fire-arms inside the city limits. Major Dinwiddie paid his fine, and Steve and I paid him for the moose meat at the rate of a dollar a pound, bones and all. That was what he paid for it. Meat was high that year.

I am only telling what I saw with my own eyes. And now I'll tell you something also. I saw that Spot fall through a water-hole. The ice was three and a half feet thick, and the current sucked him under like a straw. Three hundred yards below was the big water-hole used by the hospital. Spot crawled out of the hospital water-hole, licked off the water, bit out the ice that had formed between his toes, trotted up the bank, and whipped a big Newfoundland belonging to the Gold Commissioner.

In the fall of 1898, Steve and I poled up the Yukon on the last water, bound for Stewart River. We took the dogs along, all except Spot. We figured we'd been feeding him long enough. He'd cost us more time and trouble and money and grub than we'd got by selling him on the Chilcoot—especially grub. So Steve and I tied him down in the cabin and pulled our freight. We camped that night at the mouth of Indian River, and Steve and I were pretty facetious over having shaken him. Steve was a funny cuss, and I was just sitting up in the blankets and laughing when a tornado hit camp. The way that Spot walked into those dogs and gave them what-for was hair-raising. Now how did he get loose? It's up to you. I haven't any theory. And how did he get across the Klondike River? That's another facer. And anyway, how did he know we had gone up the Yukon? You see, we went by water, and he couldn't smell our tracks. Steve and I began to get superstitious about that dog. He got on our nerves, too; and, between you and me, we were just a mite afraid of him.

The freeze-up came on when we were at the mouth of Henderson Creek, and we traded him off for two sacks of flour to an outfit that was bound up White River after copper. Now that whole outfit was lost. Never trace nor hide nor hair of men, dogs, sleds, or anything was ever found. They dropped clean out of sight. It became one of the mysteries of the country. Steve and I plugged away up the Stewart, and six weeks afterward that Spot crawled into camp. He was a perambulating skeleton, and could just drag along; but he got there. And what I want to know is, who told him we were up the Stewart? We could have gone to a thousand other places. How did he know? You tell me, and I'll tell you.

No losing him. At the Mayo he started a row with an Indian dog. The Indian who owned the dog took a swing at Spot with an axe, missed him, and killed his own dog. Talk about magic and turning bullets aside—I, for one, consider it a blamed sight harder to turn an axe aside with a big man at the other end of it. And I saw him do it with my own eyes. That Indian didn't want to kill his own dog. You've got to show me.

I told you about Spot breaking into our meat cache. It was nearly the death of us. There wasn't any more meat to be killed, and meat was all we had to live on. The moose had gone back several hundred miles and the Indians with them. There we were. Spring was on, and we had to wait for the river to break. We got pretty thin before we decided to eat the dogs, and we decided to eat Spot first. Do you know what that dog did? He sneaked. Now how did he know our minds were made up to eat him? We sat up nights laying for him, but he never came back, and we ate the other dogs. We ate the whole team.

And now for the sequel. You know what it is when a big river breaks up and a few billion tons of ice go out, jamming and milling and grinding.

Just in the thick of it, when the Stewart went out, rumbling and roaring, we sighted Spot out in the middle. He'd got caught as he was trying to cross up above somewhere. Steve and I yelled and shouted and ran up and down the bank, tossing our hats in the air. Sometimes we'd stop and hug each other, we were that boisterous, for we saw Spot's finish. He didn't have a chance in a million. He didn't have any chance at all. After the ice-run, we got into a canoe and paddled down to the Yukon, and down the Yukon to Dawson, stopping to feed up for a week at the cabins at the mouth of Henderson Creek. And as we came in to the bank at Dawson, there sat that Spot, waiting for us, his ears pricked up, his tail wagging, his mouth smiling, extending a hearty welcome to us. Now how did he get out of that ice? How did he know we were coming to Dawson, to the very hour and minute, to be out there on the bank waiting for us?

The more I think of that Spot, the more I am convinced that there are things in this world that go beyond science. On no scientific grounds can that Spot be explained. It's psychic phenomena, or mysticism, or something of that sort, I guess, with a lot of Theosophy thrown in. The Klondike is a good country. I might have been there yet, and become a millionaire, if it hadn't been for Spot. He got on my nerves. I stood him for two years altogether, and then I guess my stamina broke. It was the summer of 1899 when I pulled out. I didn't say anything to Steve. I just sneaked. But I fixed it up all right. I wrote Steve a note, and enclosed a package of "rough-on-rats," telling him what to do with it. I was worn down to skin and bone by that Spot, and I was that nervous that I'd jump and look around when there wasn't anybody within hailing distance. But it was astonishing the way I recuperated when I got quit of him. I got back twenty pounds before I arrived in San Francisco, and by the time I'd crossed the ferry to Oakland I was my old self again, so that even my wife looked in vain for any change in me.

Steve wrote to me once, and his letter seemed irritated. He took it kind of hard because I'd left him with Spot. Also, he said he'd used the "rough-on-rats," per directions, and that there was nothing doing. A year went by. I was back in the office and prospering in all ways—even getting a bit fat. And then Steve arrived. He didn't look me up. I read his name in the steamer list, and wondered why. But I didn't wonder long. I got up one morning and found that Spot chained to the gate-post and holding up the milkman. Steve went north to Seattle, I learned, that very morning. I didn't put on any more weight. My wife made me buy him a collar and tag, and within an hour he showed his gratitude by killing her pet Persian cat. There is no getting rid of that Spot. He will be with me until I die, for he'll never die. My appetite is not so good since he arrived, and my wife says I am looking peaked. Last night that Spot got into Mr. Harvey's hen-house (Harvey is my next-door neighbour) and killed nineteen of his fancy-bred chickens. I shall have to pay for them. My neighbours on the other side quarrelled with my wife and then moved out. Spot was the cause of it. And that is why I am disappointed in Stephen Mackaye. I had no idea he was so mean a man.

14

The Sunnybank Collies

by Albert Payson Terhune

With Lad: A Dog *and stories like this one, Albert Payson Terhune has elevated collies to legendary literary status. In this tale, he's back at home with his collies, at Sunnybank.*

HERE AT "SUNNYBANK"—AT POMPTON LAKES, IN NEW JERSEY—WE raise thoroughbred collies. For many years we have been breeding them. For many years longer, I have been studying them.

The more I study them, the more I realise that there is something about a collie—a mysterious, elusive something—that makes him different from any other dog. Something nearer human than beast. And, for all that, he is one hundred per cent dog.

There is much to learn from him; much to puzzle over; as perhaps the following discursive yarns about a few members of the long line of Sunnybank collies may show.

Greatest of them all was Lad. One would as soon have thought of teaching nursery rhymes to Emerson as of teaching Lad "tricks." Beyond the common babyhood lessons of obedience and of the Place's simple Law, he went untaught. And he taught himself; being that type of dog. For example:

The Mistress had been dangerously ill, with pneumonia. (In my book, *Lad: A Dog*, I tell how Laddie kept vigil outside her door, day and night, until she was out of danger; and how he celebrated her convalescence with a brainstorm which would have disgraced a three-months puppy.)

Well, on the first day she was able to be carried out of doors, the Mistress lay in a veranda hammock, with Lad on the porch floor at her side.

Friends—several instalments of them—drove to the Place to congratulate the Mistress on her recovery; and to bring gifts of flowers, fruit, jellies, books. All morning, Lad lay there, watching the various relays of guests and eyeing the presents they laid in her lap. After the fifth group of callers had gone, the big collie got up and trotted off into the forest. For nearly an hour he was absent.

Then he came back; travelling with difficulty, by reason of the heavy burden he bore. Somewhere, far away in the woods, he had found, or revisited, the carcase of a dead horse—of an excessively dead horse. From it he had wrenched two ribs and some of the vertebrae.

Dragging this horrible gift along, he returned to the veranda. Before any of us were well aware of his presence (the wind setting in the other direction) he had mounted the steps and, with one mighty heave, had lifted the ribs and vertebræ over the hammock edge and laid them in the lap of his dismayed Mistress.

Humans had celebrated her recovery with presents. And he, watching, had imitated them. He had gone far and had toiled hard to bring her an offering that his canine mind deemed all-desirable.

It was carrion; but it represented, to a dog, everything that a present should be.

Dogs do not eat carrion. They merely rub their shoulders in it; on the same principle that women use perfumes. It is a purely aesthetic pleasure to them. And carrion is probably no more malodorous to a human being than is the reek of tobacco or of whisky or even of some $15-an-ounce scent, to a dog. It is all a matter of taste and of education. Noting that his gift awoke no joy whatever in its recipient's heart, Lad was monstrous crestfallen. Nor, from that day on, did he ever bring carrion to the Place. He even abstained henceforth from rubbing his shoulders in it. Evidently he gathered, from our reception of his present, that "it is not done."

When Lad was training his little son, Wolf, to become a decent canine citizen, he was much annoyed by the puppy's trick of watching his sire bury bones and then of exhuming and gnawing them himself. Lad did not punish the puppy for this. He adopted a shrewder and surer way of saving his buried treasures from theft.

Thereafter, he would bury the choice bone deeper in the ground than had been his habit. And, directly above it, just below the surface of the earth, he would inter a second and older bone; a bone that had long been denuded of all meat and was of no further value to any dog. Wolf, galloping eagerly up to the spot of burial, as soon as Lad moved away, would dig where his father had dug. Presently, he would unearth the topmost and worthless bone. Satisfied that he had exhausted the possibilities of the cache, he dug no deeper; but left the new and toothsome bone undiscovered.

By the way, did it ever occur to you that a dog is almost the only animal to bury food? And did you ever stop to think why? The reason is simple.

Dogs, alone of all wild animals (dogs and their blood-brethren, the wolves), used to hunt in packs. All other beasts hunted alone or, at most, in pairs. When prey was slain, the dog that did not bolt his food with all possible haste was the dog that got the smallest share or none at all. When there was more food than could be devoured at one meal, he had the sense to lay up provision for the next day's dinner.

He knew, if he left the carcase lying where it was, it would be devoured by the rest of the hungry pack. So he buried as much of it as he could, to prevent his brethren from finding and eating it.

Thus, the dog, alone of all quadrupeds, still bolts his food in huge and half-chewed mouthfuls; and the dog buries food for future use. These two traits are as purely ancestral as is the dog's habit of turning around several times before settling himself to sleep for the night. His wild ancestors did that, to crush the stiff grasses and reeds into a softer bed and to scare therefrom any lurking snakes or scorpions.

Lad's "talking" was a byword, at Sunnybank. Only to the Mistress and myself would he deign to "speak." But, to us, he would sometimes talk for five minutes at a time. Of course, there were no actual words in his speech. But no words were needed to show his meaning. His conversation used to run the full gamut of sounds, in a way that was as eerie as it was laughable. He could—and did—express every shade of meaning he chose to.

Indignation or disgust was voiced in fierce grumbles and mutters that were run together in sentence lengths. Sympathy found vent in queer crooning sounds, accompanied by swift light pats of his absurdly tiny white forepaws. Grief was expressed in something too much like human sobs to be funny. And so on through every possible emotion—except fear. The great dog did not know fear.

No one, listening when Lad "talked," could doubt he was seeking to imitate the intonation and meanings of the human voice.

Once, the Mistress and I went on a visit of sympathy to a lugubrious old woman who lived some miles from Sunnybank, and who had been laid up for weeks with a broken arm. The arm had mended. But it was still a source of mental misery to the victim. We took Lad along, on our call, because the convalescent was fond of him. We had every cause, soon, to wish we had left him at home.

From the instant we entered the old woman's house, a demon of evil mirth seemed to possess the dog. Outwardly, he was calm and sedate, as usual. He curled up beside the Mistress, and, with head gravely on one side, proceeded to listen to our hostess' tale of the long and painful illness. But, scarcely had the whiningly groaning accents framed a single sentence of the recital, when Lad took up the woeful tale on his own account.

His voice pitched in precisely the same key as the speaker's, he began to whine and to mumble. When the woman paused for breath, Lad filled in the brief interval with the most heartrendingly lamentable groans; then continued his plaint with her. And all the time, his deep-set, sorrowful eyes were fairly a-dance with mischief, and the tip of his plumy tail was quivering in a tense effort not to betray his sinful glee by wagging.

It was too much for me. I got out of the room as fast as I could. I escaped barely in time to hear the hostess moan:

"Isn't it wonderful how that dog understands my terrible suffering? He carries on, just as if it were his own agony!"

But I knew better, in spite of Lad's affirmative groan. In personal agony, Lad could never be lured into making a sound. And when the

Mistress or myself was unhappy, his swift and heart-broken sympathy did not take the form of lamentable ululations or of such impudent copying of our voices.

It was just one of Lad's jokes. He realised as well as we did that the old lady was no longer in pain and that she was a chronic calamity howler. That was his way of guying the mock-sufferer. Genuine trouble always stirred him to the depths. But, his life long, he hated fraud.

Lad's story is told in detail, elsewhere; and I have here written overlong about him. But his human traits were myriad and it is hard for me to condense an account of him.

Then there was Bruce—hero of my dogbook of the same name. Bruce's "pedigree name" was Sunnybank Goldsmith; and for many years he brought local dog-show fame to the Place by an unbroken succession of victories. A score of cups and medals and an armful of blue ribbons attest his physical perfection.

But dog-shows take no heed of a collie's mentality, nor of the thousand wistfully lovable traits which make him what he is. When we carved on Bruce's headstone the inscription, "The Dog Without a Fault," we referred less to his physical magnificence than to the soul and the heart of him.

He was wholly different from Lad. He lacked Lad's d'Artagnan-like dash and gaiety and uncanny wisdom. Yet he was clever. And he had a strange sweetness of nature that I have found in no other dog. That, and a perfect "one-man-dog" obedience and goodness.

Like Lad, he was never struck or otherwise punished; and never needed such punishment. He and Laddie were dear friends, from the moment they met. And each was the only grown male dog with which the other would consent to be on terms of cordiality.

Bruce had a melancholy dignity, behind which lurked an elusive sense of fun.

For his children—he had many dozens of them—he felt an eternal disgust; even aversion. Let visitors start to walk towards the puppy-yards, and Bruce at once lowered his head and tail and slunk away. When a group of the puppies, out for a gallop, caught sight of their sire and bore down gleefully upon him, Bruce would stalk off in utter gloom. Too chivalric to hurt or even to growl at any of the scrambling oncoming babies, he would none the less take himself out of their way with all possible haste.

But, on occasion, he could rise to a sense of his duties as a parent. As when one of the young dogs was left tied for a few minutes to a clothesline, three summers ago. The youngster gnawed the line in two and pranced merrily away on a rabbit hunt, dragging ten feet of rope with him.

When I came home and saw the severed clothesline, I knew what must be happening, somewhere out in the woods. The dangling rope was certain to catch in some bush or stump. And the puppy, in his struggles, would snarl himself inextricably. There, unless help should come, he must starve to death.

For twenty-four hours, two of the men and the Mistress and myself scoured the forests and hills for a radius of several miles. We looked everywhere a luckless puppy would be likely to entangle himself. We shouted ourselves hoarse, in hope of an answering cry from the lost one.

After a day and a night of this fruitless search, the Mistress and I set off again; this time taking Bruce along. At least, we started off taking him. After the first hundred yards, he took us. Why I bothered to follow him, I don't yet know.

He struck a bee line, through woods and brambles, travelling at a hard gallop and stopping every few moments for me to catch up with him. At the end of a mile, he plunged into a copse that was choked with briars. In the centre of this he gave tongue, with a salvo of thunderous barks. Twice before, I had searched this copse. But, at his urgency, I entered it again.

In its exact center, hidden from view by a matted screen of briars and leaves, I found the runaway. His rope had caught in a root. He had then wound himself up in it, until the line enmeshed him and held him close to earth. A twist of it, around his jaws, had kept him from making a sound. He was half dead from fright and thirst.

Having found and saved the younger dog, Bruce promptly lost all interest in him. He seemed ashamed, rather than pleased, at our laudations.

On such few times as we went motoring without him, Bruce was always on hand to greet us on our return. And his greeting took an odd form. Near the foot of the drive was a big forsythia bush. At sight of the approaching car, Bruce invariably rushed over to this bush and hid behind it. At least he bent his head until a branch of the bush hid it from view.

Then, tail a-quiver, he would crouch there; not realising that all of him except his head was in plain sight to us. When at last the car was almost alongside, he would jump out; and stand wagging his plumed tail excitedly, to note our surprise at his unforeseen presence. Never did this jest pall on him. Never did he have the faintest idea that his head was the only part of his beautiful self which was not clearly visible.

Bruce slept in my bedroom. In the morning, when one of the maids knocked at the door to wake me, he would get to his feet, cross the room to the bed, and lay his cold muzzle against my face, tapping at my arm or shoulder with his paw until I opened my eyes. Then, at once, he went back to his rug and lay down again. Nor, if I failed to climb out of bed for another two hours, would he disturb me a second time.

He had waked me, once. After that, it was up to me to obey the summons or to disregard it. That was no concern of Bruce's. His duty was done!

But how did a mere dog know that the knock on the door was a signal for me to get up? Never by any chance did he disturb me until he heard that knock.

He was psychic, too. Rex, a dog that I had had long before, used to sleep in a certain corner of the lower hall. He slept there for years. He was killed. Never afterward would Bruce set foot on the spot where Rex had been wont to lie. Time and again I have seen him skirt that part of the floor, making a semi-circular detour in order to avoid stepping there. I have tested him a dozen times, in the presence of guests. Always the result was the same.

Peace to his stately, lovable, whimsical soul! He was my dear chum. And his going has left an ache.

Wolf is Lad's son—wiry and undersized; yet he is as golden as Katherine Lee Bates' immortal "Sigurd." He inherits his sire's wonderful brain as well as Laddie's keen sense of humour.

Savage, and hating strangers, Wolf has learned the law to this extent: no one, walking or motoring down the drive from the gate and coming straight to the front door, must be molested; though no stranger crossing the grounds or prowling within their limits need be tolerated.

A guest may pat him on the head, at will; and Wolf must make no sign of resentment. But all my years of training do not prevent him from snarling in fierce menace if a visitor seeks to pat his sensitive body. Very young children are the only exceptions to this rule of his. Toddling babies may maul him to their hearts' content; and Wolf revels in the discomfort.

Like Lad, he is the Mistress' dog. Not merely because he belongs to her; but because he has adopted her for his deity.

When we leave Sunnybank, for two or three months, yearly, in mid-winter, Wolf knows we are going; even before the trunks are brought from the attic for packing. And, from that time on, he is in dire, silent misery. When at last the car carries us out of the gate, he sits down, points his muzzle skyward, and shakes the air with a series of raucous wolf-howls. After five minutes of which, he sullenly, stoically, takes up the burden of loneliness until our return.

The queer part of it is that he knows—as Lad and Bruce used to know—in some occult way, when we are coming home. And, for hours before our return, he is in a state of crazy excitement. I don't try to explain this. I have no explanation for it. But it can be proven by anyone at Sunnybank.

The ancestral herding instinct is strong in Wolf. It made itself known, first, when a car was coming down the drive towards the house, at a somewhat reckless pace, several years ago. In the center of the drive, several of the collie pups were playing. When the car was almost on top of the heedless bevy of youngsters, Wolf darted out from the veranda, rushed in among the pups, and shouldered them off the drive and up onto the bank at either side. He cleared the drive of every one of them; then bounded aside barely in time to escape the car's front wheels.

He was praised for this bit of quick thought and quicker action. And the praise made him inordinately proud. From that day on, he has hustled every pup or grown dog off the drive whenever a car has come in sight through the gateway.

When the pups are too far scattered for him to round them up and shove them out of harm's way in so short a time, he adopts a still better mode of clearing the drive. Barking in wild ecstasy, he rushes at top speed down the lawn, as though in pursuit of some highly alluring prey. No living pup can resist such a call. Every one of the youngsters dashes in pursuit. Then, as soon as the last of them is far enough away from the drive, Wolf stops and comes trotting back to the house. He has done this, again and again. To me, it savors of human reasoning.

In the car, Wolf is as efficient a guard as any policeman. When the Mistress drives alone, he sits on the front seat beside her. If she stops in front of any shop, he is at once on the alert. At such times, a woman acquaintance may come alongside for a word with her. Wolf pays no heed to the newcomer.

But let a *man* approach the car and Wolf is up on his toes, and ready for trouble. If the man lays a hand on the automobile, in the course of the chat, Wolf is at his throat. When I am driving with the Mistress, he lies on the rear seat and does not bother to act as policeman; except when we leave the car in his keeping.

People, hereabouts, know this trait of Wolf's and his aversion to any stranger. And they forbear to touch the car when talking with us. Last year, a friend came alongside while we were waiting, one evening, for the mail to be sorted. Wolf had never before seen this man. Yet, after a single glance, the dog lost his usual air of hostility. There was a slight tremble in our friend's voice as he said to us:

"My collie was run over to-day and killed. We are mighty unhappy, at our house, this evening."

As he spoke, he laid his hand on the door of the car. Wolf lurched forward, as usual. But, to our amazement, instead of attacking, he whimpered softly and licked the man's face. Never before or since, have I seen him show any sign of friendly interest in a stranger—not even to this same man, when they chanced to meet again, a few months later.

Bruce's son Jock was the finest pup, from a dog-show point of view—and in every other way—that we have been able to breed. Jock was physical perfection. And he had a brain, too; and abundant charm; and a most intensely haunting personality. He had from earliest puppyhood all the steadfast qualities of a veteran dog; and at the same time a babylike friendliness and love of play.

Nor did he know what it was to be afraid. Always, in presence of danger, he met the menace with a furious charge, accompanied by a clear, trumpet-bark of gay defiance. Once, for instance, he had been lying beside my chair on the veranda. Suddenly he jumped to his feet, with that same gay, fierce bark.

I turned to see what had excited him. A huge copperhead snake had crawled up the vines to the porch floor and had wriggled on to within a foot or two of my chair.

Jock was barely six months old. Yet he flew to the assault with more sense than would many a grown dog.

All dogs have a horror of copperheads, and Jock was no exception. By instinct, he seemed to know what the snake's tactics would be. For he strove to catch the foe by the back of the neck, before the copperhead could coil.

He was a fraction of a second too late. Yet he was nimble and wise enough to spring back out of reach, before the coiling serpent could strike. Then, with that same glad bark of defiance, he danced about his enemy, trying to take the snake from the rear and to flash in and get a neck grip before the copperhead could recoil after each futile strike.

I put an end to the battle by a bullet in the snake's ugly head. And Jock was mortally offended with me, for hours thereafter, for spoiling his fun.

When he was eight months old, I took the little chap to Paterson, to his first (and last) dog show. Never before had he been off the Place or in a house. Yet he bore himself like a seasoned traveler; and he "showed" with the perfection of a champion. He won, in class after class; annexing two silver cups and several blue ribbons. His peerless sire, Bruce, was the only collie, in the whole show, able to win over him that day.

Jock beat every other contestant. He seemed to enjoy showing and to delight in the novelty and excitement of it all. He was at the show for only a few hours; and it was a triumph-day for him.

Yet cheerfully would I give a thousand dollars not to have taken him there.

For he brought home not only his many prizes but a virulent case of distemper; as did other dogs that attended the same show.

Of course, I had had him (as well as all my other dogs) inoculated against distemper, long before; and such precautions are supposed to be effective. But the disease got through the inoculation and infected him.

He made a gallant fight of it—oh, a *gallant* fight!—the fearless little thoroughbred! But it was too much for him. For five weeks, he and I fought that grindingly losing battle.

Then, in the dim grey of a November dawn, he lifted his head from my knee, and peered through the shadows towards one black corner of the room. No one, watching him, could have doubted that he saw Something—lurking there in the dark.

Sharply, he eyed the dim room-corner for an instant. Then, from his throat burst forth that glad, fierce defiance-bark of his—his fearlessly gay battle shout. And he fell back dead.

What did he see, waiting for him, there in the murk of shadows? Perhaps nothing. Perhaps "the Arch-Fear in visible shape." Who knows?

In any case, whatever it was, he did not fear it. He challenged it as fiercely as ever he had challenged mortal foe. And his hero-spirit went forth to do battle with it—unafraid.

God grant us all so gallant an ending!

His little mother, Sunnybank Jean, had never cast Jock off, as do most dog-mothers when their pups are weaned. To the day I quarantined him for distemper, she and her son had been inseparable.

A week after Jock's death, Jean came running up to me, shaking with glad eagerness, and led me to the grave where the puppy had been buried. It was far off, and I had hoped she would not be able to find it. But she had been searching, very patiently, whenever she was free.

And now, when she had led me to the grave, she lay down close beside it. Not despondently; but wagging her plumed tail gently, and as if she had found at last a clue in her long search. Scent or some other sense told her she was nearer her baby than she had been in days. And she was well content to wait there until he should come back.

All of which is maudlin, perhaps; but it is true.

Perhaps it is also maudlin to wonder why a sane human should be fool enough to let himself care for a dog, when he knows that at best he is due for a man's size heartache within a pitifully brief span of years. Dogs live so short a time; and we humans so long!

This rambling tale of my dogs leaves no room to tell at length of the collie who was never allowed in the dining-room until the after-dinner coffee was served; and who came the length of the hall and up to the table the moment the maid brought in the coffee cups (how he timed it to the very second, none of us knew; yet not once did he miss connections by the slightest fraction of a minute).

Nor does it permit the tale of the collie pup who was proud of his stunt in learning to take the morning paper off the front steps and carry it into the dining-room; and whose pride in the accomplishment led him presently to collect all the morning papers from all the door steps within the radius of a mile and deposit them happily at my feet.

Nor can I tell of the collie that caught and followed the trail of my footsteps, through the rain, along a crowded city street; in and out of a maze of turnings; and came up with me inside of three minutes. Nor of a long line of other collies, some of whom showed human intelligence; and some, intelligence that was almost more than human.

Not even of the clown pup that was so elated over "rounding up" his first bunch of sheep that he proceeded to round up chickens and cats and every living and round-up-able creature that he could find; nor of the collie who, taught to fetch my hat, was wont to romp up to me in the presence of many outsiders; bearing proudly in his teeth an assortment of humble, not to say intimate and humiliating, garments.

Comedian dogs, spectacular dogs, gloriously human dogs, Sunnybank collies of every phase of heart and brain and soul—one common and pathetically early tragedy has waited or waits for you all! Among you, you have taught me more of true loyalty and patience and courtesy and divine forgiveness and solid sanity and fun and a hundred other worth-while lessons than all the masters I have studied under.

I wonder if it is heretical to believe that when at last my tired feet shall tread the Other Shore, a madly welcoming swirl of exultant collies—the splendid Sunnybank dogs that have been my chums here—will bound forward, circling and barking around me, to lead me Home!

Heretical or otherwise, I want to believe it. And if I fail to find them there, I shall know I have taken the Wrong Turning and have reached a goal other than I hoped for.

15

The Lead Dog

by William Francis Butler

When his book The Wild North Land *was first published in 1910,
William Francis Butler described himself: "I am become a name for
always roaming with hungry heart." This tribute to a dog is from those
travels.*

A GOOD DOG IS SO MUCH A NOBLER BEAST THAN AN INDIFFERENT MAN
that one sometimes gladly exchanges the society of one for that of the
other.

A great French writer has told us that animals were put on Earth to
show us the evil effects of passions run riot and unchecked. But it seems
to me that the reverse would be closer to the truth. The humanity which
Napoleon deemed a dog taught to man on Bassano's battlefield is not the
only virtue we can learn from that lower world which is bound to us by
such close ties, and yet lies so strangely apart from us. Be that as it may, a
man can seldom feel alone if he has a dog to share his supper, to stretch
near him under the starlight, to answer him with tail-wag, or glance of
eye, or prick of ear.

Day after day Cerf-vola and his comrades trotted on in all the freedom
which summer and autumn give to the great dog family in the north. Now
chasing a badger, who invariably popped into his twenty-sixth burrow in
time to save his skin; now sending a pack of prairie grouse flying from the
long grass; now wading breast-deep into a lake where a few wild ducks
still lingered, loath to quit their summer nesting-haunts.

Of all the dogs I have known, Cerf-vola possessed the largest share of tact. He never fought a pitched battle, yet no dog dared dispute his supremacy. Other dogs had to maintain their leadership by many a deadly conflict, but he quietly assumed it, and invariably his assumption was left unchallenged; nay, even upon his arrival at some Hudson Bay fort, some place wherein he had never before set foot, he was wont to instantly appoint himself director-general of all the Company's dogs, whose days from earliest puppyhood had been passed within the palisades. I have often watched him at this work, and marvelled by what mysterious power he held his sway. I have seen two or three large dogs flee before a couple of bounds merely made by him in their direction, while a certain will-some-one-hold-me-back? kind of look pervaded his face, as though he was only prevented from rending his enemy into small pieces by the restraining influence which the surface of the ground exercised upon his legs.

His great weight no doubt carried respect with it. At the lazy time of the year he weighed nearly 100 pounds, and his size was in no way diminished by the immense coat of hair and fine fur which enveloped him. Had Sir Boyle Roche known this dog, he would not have given to a bird alone the faculty of being in two places at once, for no mortal eye could measure the interval between Cerf-vola's demolishment of two pieces of dogmeat, or Pemmican, flung in different directions at the same moment.

Thus we journeyed on. Sometimes when the sheen of a lake suggested the evening camp, while yet the sun was above the horizon, my three friends would accompany me on a ramble through the thicket-lined hills. At such times, had any Indian watched from sedgy shore or bordering willow copse the solitary wanderer who, with dogs following close, treaded the lonely lake shore, he would have probably carried to his brethren a strange story of the "white man's medicine." He would have averred that he had heard a white man talking to a big, bushy-tailed dog, somewhere amidst the Touchwood Hills, and singing to him a "great medicine song" when the sun went down.

And if now we reproduce for the reader the medicine song which the white man strung together for his bushy-tailed dog, we may perhaps forestall some critic's verdict by prefixing to it the singularly appropriate title of

DOGGEREL

And so, old friend, we are met again, companions still to be,
Across the waves of drifted snow, across the prairie sea.
Again we'll tread the silent lake, the frozen swamp, the fen,
Beneath the snow-crown'd sombre pine we'll build our camp again:
And long before the icy dawn, while hush'd all nature lies,
And weird and wan the white lights flash across the northern skies;
Thy place, as in past days thou'lt take, the leader of the train,
To steer until the stars die out above the dusky plain;
Then on, thro' space by wood and hill, until the wintry day
In pale gleams o'er the snow-capped ridge has worn itself away,
And twilight bids us seek the brake, where midst the pines once more
The fire will gleam before us, the stars will glimmer o'er.
There stretch'd upon the snow-drift, before the pine log's glare,
Thy master's couch and supper with welcome thou wilt share,
To rest, unless some prowling wolf should keep thee watchful still,
While lonely through the midnight sounds his wail upon the hill.

And when the storm raves around, and thick and blinding snow
Comes whirling in wild eddies around, above, below;
Still all unmoved thou'lt keep thy pace as manfully as when
Thy matchless mettle first I tried in lone Pasquia's glen.
Thus day by day we'll pierce the wilds where rolls the Arctic stream,
Where Athabasca's silent lakes, through whispering pine-trees gleam.
Until, where far Unchagah's flood by giant cliffs is crown'd,
Thy bells will feed the echoes, long hungering for a sound.
Old dog, they say thou hast no life beyond this earth of ours,
That toil and truth give thee no place amidst Elysian bowers.
Ah well, e'en so, I look for thee when all our danger's past,
That on some hearth-rug, far at home, thou'lt rest thy limbs at last.

16

Uncle Dick's Rolf

by Georgiana Marion Craik

Even though this is a story of a dog's loyalty and uncanny pre-science, mistreatment is suggested. Rolf's owner strikes out at him when the dog's behavior grows irrational. But that does not deter Rolf from risking his own life to save Uncle Dick from the jaws of death—literally.

"I HAD BEEN RIDING FOR FIVE OR SIX MILES ONE PLEASANT AFTERNOON. It was a delicious afternoon, like the afternoon of an English summer day. You always imagine it hotter out in Africa by a good deal than it is in England, don't you? Well, so it is, in a general way, a vast deal hotter; but every now and then, after the rains have fallen and the wind comes blowing from the sea, we get a day as much like one of our own best summer days as you ever felt anywhere. This afternoon was just like an English summer afternoon, with the fresh sweet breeze rustling amongst the green leaves, and the great bright sea stretching out all blue and golden, and meeting the blue sky miles and miles away.

"It wasn't very hot, but it was just hot enough to make the thought of a swim delicious; so after I had been riding leisurely along for some little time, shooting a bird or two as I went—for I wanted some bright feathers to send home to a little cousin that I had in England—I alighted from my horse, and, letting him loose to graze, lay down for a quarter of an hour to cool myself, and then began to make ready for my plunge.

"I was standing on a little ledge of cliff, some six or seven feet above the sea. It was high tide, and the water at my feet was about a fathom deep. 'I shall have a delightful swim,' I thought to myself as I threw off my coat; and as just at that moment Rolf in a very excited way flung himself upon me, evidently understanding the meaning of the proceeding, and, as I thought, anxious to show his sympathy with it, I repeated the remark aloud. 'Yes, we'll have a delightful swim, you and I together,' I said. 'A grand swim, my old lad'; and I clapped his back as I spoke, and encouraged him, as I was in the habit of doing, to express his feelings without reserve. But, rather to my surprise, instead of wagging his tail, and wrinkling his nose, and performing any of his usual antics, the creature only lifted up his face and began to whine. He had lain, for the quarter of an hour while I had been resting, at the edge of the little cliff, with his head dropped over it; but whether he had been taking a sleep in that position, or had been amusing himself by watching the waves, was more than I knew. He was a capital one for sleeping even then, and generally made a point of snatching a doze at every convenient opportunity; so I had naturally troubled my head very little about him, taking it for granted that he was at his usual occupation. But, whether he had been asleep before or not, at any rate he was wide awake now, and, as it seemed to me, in a very odd humor indeed.

"'What's the matter, old fellow?' I said to him when he set up this dismal howl. 'Don't you want to have a swim? Well, you needn't unless you like, only *I* mean to have one; so down with you, and let me get my clothes off.' But, instead of getting down, the creature began to conduct himself in the most incomprehensible way, first seizing me by the trousers with his teeth and pulling me to the edge of the rock, as if he wanted me to plunge in dressed as I was; then catching me again and dragging me back, much as though I was a big rat that he was trying to worry; and this pantomime, I declare, he went through three separate times, barking and whining all the while, till I began to think he was going out of his mind.

"Well, God forgive me! but at last I got into a passion with the beast. I couldn't conceive what he meant. For two or three minutes I tried to pacify him, and as long as I took no more steps to get my clothes off he was willing to be pacified; but the instant I fell to undressing myself again he was on me once more, pulling me this way and that, hanging on my arms, slobbering over me, howling with his mouth up in the air. And so at last I lost my temper, and I snatched up my gun and struck him with the butt-end of it. My poor Rolf!" said Uncle Dick, all at once, with a falter in his voice; and he stopped abruptly, and stooped down and laid his hand on the great black head.

"He was quieter after I had struck him," said Uncle Dick, after a little pause. "For a few moments he lay quite still at my feet, and I had begun to think that his crazy fit was over, and that he was going to give me no more trouble, when all at once, just as I had got ready to jump into the water, the creature sprang to his feet and flung himself upon me again. He threw himself with all his might upon my breast and drove me backwards, howling so wildly that many a time since, boys, I have thought I must have been no better than a blind, perverse fool not to have guessed what the trouble was; but the fact is, I was a conceited young fellow (as most young fellows are), and because I imagined the poor beast was trying for some reason of his own to get his own way, I thought it was my business to teach him that he was not to get his own way, but that I was to get mine; and so I beat him down somehow—I don't like to think of it now; I struck him again three or four times with the end of my gun, till at last I got myself freed from him.

"He gave a cry when he fell back. I call it a cry, for it was more like something human than a dog's howl—something so wild and pathetic that, angry as I was, it startled me, and I almost think, if time enough had been given me, I would have made some last attempt then to understand what the creature meant; but I had no time after that. I was standing a few feet in from the water, and as soon as I had shaken him off he went to the edge of the bit of cliff, and stood there for a moment till I came up to him, and then—just as in another second I should have jumped into the sea—my brave dog, my noble dog, gave one last whine and one look into my face, and took the leap before me. And then, boys, in another instant I saw what he had meant. He had scarcely touched the water when I saw a crocodile slip like lightning from a sunny ledge of the cliff, and grip him by the hinder legs.

"You know that I had my gun close at hand, and in the whole course of my life I never was so glad to have my gun beside me. It was loaded, too, and a revolver. I caught it up, and fired into the water. I fired three times, and two of the shots went into the brute's head. One missed him, and the first seemed not to harm him much, but the third hit him in some vital place, I hope—some sensitive place, at any rate, for the hideous jaws started wide. Then, with my gun in my hand still, I began with all my might to shout out, 'Rolf!' I couldn't leave my post, for the brute, though he had let Rolf go, and had dived for a moment, might make another spring, and I didn't dare to take my eyes off the spot where he had gone down; but I called to my wounded beast with all my might, and when he had struggled through the water and gained a moment's hold of the rock, I jumped down and caught him, and somehow—I don't know how— half carried and half dragged him up the little bit of steep ascent, till we were safe on the top—on the dry land again. And then upon my word, I don't know what I did next, only I think, as I looked at my darling's poor crushed limbs, with the blood oozing from them, and heard his choking gasps for breath—I—I forgot for a moment or two that I was a man at all, and burst out crying like a child.

"Boys, you don't know what it is to feel that a living creature has tried to give up his life for you, even though the creature is only a soulless dog. Do you think I had another friend in the world who would have done what Rolf had done for me? If I had, I did not know it. And then when I thought that it was while he had been trying to save my life that I had taken up my gun and struck him! There are some things, my lads, that a man does without meaning any harm by them, which yet, when he sees them by the light of after events, he can never bear to look back upon without a sort of agony; and those blows I gave to Rolf are of that sort. He forgave them—my noble dog; but I have never forgiven myself for them to this hour. When I saw him lying before me, with his blood trickling out upon the sand, I think I would have given my right hand to save his life. And well I might, too, for he had done ten times more than that to save mine.

"He licked the tears off my cheeks, my poor old fellow; I remember that. We looked a strange pair, I dare say, as we lay on the ground together, with our heads side by side. It's a noble old head still, isn't it, boys? (I don't mean mine, but this big one down here. All right, Rolf! We're only talking of your beauty, my lad.) It's as grand a head as ever a dog had. I had his picture taken after I came home. I've had him painted more than once, but somehow I don't think the painters have ever seen quite into the bottom of his heart. At least, I fancy that if I were a painter I could make something better of him than any of them have done yet. Perhaps it's only a notion of mine, but, to tell the truth, I've only a dozen times or so in my life seen a painting of a grand dog that looks quite right. But I'm wandering from my story, though, indeed, my story is almost at an end.

"When I had come to my senses a little, I had to try to get my poor Rolf moved. We were a long way from any house, and the creature couldn't walk a step. I tore up my shirt, and bound his wounds as well as I could, and then I got my clothes on, and called to my horse, and in some way, as gently as I could—though it was no easy thing to do it—I got him and myself together upon the horse's back, and we began our ride. There was a village about four or five miles off, and I made for that. It was a long, hard jolt for a poor fellow with both his hind legs broken, but he bore it as patiently as if he had been a Christian. I never spoke to him but, panting as he was, he was ready to lick my hands and look lovingly up into my face. I've wondered since, many a time, what he could have thought about it all; and the only thing I am sure of is that he never thought much of the thing that he himself had done. That seemed, I know, all natural and simple to him; I don't believe that he has ever understood to this day what anybody wondered at in it, or made a hero of him for. For the noblest people are the people who are noble without knowing it; and the same rule, I fancy, holds good, too, for dogs.

"I got him to a resting-place at last, after a weary ride, and then I had his wounds dressed; but it was weeks before he could stand upon his feet again, and when at last he began to walk he limped, and he has gone on limping ever since. The bone of one leg was so crushed that it couldn't be set properly, and so that limb is shorter than the other three. *He* doesn't mind it much, I dare say—I don't think he ever did—but it has been a pathetic lameness to me, boys. It's all an old story now, you know," said Uncle Dick, abruptly, "but it's one of those things that a man doesn't forget, and that it would be a shame to him if he ever *could* forget as long as his life lasts."

Uncle Dick stooped down again as he ceased to speak, and Rolf, disturbed by the silence, raised his head to look about him. As his master had said, it was a grand old head still, though the eyes were growing dim now with age. Uncle Dick laid his hand upon it, and the bushy tail began to wag. It had wagged at the touch of that hand for many a long day.

"We've been together for fifteen years. He's getting old now," said Uncle Dick.

17

Ulysses and the Dogman

by O. Henry

A master of the surprise ending, O. Henry leaves us guessing in this tale. It is difficult to be sure who is the pet—the bulldog on the leash or the former cowhand who walks him every night at the behest of his wealthy, citified wife. When the husband at last declares his independence, it is the dog, and not the wife, who takes the brunt of his master's frustration.

DO YOU KNOW THE TIME OF THE DOGMEN?

When the forefinger of twilight begins to smudge the clear-drawn lines of the Big City, there is inaugurated an hour devoted to one of the most melancholy sights of urban life.

Out from the towering flat crags and apartment peaks of the cliff-dwellers of New York steals an army of beings that were once men. Even yet they go upright upon two limbs and retain human form and speech; but you will observe that they are behind animals in progress. Each of these beings follows a dog, to which he is fastened by an artificial ligament.

These men are all victims to Circe. Not willingly do they become flunkeys to Fido, bell-boys to bull terriers, and toddlers after Towzer. Modern Circe, instead of turning them into animals, has kindly left the difference of a six-foot leash between them. Every one of these dogmen has been either cajoled, bribed, or commanded by his own particular Circe to take the dear household pet out for an airing.

By their faces and manner you can tell that the dogmen are bound in a hopeless enchantment. Never will there come even a dog-catcher Ulysses to remove the spell.

The faces of some are stonily set. They are past the commiseration, the curiosity, or the jeers of their fellow-beings. Years of matrimony, of continuous compulsory canine constitutionals, have made them callous. They unwind their beasts from lamp-posts, or the ensnared legs of profane pedestrians, with the stolidity of mandarins manipulating the strings of their kites.

Others, more recently reduced to the ranks of Rover's retinue, take their medicine sulkily and fiercely. They play the dog on the end of their line with the pleasure felt by the girl out fishing when she catches a sea-robin on her hook. They glare at you threateningly if you look at them, as if it would be their delight to let slip the dogs of war. These are half-mutinous dogmen, not quite Circe-ized, and you will do well not to kick their charges, should they sniff around your ankles.

Others of the tribe do not seem to feel so keenly. They are mostly unfresh youths, with gold caps and drooping cigarettes, who do not harmonize with their dogs. The animals they attend wear satin bows in their collars; and the young men steer them so assiduously that you are tempted to the theory that some personal advantage, contingent upon satisfactory service, waits upon the execution of their duties.

The dogs thus personally conducted are of many varieties; but they are one in fatness, in pampered, diseased vileness of temper, in insolent, snarling capriciousness of behavior. They tug at the leash fractiously, they make leisurely nasal inventory of every doorstep, railing, and post. They sit down to rest when they choose; they wheeze like the winner of a Third Avenue beefsteak-eating contest; they blunder clumsily into open cellars and coal holes; they lead the dogmen a merry dance.

These unfortunate dry nurses of dogdom, the cur cuddlers, mongrel managers, Spitz stalkers, poodle pullers, Skye scrapers, dachshund dandlers, terrier trailers and Pomeranian pushers of the cliff-dwelling Circes follow their charges meekly. The doggies neither fear nor respect them. Masters of the house these men whom they hold in leash may be, but they are not masters of them. From cozy corner to fire-escape, from divan to dumb-waiter, doggy's snarl easily drives this two-legged being who is commissioned to walk at the other end of his string during his outing.

One twilight the dogmen came forth as usual at their Circes' pleading, guerdon, or crack of the whip. One among them was a strong man, apparently of too solid virtues for this airy vocation. His expression was melancholic, his manner depressed. He was leashed to a vile, white dog, loathsomely fat, fiendishly ill-natured, gloatingly intractable toward his despised conductor.

At a corner nearest to his apartment-house the dogman turned down a side-street, hoping for fewer witnesses to his ignominy. The surfeited beast waddled before him, panting with spleen and the labor of motion.

Suddenly the dog stopped. A tall, brown, long-coated, wide-brimmed man stood like a Colossus blocking the sidewalk and declaring:

"Well, I'm a son of a gun!"

"Jim Berry!" breathed the dogman, with exclamation points in his voice.

"Sam Telfair," cried Wide-Brim again, "you ding-basted old willy-walloo, give us your hoof!"

Their hands clasped in the brief, tight greeting of the West that is death to the handshake microbe.

"You old fat rascal!" continued Wide-Brim, with a wrinkled, brown smile; "it's been five years since I seen you. I been in this town a week, but you can't find nobody in such a place. Well, you dinged old married man, how are they coming?"

Something mushy and heavily soft like raised dough leaned against Jim's leg and chewed his trousers with a yeasty growl.

"Get to work," said Jim, "and explain this yard-wide hydrophobia yearling you've throwed your lasso over. Are you the pound-master of this burg? Do you call that a dog or what?"

"I need a drink," said the dogman, dejected at the reminder of his old dog of the sea. "Come on."

Hard by was a café. 'Tis ever so in the big city.

They sat at a table, and the bloated monster yelped and scrambled at the end of his leash to get at the café cat.

"Whisky," said Jim to the waiter. "Make it two," said the dogman.

"You're fatter," said Jim, "and you look subjugated. I don't know about the East agreeing with you. All the boys asked me to hunt you up when I started. Sandy King, he went to the Klondike. Watson Burrel, he married the oldest Peters girl. I made some money buying beeves, and I bought a lot of wild land up on the Little Powder. Going to fence next fall. Bill Rawlins, he's gone to farming. You remember Bill, of course—he was courting Marcella—excuse me, Sam—I mean the lady you married, while she was teaching school at Prairie View. But you was the lucky man. How is Missis Telfair?"

"S-h-h-h!" said the dogman, signaling the waiter; "give it a name."

"Whisky," said Jim.

"Make it two," said the dogman.

"She's well," he continued, after his chaser. "She refused to live anywhere but in New York, where she came from. We live in a flat. Every evening at six I take that dog out for a walk. It's Marcella's pet. There never were two animals on earth, Jim, that hated one another like me and that dog does. His name's Lovekins. Marcella dresses for dinner while we're out. We eat tabble dote. Ever tried one of them, Jim?"

"No, I never," said Jim. "I seen the signs, but I thought they said 'table de hole.' I thought it was French for pool tables. How does it taste?"

"If you're going to be in the city for awhile we will—"

"No, sir-ee. I'm starting for home this evening on the 7:25. Like to stay longer, but I can't."

"I'll walk down to the ferry with you," said the dogman.

The dog had bound a leg each of Jim and the chair together, and had sunk into a comatose slumber. Jim stumbled and the leash was slightly wrenched. The shrieks of the awakened beast rang for a block around.

"If that's your dog," said Jim, when they were on the street again, "what's to hinder you from running that habeas corpus you've got around his neck over a limb and walking off and forgetting him?"

"I'd never dare to," said the dogman, awed at the bold proposition. "He sleeps in the bed. I sleep on a lounge. He runs howling to Marcella if I look at him. Some night, Jim, I'm going to get even with that dog.

I've made up my mind to do it. I'm going to creep over with a knife and cut a hole in his mosquito bar so they can get in to him. See if I don't do it!"

"You ain't yourself, Sam Telfair. You ain't what you was once. I don't know about these cities and flats over here. With my own eyes I seen you stand off both the Tillotson boys in Prairie View with the brass faucet out of a molasses barrel. And I seen you rope and tie the wildest steer on Little Powder."

"I did, didn't I?" said the other, with a temporary gleam in his eye. "But that was before I was dogmatized."

"Does Missis Telfair—" began Jim.

"Hush!" said the dogman. "Here's another café."

They lined up at the bar. The dog fell asleep at their feet.

"Whisky," said Jim.

"Make it two," said the dogman.

"I thought about you," said Jim, "when I bought that wild land. I wished you was out there to help me with the stock."

"Last Tuesday," said the dogman, "he bit me on the ankle because I asked for cream in my coffee. He always gets the cream."

"You'd like Prairie View now," said Jim. "The boys from the roundups for fifty miles around ride in there. One corner of my pasture is in sixteen miles of the town. There's a straight forty miles of wire on one side of it."

"You pass through the kitchen to get to the bedroom," said the dogman, "and you pass through the parlor to get to the bathroom, and you back out through the dining-room to get into the bedroom so you can turn around and leave by the kitchen. And he snores and barks in his sleep, and I have to smoke in the park on account of his asthma."

"Don't Missis Telfair—" began Jim.

"Oh, shut up!" said the dogman. "What is it this time?"

"Whisky," said Jim.

"Make it two," said the dogman.

"Well, I'll be racking along down toward the ferry," said the other.

"Come on, there, you mangy, turtle-backed, snake-headed, bench-legged ton-and-a-half of soap-grease!" shouted the dogman, with a new note in his voice and a new hand on the leash. The dog scrambled after them, with an angry whine at such unusual language from his guardian.

At the foot of Twenty-third Street the dogman led the way through swinging doors.

"Last chance," said he. "Speak up."

"Whisky," said Jim.

"Make it two," said the dogman.

"I don't know," said the ranchman, "where I'll find the man I want to take charge of the Little Powder outfit. I want somebody I know something about. Finest stretch of prairie and timber you ever squinted your eye over, Sam. Now, if you was—"

"Speaking of hydrophobia," said the dogman, "the other night he chewed a piece out of my leg because I knocked a fly off of Marcella's arm. 'It ought to be cauterized,' says Marcella, and I was thinking so myself. I telephones for the doctor, and when he comes Marcella says to me: 'Help me hold the poor dear while the doctor fixes his mouth. Oh, I hope he got no virus on any of his toofies when he bit you.' Now what do you think of that?"

"Does Missis Telfair—" began Jim.

"Oh, drop it," said the dogman. "Come again!"

"Whisky," said Jim.

"Make it two," said the dogman.

They walked on to the ferry. The ranchman stepped to the ticket-window.

Suddenly the swift landing of three or four heavy kicks was heard, the air was rent by piercing canine shrieks, and a pained, outraged, lubberly, bow-legged pudding of a dog ran frenziedly up the street alone.

"Ticket to Denver," said Jim.

"Make it two," shouted the ex-dogman, reaching for his inside pocket.

18

Brown Wolf

by Jack London

Jack London, author of The Call of the Wild *and* White Fang, *among a host of gripping and gritty dog stories, creates a poignant tale of torn loyalties in "Brown Wolf." Wolf is a dog with a past, but the young couple who try to tame him when he turns up wounded at their ranch can have no way of knowing his origins. What is more puzzling are his constant attempts to run away—heading always to the north. It is only by sheerest coincidence that they discover the truth about their wandering dog, a painful truth that draws them into a contest that only the most loving and generous owners would agree to.*

SHE HAD DELAYED, BECAUSE OF THE DEW-WET GRASS, IN ORDER TO PUT on her overshoes, and when she emerged from the house found her waiting husband absorbed in the wonder of a bursting almond-bud. She sent a questing glance across the tall grass and in and out among the orchard trees.

"Where's Wolf?" she asked.

"He was here a moment ago." Walt Irvine drew himself away with a jerk from the metaphysics and poetry of the organic miracle of blossom, and surveyed the landscape. "He was running a rabbit the last I saw of him."

"Wolf! Wolf! Here, Wolf!" she called, as they left the clearing and took the trail that led down through the waxen-belled manzanita jungle to the county road.

Irvine thrust between his lips the little finger of each hand and lent to her efforts a shrill whistling.

She covered her ears hastily and made a wry grimace.

"My! For a poet, delicately attuned and all the rest of it, you can make unlovely noises. My eardrums are pierced. You outwhistle—"

"Orpheus."

"I was about to say a street-Arab," she concluded severely.

"Poesy does not prevent one from being practical—at least it doesn't prevent *me*. Mine is no futility of genius that can't sell gems to the magazines."

He assumed a mock extravagance, and went on:

"I am no attic singer, no ballroom warbler. And why? Because I am practical. Mine is no squalor of song that cannot transmute itself, with proper exchange value, into a flower-crowned cottage, a sweet mountain-meadow, a grove of red-woods, an orchard of thirty-seven trees, one long row of blackberries and two short rows of strawberries, to say nothing of a quarter of a mile of gurgling brook. I am a beauty-merchant, a trader in song, and I pursue utility, dear Madge. I sing a song, and thanks to the magazine editors I transmute my song into a waft of the west wind sighing through our redwoods, into a murmur of waters over mossy stones that sings back to me another song than the one I sang and yet the same song wonderfully—er—transmuted."

"O that all your song-transmutations were as successful!" she laughed.

"Name one that wasn't."

"Those two beautiful sonnets that you transmuted into the cow that was accounted the worst milker in the township."

"She was beautiful—" he began.

"But she didn't give milk," Madge interrupted.

"But she *was* beautiful, now, wasn't she?" he insisted.

"And here's where beauty and utility fall out," was her reply. "And there's the Wolf!"

From the thicket-covered hillside came a crashing of underbrush, and then, forty feet above them, on the edge of the sheer wall of rock, appeared a wolf's head and shoulders. His braced forepaws dislodged a pebble, and with sharp-pricked ears and peering eyes he watched the fall of the pebble till it struck at their feet. Then he transferred his gaze and with open mouth laughed down at them.

"You Wolf, you!" and "You blessed Wolf!" the man and woman called out to him.

The ears flattened back and down at the sound, and the head seemed to snuggle under the caress of an invisible hand.

They watched him scramble backward into the thicket, then proceeded on their way. Several minutes later, rounding a turn in the trail where the descent was less precipitous, he joined them in the midst of a miniature avalanche of pebbles and loose soil. He was not demonstrative. A pat and a rub around the ears from the man, and a more prolonged caressing from the woman, and he was away down the trail in front of them, gliding effortlessly over the ground in true wolf fashion.

In build and coat and brush he was a huge timber-wolf; but the lie was given to his wolf-hood by his color and marking. There the dog unmistakably advertised itself. No wolf was ever colored like him. He was brown, deep brown, red-brown, an orgy of browns. Back and shoulders were a warm brown that paled on the sides and underneath to a yellow that was dingy because of the brown that lingered in it. The white of the throat and paws and the spots over the eyes was dirty because of the persistent and ineradicable brown, while the eyes themselves were twin topazes, golden and brown.

The man and woman loved the dog very much; perhaps this was because it had been such a task to win his love. It had been no easy matter when he first drifted in mysteriously out of nowhere to their little mountain cottage. Footsore and famished, he had killed a rabbit under their very noses and under their very windows, and then crawled away and slept by the spring at the foot of the blackberry bushes. When Walt Irvine went down to inspect the intruder, he was snarled at for his pains, and Madge likewise was snarled at when she went down to present, as a peace-offering, a large pan of bread and milk.

A most unsociable dog he proved to be, resenting all their advances, refusing to let them lay hands on him, menacing them with bared fangs and bristling hair. Nevertheless he remained, sleeping and resting by the spring, and eating the food they gave him after they set it down at a safe distance and retreated. His wretched physical condition explained why he lingered; and when he had recuperated, after several days' sojourn, he disappeared.

And this would have been the end of him, so far as Irvine and his wife were concerned, had not Irvine at that particular time been called away into the northern part of the state. Riding along on the train, near to the line between California and Oregon, he chanced to look out of the window and saw his unsociable guest sliding along the wagon road, brown and wolfish, tired yet tireless, dust-covered and soiled with two hundred miles of travel.

Now Irvine was a man of impulse, a poet. He got off the train at the next station, bought a piece of meat at a butcher shop, and captured the vagrant on the outskirts of the town. The return trip was made in the baggage car, and so Wolf came a second time to the mountain cottage. Here he was tied up for a week and made love to by the man and woman. But it was very circumspect lovemaking. Remote and alien as a traveler from another planet, he snarled down their soft-spoken love-words. He never barked. In all the time they had him he was never known to bark.

To win him became a problem. Irvine liked problems. He had a metal plate made, on which was stamped: "Return to Walt Irvine, Glen Ellen, Sonoma County, California." This was riveted to a collar and strapped about the dog's neck. Then he was turned loose, and promptly he disappeared. A day later came a telegram from Mendocino County. In twenty hours he had made over a hundred miles to the north, and was still going when captured.

He came back by Wells Fargo Express, was tied up three days, and was loosed on the fourth and lost. This time he gained southern Oregon before he was caught and returned. Always, as soon as he received his liberty, he fled away, and always he fled north. He was possessed of an obsession that drove him north. The homing instinct, Irvine called it, after he had expended the selling price of a sonnet in getting the animal back from northern Oregon.

Another time the brown wanderer succeeded in traversing half the length of California, all of Oregon, and most of Washington before he was picked up and returned "Collect." A remarkable thing was the speed with which he traveled. Fed up and rested, as soon as he was loosed he devoted all his energy to getting over the ground. On the first day's run he was known to cover as high as a hundred and fifty miles, and after that he would average a hundred miles a day until caught. He always arrived back lean and hungry and savage, and always departed fresh and vigorous, cleaving his way northward in response to some prompting of his being that no one could understand.

But at last, after a futile year of flight, he accepted the inevitable and elected to remain at the cottage where first he had killed the rabbit and slept by the spring. Even after that, a long time elapsed before the man and woman succeeded in patting him. It was a great victory, for they alone were allowed to put hands on him. He was fastidiously exclusive, and no guest at the cottage ever succeeded in making up to him. A low growl greeted such approach; if anyone had the hardihood to come nearer, the lips lifted, the naked fangs appeared, and the growl became a snarl—a snarl so terrible and malignant that it awed the stoutest of them, as it likewise awed the farmers' dogs that knew ordinary dog-snarling, but had never seen wolf-snarling before.

He was without antecedents. His history began with Walt and Madge. He had come up from the south, but never a clue did they get of the owner from whom he had evidently fled. Mrs. Johnson, their nearest neighbor and the one who supplied them with milk, proclaimed him a Klondike dog. Her brother was burrowing for frozen pay-streaks in that far country, and so she constituted herself an authority on the subject.

But they did not dispute her. There were the tips of Wolf's ears, obviously so severely frozen at some time that they would never quite heal again. Besides, he looked like the photographs of the Alaskan dogs they saw published in magazines and newspapers. They often speculated over his past, and tried to conjure up (from what they had read and heard) what his northland life had been. That the northland still drew him, they knew; for at night they sometimes heard him crying softly; and when the north wind blew and the bite of frost was in the air, a great restlessness would come upon him and he would lift a mournful lament which they knew to be the long wolf-howl. Yet he never barked. No provocation was great enough to draw from him that canine cry.

Long discussion they had, during the time of winning him, as to whose dog he was. Each claimed him, and each proclaimed loudly any expression of affection made by him. But the man had the better of it at first, chiefly because he was a man. It was patent that Wolf had had no experience with women. He did not understand women. Madge's skirts were something he never quite accepted. The swish of them was enough to set him a-bristle with suspicion, and on a windy day she could not approach him at all.

On the other hand, it was Madge who fed him; also it was she who ruled the kitchen, and it was by her favor, and her favor alone, that he was permitted to come within that sacred precinct. It was because of these things that she bade fair to overcome the handicap of her garments. Then it was that Walt put forth special effort, making it a practice to have Wolf lie at his feet while he wrote, and, between petting and talking, losing much time from his work. Walt won in the end, and his victory was most probably due to the fact that he was a man, though Madge averred that they would have had another quarter of a mile of gurgling brook, and at least two west winds sighing through their redwoods, had Walt properly devoted his energies to song-transmutation and left Wolf alone to exercise a natural taste and an unbiased judgment.

"It's about time I heard from those triolets," Walt said, after a silence of five minutes, during which they had swung steadily down the trail. "There'll be a check at the post-office, I know, and we'll transmute it into beautiful buckwheat flour, a gallon of maple syrup, and a new pair of overshoes for you."

"And into beautiful milk from Mrs. Johnson's beautiful cow," Madge added. "Tomorrow's the first of the month, you know."

Walt scowled unconsciously; then his face brightened, and he clapped his hand to his breast pocket.

"Never mind. I have here a nice beautiful new cow, the best milker in California."

"When did you write it?" she demanded eagerly. Then, reproachfully, "And you never showed it to me."

"I saved it to read to you on the way to the post office, in a spot remarkably like this one," he answered, indicating, with a wave of his hand, a dry log on which to sit.

A tiny stream flowed out of a dense fern-brake, slipped down a mossy-lipped stone, and ran across the path at their feet. From the valley arose the mellow song of meadowlarks, while about them, in and out, through sunshine and shadow, fluttered great yellow butterflies.

Up from below came another sound that broke in upon Walt reading softly from his manuscript. It was a crunching of heavy feet, punctuated now and again by the clattering of a displaced stone. As Walt finished and looked to his wife for approval, a man came into view around the turn of the trail. He was bareheaded and sweaty. With a handkerchief in one hand he mopped his face, while in the other hand he carried a new hat and a wilted starched collar which he had removed from his neck. He was a well-built man, and his muscles seemed on the point of bursting out of the painfully new and ready-made black clothes he wore.

"Warm day," Walt greeted him. Walt believed in country democracy, and never missed an opportunity to practice it.

The man paused and nodded.

"I guess I ain't used much to the warm," he vouchsafed half apologetically. "I'm more accustomed to zero weather."

"You don't find any of that in this country," Walt laughed.

"Should say not," the man answered. "An' I ain't here a-lookin' for it neither. I'm tryin' to find my sister. Mebbe you know where she lives. Her name's Johnson, Mrs. William Johnson."

"You're not her Klondike brother!" Madge cried, her eyes bright with interest, "about whom we've heard so much?"

"Yes'm, that's me," he answered modestly. "My name's Miller, Skiff Miller. I just thought I'd s'prise her."

"You are on the right track then. Only you've come by the footpath." Madge stood up to direct him, pointing up the canyon a quarter of a mile. "You see that blasted redwood? Take the little trail turning off to the right. It's the short cut to her house. You can't miss it."

"Yes'm, thank you, ma'am," he said. He made tentative efforts to go, but seemed awkwardly rooted to the spot. He was gazing at her with an open admiration of which he was quite unconscious, and which was drowning, along with him, in the rising sea of embarrassment in which he floundered.

"We'd like to hear you tell about the Klondike," Madge said. "Mayn't we come over some day while you are at your sister's? Or, better yet, won't you come over and have dinner with us?"

"Yes'm, thank you, ma'am," he mumbled mechanically. Then he caught himself up and added: "I ain't stoppin' long. I got to be pullin' north again. I go out on tonight's train. You see, I've got a mail contract with the government."

When Madge had said that it was too bad, he made another futile effort to go. But he could not take his eyes from her face. He forgot his embarrassment in his admiration, and it was her turn to flush and feel uncomfortable.

It was at this juncture, when Walt had just decided it was time for him to be saying something to relieve the strain, that Wolf, who had been away nosing through the brush, trotted wolf-like into view.

Skiff Miller's abstraction disappeared. The pretty woman before him passed out of his field of vision. He had eyes only for the dog, and a great wonder came into his face.

"Well, I'll be damned!" he enunciated slowly and solemnly.

He sat down ponderingly on the log, leaving Madge standing. At the sound of his voice, Wolf's ears had flattened down, then his mouth had opened in a laugh. He trotted slowly up to the stranger and first smelled his hands, then licked them with his tongue.

Skiff Miller patted the dog's head, and slowly and solemnly repeated, "Well, I'll be damned!"

"Excuse me, ma'am," he said the next moment, "I was just s'prised some, that was all."

"We're surprised, too," she answered lightly. "We never saw Wolf make up to a stranger before."

"Is that what you call him—Wolf?" the man asked.

Madge nodded. "But I can't understand his friendliness toward you—unless it's because you're from the Klondike. He's a Klondike dog, you know."

"Yes'm," Miller said absently. He lifted one of Wolf's forelegs and examined the foot-pads, pressing them and denting them with his thumb. "Kind of soft," he remarked. "He ain't been on trail for a long time."

"I say," Walt broke in, "it is remarkable the way he lets you handle him."

Skiff Miller arose, no longer awkward with admiration of Madge, and in a sharp, businesslike manner asked, "How long have you had him?"

But just then the dog, squirming and rubbing against the newcomer's legs, opened his mouth and barked. It was an explosive bark, brief and joyous, but a bark.

"That's a new one on me," Skiff Miller remarked.

Walt and Madge stared at each other. The miracle had happened. Wolf had barked.

"It's the first time he ever barked," Madge said.

"First time I ever heard him, too," Miller volunteered. Madge smiled at him. The man was evidently a humorist.

"Of course," she said, "since you have only seen him for five minutes."

Skiff Miller looked at her sharply, seeking in her face the guile her words had led him to suspect.

"I thought you understood," he said slowly. "I thought you'd tumbled to it from his makin' up to me. He's my dog. His name ain't Wolf. It's Brown."

"Oh, Walt!" was Madge's instinctive cry to her husband.

Walt was on the defensive at once.

"How do you know he's your dog?" he demanded.

"Because he is," was the reply.

"Mere assertion," Walt said sharply.

In his slow and pondering way, Skiff Miller looked at him, then asked, with a nod of his head toward Madge:

"How d'you know she's your wife? You just say, 'Because she is,' and I'll say it's mere assertion. The dog's mine. I bred 'm an' raised 'm, an' I guess I ought to know. Look here. I'll prove it to you."

Skiff Miller turned to the dog. "Brown!" His voice rang out sharply, and at the sound the dog's ears flattened down as to a caress. "Gee!" The dog made a swinging turn to the right. "Now mush-on!" And the dog ceased his swing abruptly and started straight ahead, halting obediently at command.

"I can do it with whistles," Skiff Miller said proudly. "He was my lead dog."

"But you are not going to take him away with you?" Madge asked tremulously.

The man nodded.

"Back into that awful Klondike world of suffering?"

He nodded and added: "Oh, it ain't so bad as all that. Look at me. Pretty healthy specimen, ain't I?"

"But the dogs! The terrible hardship, the heart-breaking toil, the starvation, the frost! Oh, I've read about it and I know."

"I nearly ate him once, over on Little Fish River," Miller volunteered grimly. "If I hadn't got a moose that day was all that saved 'm."

"I'd have died first!" Madge cried.

"Things is different down here," Miller explained. "You don't have to eat dogs. You think different just about the time you're all in. You've never been all in, so you don't know anything about it."

"That's the very point," she argued warmly. "Dogs are not eaten in California. Why not leave him here? He is happy. He'll never want for food—you know that. He'll never suffer from cold and hardship. Here all is softness and gentleness. Neither the human nor nature is savage. He will never know a whip lash again. And as for the weather—why, it never snows here."

"But it's all-fired hot in summer, beggin' your pardon," Skiff Miller laughed.

"But you do not answer," Madge continued passionately. "What have you to offer him in that northland life?"

"Grub, when I've got it, and that's most of the time," came the answer.

"And the rest of the time?"

"No grub."

"And the work?"

"Yes, plenty of work," Miller blurted out impatiently. "Work without end, an' famine, an' frost, an' all the rest of the miseries—that's what he'll get when he comes with me. But he likes it. He is used to it. He knows that life. He was born to it an' brought up to it. An' you don't know anything about it. You don't know what you're talking about. That's where the dog belongs, and that's where he'll be happiest."

"The dog doesn't go," Walt announced in a determined voice. "So there is no need of further discussion."

"What's that?" Skiff Miller demanded, his brows lowering and an obstinate flush of blood reddening his forehead.

"I said the dog doesn't go, and that settles it. I don't believe he's your dog. You may have seen him sometime. You may even sometime have driven him for his owner. But his obeying the ordinary driving commands of the Alaskan trail is no demonstration that he is yours. Any dog in Alaska would obey you as he obeyed. Besides, he is undoubtedly a valuable dog, as dogs go in Alaska, and that is sufficient explanation of your desire to get possession of him. Anyway, you've got to prove property."

Skiff Miller, cool and collected, the obstinate flush a trifle deeper on his forehead, his huge muscles bulging under the black cloth of his coat, carefully looked the poet up and down as though measuring the strength of his slenderness.

The Klondiker's face took on a contemptuous expression as he said finally, "I reckon there's nothin' in sight to prevent me takin' the dog right here an' now."

Walt's face reddened, and the striking-muscles of his arms and shoulders seemed to stiffen and grow tense. His wife fluttered apprehensively into the breach.

"Maybe Mr. Miller is right," she said. "I am afraid that he is. Wolf does seem to know him, and certainly he answers to the name of 'Brown.'

He made friends with him instantly, and you know that's something he never did with anybody before. Besides, look at the way he barked. He was just bursting with joy. Joy over what? Without doubt at finding Mr. Miller."

Walt's striking-muscles relaxed, and his shoulders seemed to droop with hopelessness.

"I guess you're right, Madge," he said. "Wolf isn't Wolf, but Brown, and he must belong to Mr. Miller."

"Perhaps Mr. Miller will sell him," she suggested. "We can buy him."

Skiff Miller shook his head, no longer belligerent, but kindly, quick to be generous in response to generousness.

"I had five dogs," he said, casting about for the easiest way to temper his refusal. "He was the leader. They was the crack team of Alaska. Nothin' could touch 'em. In 1898 I refused five thousand dollars for the bunch. Dogs was high, then, anyway; but that wasn't what made the fancy price. It was the team itself. Brown was the best in the team. That winter I refused twelve hundred for 'm. I didn't sell 'm then, an' I ain't a-sellin' 'm now. Besides, I think a mighty lot of that dog. I've been lookin' for 'm for three years. It made me fair sick when I found he'd been stole—not the value of him, but the—well, I liked 'm like hell, that's all, beggin' your pardon. I couldn't believe my eyes when I seen 'm just now. I thought I was dreamin'. It was too good to be true. Why, I was his wet-nurse. I put 'm to bed, snug every night. His mother died, and I brought 'm up on condensed milk at two dollars a can when I couldn't afford it in my own coffee. He never knew any mother but me. He used to suck my finger regular, the darn little cuss—that finger right there!"

And Skiff Miller, too overwrought for speech, held up a forefinger for them to see.

"That very finger," he managed to articulate, as though it somehow clinched the proof of ownership and the bond of affection.

He was still gazing at his extended finger when Madge began to speak.

"But the dog," she said. "You haven't considered the dog."

Skiff Miller looked puzzled.

"Have you thought about him?" she asked.

"Don't know what you're drivin' at," was the response.

"Maybe the dog has some choice in the matter," Madge went on. "Maybe he has his likes and desires. You have not considered him. You give him no choice. It has never entered your mind that possibly he might prefer California to Alaska. You consider only what you like. You do with him as you would with a sack of potatoes or a bale of hay."

This was a new way of looking at it, and Miller was visibly impressed as he debated it in his mind. Madge took advantage of his indecision.

"If you really love him, what would be happiness to him would be your happiness also," she urged.

Skiff Miller continued to debate with himself, and Madge stole a glance of exultation to her husband, who looked back with warm approval.

"What do you think?" the Klondiker suddenly demanded.

It was her turn to be puzzled. "What do you mean?" she asked.

"D'ye think he'd sooner stay in California?"

She nodded her head with positiveness. "I am sure of it."

Skiff Miller again debated with himself, though this time aloud, at the same time running his gaze in a judicial way over the mooted animal.

"He was a good worker. He's done a heap of work for me. He never loafed on me, an' he was a joe-dandy at hammerin' a raw team into shape. He's got a head on him. He can do everything but talk. He knows what you say to him. Look at 'm now. He knows we're talkin' about him."

The dog was lying at Skiff Miller's feet, head close down on paws, ears erect and listening, and eyes that were quick and eager to follow the sound of speech as it fell from the lips of first one and then the other.

"An' there's a lot of work in 'm yet. He's good for years to come. An' I do like him. I like him like hell."

Once or twice after that Skiff Miller opened his mouth and closed it again without speaking. Finally he said:

"I'll tell you what I'll do. Your remarks, ma'am, has some weight in them. The dog's worked hard, and maybe he's earned a soft berth an' has got a right to choose. Anyway, we'll leave it up to him. Whatever he says, goes. You people stay right here settin' down. I'll say good-by and walk off casual-like. If he wants to stay, he can stay. If he wants to come with me, let 'm come. I won't call 'm to come an' don't you call 'm to come back."

He looked with sudden suspicion at Madge, and added, "Only you must play fair. No persuadin' after my back is turned."

"We'll play fair," Madge began, but Skiff Miller broke in on her assurances.

"I know the ways of women," he announced. "Their hearts is soft. When their hearts is touched they're likely to stack the cards, look at the bottom of the deck, an' lie like the devil—beggin' your pardon, ma'am. I'm only discoursin' about women in general."

"I don't know how to thank you," Madge quavered.

"I don't see as you've got any call to thank me," he replied. "Brown ain't decided yet. Now you won't mind if I go away slow? It's no more'n fair, seein' I'll be out of sight inside a hundred yards."

Madge agreed, and added, "And I promise you faithfully that we won't do anything to influence him."

"Well, then, I might as well be gettin' along," Skiff Miller said in the ordinary tones of one departing.

At this change in his voice, Wolf lifted his head quickly, and still more quickly got to his feet when the man and woman shook hands. He sprang up on his hind legs, resting his fore paws on her hip and at the same time licking Skiff Miller's hand. When the latter shook hands with Walt, Wolf repeated his act, resting his weight on Walt and licking both men's hands.

"It ain't no picnic, I can tell you that," were the Klondiker's last words, as he turned and went slowly up the trail.

For the distance of twenty feet Wolf watched him go, himself all eagerness and expectancy, as though waiting for the man to turn and retrace his steps. Then, with a quick low whine, Wolf sprang after him, overtook him, caught his hand between his teeth with reluctant tenderness, and strove gently to make him pause.

Failing in this, Wolf raced back to where Walt Irvine sat, catching his coat-sleeve in his teeth and trying vainly to drag him after the retreating man.

Wolf's perturbation began to wax. He desired ubiquity. He wanted to be in two places at the same time, with the old master and the new, and steadily the distance between them was increasing. He sprang about excitedly, making short nervous leaps and twists, now toward one, now toward the other, in painful indecision, not knowing his own mind, desiring both and unable to choose, uttering quick sharp whines and beginning to pant.

He sat down abruptly on his haunches, thrusting his nose upward, the mouth opening and closing with jerking movements, each time opening wider. These jerking movements were in unison with the recurrent spasms that attacked the throat, each spasm severer and more intense than the preceding one. And in accord with jerks and spasms the larynx began to vibrate, at first silently, accompanied by the rush of air expelled from the lungs, then sounding a low, deep note, the lowest in the register of the human ear. All this was the nervous and muscular preliminary to howling.

But just as the howl was on the verge of bursting from the full throat, the wide-opened mouth was closed, the paroxysms ceased, and he looked long and steadily at the retreating man. Suddenly Wolf turned his head, and over his shoulder just as steadily regarded Walt. The appeal was unanswered. Not a word nor a sign did the dog receive, no suggestion and no clue as to what his conduct should be.

A glance ahead to where the old master was nearing the curve of the trail excited him again. He sprang to his feet with a whine, and then, struck by a new idea, turned his attention to Madge. Hitherto he had ignored her, but now, both masters failing him, she alone was left. He went over to her and snuggled his head in her lap, nudging her arm with his nose—an old trick of his when begging for favors. He backed away from her and began writhing and twisting playfully, curveting and prancing, half rearing and striking his fore paws to the earth, struggling with all his body, from the wheedling eyes and flattening ears to the wagging tail, to express the thought that was in him and that was denied him utterance.

This, too, he soon abandoned. He was depressed by the coldness of these humans who had never been cold before. No response could he draw from them, no help could he get. They did not consider him. They were as dead.

He turned and silently gazed after the old master. Skiff Miller was rounding the curve. In a moment he would be gone from view. Yet he never turned his head, plodding straight onward, slowly and methodically, as though possessed of no interest in what was occurring behind his back.

And in this fashion he went out of view. Wolf waited for him to reappear. He waited a long minute, silently, quietly, without movement, as though turned to stone—withal stone quick with eagerness and desire. He barked once, and waited. Then he turned and trotted back to Walt Irvine. He sniffed his hand and dropped down heavily at his feet, watching the trail where it curved emptily from view.

The tiny stream slipping down the mossy-lipped stone seemed suddenly to increase the volume of its gurgling noise. Save for the meadow-larks, there was no other sound. The great yellow butterflies drifted silently through the sunshine and lost themselves in the drowsy shadows. Madge gazed triumphantly at her husband.

A few minutes later Wolf got upon his feet. Decision and deliberation marked his movements. He did not glance at the man and woman. His eyes were fixed up the trail. He had made up his mind.

They knew it. And they knew, so far as they were concerned, that the ordeal had just begun.

He broke into a trot, and Madge's lips pursed, forming an avenue for the caressing sound that it was the will of her to send forth. But the caressing sound was not made. She was impelled to look at her husband, and she saw the sternness with which he watched her. The pursed lips relaxed, and she sighed inaudibly.

Wolf's trot broke into a run. Wider and wider were the leaps he made. Not once did he turn his head, his wolf's brush standing out straight behind him. He cut sharply across the curve of the trail and was gone.

19

Tito: The Story of the Coyote That Learned How

by Ernest Thompson Seton

"Tito: The Story of the Coyote That Learned How" is another offering from wildlife fiction mainstay Ernest Thompson Seton. While still a pup, Tito is captured by a rancher, and quickly learns the ways of men. When her wild nature stirs, she returns to the life she was born for— taking a mate and bearing her own litter of pups. But trouble lurks nearby as an old adversary stalks Tito's new family, and she must use all the wiles she acquired in captivity to best her enemy. This is a truly tender evocation of a wild parent and her offspring, quite unusual for the time it was written. Without anthropomorphizing Tito, the author makes her spring to life, as finely drawn and compelling as any human protagonist.

RAINDROP MAY DEFLECT A THUNDERBOLT, OR A HAIR MAY RUIN AN EM-pire, as surely as a spider-web once turned the history of Scotland; and if it had not been for one little pebble, this history of Tito might never have happened.

That pebble was lying on a trail in the Dakota Badlands, and one hot, dark night it lodged in the foot of a Horse that was ridden by a tipsy cowboy. The man got off, as a matter of habit, to know what was laming his Horse. But he left the reins on its neck instead of on the ground, and the Horse, taking advantage of this technicality, ran off in the darkness.

Then the cowboy, realizing that he was afoot, lay down in a hollow under some buffalo-bushes and slept the loggish sleep of the befuddled.

The golden beams of the early summer sun were leaping from top to top of the wonderful Badland Buttes, when an old Coyote might have been seen trotting homeward along the Garner's Creek Trail with a Rabbit in her jaws to supply her family's breakfast.

Fierce war had for a long time been waged against the Coyote kind by the cattlemen of Billings County. Traps, guns, poison, and Hounds had reduced their number nearly to zero, and the few survivors had learned the bitter need of caution at every step. But the destructive ingenuity of man knew no bounds, and their numbers continued to dwindle.

The old Coyote quit the trail very soon, for nothing that man has made is friendly. She skirted along a low ridge, then across a little hollow where grew a few buffalo-bushes, and, after a careful sniff at a very stale human trail-scent, she crossed another near ridge on whose sunny side was the home of her brood. Again she cautiously circled, peered about, and sniffed, but, finding no sign of danger, went down to the doorway and uttered a low *woof-woof.* Out of the den, beside a sage-bush, there poured a procession of little Coyotes, merrily tumbling over one another. Then, barking little barks and growling little puppy growls, they fell upon the feast that their mother had brought, and gobbled and tussled while she looked on and enjoyed their joy.

Wolver Jake, the cowboy, had awakened from his chilly sleep about sunrise, in time to catch a glimpse of the Coyote passing over the ridge. As soon as she was out of sight he got on his feet and went to the edge, there to witness the interesting scene of the family breakfasting and frisking about within a few yards of him, utterly unconscious of any danger.

But the only appeal the scene had to him lay in the fact that the county had set a price on every one of these Coyotes' lives. So he got out his big .45 navy revolver, and notwithstanding his shaky condition, he managed somehow to get a sight on the mother as she was caressing one of the little ones that had finished its breakfast, and shot her dead on the spot.

The terrified cubs fled into the den, and Jake, failing to kill another with his revolver, came forward, blocked up the hole with stones, and leaving the seven little prisoners quaking at the far end, set off on foot for the nearest ranch, cursing his faithless Horse as he went.

In the afternoon he returned with his pard and tools for digging. The little ones had cowered all day in the darkened hole, wondering why their mother did not come to feed them, wondering at the darkness and the change. But late that day they heard sounds at the door. Then light was again let in. Some of the less cautious young ones ran forward to meet their mother, but their mother was not there—only two great rough brutes that began tearing open their home.

After an hour or more the diggers came to the end of the den, and here were the woolly, bright-eyed, little ones, all huddled in a pile at the farthest corner. Their innocent puppy faces and ways were not noticed by the huge enemy. One by one they were seized. A sharp blow, and each quivering, limp form was thrown into a sack to be carried to the nearest magistrate who was empowered to pay the bounties.

Even at this stage there was a certain individuality of character among the puppies. Some of them squealed and some of them growled when dragged out to die. One or two tried to bite. The one that had been slowest to comprehend the danger, had been the last to retreat, and so was on top of the pile, and therefore the first killed. The one that had first realized the peril had retreated first, and now crouched at the bottom of the pile. Coolly and remorselessly the others were killed one by one, and then this prudent little puppy was seen to be the last of the family. It lay perfectly still, even when touched, its eyes being half closed, as, guided by instinct, it tried to "play possum." One of the men picked it up. It neither squealed nor resisted. Then Jake, realizing ever the importance of "standing in with the boss," said: "Say, let's keep that 'un for the children." So the last of the family was thrown alive into the same bag with its dead brothers, and, bruised and frightened, lay there very still, understanding nothing, knowing only that after a long time of great noise and cruel jolting it was again half strangled by a grip on its neck and dragged out, where were a lot of creatures like the diggers.

These were really the inhabitants of the Chimneypot Ranch, whose brand is the Broad-arrow; and among them were the children for whom the cub had been brought. The boss had no difficulty in getting Jake to accept the dollar that the cub Coyote would have brought in bounty-money, and his present was turned over to the children. In answer to their question, "What is it?" a Mexican cow-hand present said it was a Coyotito—that is, a "little Coyote"—and this, afterward shortened to "Tito," became the captive's name.

Tito was a pretty little creature, with woolly body, a puppy-like expression, and a head that was singularly broad between the ears.

But, as a children's pet, she—for it proved to be a female—was not a success. She was distant and distrustful. She ate her food and seemed healthy, but never responded to friendly advances; never even learned to come out of the box when called. This probably was due to the fact that the kindness of the small children was offset by the roughness of the men and boys, who did not hesitate to drag her out by the chain when they wished to see her. On these occasions she would suffer in silence, playing possum, shamming dead, for she seemed to know that that was the best thing to do. But as soon as released she would once more retire into the darkest corner of her box and watch her tormentors with eyes that, at the proper angle, showed a telling glint of green. Among the children of the ranchmen was a thirteen-year-old boy.

The fact that he grew up to be like his father, a kind, strong, and thoughtful man, did not prevent him being, at this age, a shameless little brute.

Like all boys in that country, he practiced lasso-throwing, with a view to being a cowboy. Posts and stumps are uninteresting things to catch. His little brothers and sisters were under special protection of the Home Government. The Dogs ran far away whenever they saw him coming with the rope in his hands. So he must needs practice on the unfortunate Coyotito. She soon learned that her only hope for peace was to hide in the kennel, or, if thrown at when outside, to dodge the rope by lying as flat as possible on the ground. Thus Lincoln unwittingly taught the Coyote the dangers and limitations of a rope, and so he proved a blessing in disguise—a very perfect disguise. When the Coyote had thoroughly learned how to baffle the lasso, the boy terror devised a new amusement. He got a large trap of the kind known as "Fox-size." This he set in the dust as he had seen Jake set a Wolf-trap, close to the kennel, and over it he scattered scraps of meat, in the most approved style for Wolf-trapping. After a while Tito, drawn by the smell of the meat, came hungrily sneaking out toward it, and almost immediately was caught in the trap by one foot. The boy terror was watching from a near hiding-place. He gave a wild Indian whoop of delight, then rushed forward to drag the Coyote out of the box into which she had retreated. After some more delightful thrills of excitement and struggle he got his lasso on Tito's body, and, helped by a younger brother, a most promising pupil, he succeeded in setting the Coyote free from the trap before the grownups had discovered his amusement. One or two experiences like this taught her a mortal terror of traps. She soon learned the smell of the steel, and could detect and avoid it, no matter how cleverly Master Lincoln might bury it in the dust while the younger brother screened the operation from the intended victim by holding his coat over the door of Tito's kennel.

One day the fastening of her chain gave way, and Tito went off in an uncertain fashion, trailing her chain behind her. But she was seen by one of the men, who fired a charge of bird-shot at her. The burning, stinging, and surprise of it all caused her to retreat to the one place she knew, her own kennel. The chain was fastened again, and Tito added to her ideas this, a horror of guns and the smell of gunpowder; and this also, that the one safety from them is to "lay low."

There were yet other rude experiences in store for the captive.

Poisoning Wolves was a topic of daily talk at the Ranch, so it was not surprising that Lincoln should privately experiment on Coyotito. The deadly strychnine was too well guarded to be available. So Lincoln hid some Rough on Rats in a piece of meat, threw it to the captive, and sat by to watch, as blithe and conscience-clear as any professor of chemistry trying a new combination.

Tito smelled the meat—everything had to be passed on by her nose. Her nose was in doubt. There was a good smell of meat, a familiar but unpleasant smell of human hands, and a strange new odor, but not the odor of the trap; so she bolted the morsel. Within a few minutes she began to have fearful pains in her stomach, followed by cramps. Now in all the Wolf tribe there is the instinctive habit to throw up anything that disagrees with them, and after a minute or two of suffering the Coyote sought relief in this way; and to make it doubly sure she hastily gobbled some blades of grass, and in less than an hour was quite well again.

Lincoln had put in poison enough for a dozen Coyotes. Had he put in less she could not have felt the pang till too late, but she recovered and never forgot that peculiar smell that means such awful after-pains. More than that, she was ready thenceforth to fly at once to the herbal cure that Nature had everywhere provided. An instinct of this kind grows quickly, once followed. It had taken minutes of suffering in the first place to drive her to the easement. Thenceforth, having learned, it was her first thought on feeling pain. The little miscreant did indeed succeed in having her swallow another bait with a small dose of poison, but she knew what to do now and had almost no suffering.

Later on, a relative sent Lincoln a Bull-terrier, and the new combination was a fresh source of spectacular interest for the boy, and of tribulation for the Coyote. It all emphasized for her that old idea to "lay low"—that is, to be quiet, unobtrusive, and hide when danger is in sight. The grown-ups of the household at length forbade these persecutions, and the Terrier was kept away from the little yard where the Coyote was chained up.

It must not be supposed that, in all this, Tito was a sweet, innocent victim. She had learned to bite. She had caught and killed several chickens by shamming sleep while they ventured to forage within the radius of her chain. And she had an inborn hankering to sing a morning and evening hymn, which procured for her many beatings. But she learned to shut up the moment her opening notes were followed by a rattle of doors or windows, for these sounds of human nearness had frequently been followed by a *bang* and a charge of bird-shot, which somehow did no serious harm, though it severely stung her hide. And these experiences all helped to deepen her terror of guns and of those who used them. The object of these musical outpourings was not clear. They happened usually at dawn or dusk, but sometimes a loud noise at high noon would set her going. The song consisted of a volley of short barks, mixed with doleful squalls that never failed to set the Dogs astir in a responsive uproar, and once or twice had begotten a far-away answer from some wild Coyote in the hills.

There was one little trick that she had developed which was purely instinctive—that is, an inherited habit. In the back end of her kennel she had a little cache of bones, and knew exactly where one or two lumps of unsavory meat were buried within the radius of her chain, for a time of famine which never came. If anyone approached these hidden treasures she watched with anxious eyes, but made no other demonstration. If she saw that the meddler knew the exact place, she took an early opportunity to secrete them elsewhere.

After a year of this life Tito had grown to full size, and had learned many things that her wild kinsmen could not have learned without losing their lives in doing it. She knew and feared traps. She had learned to avoid poison baits, and knew what to do at once if, by some mistake, she should take one. She knew what guns were. She had learned to cut her morning and evening song very short. She had some acquaintance with Dogs, enough to make her hate and distrust them all. But, above all, she had this idea: whenever danger is near, the very best move possible is to lay low, be very quiet, do nothing to attract notice. Perhaps the little brain that looked out of those changing yellow eyes was the storehouse of much other knowledge about men, but what it was did not appear.

The Coyote was fully grown when the boss of the outfit bought a couple of thoroughbred Greyhounds, wonderful runners, to see whether he could not entirely extirpate the remnant of the Coyotes that still destroyed occasional Sheep and Calves on the range, and at the same time find amusement in the sport. He was tired of seeing that Coyote in the yard; so, deciding to use her for training the Dogs, he had her roughly thrown into a bag, then carried a quarter of a mile away and dumped out. At the same time the Greyhounds were slipped and chivvied on. Away they went bounding at their matchless pace, that nothing else on four legs could equal, and away went the Coyote, frightened by the noise of the men, frightened even to find herself free. Her quarter-mile start quickly shrank to one hundred yards, the one hundred to fifty, and on sped the flying Dogs. Clearly there was no chance for her. On and nearer they came. In another minute she would have been stretched out—not a doubt of it. But on a sudden she stopped, turned, and walked toward the Dogs with her tail serenely waving in the air and a friendly cock to her ears. Greyhounds are peculiar Dogs. Anything that runs away, they are going to catch and kill if they can. Anything that is calmly facing them becomes at once a non-combatant. They bounded over and past the Coyote before they could curb their own impetuosity, and returned completely nonplussed. Possibly they recognized the Coyote of the house-yard as she stood there wagging her tail. The ranchmen were nonplussed too. Everyone was utterly taken aback, had a sense of failure, and the real victor in the situation was felt to be the audacious little Coyote.

The Greyhounds refused to attack an animal that wagged its tail and would not run; and the men, on seeing that the Coyote could walk far enough away to avoid being caught by hand, took their ropes (lassoes), and soon made her a prisoner once more. The next day they decided to try again, but this time they added the white Bull-terrier to the chasers. The Coyote did as before. The Greyhounds declined to be party to any attack on such a mild and friendly acquaintance. But the Bull-terrier, who came puffing and panting on the scene three minutes later, had no such scruples. He was not so tall, but he was heavier than the Coyote, and, seizing her by her wool-protected neck, he shook her till, in a surprisingly short time, she lay limp and lifeless, at which all the men seemed pleased, and congratulated the Terrier, while the Greyhounds pottered around in restless perplexity.

A stranger in the party, a newly arrived Englishman, asked if he might have the brush—the tail, he explained—and on being told to help him-self, he picked up the victim by the tail, and with one awkward chop of his knife he cut it off at the middle, and the Coyote dropped, but gave a shrill yelp of pain. She was not dead, only playing possum, and now she leaped up and vanished into a near-by thicket of cactus and sage.

With Greyhounds a running animal is the signal for a run, so the two long-legged Dogs and the white broad-chested Dog dashed after the Coyote. But right across their path, by happy chance, there flashed a brown streak ridden by a snowy powder-puff, the visible but evanescent sign for Cottontail Rabbit. The Coyote was not in sight now. The Rabbit was, so the Greyhounds dashed after the Cottontail, who took advantage of a Prairie-dog's hole to seek safety in the bosom of Mother Earth, and the Coyote made good her escape.

She had been a good deal jarred by the rude treatment of the Terrier, and her mutilated tail gave her some pain. But otherwise she was all right, and she loped lightly away, keeping out of sight in the hollows, and so escaped among the fantastic buttes of the Badlands, to be eventually the founder of a new life among the Coyotes of the Little Missouri.

Moses was preserved by the Egyptians till he had outlived the dangerous period, and learned from them wisdom enough to be the savior of his people against those same Egyptians. So the bobtailed Coyote was not only saved by man and carried over the dangerous period of puppyhood; she was also unwittingly taught by him how to baffle the traps, poisons, lassoes, guns, and Dogs that had so long waged a war of extermination against her race.

Thus Tito escaped from man, and for the first time found herself face to face with the whole problem of life; for now she had her own living to get.

A wild animal has three sources of wisdom:

First, *the experience of its ancestors*, in the form of instinct, which is inborn learning, hammered into the race by ages of selection and tribulation. This is the most important to begin with, because it guards him from the moment he is born.

Second, *the experience of his parents and comrades*, learned chiefly by example. This becomes most important as soon as the young can run.

Third, *the personal experience* of the animal itself. This grows in importance as the animal ages.

The weakness of the first is its fixity; it cannot change to meet quickly changing conditions. The weakness of the second is the animal's inability freely to exchange ideas by language. The weakness of the third is the danger in acquiring it. But the three together are a strong arch.

Now, Tito was in a new case. Perhaps never before had a Coyote faced life with unusual advantages in the third kind of knowledge, none at all in the second, and with the first dormant. She traveled rapidly away from the ranchmen, keeping out of sight, and sitting down once in a while to lick her wounded tail-stump. She came at last to a Prairie-dog town. Many of the inhabitants were out, and they barked at the intruder, but all dodged down as soon as she came near. Her instinct taught her to try and catch one, but she ran about in vain for some time, and then gave it up. She would have gone hungry that night but that she found a couple of Mice in the long grass by the river. Her mother had not taught her to hunt, but her instinct did, and the accident that she had an unusual brain made her profit very quickly by her experience.

In the days that followed she quickly learned how to make a living; for Mice, Ground Squirrels, Prairie-dogs, Rabbits, and Lizards were abundant, and many of these could be captured in open chase. But open chase, and sneaking as near as possible before beginning the open chase, lead naturally to stalking for a final spring. And before the moon had changed the Coyote had learned how to make a comfortable living.

Once or twice she saw the men with the Greyhounds coming her way. Most Coyotes would, perhaps, have barked in bravado, or would have gone up to some high place whence they could watch the enemy; but Tito did no such foolish thing. Had she run, her moving form would have caught the eyes of the Dogs, and then nothing could have saved her. She dropped where she was, and lay flat until the danger had passed. Thus her ranch training to lay low began to stand her in good stead, and so it came about that her weakness was her strength. The Coyote kind had so long been famous for their speed, had so long learned to trust in their legs, that they never dreamed of a creature that could run them down. They were accustomed to play with their pursuers, and so rarely bestirred themselves to run from Greyhounds, till it was too late. But Tito, brought up at the end of a chain, was a poor runner. She had no reason to trust her legs. She rather trusted her wits, and so lived.

During that summer she stayed about the Little Missouri, learning the tricks of small-game hunting that she should have learned before she shed her milk-teeth, and gaining in strength and speed. She kept far away from all the ranches, and always hid on seeing a man or a strange beast, and so passed the summer alone. During the daytime she was not lonely, but when the sun went down she would feel the impulse to sing that wild song of the West which means so much to the Coyotes. It is not the invention of an individual nor of the present, but was slowly built out of the feelings of all Coyotes in all ages. It expresses their nature and the Plains that made their nature. When one begins it, it takes hold of the rest, as the fife and drum do with soldiers, or the ki-yi war-song with Indian braves. They respond to it as a bell-glass does to a certain note the moment that note is struck, ignoring other sounds. So the Coyote, no matter how brought up, must vibrate at the night song of the Plains, for it touches something in himself.

They sing it after sundown, when it becomes the rallying cry of their race and the friendly call to a neighbor; and they sing it as one boy in the woods holloas to another to say, "All's well! Here am I. Where are you?" A form of it they sing to the rising moon, for this is the time for good hunting to begin. They sing when they see the new camp-fire, for the same reason that a Dog barks at a stranger. Yet another weird chant they have for the dawning before they steal quietly away from the offing of the camp—a wild, weird, squalling refrain: *Wow-wow-wow-wow-wow-w-o-o-o-o-o-o-w*, again and again; and doubtless with many another change that man cannot distinguish any more than the Coyote can distinguish the words in the cowboy's anathemas.

Tito instinctively uttered her music at the proper times. But sad experiences had taught her to cut it short and keep it low. Once or twice she had got a far-away reply from one of her own race, whereupon she had quickly ceased and timidly quit the neighborhood.

One day, when on the Upper Garner's Creek, she found the trail where a piece of meat had been dragged along. It was a singularly inviting odor, and she followed it, partly out of curiosity. Presently she came on a piece of the meat itself. She was hungry; she was always hungry now. It was tempting, and although it had a peculiar odor, she swallowed it. Within a few minutes she felt a terrific pain. The memory of the poisoned meat the boy had given her was fresh. With trembling, foaming jaws she seized some blades of grass, and her stomach threw off the meat; but she fell in convulsions on the ground.

The trail of meat dragged along and the poison baits had been laid the day before by Wolfer Jake. This morning he was riding the drag, and on coming up from the draw he saw, far ahead, the Coyote struggling. He knew, of course, that it was poisoned, and rode quickly up; but the convulsions passed as he neared. By a mighty effort, at the sound of the Horse's hoofs the Coyote arose to her front feet. Jake drew his revolver and fired, but the only effect was fully to alarm her. She tried to run, but her hind legs were paralyzed. She put forth all her strength, dragging her hind legs. Now, when the poison was no longer in the stomach, will-power could do a great deal. Had she been allowed to lie down then she would have been dead in five minutes; but the revolver shots and the man coming stirred her to strenuous action. Madly she struggled again and again to get her hind legs to work. All the force of desperate intent she brought to bear. It was like putting forth tenfold power to force the nervous fluids through their blocked-up channels as she dragged herself with marvelous speed downhill. What is nerve but will? The dead wires of her legs were hot with this fresh power, multiplied, injected, blasted into them. They had to give in. She felt them thrill with life again. Each wild shot from the gun lent vital help. Another fierce attempt, and one hind leg obeyed the call to duty. A few more bounds, and the other, too, fell in. Then lightly she loped away among the broken buttes, defying the agonizing gripe that still kept on inside.

Had Jake held off then she would yet have laid down and died; but he followed and fired and fired, till in another mile she bounded free from pain, saved from her enemy by himself. He had compelled her to take the only cure, so she escaped.

And these were the ideas that she harvested that day: That curious smell on the meat stands for mortal agony. Let it alone! And she never forgot it; thenceforth she knew strychnine.

Fortunately, Dogs, traps, and strychnine do not wage war at once, for the Dogs are as apt to be caught or poisoned as the Coyotes. Had there been a single Dog in the hunt that day, Tito's history would have ended.

When the weather grew cooler toward the end of Autumn, Tito had gone far toward repairing the defects in her early training. She was more like an ordinary Coyote in her habits now, and she was more disposed to sing the sundown song. One night, when she got a response, she yielded to the impulse again to call, and soon afterward a large, dark Coyote appeared. The fact that he was there at all was a guarantee of unusual gifts, for the war against his race was waged relentlessly by the cattlemen. He approached with caution. Tito's mane bristled with mixed feelings at the sight of one of her own kind. She crouched flat on the ground and waited. The newcomer came stiffly forward, nosing the wind; then up the wind nearly to her. Then he walked around so that she should wind him and, raising his tail, gently waved it. The first acts meant armed neutrality, but the last was a distinctly friendly signal. Then he approached and she rose up suddenly and stood as high as she could to be smelled. Then she wagged the stump of her tail, and they considered themselves acquainted.

The newcomer was a very large Coyote, half as tall again as Tito, and the dark patch on his shoulders was so large and black that the cowboys, when they came to know him, called him Saddleback. From that time these two continued more or less together. They were not always close together, often were miles apart during the day, but toward night one or the other would get on some high open place and sing the loud

Yap-yap-yap-yow-wow-wow-wow-wow,

and they would forgather for some foray on hand.

The physical advantages were with Saddleback, but the greater cunning was Tito's, so that she in time became the leader. Before a month a third Coyote had appeared on the scene and become also a member of this loose-bound fraternity, and later two more appeared. Nothing succeeds like success. The little bobtailed Coyote had had rare advantages of training just where the others were lacking: she knew the devices of man. She could not tell about these in words, but she could by the aid of a few signs and a great deal of example. It soon became evident that her methods of hunting were successful, whereas, when they went without her, they often had hard luck. A man at Boxelder Ranch had twenty Sheep. The rules of the county did not allow anyone to own more, as this was a Cattle-range. The Sheep were guarded by a large and fierce Collie. One day in winter two of the Coyotes tried to raid this flock by a bold dash, and all they got was a mauling from the Collie. A few days later the band returned at dusk. Just how Tito arranged it, man cannot tell. We can only guess how she taught them their parts, but we know that she surely did. The Coyotes hid in the willows. Then Saddleback, the bold and swift, walked openly toward the Sheep and barked a loud defiance. The Collie jumped up with bristling mane and furious growl, then, seeing the foe, dashed straight at him. Now was the time for the steady nerve and the unfailing limbs. Saddleback let the Dog come near enough almost to catch him, and so beguiled him far and away into the woods, while the other Coyotes, led by Tito, stampeded the Sheep in twenty directions; then following the farthest, they killed several and left them in the snow. In the gloom of descending night the Dog and his master labored till they had gathered the bleating survivors; but next morning they found that four had been driven far away and killed, and the Coyotes had had a banquet royal.

The shepherd poisoned the carcasses and left them. Next night the Coyotes returned. Tito sniffed the now frozen meat, detected the poison, gave a warning growl, and scattered filth over the meat, so that none of the band should touch it. One, however, who was fast and foolish, persisted in feeding in spite of Tito's warning, and when they came away he was lying poisoned and dead in the snow.

Jake now heard on all sides that the Coyotes were getting worse. So he set to work with many traps and much poison to destroy those on the Garner's Creek, and every little while he would go with the Hounds and scour the Little Missouri south and east of the Chimney-pot Ranch; for it was understood that he must never run the Dogs in country where traps and poison were laid. He worked in his erratic way all winter, and certainly did have some success. He killed a couple of Grey Wolves, said to be the last of their race, and several Coyotes, some of which, no doubt, were of the Bobtailed pack, which thereby lost those members which were lacking in wisdom.

Yet that winter was marked by a series of Coyote raids and exploits; and usually the track in the snow or the testimony of eye-witnesses told that the master spirit of it all was a little Bobtailed Coyote.

One of these adventures was the cause of much talk. The Coyote challenge sounded close to the Chimney-pot Ranch after sundown. A dozen Dogs responded with the usual clamor. But only the Bull-terrier dashed away toward the place whence the Coyotes had called, for the reason that he only was loose. His chase was fruitless, and he came back growling. Twenty minutes later there was another Coyote yell close at hand. Off dashed the Terrier as before. In a minute his excited yapping told that he had sighted his game and was in full chase. Away he went, furiously barking, until his voice was lost afar, and nevermore was heard. In the morning the men read in the snow the tale of the night. The first cry of the Coyotes was to find out if all the Dogs were loose; then, having found that only one was free, they laid a plan. Five Coyotes hid along the side of the trail; one went forward and called till it had decoyed the rash Terrier, and then led him right into the ambush. What chance had he with six? They tore him limb from limb, and devoured him, too, at the very spot where once he had worried Coyotito. And next morning, when the men came, they saw by the signs that the whole thing had been planned, and that the leader whose cunning had made it a success was a little Bob-tailed Coyote.

The men were angry, and Lincoln was furious; but Jake remarked: "Well, I guess that Bobtail came back and got even with that Terrier."

When spring was near, the annual love-season of the Coyotes came on. Saddleback and Tito had been together merely as companions all winter, but now a new feeling was born. There was not much courting. Saddleback simply showed his teeth to possible rivals. There was no ceremony. They had been friends for months, and now, in the light of the new feeling, they naturally took to each other and were mated. Coyotes do not give each other names as do mankind, but have one sound like a growl and short howl, which stands for "mate" or "husband" or "wife." This they use in calling to each other, and it is by recognizing the tone of the voice that they know who is calling.

The loose rambling brotherhood of the Coyotes was broken up now, for the others also paired off, and since the returning warm weather was bringing out the Prairie-dogs and small game, there was less need to combine for hunting. Ordinarily Coyotes do not sleep in dens or in any fixed place. They move about all night while it is cool, then during the daytime they get a few hours' sleep in the sun, on some quiet hillside that also gives a chance to watch out. But the mating season changes this habit somewhat.

As the weather grew warm Tito and Saddleback set about preparing a den for the expected family. In a warm little hollow, an old Badger abode was cleaned out, enlarged, and deepened. A quantity of leaves and grass was carried into it and arranged in a comfortable nest. The place selected for it was a dry sunny nook among the hills, half a mile west of the Little Missouri. Thirty yards from it was a ridge which commanded a wide view of the grassy slopes and cottonwood groves by the river. Men would have called the spot very beautiful, but it is tolerably certain that that side of it never touched the Coyotes at all.

Tito began to be much preoccupied with her impending duties. She stayed quietly in the neighborhood of the den, and lived on such food as Saddleback brought her, or she herself could easily catch, and also on the little stores that she had buried at other times. She knew every Prairie-dog town in the region, as well as all the best places for Mice and Rabbits.

Not far from the den was the very Dog-town that first she had crossed, the day she had gained her liberty and lost her tail. If she were capable of such retrospect, she must have laughed to herself to think what a fool she was then. The change in her methods was now shown. Somewhat removed from the others, a Prairie-dog had made his den in the most approved style, and now when Tito peered over he was feeding on the grass ten yards from his own door. A Prairie-dog away from the others is, of course, easier to catch than one in the middle of the town, for he has but one pair of eyes to guard him; so Tito set about stalking this one. How was she to do it when there was no cover, nothing but short grass and a few low weeds? The White-bear knows how to approach the Seal on the flat ice, and the Indian how to get within striking distance of the grazing Deer. Tito knew how to do the same trick, and although one of the town Owls flew over with a warning chuckle, Tito set about her plan. A Prairie-dog cannot see well unless he is sitting up on his hind legs; his eyes are of little use when he is nosing in the grass; and Tito knew this. Further, a yellowish-gray animal on a yellowish-gray landscape is invisible till it moves. Tito seemed to know that. So, without any attempt to crawl or hide, she walked gently up-wind toward the Prairie-dog. Upwind, not in order to prevent the Prairie-dog smelling her, but so that she could smell him, which came to the same thing. As soon as the Prairie-dog sat up with some food in his hand, she froze into a statue. As soon as he dropped again to nose in the grass, she walked steadily nearer, watching his every move so that she might be motionless each time he sat up to see what his distant brothers were barking at. Once or twice he seemed alarmed by the calls of his friends, but he saw nothing and resumed his feeding. She soon cut the fifty yards down to ten, and the ten to five, and still was undiscovered. Then, when again the Prairie-dog dropped down to seek more fodder, she made a quick dash, and bore him off kicking and squealing. Thus does the angel of the pruning-knife lop off those that are heedless and foolishly indifferent to the advantages of society.

Tito had many adventures in which she did not come out so well. Once she nearly caught an Antelope fawn, but the hunt was spoiled by the sudden appearance of the mother, who gave Tito a stinging blow on the side of the head and ended her hunt for that day. She never again made that mistake—she had sense. Once or twice she had to jump to escape the strike of a Rattlesnake. Several times she had been fired at by hunters with long-range rifles. And more and more she had to look out for the terrible Grey Wolves. The Grey Wolf, of course, is much larger and stronger than the Coyote, but the Coyote has the advantage of speed, and can always escape in the open. All it must beware of is being caught in a corner. Usually when a Grey Wolf howls the Coyotes go quietly about their business elsewhere.

Tito had a curious fad, occasionally seen among the Wolves and Coyotes, of carrying in her mouth, for miles, such things as seemed to be interesting and yet were not tempting as eatables. Many a time had she trotted a mile or two with an old Buffalo-horn or a cast-off shoe, only to drop it when something else attracted her attention. The cowboys who remark these things have various odd explanations to offer: one, that it is done to stretch the jaws, or keep them in practice, just as a man in training carries weights. Coyotes have, in common with Dogs and Wolves, the habit of calling at certain stations along their line of travel, to leave a record of their visit. These stations may be a stone, a tree, a post, or an old Buffalo-skull, and the Coyote calling there can learn, by the odor and track of the last comer, just who the caller was, whence he came, and whither he went. The whole country is marked out by these intelligence depots. Now it often happens that a Coyote that has not much else to do will carry a dry bone or some other useless object in its mouth, but sighting the signal-post, will go toward it to get the news, lay down the bone, and afterwards forget to take it along, so that the signal-posts in time become further marked with a curious collection of odds and ends.

This singular habit was the cause of a disaster to the Chimney-pot Wolf-hounds, and a corresponding advantage to the Coyotes in the war. Jake had laid a line of poison baits on the western bluffs. Tito knew what they were, and spurned them as usual; but finding more later, she gathered up three or four and crossed the Little Missouri toward the ranchhouse. This she circled at a safe distance; but when something made the pack of Dogs break out into clamor, Tito dropped the baits, and next day, when the Dogs were taken out for exercise they found and devoured these scraps of meat, so that in ten minutes, there were four hundred dollars' worth of Greyhounds lying dead. This led to an edict against poisoning in that district, and thus was a great boon to the Coyotes.

Tito quickly learned that not only each kind of game must be hunted in a special way, but also different ones of each kind may require quite different treatment. The Prairie-dog with the outlying den was really an easy prey, but the town was quite compact now that he was gone. Near the center of it was a fine, big, fat Prairie-dog, a perfect alderman, that she had made several vain attempts to capture. On one occasion she had crawled almost within leaping distance, when the angry buzz of a Rattlesnake just ahead warned her that she was in danger. Not that the Rattler cared anything about the Prairie-dog, but he did not wish to be disturbed; and Tito, who had an instinctive fear of the Snake, was forced to abandon the hunt. The open stalk proved an utter failure with the Alderman, for the situation of his den made every Dog in the town his sentinel; but he was too good to lose, and Tito waited until circumstances made a new plan.

All Coyotes have a trick of watching from a high look-out whatever passes along the roads. After it has passed they go down and examine its track. Tito had this habit, except that she was always careful to keep out of sight herself.

One day a wagon passed from the town to the southward. Tito lay low and watched it. Something dropped on the road. When the wagon was out of sight Tito sneaked down, first to smell the trail as a matter of habit, second to see what it was that had dropped. The object was really an apple, but Tito saw only an unattractive round green thing like a cactus-leaf without spines, and of a peculiar smell. She snuffed it, spurned it, and was about to pass on; but the sun shone on it so brightly, and it rolled so curiously when she pawed, that she picked it up in a mechanical way and trotted back over the rise, where are found herself at the Dog-town. Just then two great Prairie-hawks came skimming like pirates over the plain. As soon as they were in sight the Prairie-dogs all barked, jerking their tails at each bark, and hid below. When all were gone Tito walked on toward the hole of the big fat fellow whose body she coveted, and dropping the apple on the ground a couple of feet from the rim of the crater that formed his home, she put her nose down to enjoy the delicious smell of Dog-fat. Even his den smelled more fragrant than those of the rest. Then she went quietly behind a greasewood bush, in a lower place some twenty yards away, and lay flat. After a few seconds some venturesome Prairie-dog looked out, and seeing nothing, gave the "all's well" bark. One by one they came out, and in twenty minutes the town was alive as before. One of the last to come out was the fat old Alderman. He always took good care of his own precious self. He peered out cautiously a few times, then climbed to the top of his look-out. A Prairie-dog hole is shaped like a funnel, going straight down. Around the top of this is built a high ridge which serves as a look-out, and also makes sure that, no matter how they may slip in their hurry, they are certain to drop into the funnel and be swallowed up by the all-protecting earth. On the outside the ground slopes away gently from the funnel. Now, when the Alderman saw that strange round thing at his threshold he was afraid. Second inspection led him to believe that it was not dangerous, but was probably interesting. He went cautiously toward it, smelled it, and tried to nibble it; but the apple rolled away, for it was round, and the ground was smooth as well as sloping. The Prairie-dog followed and gave it a nip which satisfied him that the strange object would make good eating. But each time he nibbled, it rolled farther away. The coast seemed clear, all the other Prairie-dogs were out, so the fat Alderman did not hesitate to follow up the dodging, shifting apple.

This way and that it wriggled, and he followed. Of course it worked toward the low place where grew the greasewood bush. The little tastes of apple that he got only whetted his appetite. The Alderman was more and more interested. Foot by foot he was led from his hole toward that old, familiar bush and had no thought of anything but the joy of eating. And Tito curled herself and braced her sinewy legs, and measured the distance between, until it dwindled to not more than three good jumps; then up and like an arrow she went, and grabbed and bore him off at last.

It will never be known whether it was accident or design that led to the placing of that apple, but it proved important, and if such a thing were to happen once or twice to a smart Coyote,—and it is usually clever ones that get such chances,—it might easily grow into a new trick of hunting.

After a hearty meal Tito buried the rest in a cold place, not to get rid of it, but to hide it for future use; and a little later, when she was too weak to hunt much, her various hoards of this sort came in very useful. True, the meat had turned very strong; but Tito was not critical, and she had no fears or theories of microbes, so suffered no ill effects.

The lovely Hiawathan spring was touching all things in the fairy Badlands. Oh, why are they called Badlands? If Nature sat down deliberately on the eighth day of creation and said, "Now work is done, let's play; let's make a place that shall combine everything that is finished and wonderful and beautiful—a paradise for man and bird and beast," it was surely then that she made these wild, fantastic hills, teeming with life, radiant with gayest flowers, varied with sylvan groves, bright with prairie sweeps and brimming lakes and streams. In foreground, offing, and distant hills that change at every step, we find some proof that Nature squandered here the riches that in other lands she used as sparingly as gold, with colorful sky above and colorful land below, and the distance blocked by sculptured buttes that are built of precious stones and ores, and tinged as by a lasting and unspeakable sunset. And yet, for all this ten times gorgeous wonderland enchanted, blind man has found no better name than one which says, *the road to it is hard.*

The little hollow west of Chimney Butte was freshly grassed. The dangerous-looking Spanish bayonets, that through the bygone winter had waged war with all things, now sent out their contribution to the peaceful triumph of the spring, in flowers that have stirred even the chilly scientists to name them Gloriosa; and the cactus, poisonous, most reptilian of herbs, surprised the world with a splendid bloom as little like itself as the pearl is like its mother shell-fish. The sage and the greasewood lent their gold, and the sand-anemone tinged the Badland hills like bluish snow; and in the air and earth and hills on every hand was felt the fecund promise of the spring. This was the end of the winter famine, the beginning of the summer feast, and this was the time by the All-mother, ordained when first the little Coyotes should see the light of day.

A mother does not have to learn to love her helpless, squirming brood. They bring the love with them—not much or little, not measurable, but perfect love. And in that dimly lighted warm abode she fondled them and licked them and cuddled them with heartful warmth of tenderness that was as much a new epoch in her life as in theirs.

But the pleasure of loving them was measured in the same measure as anxiety for their safety. In bygone days her care had been mainly for herself. All she had learned in her strange puppyhood, all she had picked up since, was bent to the main idea of self-preservation. Now she was ousted from her own affections by her brood. Her chief care was to keep their home concealed, and this was not very hard at first, for she left them only when she must, to supply her own wants.

She came and went with great care, and only after spying well the land so that none should see and find the place of her treasure. If it were possible for the little ones' idea of their mother and the cowboys' idea to be set side by side, they would be found to have nothing in common, though both were right in their point of view. The ranchmen knew the Coyote only as a pair of despicable, cruel jaws, borne around on tireless legs, steered by incredible cunning, and leaving behind a track of destruction. The little ones knew her as a loving, gentle, all-powerful guardian. For them her breast was soft and warm and infinitely tender. She fed and warmed them, she was their wise and watchful keeper. She was always at hand with food when they hungered, with wisdom to foil the cunning of their foes, and with a heart of courage tried to crown her well-laid plans for them with uniform success.

A baby Coyote is a shapeless, senseless, wriggling, and—to every one but its mother—a most uninteresting little lump. But after its eyes are open, after it has developed its legs, after it has learned to play in the sun with its brothers, or run at the gentle call of its mother when she brings home game for it to feed on, the baby Coyote becomes one of the cutest, dearest little rascals on earth. And when the nine that made up Coyotito's brood had reached this stage, it did not require the glamour of motherhood to make them objects of the greatest interest. The summer was now on. The little ones were beginning to eat flesh-meat, and Tito, with some assistance from Saddleback, was kept busy to supply both themselves and the brood. Sometimes she brought them a Prairie-dog, at other times she would come home with a whole bunch of Gophers and Mice in her jaws; and once or twice, by the clever trick of relay-chasing, she succeeded in getting one of the big Northern Jack-rabbits for the little folks at home.

After they had feasted they would lie around in the sun for a time. Tito would mount guard on a bank and scan the earth and air with her keen, brassy eye, lest any dangerous foe should find their happy valley; and the merry pups played little games of tag, or chased the Butterflies, or had apparently desperate encounters with each other, or tore and worried the bones and feathers that now lay about the threshold of the home. One, the least, for there is usually a runt, stayed near the mother and climbed on her back or pulled at her tail. They made a lovely picture as they played, and the wrestling group in the middle seemed the focus of it all at first; but a keener, later look would have rested on the mother, quiet, watchful, not without anxiety, but, above all, with a face full of motherly tenderness. Oh, she was so proud and happy, and she would sit there and watch them and silently love them till it was time to go home, or until some sign of distant danger showed. Then, with a low growl, she gave the signal, and all disappeared from sight in a twinkling, after which she would set off to meet and turn the danger, or go on a fresh hunt for food.

Oliver Jake had several plans for making a fortune, but each in turn was abandoned as soon as he found that it meant work. At one time or other most men of this kind see the chance of their lives in a poultry-farm. They cherish the idea that somehow the poultry do all the work. And without troubling himself about the details, Jake devoted an unexpected windfall to the purchase of a dozen Turkeys for his latest scheme. The Turkeys were duly housed in one end of Jake's shanty, so as to be well guarded, and for a couple of days were the object of absorbing interest, and had the best of care—too much, really. But Jake's ardor waned about the third day; then the recurrent necessity for long celebrations at Medora, and the ancient allurements of idle hours spent lying on the tops of sunny buttes and of days spent sponging on the hospitality of distant ranches, swept away the last pretence of attention to his poultry-farm. The Turkeys were utterly neglected—left to forage for themselves; and each time that Jake returned to his uninviting shanty, after a few days' absence, he found fewer birds, till at last none but the old Gobbler was left.

Jake cared little about the loss, but was filled with indignation against the thief.

He was now installed as wolver to the Broadarrow outfit. That is, he was supplied with poison, traps, and Horses, and was also entitled to all he could make out of Wolf bounties. A reliable man would have gotten pay in addition, for the ranchmen are generous, but Jake was not reliable.

Every wolver knows, of course, that his business naturally drops into several well-marked periods.

In the late winter and early spring—the love-season—the Hounds will not hunt a She-wolf. They will quit the trail of a He-wolf at this time—to take up that of a She-wolf, but when they do overtake her, they, for some sentimental reason, invariably let her go in peace. In August and September the young Coyotes and Wolves are just beginning to run alone, and they are then easily trapped and poisoned. A month or so later the survivors have learned how to take care of themselves, but in the early summer the wolver knows that there are dens full of little ones all through the hills. Each den has from five to fifteen pups, and the only difficulty is to know the whereabouts of these family homes.

One way of finding the dens is to watch from some tall butte for a Coyote carrying food to its brood. As this kind of wolving involved much lying still, it suited Jake very well. So, equipped with a Broadarrow Horse and the boss's field-glasses, he put in week after week at den-hunting— that is, lying asleep in some possible look-out, with an occasional glance over the country when it seemed easier to do that than to lie still.

The Coyotes had learned to avoid the open. They generally went homeward along the sheltered hollows; but this was not always possible, and one day, while exercising his arduous profession in the country west of Chimney Butte, Jake's glasses and glance fell by chance on a dark spot which moved along an open hillside. It was gray, and . . . even Jake knew that that meant Coyote. If it had been a Gray Wolf it would have been with tail up. A Fox would have had the large ears and tail, and the yellow color would have marked it. That dark shade from the front end meant something in his mouth—probably something being carried home—and that would mean a den of little ones.

He made careful note of the place, and returned there next day to watch, selecting a high butte near where he had seen the Coyote carrying the food. But all day passed, and he saw nothing. Next day, however, he descried a dark Coyote, old Saddleback, carrying a large Bird, and by the help of the glasses he made out that it was a Turkey, and then he knew that the yard at home was quite empty, and he also knew where the rest of them had gone, and vowed terrible vengeance when he should find the den. He followed Saddleback with his eyes as far as possible, and that was no great way, then went to the place to see if he could track him any farther; but he found no guiding signs, and he did not chance on the little hollow the was the playground of Tito's brood. Meanwhile Saddleback came to the little hollow and gave the low call that always conjured from the earth the unruly procession of the nine riotous little pups, and they dashed at the Turkey and pulled and worried till it was torn up, and each that got a piece ran to one side alone and silently proceeded to eat, seizing his portion in his jaws when another came near, and growling his tiny growl as he showed the brownish whites of his eyes in his effort to watch the intruder. Those that got the softer parts to feed on were well fed. But the three that did not turned all their energies on the frame of the Gobbler, and over that there waged a battle royal. This way and that they tugged and tussled, getting off occasional scraps, but really hindering each other feeding, till Tito glided in and deftly cut the Turkey into three or four, when each dashed off with a prize, over which he sat and chewed and smacked his lips and jammed his head down sideways to bring the backmost teeth to bear, while the baby runt scrambled into the home den, carrying in triumph his share—the Gobbler's grotesque head and neck.

Jake felt that he had been grievously wronged, indeed ruined, by that Coyote that stole his Turkeys. He vowed he would skin them alive when he found the pups, and took pleasure in thinking about how he would do it. His attempt to follow Saddleback by trailing was a failure, and all his searching for the den was useless, but he had come prepared for any emergency. In case he found the den he had brought a pick and shovel; in case he did not he had brought a living white Hen.

The Hen he now took to a broad open place near where he had seen Saddleback, and there he tethered her to a stick of wood that she could barely drag. Then he made himself comfortable on a look-out that was near, and lay still to watch. The Hen, of course, ran to the end of the string, and then lay on the ground flopping stupidly. Presently the log gave enough to ease the strain, she turned by mere chance in another direction, and so, for a time, stood up to look around.

The day went slowly by, and Jake lazily stretched himself on the blanket in his spying-place. Toward evening Tito came by on a hunt. This was not surprising, for the den was only half a mile away. Tito had learned, among other rules, this, "Never show yourself on the sky-line." In former days the Coyotes used to trot along the tops of the ridges for the sake of the chance to watch both sides. But men and guns had taught Tito that in this way you are sure to be seen. She therefore made a practice of running along near the top, and once in a while peeping over.

This was what she did that evening as she went out to hunt for the children's supper, and her keen eyes fell on the white Hen, stupidly stalking about and turning up its eyes in a wise way each time a harmless Turkey-buzzard came in sight against a huge white cloud.

Tito was puzzled. This was something new. It *looked* like game, but she feared to take any chances. She circled all around without showing herself, then decided that, whatever it might be, it was better let alone. As she passed on, a faint whiff of smoke caught her attention. She followed cautiously, and under a butte far from the Hen she found Jake's camp. His bed was there, his Horse was picketed, and on the remains of the fire was a pot which gave out a smell which she well knew about men's camps— the smell of coffee. Tito felt uneasy at this proof that a man was staying so near her home, but she went off quietly on her hunt, keeping out of sight, and Jake knew nothing of her visit.

About sundown he took in his decoy Hen, as Owls were abundant, and went back to his camp.

Next day the Hen was again put out, and late that afternoon Saddleback came trotting by. As soon as his eye fell on the white Hen he stopped short, his head on one side, and gazed. Then he circled to get the wind, and went cautiously sneaking nearer, very cautiously, somewhat puzzled, till he got a whiff that reminded him of the place where he had found those Turkeys. The Hen took alarm and tried to run away; but Saddleback made a rush, seized the Hen so fiercely that the string was broken, and away he dashed toward the home valley.

Jake had fallen asleep, but the squawk of the Hen happened to awaken him, and he sat up in time to see her borne away in old Saddleback's jaws. As soon as they were out of sight Jake took up the white-feather trail. At first it was easily followed, for the Hen had shed plenty of plumes in her struggles; but once she was dead in Saddleback's jaws, very few feathers were dropped except where she was carried through the brush. But Jake was following quietly and certainly, for Saddleback had gone nearly in a straight line home to the little ones with the dangerous tell-tale prize. Once or twice there was a puzzling delay when the Coyote had changed his course or gone over an open place; but one white feather was good for fifty yards, and when the daylight was gone, Jake was not two hundred yards from the hollow, in which at that very moment were the nine little pups, having a perfectly delightful time with the Hen, pulling it to pieces, feasting and growling, sneezing the white feathers from their noses or coughing them from their throats.

If a puff of wind had now blown from them toward Jake, it might have carried a flurry of snowy plumes or even the merry cries of the little revelers, and the den would have been discovered at once. But, as luck would have it, the evening lull was on, and all distant sounds were hidden by the crashing that Jake made in trying to trace his feather guides through the last thicket.

About this time Tito was returning home with a Magpie that she had captured by watching till it went to feed within the ribs of a dead Horse, when she ran across Jake's trail. Now, a man on foot is always a suspicious character in this country. She followed the trail for a little to see where he was going, and that she knew at once from the scent. How it tells her no one can say, yet all hunters know that it does. And Tito marked that it was going straight toward her home. Thrilled with new fear, she hid the bird she was carrying, then followed the trail of the man. Within a few minutes she could hear him in the thicket, and Tito realized the terrible danger that was threatening. She went swiftly, quietly around to the den hollow, came on the heedless little roisterers, after giving the signal-call, which prevented them taking alarm at her approach; but she must have had a shock when she saw how marked the hollow and the den were now, all drifted over with feathers white as snow. Then she gave the danger-call that sent them all to earth, and the little glade was still.

Her own nose was so thoroughly and always her guide that it was not likely she thought of the white-feathers being the telltale. But now she realized that a man, one she knew of old as a treacherous character, one whose scent had always meant mischief to her, that had been associated with all her own troubles and the cause of nearly all her desperate danger, was close to her darlings; was tracking them down, in a few minutes would surely have them in his merciless power.

Oh, the wrench to the mother's heart at the thought of what she could foresee! But the warmth of the mother-love lent life to the mother-wit. Having sent her little ones out of sight, and by a sign conveyed to Saddleback her alarm, she swiftly came back to the man, then she crossed before him, thinking, in her half-reasoning way, that the man must be following a foot-scent just as she herself would do, but would, of course, take the stronger line of tracks she was now laying. She did not realize that the failing daylight made any difference. Then she trotted to one side, and to make doubly sure of being followed, she uttered the fiercest challenge she could, just as many a time she had done to make the Dogs pursue her:

Grrr-wow-wow-wa-a-a-a-h,

and stood still; then ran a little nearer and did it again, and then again much nearer, and repeated her bark, she was so determined that the wolver should follow her.

Of course the wolver could see nothing of the Coyote, for the shades were falling. He had to give up the hunt anyway. His understanding of the details was as different as possible from that the Mother Coyote had, and yet it came to the same thing. He recognized that the Coyote's bark was the voice of the distressed mother trying to call him away. So he knew the brood must be close at hand, and all he now had to do was return in the morning and complete his search. So he made his way back to his camp.

Saddleback thought they had won the victory. He felt secure, because the foot-scent that he might have supposed the man to be following would be stale by morning. Tito did not feel so safe. That two-legged beast was close to her home and her little ones; had barely been turned aside; might come back yet.

The wolver watered and repicketed his Horse, kindled the fire anew, made his coffee and ate his evening meal, then smoked awhile before lying down to sleep, thinking occasionally of the little woolly scalps he expected to gather in the morning.

He was about to roll up in his blanket when, out of the dark distance, there sounded the evening cry of the Coyote, the rolling challenge of more than one voice. Jake grinned in fiendish glee, and said: "There you are all right. Howl some more. I'll see you in the morning." It was the ordinary, or rather one of the ordinary, camp-calls of the Coyote. It was sounded once, and then all was still. Jake soon forgot it in his loggish slumber.

The callers were Tito and Saddleback. The challenge was not an empty bluff. It had a distinct purpose behind it—to know for sure whether the enemy had any dogs with him; and because there was no responsive bark Tito knew that he had none.

Then Tito waited for an hour or so till the flickering fire had gone dead, and the only sound of life about the camp was the cropping of the grass by the picketed Horse. Tito crept near softly, so softly that the Horse did not see her till she was within twenty feet; then he gave a start that swung the tightened picket-rope up into the air, and snorted gently. Tito went quietly forward, and opening her wide gape, took the rope in, almost under her ears, between the great scissor-like back teeth, then chewed it for a few seconds. The fibers quickly frayed, and, aided by the strain the nervous Horse still kept up, the last of the strands gave way, and the Horse was free. He was not much alarmed; he knew the smell of Coyote; and after jumping three steps and walking six, he stopped.

The sounding thumps of his hoofs on the ground awoke the sleeper. He looked up, but, seeing the Horse standing there, he went calmly off to sleep again, supposing that all went well.

Tito had sneaked away, but she now returned like a shadow, avoided the sleeper, but came around, sniffed doubtfully at the coffee, and then puzzled over a tin can, while Saddleback examined the frying-pan full of "camp-sinkers" and then defiled both cakes and pan with dirt. The bridle hung on a low bush; the Coyotes did not know what it was, but just for luck they cut it into several pieces, then, taking the sacks that held Jake's bacon and flour, they carried them far away and buried them in the sand.

Having done all the mischief she could, Tito, followed by her mate, now set off for a wooded gully some miles away, where was a hole that had been made first by a Chipmunk, but enlarged by several other animals, including a Fox that had tried to dig out its occupants. Tito stopped and looked at many possible places before she settled on this. Then she set to work to dig. Saddleback had followed in a half-comprehending way, till he saw what she was doing. Then when she, tired with digging, came out, he went into the hole, and after snuffing about went on with the work, throwing out the earth between his hind legs; and when it was piled up behind he would come out and push it yet farther away.

And so they worked for hours, not a word said and yet with a sufficient comprehension of the object in view to work in relief of each other. And by the time the morning came they had a den big enough to do for their home, in case they must move, though it would not compare with the one in the grassy hollow.

It was nearly sunrise before the wolver awoke. With the true instinct of a plainsman he turned to look for his Horse. *It was gone.* What his ship is to the sailor, what wings are to the Bird, what money is to the merchant, the Horse is to the plainsman. Without it he is helpless, lost at sea, wing broken, crippled in business. Afoot on the plains is the sum of earthly terrors. Even Jake realized this, and ere his foggy wits had fully felt the shock he sighted the steed afar on a flat, grazing and stepping ever farther from the camp. At a second glance Jake noticed that the Horse was trailing the rope. If the rope had been left behind Jake would have known that it was hopeless to try to catch him; he would have finished his den-hunt and found the little Coyotes. But, with the trailing rope, there was a good chance of catching the Horse; so Jake set out to try.

Of all the maddening things there is nothing worse than to be almost, but not quite, able to catch your Horse. Do what he might, Jake could not get quite near enough to seize that short rope, and the Horse led him on and on, until at last they were well on the homeward trail.

Now Jake was afoot anyhow, so seeing no better plan, he set out to follow that Horse right back to the Ranch.

But when about seven miles were covered Jake succeeded in catching him. He rigged up a rough jaquima with the rope and rode barebacked in fifteen minutes over the three miles that lay between him and the Sheepranch, giving vent all the way to his pent-up feelings in cruel abuse of that Horse. Of course it did not do any good, and he knew that, but he considered it was heaps of satisfaction. Here Jake got a meal and borrowed a saddle and a mongrel Hound that could run a trail, and returned late in the afternoon to finish his den-hunt. Had he known it, he now could have found it without the aid of the cur, for it was really close at hand when he took up the feather-trail where he last had left it. Within one hundred yards he rose to the top of the little ridge; then just over it, almost face to face, he came on a Coyote, carrying in its mouth a large Rabbit. The Coyote leaped just at the same moment that Jake fired his revolver, and the Dog broke into a fierce yelling and dashed off in pursuit, while Jake blazed and blazed away, without effect, and wondered why the Coyote should still hang on to that Rabbit as she ran for her life with the Dog yelling at her heels. Jake followed as far as he could and fired at each chance, but scored no hit. So when they had vanished among the buttes he left the Dog to follow or come back as he pleased, while he returned to the den, which, of course, was plain enough now. Jake knew that the pups were there yet. Had he not seen the mother bringing a Rabbit for them?

So he set to work with pick and shovel all the rest of that day. There were plenty of signs that the den had inhabitants, and, duly encouraged, he dug on, and after several hours of the hardest work he had ever done, he came to the end of the den—*only to find it empty*. After cursing his luck at the first shock of disgust, he put on his strong leather glove and groped about in the nest. He felt something firm and drew it out. It was the head and neck of his own Turkey Gobbler, and that was all he got for his pains.

Tito had not been idle during the time that the enemy was Horse-hunting. Whatever Saddleback might have done, Tito would live in no fool's paradise. Having finished the new den, she trotted back to the little valley of feathers, and the first young one that came to meet her at the door of this home was a broad-headed one much like herself. She seized him by the neck and set off, carrying him across country toward the new den, a couple of miles away. Every little while she had to put her offspring down to rest and give it a chance to breathe. This made the moving slow, and the labor of transporting the pups occupied all that day, for Saddleback was not allowed to carry any of them, probably because he was too rough. Beginning with the biggest and brightest, they were carried away one at a time, and late in the afternoon only the runt was left. Tito had not only worked at digging all night, she had also trotted over thirty miles, half of it with a heavy baby to carry. But she did not rest. She was just coming out of the den, carrying her youngest in her mouth, when over the very edge of this hollow appeared the mongrel Hound, and a little way behind him Wolver Jake.

Away went Tito, holding the baby tight, and away went the Dog behind her.

Bang! bang! bang! said the revolver.

But not a shot touched her. Then over the ridge they dashed, where the revolver could not reach her, and sped across a flat, the tired Coyote and her baby, and the big fierce Hound behind her, bounding his hardest. Had she been fresh and unweighted she could soon have left the clumsy cur that now was barking furiously on her track and rather gaining than losing in the race. But she put forth all her strength, careered along a slope, where she gained a little, then down across a brushy flat where the cruel bushes robbed her of all she had gained. But again into the open they came, and the wolver, laboring far behind, got sight of them and fired again and again with his revolver, and only stirred the dust, but still it made her dodge and lose time, and it also spurred the Dog. The hunter saw the Coyote, his old acquaintance of the bobtail, carrying still, as he thought, the Jack-rabbit she had been bringing to her brood, and wondered at her strange persistence.

"Why doesn't she drop that weight when flying for her life?" But on she went and gamely bore her load over the hills, the man cursing his luck that he had not brought his Horse, and the mongrel bounding in deadly earnest but thirty feet behind her. Then suddenly in front of Tito yawned a little cut-bank gully. Tired and weighted, she dared not try the leap; she skirted around. But the Dog was fresh; he cleared it easily, and the mother's start was cut down by half. But on she went, straining to hold the little one high above the scratching brush and the dangerous bayonet-spikes; but straining too much, for the helpless cub was choking in his mother's grip. She must lay him down or strangle him; with such a weight she could not much longer keep out of reach. She tried to give the howl for help, but her voice was muffled by the cub, now struggling for breath, and as she tried to ease her grip on him a sudden wrench jerked him from her mouth into the grass—into the power of the merciless Hound. Tito was far smaller than the Dog; ordinarily she would have held him in fear; but her little one, her baby, was the only thought now, and as the brute sprang forward to tear it in his wicked jaws, she leaped between and stood facing him with all her mane erect, her teeth exposed, and plainly showed her resolve to save her young one at any price. The Dog was not brave, only confident that he was bigger and had the man behind him. But the man was far away, and balked in his first rush at the trembling little Coyote that tried to hide in the grass, the cur hesitated a moment, and Tito howled the long howl for help—the muster-call:

Yap-yap-yap-yah-yah-yah-h-h-h-h Yap-yap-yap-yah-yah-yah-h-h-h-h,

and made the buttes around re-echo so that Jake could not tell where it came from; but someone else there was that heard and did know whence it came. The Dog's courage revived on hearing something like a far-away shout. Again he sprang at the little one, but again the mother balked him with her own body, and then they closed in deadly struggle. "Oh, if Saddleback would only come!" But no one came, and now she had no further chance to call. Weight is everything in a closing fight, and Tito soon went down, bravely fighting to the last, but clearly worsted; and the Hound's courage grew with the sight of victory, and all he thought of now was to finish her and then kill her helpless baby in its turn. He had no ears or eyes for any other thing, till out of the nearest sage there flashed a streak of gray, and in a trice the big-voiced coward was hurled back by a foe almost as heavy as himself—hurled back with a crippled shoulder. Dash, chop, and staunch old Saddleback sprang on him again. Tito struggled to her feet, and they closed on him together. His courage fled at once when he saw the odds, and all he wanted now was safe escape—escape from Saddleback, whose speed was like the wind, escape from Tito, whose baby's life was at stake. Not twenty jumps away did he get; not breath enough had he to howl for help to his master in the distant hills; not fifteen yards away from her little one that he meant to tear, they tore him all to bits.

And Tito lifted the rescued young one, and traveling as slowly as she wished, they reached the new-made den. There the family safely reunited, far away from danger of further attack by Wolver Jake or his kind.

And there they lived in peace till their mother had finished their training, and every one of them grew up wise in the ancient learning of the plains, wise in the later wisdom that the ranchers' war has forced upon them, and not only they, but their children's children, too. The Buffalo herds have gone; they have succumbed to the rifles of the hunters. The Antelope droves are nearly gone; Hound and lead were too much for them. The Blacktail bands have dwindled before axe and fence. The ancient dwellers of the Badlands have faded like snow under the new conditions, but the Coyotes are no more in fear of extinction. Their morning and evening song still sounds from the level buttes, as it did long years ago when every plain was a teeming land of game. They have learned the deadly secrets of traps and poisons, they know how to baffle the gunner and Hound, they have matched their wits with the hunter's wits. They have learned how to prosper in a land of man-made plenty, in spite of the worst that man can do, and it was Tito that taught them how.

20

Scrap

by Lucia Chamberlain

*Generally speaking, soldiers get along well with dogs—especially a dog
like this one.*

AT THE GRAY END OF THE AFTERNOON THE REGIMENT OF TWELVE COM-
panies went through Monterey on its way to the summer camp, a mile out
on the salt-meadows; and it was here that Scrap joined it.

He did not tag at the heels of the boys who tagged the last company,
or rush out with the other dogs who barked at the band; but he appeared
somehow independent of any surroundings, and marched, ears alert,
stump tail erect, one foot in front of the tall first lieutenant who walked
on the wing of Company A.

The lieutenant was self-conscious and so fresh to the service that his
shoulder-straps hurt him. He failed to see Scrap, who was very small and
very yellow, until, in quickening step, he stumbled over him and all but
measured his long length. He aimed an accurate kick that sent Scrap
flying, surprised but not vindictive, to the side lines, where he considered,
his head cocked. With the scratched ear pricked and the bitten ear flat,
he passed the regiment in review until Company K, with old Muldoon,
sergeant on the flank, came by.

As lean, as mongrel, as tough, and as scarred as Scrap, he carried his
wiry body with a devil-may-care assurance, in which Scrap may have recognized a kindred spirit. He decided in a flash. He made a dart and fell
in abreast the sergeant of Company K. Muldoon saw and growled at him.

"Gr-r-r-r!" said Scrap, not ill-naturedly, and fell back a pace. But he did not slink. He had the secret of success. He kept as close as he could and yet escape Muldoon's boot. With his head high, ears stiff, tail up, he stepped out to the music.

Muldoon looked back with a threat that sent Scrap retreating, heels over ears. The sergeant was satisfied that the dog had gone; but when camp was reached and ranks were broken he found himself confronted by a disreputable yellow cur with a ragged ear cocked over his nose.

"Well, I'm domned!" said Muldoon. His heart, probably the toughest thing about him, was touched by this fearless persistence.

"Ar-ren't ye afraid o' nothin', ye little scrap?" he said. Scrap, answering the first name he had ever known, barked shrilly.

"What's that dog doing here?" said the tall lieutenant of Company A, disapprovingly.

"I'm afther kickin' him out, sor," explained Muldoon, and, upon the lieutenant's departure, was seen retreating in the direction of the cook-tent, with the meager and expectant Scrap inconspicuously at his heels.

He went to sleep at taps in Muldoon's tent, curled up inside Muldoon's cartridge-belt; but at reveille the next morning the sergeant missed him. Between drill and drill Muldoon sought diligently, with insinuations as to the character of dog-stealers that were near to precipitating personal conflict. He found the stray finally, in Company B street, leaping for bones amid the applause of the habitants.

Arraigned collectively as thieves, Company B declared that the dog had strayed in and remained only because he could not be kicked out. But their pride in the height of his leaps was too evidently the pride of possession; and Muldoon, after vain attempts to catch the excited Scrap, who was eager only for bones, retired with threats of some vague disaster to befall Company B the next day if *his* dog were not returned.

The responsibility, with its consequences, was taken out of Company B's hands by Scrap's departure from their lines immediately after supper. He was not seen to go. He slid away silently, among the broken shadows of the tents. Company B reviled Muldoon. Scrap spent the night in a bugler's cape, among a wilderness of brasses, and reappeared the next morning at guard mount, deftly following the stately maneuvers of the band.

"Talk about a dorg's gratitude!" said the sergeant of Company B, bitterly, remembering Scrap's entertainment of the previous evening.

"I'm on to his game!" muttered old Muldoon. "Don't ye see, ye fool, he don't belong to any *wan* of us. He belongs to the crowd—to the regiment. That's what he's tryin' to show us. He's what that Frinchman down in F calls a—a mascot; and, be jabers, he moves like a soldier!"

The regiment's enthusiasm for Scrap, as voiced by Muldoon, was not extended to the commanding officer, who felt that the impressiveness of guard mount was detracted from by Scrap's deployments. Also the tall lieutenant of Company A disliked the sensation of being accompanied in his social excursions among ladies who had driven out to band practice by a lawless yellow pup with a bitten ear. The lieutenant, good fellow at bottom, was yet a bit of a snob, and he would have preferred the colonel's foolish Newfoundland to the spirited but unregenerate Scrap.

But the privates and "non-coms" judged by the spirit, and bid for the favor of their favorite, and lost money at canteen on the next company to be distinguished as Scrap's temporary entertainers. He was cordial, even demonstrative, but royally impartial, devoting a day to a company with a method that was military. He had personal friends—Muldoon for one, the cook for another—but there was no man in the regiment who could expect Scrap to run to his whistle.

Yet independent as he was of individuals, he obeyed regimental regulations like a soldier. He learned the guns and the bugles, what actions were signified by certain sounds. He was up in the morning with the roll of the drums. He was with every drill that was informal enough not to require the presence of the commanding officer, and during dress parade languished, lamenting, in Muldoon's tent. Barking furiously, he was the most enthusiastic spectator of target practice. He learned to find the straying balls when the regimental nine practiced during "release," and betrayed a frantic desire to "retrieve" the shot that went crashing seaward from the sullen-mouthed cannon on the shore. More than once he made one of the company that crossed the lines at an unlawful hour to spend a night among the crooked ways of Monterey.

The regiment was tiresome with tales of his tricks. The height of his highest leap was registered in the mess, and the number of rats that had died in his teeth were an ever increasing score in the canteen. He was fairly aquiver with the mere excitement and curiosity of living. There was no spot in the camp too secure or too sacred for Scrap to penetrate. His invasions were without impertinence; but the regiment was his, and he deposited dead rats in the lieutenant's shoes as casually as he concealed bones in the French horn; and slumbered in the major's hat-box with the same equanimity with which he slept in Muldoon's jacket.

The major evicted Scrap violently, but, being a good-natured man, said nothing to the colonel, who was not. But it happened, only a day after the episode of the hat-box, that the colonel entered his quarters to find the yellow mascot, fresh from a plunge in the surf and a roll in the dirt, reposing on his overcoat.

To say that the colonel was angry would be weak; but, overwhelmed as he was, he managed to find words and deeds. Scrap fled with a sharp yelp as a boot-tree caught him just above the tail.

His exit did not fail to attract attention in the company street. The men were uneasy, for the colonel was noticeably a man of action as well as of temper. Their premonitions were fulfilled when at assembly the next morning, an official announcement was read to the attentive regiment. The colonel, who was a strategist as well as a fighter, had considered the matter more calmly overnight. He was annoyed by the multiplicity of Scrap's appearances at times and places where he was officially a nuisance. He was more than annoyed by the local paper's recent reference to "our crack yellow-dog regiment." But he knew the strength of regimental sentiment concerning Scrap and the military superstition of the mascot, and he did not want to harrow the feelings of the "summer camp" by detailing a firing squad. Therefore he left a loop-hole for Scrap's escape alive. The announcement read: "All dogs found in camp not wearing collars will be shot, by order of the commanding officer."

Now there were but two dogs in camp, and the colonel's wore a collar. The regiment heard the order with consternation.

"That'll fix it," said the colonel, comfortably.

"Suppose some one gets a collar?" suggested the major, with a hint of hopefulness in his voice.

"I know my regiment," said the colonel. "There isn't enough money in it three days before pay day to buy a button. They'll send him out to-night."

Immediately after drill there was a council of war in Muldoon's tent, Muldoon holding Scrap between his knees. Scrap's scratched ear, which habitually stood cocked, flopped forlornly; his stump tail drooped dismally. The atmosphere of anxiety oppressed his sensitive spirit. He desired to play, and Muldoon only sat and rolled his argumentative tongue. From this conference those who had been present went about the business of the day with a preternatural gloom that gradually permeated the regiment. The business of the day was varied, since the next day was to be a field day, with a review in the morning and cavalry maneuvers in the afternoon.

All day Scrap was conspicuous in every quarter of the camp, but at supper-time the lieutenant of Company A noted his absence from his habitual place at the left of Muldoon in the men's mess-tent. The lieutenant was annoyed by his own anxiety.

"Of course they'll get him out, sir?" he said to the major.

"Of course," the major assented, with more confidence than he felt. The colonel was fairly irritable in his uncertainty over it.

Next morning the sentries, who had been most strictly enjoined to vigilant observation, reported that no one had left camp that night, though a man on beat four must have failed in an extraordinary way to see a private crossing his line six feet in front of him.

The muster failed to produce any rag-eared, stub-tailed, eager-eyed, collarless yellow cur. Nor did the mess-call raise his shrill bark in the vicinity of the cook's tent. The lieutenant felt disappointed.

He thought that the regiment should at least have made some sort of demonstration in Scrap's defense. It seemed a poor return for such confidence and loyalty to be hustled out of the way on an official threat. It seemed to him the regiment was infernally light-hearted, as, pipe-clay white and nickel bright in the morning sun, it swung out of camp for the parade-ground, where the dog-carts and runabouts and automobiles were gathering from Del Monte and the cottages along the shore.

The sight of the twelve companies moving across the field with the step of one warmed the cockles of the colonel's pride. The regiment came to parade rest, and the band went swinging past their front, past the reviewing-stand. As it wheeled into place, the colonel, who had been speaking to the adjutant, who was the lieutenant of Company A, bit his sentence in the middle, and glared at something that moved, glittering, at the heels of the drum-major.

The colonel turned bright red. His glass fell out of his eye-socket. "What the devil is the matter with that dog?" he whispered softly.

And the adjutant, who had also seen and was suffocating, managed to articulate, "Collars!"

The colonel put his glass back in his eye. His shoulders shook. He coughed violently as he addressed the adjutant:

"Have that dog removed—no, let him alone—no, adjutant, bring him here!"

So the adjutant, biting his lip, motioned Muldoon to fall out. Tough old Muldoon tucked Scrap, struggling, squirming, glittering like a hardware shop, under his arm, and saluted his commander, while the review waited.

The colonel was blinking through his glass and trying not to grin. "Sergeant, how many collars has that dog got on?"

"Thirteen, sor," said Muldoon.

"What for?" said the colonel, severely.

"Wan for each company, sor, an' wan for the band."

Bruce

by Albert Payson Terhune

*From the trenches of France in World War I comes another tale from
the master of collie literature.*

"YES, IT'S AN EASY ENOUGH TRADE TO PICK UP," LECTURED TOP SERGEANT
Mahan, formerly of the regular army. "You've just got to remember a few
things. But you've got to keep on remembering those few, all the time. If
you forget one of 'em, it's the last bit of forgetting you're ever likely to do."

Top Sergeant Mahan, of the mixed French-and-American regiment
known as "Here We Come," was squatting at ease on the trench fir-
ing-step. From that professorial seat he was dispensing useful knowledge
to a group of fellow-countrymen—newly arrived from the base, to pad
the "Here-We-Come" ranks, which had been thinned at the Rache attack.

"What sort of things have we got to remember, Sergeant?" jauntily
asked a lanky Missourian. "We've got the drill pretty pat; and the trench
instructions and—"

"Gee!" ejaculated Mahan. "I had no idea of that! Then why don't you
walk straight ahead into Berlin? If you know all you say you do about
war, there's nothing more for you to learn. I'll drop a line to General Foch
and suggest to him that you rookies be detailed to teach the game to us
oldsters."

"I didn't mean to be fresh," apologized the jaunty one. "Won't you go
ahead and tell us the things we need to remember?"

"Well," exhorted Mahan, appeased by the newcomer's humility, "there aren't so many of them, after all. Learn to duck when you hear a Minnie grunt or a whizz-bang cut loose; or a five-nine begin to whimper. Learn not to bother to duck when the rifles get to jabbering—for you'll never hear the bullet that gets you. Study the nocturnal habits of machine-guns and the ways of snipers and the right time not to play the fool. And keep saying to yourself: 'The bullet ain't molded that can get *me!*' Mean it when you say it. When you've learned those few things, the rest of the war-game is dead easy."

"Except," timidly amended old Sergeant Vivier, the gray little Frenchman, "except when eyes are—are what you call it, no use."

"That's right," assented Mahan. "In the times when eyes are no use, all rules fail. And then the only thing you can do is to trust to your Yankee luck. I remember—"

"'When eyes are no use'?" repeated the recruit. "If you mean after dark, at night—haven't we got the searchlights and the star-shells and all that?"

"Son," replied Mahan, "we have. Though I don't see how you ever guessed such an important secret. But since you know everything, maybe you'll just kindly tell us what good all the lights in the world are going to do us when the filthy yellow-gray fog begins to ooze up out of the mud and the shell-holes, and the filthy gray mist oozes down from the clouds to meet it. Fog is the one thing that all the war-science won't overcome. A fog-penetrator hasn't been invented yet. If it had been, there'd be many a husky lad living today who has gone West this past few years, on account of the fogs. Fog is the boche's pet. It gives Fritzy a lovely chance to creep up on us. It—"

"It is the helper of *us,* too," suggested old Vivier. "More than one time, it has kept me safe when I was on patrol. And did it not help to save us at Rache, when—"

"The fog may have helped us, one per cent, at Rache," admitted Mahan. "But Bruce did ninety-nine per cent of the saving."

"A Scotch general?" asked the recruit, as Vivier nodded cordial affirmation of Mahan's words, and as others of the old-timers muttered approval.

"No," contradicted Mahan. "A Scotch collie. If you were dry behind the ears, in this life, you wouldn't have to ask who Bruce is."

"I don't understand," faltered the rookie, suspicious of a possible joke.

"You will soon," Mahan told him. "Bruce will be here to-day. I heard the K.O. saying the big dog is going to be sent down with some dispatches or something, from headquarters. It's his first trip since he was cut up so."

"I am saving him—this!" proclaimed Vivier, disgorging from the flotsam of his pocket a lump of once-white sugar. "My wife, she smuggle three of these to me in her last *paquet*. One I eat in my *café noir*, one I present to *mon cher vieux, ce bon* Mahan; one I keep for the grand dog what save us all that day."

"What's the idea?" queried the mystified rookie. "I don't—"

"We were stuck in the front line of the Rache salient," explained Mahan, eager to recount his dog-friend's prowess. "On both sides our supports got word to fall back. We couldn't get the word, because our telephone connection was knocked galley-west. There we were, waiting for a Hun attack to wipe us out. We couldn't fall back, for they were peppering the hill-slope behind us. We were at the bottom. They'd have cut us to ribbons if we'd shown our carcasses in the open. Bruce was here, with a message he'd brought. The K.O. sent him back to headquarters for the reserves. The boche heavies and snipers and machine-guns all cut loose to stop him as he scooted up the hill. And a measly giant of a German police dog tried to kill him, too. Bruce got through the lot of them; and he reached headquarters with the S.O.S. call that saved us. The poor chap was cut and gouged and torn by bullets and shell-scraps, and he was nearly dead from shell-shock, too. But the surgeon-general worked over him, himself, and pulled him back to life. He—"

"He is a loved pet of a man and a woman in your America, I have heard one say," chimed in Vivier. "And his home, there, was in the quiet country. He was lent to the cause, as a patriotic offering, *ce brave*! And of a certainty, he has earned his welcome."

When Bruce, an hour later, trotted into the trenches on the way to the "Here-We-Come" colonel's quarters, he was received like a visiting potentate. Dozens of men hailed him eagerly by name as he made his way to his destination with the message affixed to his collar.

Many of these men were his well-remembered friends and comrades. Mahan and Vivier, and one or two more, he had grown to like—as well as he could like any one in that land of horrors, three thousand miles away from The Place, where he was born, and from the Mistress and the Master, who were his loyally worshiped gods.

Moreover, being only mortal and afflicted with a hearty appetite, Bruce loved the food and other delicacies the men were forever offering him as a variation on the stodgy fare dished out to him and his fellow-war-dogs.

As much to amuse and interest the soldiers whose hero he was as for any special importance in the dispatch he carried, Bruce had been sent now to the trenches of the "Here-We-Comes." It was his first visit to the regiment he had saved since the days of the Rache assault two months earlier. Thanks to supremely clever surgery and to tender care, the dog was little the worse for his wounds. His hearing gradually had come back. In one shoulder he had a very slight stiffness which was not a limp, and a new-healed furrow scarred the left side of his tawny coat. Otherwise he was as good as new.

As Bruce trotted toward the group that so recently had been talking of him, the Missouri recruit watched with interest for the dog's joy at this reunion with his old friends. Bruce's snowy chest and black-stippled coat were fluffed out by many recent baths. His splendid head high and his dark eyes bright, the collie advanced toward the group.

Mahan greeted him joyously. Vivier stretched out a hand which displayed temptingly the long-hoarded lump of sugar. A third man produced, from nowhere in particular, a large and meat-fringed soup-bone. "I wonder which of you he'll come to first," said the interested Missourian.

The question was answered at once, and right humiliatingly. For Bruce did not falter in his swinging stride as he came abreast of the group. Not by so much as a second glance did he notice Mahan's hail and the tempting food.

As he passed within six inches of the lump of sugar which Vivier was holding out to him, the dog's silken ears quivered slightly—sure sign of hard-repressed emotion in a thoroughbred collie—but he gave no other manifestation that he knew any one was there.

"Well, I'll be blessed!" snickered the Missourian in high derision, as Bruce passed out of sight around an angle of the trench. "So *that's* the pup who is such a pal of you fellows, is he? Gee, but it was a treat to see how tickled he was to meet you again!"

To the rookie's amazement none of his hearers seemed in the least chagrined over the dog's chilling disregard of them. Instead, Mahan actually grunted approbation.

"He'll be back," prophesied the Sergeant. "Don't you worry. He'll be back. We ought to have had more sense than try to stop him when he's on duty. He has better discipline than the rest of us. That's one of the very first things they teach a courier-dog—to pay no attention to anybody when he's on dispatch duty. When Bruce has delivered his message to the K.O., he'll have the right to hunt up his chums. And no one knows it better'n Bruce himself."

"It was a sin—a thoughtlessness—of me to hold the sugar at him," said old Vivier. "Ah, but he is a so good soldier, *ce brave* Bruce! He look not to the left nor yet to the right, nor yet to the so-desired sugar-lump. He keep his head at attention! All but the furry tips of his ears. Them he has not yet taught to be good soldiers. They tremble, when he smell the sugar and the good soup-bone. They quiver like the little leaf. But he keep on. He—"

There was a scurry of fast-cantering feet. Around the angle of the trench dashed Bruce. Head erect, soft dark eyes shining with a light of gay mischief, he galloped up to the grinning Sergeant Vivier and stood. The dog's great plume of a tail was wagging violently. His tulip ears were cocked. His whole interest in life was fixed on the precious lump of sugar which Vivier held out to him.

From puppyhood, Bruce had adored lump sugar. Even at The Place, sugar had been a rarity for him, for the Mistress and the Master had known the damage it can wreak upon a dog's teeth and digestion. Yet, once in a while, as a special luxury, the Mistress had been wont to give him a solitary lump of sugar.

Since his arrival in France, the dog had never seen nor scented such a thing until now. Yet he did not jump for the gift. He did not try to snatch it from Vivier. Instead, he waited until the old Frenchman held it closer toward him, with the invitation:

"Take it, *mon vieux*! It is for you."

Then and then only did Bruce reach daintily forward and grip the grimy bit of sugar between his mighty jaws. Vivier stroked the collie's head while Bruce wagged his tail and munched the sugar and blinked gratefully up at the donor. Mahan looked on, enviously.

"A dog's got forty-two teeth, instead of the thirty-two that us humans have to chew on," observed the Sergeant. "A vet' told me that once. And sugar is bad for all forty-two of 'em. Maybe you didn't know that, Monsoo Vivier? Likely, at this rate, we'll have to chip in before long and buy poor Brucie a double set of false teeth. Just because you've put his real ones out of business with lumps of sugar!"

Vivier looked genuinely concerned at this grim forecast. Bruce wandered across to the place where the donor of the soup-bone brandished his offering. Other men, too, were crowding around with gifts.

Between petting and feeding, the collie spent a busy hour among his comrades-at-arms. He was to stay with the "Here-We-Comes" until the following day, and then carry back to headquarters a reconnaissance report.

At four o'clock that afternoon the sky was softly blue and the air was unwontedly clear. By five o'clock a gentle India-summer haze blurred the world's sharper outlines. By six a blanket-fog rolled in, and the air was wetly unbreatheable. The fog lay so thick over the soggy earth that objects ten feet away were invisible.

"This," commented Sergeant Mahan, "is one of the times I was talking about this morning—when eyes are no use. This is sure the country for fogs, in war-time. The cockneys tell me the London fogs aren't a patch on 'em."

The "Here-We-Comes" were encamped, for the while, at the edge of a sector from whence all military importance had recently been removed by a convulsive twist of a hundred-mile battle-front. In this dull hole-in-a-corner the new-arrived rivets were in process of welding into the more veteran structure of the mixed regiment.

Not a quarter-mile away—across No Man's Land and athwart two barriers of barbed wire—lay a series of German trenches. Now, in all probability, and from all outward signs, the occupants of this boche position consisted only of a regiment or two which had been so badly cut up in a foiled drive as to need a month of non-exciting routine before going back into more perilous service.

Yet the commander of the division to which the "Here-We-Comes" were attached did not trust to probabilities nor to outward signs. He had been at the front long enough to realize that the only thing likely to happen was the thing which seemed unlikeliest. And he felt a morbid curiosity to learn more about the personnel of those dormant German trenches.

Wherefore he had sent an order that a handful of the "Here-We-Comes" go forth into No Man's Land on the first favorable night and try to pick up a boche prisoner or two for questioning-purposes. A scouring of the doubly wired area between the hostile lines might readily harvest some solitary sentinel or some other man on special duty, or even the occupants of a listening-post. And the division commander earnestly desired to question such prisoner or prisoners. The fog furnished an ideal night for such an expedition.

Thus it was that a very young lieutenant and Sergeant Mahan and ten privates—the lanky Missourian among them—were detailed for the prisoner-seeking job. At eleven o'clock, they crept over the top, single file.

It was a night wherein a hundred searchlights and a million star-flares would not have made more impression on the density of the fog than would the striking of a safety match. Yet the twelve reconnoiterers were instructed to proceed in the cautious manner customary to such nocturnal expeditions into No Man's Land. They moved forward at the lieutenant's order, tiptoeing abreast, some twenty feet apart from one another, and advancing in three-foot strides. At every thirty steps the entire line was required to halt and to reestablish contact—in other words, to "dress" on the lieutenant, who was at the extreme right.

This maneuver was more time-wasting and less simple than its recital would imply. For in the dark, unaccustomed legs are liable to miscalculation in the matter of length of stride, even when shell-holes and other inequalities of ground do not complicate the calculations still further. And it is hard to maintain a perfectly straight line when moving forward through choking fog and over scores of obstacles.

The halts for realignment consumed much time and caused no little confusion. Nervousness began to encompass the Missouri recruit. He was as brave as the next man. But there is something creepy about walking with measured tread through an invisible space, with no sound but the stealthy *pad-pad-pad* of equally hesitant footsteps twenty feet away on either side. The Missourian was grateful for the intervals that brought the men into mutual contact, as the eerie march continued.

The first line of barbed wire was cut and passed. Then followed an endless groping progress across No Man's Land, and several delays, as one man or another had trouble in finding contact with his neighbor. At last the party came to the German wires. The lieutenant had drawn on a rubber glove. In his gloved hand he grasped a strip of steel which he held in front of him, like a wand, fanning the air with it.

As he came to the entanglement, he probed the barbed wire carefully with his wand, watching for an ensuing spark. For the Germans more than once had been known to electrify their wires, with fatal results to luckless prowlers.

These wires, to-night, were not charged. And, with pliers, the lieutenant and Mahan started to cut a passageway through them.

As the very first strand parted under his pressure, Mahan laid one hand warningly on the lieutenant's sleeve, and then passed the same pre-arranged warning down the line to the left.

Silence—moveless, tense, sharply listening silence—followed his motion. Then the rest of the party heard the sound which Mahan's keener ears had caught a moment earlier—the thud of many marching feet.

Here was no furtive creeping, as when the twelve Yankees had moved along. Rather was it the rhythmic beat of at least a hundred pairs of shapeless army boots—perhaps of more. The unseen marchers were moving wordlessly, but with no effort at muffling the even tread of their multiple feet.

"They're coming this way!" breathed Sergeant Mahan almost without sound, his lips close to the excited young lieutenant's ear. "And they're not fifty paces off. That means they're boches. So near the German wire, *our* men would either be crawling or else charging, not marching! It's a company—maybe a battalion—coming back from a reconnaissance, and making for a gap in their own wire somewhere near here. If we lay low there's an off chance they may pass us by."

Without awaiting the lieutenant's order, Mahan passed along the signal for every man to drop to earth and lie there. He all but forced the eagerly gesticulating lieutenant to the ground.

On came the swinging tread of the Germans. Mahan, listening breathlessly, tried to gauge the distance and the direction. He figured, presently, that the break the Germans had made in their wire could be only a few yards below the spot where he and the lieutenant had been at work with the pliers. Thus the intruders, from their present course, must inevitably pass very close to the prostrate Americans—so close, perhaps, as to brush against the nearest of them, or even to step on one or more of the crouching figures.

Mahan whispered to the man on his immediate left, the rookie from Missouri:

"Edge closer to the wire—close as you can wiggle, and lie flat. Pass on the word."

The Missourian obeyed. Before writhing his long body forward against the bristly mass of wire he passed the instructions on to the man at his own left.

But his nerves were at breaking-point.

It had been bad enough to crawl through the blind fog, with the ghostly steps of his comrades pattering softly at either side of him. But it was a thousand times harder to lie helpless here, in the choking fog and on the soaked ground, while countless enemies were bearing down, unseen, upon him, on one side, and an impenetrable wire cut off his retreat on the other.

The Missourian had let his imagination begin to work—always a mistake in a private soldier. He was visualizing the moment when this tramping German force should become aware of the presence of their puny foes and should slaughter them against the merciless wires. It would not be a fair stand-up fight, this murder-rush of hundreds of men against twelve who were penned in and could not maneuver nor escape. And the thought of it was doing queer things to the rookie's overwrought nerves.

Having passed the word to creep closer to the wires, he began to execute the order in person, with no delay at all. But he was a fraction of a second too late. The Germans were moving in hike-formation with "points" thrown out in advance to either side—a "point" being a private soldier who, for scouting and other purposes, marches at some distance from the main body.

The point, ahead of the platoon, had swerved too far to the left in the blackness—an error that would infalliby have brought him up against the wires, with considerable force, in another two steps. But the Missourian was between him and the wires. And the point's heavy-shod foot came down, heel first, on the back of the rookie's out-groping hand. Such a crushing impact on the hand-back is one of the most agonizing minor injuries a man can sustain. And this fact the Missourian discovered with great suddenness.

His too-taut nerves forced from his throat a yell that split the deathly stillness with an ear-piercing vehemence. He sprang to his feet, forgetful of orders—intent only on thrusting his bayonet through the Hun who had caused such acute torture to his hand. Halfway up, the rookie's feet went out from under him in the slimy mud. He caromed against the point, then fell headlong.

The German, doubtless thinking he had stumbled upon a single stray American scout, whirled his own rifle aloft to dash out the brains of his luckless foe. But before the upflung butt could descend—before the rookie could rise or dodge—the point added his quota to the rude breaking of the night's silence. He screamed in panic terror, dropped his brandished gun and reeled backward, clawing at his own throat.

For out of the eerie darkness, something had launched itself at him—something silent and terrible that had flown to the Missourian's aid. Down with a crash went the German, on his back. He rolled against the Missourian, who promptly sought to grapple with him.

But even as he clawed for the German, the rookie's nerves wrung from him a second yell—this time less of rage than of horror.

"Sufferin' cats!" he bellowed. "Why didn't anybody ever tell me Germans was covered with fur instead of clothes?"

The boche platoon was no longer striding along in hike-formation. It was broken up into masses of wildly running men, all of them bearing down upon the place whence issued this ungodly racket and turmoil. Stumbling, reeling, blindly falling and rising again, they came on.

Some one among them loosed a rifle-shot in the general direction of the yelling. A second and a third German rifleman followed the example of the first. From the distant American trenches, one or two snipers began to pepper away toward the enemy lines, though the fog was too thick for them to see the German rifle-flashes.

The boches farthest to the left, in the blind rush, fouled with the wires. German snipers, from behind the Hun parapets, opened fire. A minute earlier the night had been still as the grave. Now it fairly vibrated with clangor. All because one rookie's nerves had been less stanch than his courage, and because that same rookie had not only had his hand stepped on in the dark, but had encountered something swirling and hairy when he grabbed for the soldier who had stepped on him!

The American lieutenant, at the onset of the clamor, sprang to his feet, whipping out his pistol; his dry lips parted in a command to charge—a command which, naturally, would have reduced his eleven men and himself to twelve corpses or to an equal number of mishandled prisoners within the next few seconds. But a big hand was clapped unceremoniously across the young officer's mouth, silencing the half-spoken suicidal order.

Sergeant Mahan's career in the regular army had given him an almost uncanny power of sizing up his fellowmen. And he had long ago decided that this was the sort of thing his untried lieutenant would be likely to do, in just such an emergency. Wherefore his flagrant breach of discipline in shoving his palm across the mouth of his superior officer.

And as he was committing this breach of discipline, he heard the Missourian's strangled gasp of:

"Why didn't anybody ever tell me Germans was covered with fur?"

In a flash Mahan understood. Wheeling, he stooped low and flung out both arms in a wide-sweeping circle. Luckily his right hand's finger-tips, as they completed the circle, touched something fast-moving and furry.

"Bruce!" he whispered fiercely, tightening his precarious grip on the wisp of fur his fingers had touched. "Bruce! Stand still, boy! It's *you* who's got to get us clear of this! Nobody else, short of the good Lord, can do it!"

Bruce had had a pleasantly lazy day with his friends in the first-line trenches. There had been much good food and more petting. And at last, comfortably tired of it all, he had gone to sleep. He had awakened in a most friendly mood, and a little hungry. Wherefore he had sallied forth in search of human companionship. He found plenty of soldiers who were more than willing to talk to him and make much of him. But, a little farther ahead, he saw his good friend, Sergeant Mahan, and other of his acquaintances, starting over the parapet on what promised to be a jolly evening stroll.

All dogs find it hard to resist the mysterious lure of a walk in human companionship. True, the night was not an ideal one for a ramble, and the fog had a way of congealing wetly on Bruce's shaggy coat. Still, a damp coat was not enough of a discomfort to offset the joy of a stroll with his friends. So Bruce had followed the twelve men quietly into No Man's Land, falling decorously into step behind Mahan.

It had not been much of a walk, for speed or for fun. For the humans went ridiculously slowly, and had an eccentric way of bunching together, every now and again, and then of stringing out into a shambling line. Still, it was a walk, and therefore better than loafing behind in the trenches. And Bruce had kept his noiseless place at the Sergeant's heels.

Then—long before Mahan heard the approaching tramp of feet—Bruce caught not only the sound but the scent of the German platoon. The scent at once told him that the strangers were not of his own army.

A German soldier and an American soldier—because of their difference in diet as well as for certain other and more cogent reasons—have by no means the same odor to a collie's trained scent, nor to that of other breeds of war-dogs. Official records of dog-sentinels prove that.

Aliens were nearing Bruce's friends. And the dog's ruff began to stand up. But Mahan and the rest seemed in no way concerned in spirit thereby—though, to the dog's understanding, they must surely be aware of the approach. So Bruce gave no further sign of displeasure. He was out for a walk, as a guest. He was not on sentry-duty.

But when the nearest German was almost upon them, and all twelve Americans dropped to the ground, the collie became interested once more. A German stepped on the hand of one of his newest friends. And the friend yelled in pain. Whereat the German made as if to strike the stepped-on man.

This was quite enough for loyal Bruce. Without so much as a growl of warning, he jumped at the offender.

Dog and man tumbled earthward together. Then after an instant of flurry and noise, Bruce felt Mahan's fingers on his shoulder and heard the stark appeal of Mahan's whispered voice. Instantly the dog was a professional soldier once more—alertly obedient and resourceful.

"Catch hold my left arm, Lieutenant!" Mahan was exhorting. "Close up, there, boys—every man's hand grabbing tight to the shoulder of the man on his left! Pass the word. And you, Missouri, hang onto the Lieutenant! Quick, there! And tread soft and tread fast, and don't let go, whatever happens! Not a sound out of any one! I'm leading the way. And Bruce is going to lead *me*."

There was a scurrying scramble as the men groped for one another. Mahan tightened his hold on Bruce's mane.

"Bruce!" he said, very low, but with a strength of appeal that was not lost on the listening dog. "Bruce! Camp! Back to *camp*! And keep *quiet*! Back to camp, boy! *Camp!*"

He had no need to repeat his command so often and so strenuously. Bruce was a trained courier. The one word "Camp!" was quite enough to tell him what he was to do.

Turning, he faced the American lines and tried to break into a gallop. His scent and his knowledge of direction were all the guides he needed. A dog always relies on his nose first and his eyes last. The fog was no obstacle at all to the collie. He understood the Sergeant's order, and he set out at once to obey it.

But at the very first step, he was checked. Mahan did not release that feverishly tight hold on his mane, but merely shifted to his collar.

Bruce glanced back, impatient at the delay. But Mahan did not let go. Instead he said once more:

"*Camp*, boy!"

And Bruce understood he was expected to make his way to camp, with Mahan hanging on to his collar.

Bruce did not enjoy this mode of locomotion. It was inconvenient, and there seemed no sense in it; but there were many things about this strenuous war-trade that Bruce neither enjoyed nor comprehended, yet which he performed at command.

So again he turned campward, Mahan at his collar and an annoyingly hindering tail of men stumbling silently on behind them. All around were the Germans—butting drunkenly through the blanket-dense fog, swinging their rifles like flails, shouting confused orders, occasionally firing. Now and then two or more of them would collide and would wrestle in blind fury, thinking they had encountered an American.

Impeded by their own sightlessly swarming numbers, as much as by the impenetrable darkness, they sought the foe. And but for Bruce they must quickly have found what they sought. Even in compact form, the Americans could not have had the sheer luck to dodge every scattered contingent of Huns which starred the German end of No Man's Land—most of them between the fugitives and the American lines.

But Bruce was on dispatch duty. It was his work to obey commands and to get back to camp at once. It was bad enough to be handicapped by Mahan's grasp on his collar. He was not minded to suffer further delay by running into any of the clumps of gesticulating and cabbage-reeking Germans between him and his goal. So he steered clear of such groups, making several wide detours in order to do so. Once or twice he stopped short to let some of the Germans grope past him, not six feet away. Again he veered sharply to the left—increasing his pace and forcing Mahan and the rest to increase theirs—to avoid a squad of thirty men who were quartering the field in close formation, and who all but jostled the dog as they strode sightlessly by.

An occasional rifle-shot spat forth its challenge. From both trench-lines men were firing at a venture. A few of the bullets sang nastily close to the twelve huddled men and their canine leader. Once a German, not three yards away, screamed aloud and fell sprawling and kicking, as one such chance bullet found him. Above and behind, sounded the *plop* of star-shells sent up by the enemy in futile hope of penetrating the viscid fog. And everywhere was heard the shuffle and stumbling of innumerable boots.

At last the noise of feet began to die away, and the uneven groping tread of the twelve Americans to sound more distinctly for the lessening of the surrounding turmoil. And in another few seconds Bruce came to a halt—not to an abrupt stop, as when he had allowed an enemy squad to pass in front of him, but a leisurely checking of speed, to denote that he could go no farther with the load he was helping to haul.

Mahan put out his free hand. It encountered the American wires. Bruce had stopped at the spot where the party had cut a narrow path through the entanglement on the outward journey. Alone, the dog could easily have passed through the gap, but he could not be certain of pulling Mahan with him. Wherefore the halt.

The last of the twelve men scrambled down to safety in the American first-line trench, Bruce among them. The lieutenant went straight to his commanding officer, to make his report. Sergeant Mahan went straight to his company cook, whom he woke from a snoreful sleep. Presently Mahan ran back to where the soldiers were gathered admiringly around Bruce.

The Sergeant carried a chunk of fried beef, for which he had just given the cook his entire remaining stock of cigarettes.

"Here you are, Bruce!" he exclaimed. "The best in the shop is none too good for the dog that got us safe out of that filthy mess. Eat hearty!"

Bruce did not so much as sniff at the (more or less) tempting bit of meat. Coldly he looked up at Mahan. Then, with sensitive ears laid flat against his silken head, in token of strong contempt, he turned his back on the Sergeant and walked away.

Which was Bruce's method of showing what he thought of a human fool who would give him a command and who would then hold so tightly to him that the dog could hardly carry out the order.

22

How the Dog Tax Was Paid

by Sarah Knowles Bolton

*Not all dog-story authors are well-known. Still, they write stories that
are engaging and illuminating.*

TWO LITTLE CHILDREN, ANNIE AND JAMES, WERE PICKING UP STRAY
pieces of coal near the railroad to carry to a very poor home. Suddenly they
espied a black lump that looked like coal, only it moved. With childish
curiosity they crept towards it and found a thin, frightened, hungry dog
that had been crippled and beaten by boys.

"Do you dare touch her?" said the girl of nine years. "She might bite."

"Oh, yes," said Jimmie, a rugged and alert little fellow of seven. "See,
she wags her short tail, and I guess she wants to go home with us."

"But mother couldn't take care of her, we're so poor, and baby Ned
and Willie have to eat and have clothes."

"Oh, I'll give her some of my bread and milk every night, and Mrs.
Martin next door will give her bones, I guess. She hasn't any boy and she
is good to me."

The girl put her fingers carefully along the black dog's forehead, and
the animal pushed her cold nose against the child's hand and licked it.
She was not used to kind voices, and a girl's fingers upon her head gave
her courage. She half rose to her feet, looked from one to the other and
seemed to say, "I will go with you if you will only take me."

"I wouldn't pick her up, Jimmie; she'll follow us."

"She can't walk much," said the boy, "but I'll help her over the bad places if you'll carry the basket of coal."

The dog seemed to realize the conversation, for when the coal was ready to be moved, she was also ready, and hobbled on after the children.

"You must be tired, poor thing!" said Jimmie, taking her up as they crossed a muddy street, and thereby getting his torn jacket stained from her hurt back and bleeding foot.

The dog nestled up to him and seemed happy. When they reached home Jimmie ran ahead, showing his poor bruised friend to his mother.

"Why, Jimmie, what can you do with a dog?"

"Keep her to play with, and to guard the house when you are away washing."

"I don't know how we'll feed her," said Mrs. Conlon, who looked about as poor as the dog, "but we'll try. We can keep her warm anyway if you'll pick up enough coal."

"We shall love her so," said the boy, "and the baby will play with her when she gets well. Let's call her 'Pet,' because we never have anything to play with."

The dog crawled behind the stove and closed her eyes, as though thankful for a place to rest, where at least boys would not throw stones, and men would not kick her with their rough boots.

Days and weeks went by. The black dog, though not having a great supply of food, was living like a prince compared with the starvation of the street. Her bruises healed, her coat became blacker and her eyes brighter. She was indeed the baby's pet, and the idol of the other children. She went with Annie and Jimmie as they gathered coal. She slept on the floor beside their humble bed at night, and guarded the household when the mother was absent. She shared their food, and would have returned their kindness with her life if need be. The whole family were happier and kinder since she came into it, as is always the case when a pet animal is in the home.

Though poverty was a constant guest at the Conlon abode, with its bare floors, poor clothes, and common fare, yet they were not unhappy. The mother worked too hard to philosophize much about circumstances, and the children were too young to realize what was before them of struggle. A cloud was coming, and a man's hand brought it. It was the arrival of the tax-gatherer.

A high official in the State found that the treasury was low, and decided that money must be raised in some way. Of course it was generally conceded that the liquor traffic caused so much of the poverty, crime, and sorrow that it would be wise to make it pay for some of its evil results. This was a difficult matter, however, as saloon keepers and their customers had votes. Corporations could be taxed more heavily, but corporations sometimes paid money to help carry elections.

There was at least one class that had no votes, and consequently little influence. Dogs could therefore be taxed. The rich could easily pay the tax, and if the poor could not, their dogs could be killed. Who stopped to think whether money raised through the sorrow of the poor, or the death of helpless animals, might prove a bane rather than a blessing? Who asked whether a dog did not love life as well as his master, and whether, for his devotion and courage and guarding of homes, he was not entitled to the consideration of the city and the State, rather than to be killed because his owner could not or did not pay a tax or a license fee? The dog had done no wrong, and though somebody loved him, as he could not earn the fee himself he must needs be destroyed.

The tax-gatherer, endowed with power by the officials, came to the Conlon home. There was little that could be taken from so poor a place, thought the collector, until he espied the black dog beside the baby's cradle. "Your dog, madam, must be paid for. The fee is five dollars."

"I haven't the money," said the woman. "Why, I couldn't raise so much! I can hardly fill these four mouths with food."

"Well, madam, then you shouldn't keep a dog."

"But she guards the children while I work, and she is such a comfort to them!"

"The law doesn't take sentiment into the account. If you were a man I should arrest you, and shoot the dog. As it is, I will only shoot the dog. Bring the animal out and I will call that policeman over."

"You wouldn't shoot her before these crying children?"—for three of them had begun to cry, and were clasping the dog to their hearts, while the baby looked scared, and pressed his lips together, as though he realized that something was wrong.

"As I said before, madam, the law has no regard for sentiment. The State must have money."

"I wish they would tax the saloons. If my husband hadn't lost his money in them before he died we should have the money now to pay the tax for our dog. Could you wait a little for the money? I can give you a dollar, and perhaps I can borrow another, but I can't possibly raise five dollars. Can you come to-morrow?"

"Yes, I'll give you a trial, but it's a long walk here. I'm afraid you'll turn the dog on the street and then say you haven't any."

"Oh, no, sir, we are not as mean as that, even if we are poor! Pet would suffer and perhaps starve, and we all love her too much for that."

After the man was gone Mrs. Conlon put on her faded shawl and bonnet and went to her neighbors, as poor as herself. One loaned her a quarter, another a half, till the whole dollar was secured.

When the assessor came on the following day, being somewhat impressed by the devotion of both family and dog, he took the two dollars and promised to wait a reasonable time for the remaining three. Various plans were talked over in the Conlon home for the raising of the extra money. There was comparatively little work to be obtained, rent must be met or they would be turned upon the street, and there were five mouths to feed besides that of Pet.

Jimmie declared that a letter to the Governor of the State ought to do good, and Annie should write it. Accordingly a sheet of paper and an envelope were procured that very afternoon, and a letter was penned to that official. It read as follows:

Dear Mr. Governor:

We have a beautiful [this was a stretch of the imagination] black dog that we found sick and hurt, and we love her dearly, but can't pay the tax of five dollars. Mother works, and I take care of the children, but I can't earn any money for poor dear Pet. The police have killed lots of dogs on our street. One belonged to Mamie Fisher, my best friend, and we went together and found him in a pile of dogs, all dead. Mamie took him up in her arms and cried dreadfully. I helped her carry him, and we dug a grave in their little yard and buried him, and we took five cents that a lady gave me and bought two roses and laid on his grave. He was a big yellow puppy, and was so kind.

Now, Mr. Governor, would you be willing to lend us three dollars till we can earn it, and pay you back? She has two dollars already. We wish there wasn't any tax on dogs, for they make us poor children so happy. Perhaps you can stop the law.

Yours most respectful,
Annie Conlon.

All pronounced this a proper letter, and Jimmie dropped it into the mail-box. All the family waited prayerfully for the answer.

The Governor was touched as he read this letter from a child. "I will give her the three dollars," he said to his wife. "I didn't suppose the enforcement of a dog tax would bring so much sorrow to little hearts and large ones too. I really wish there were no tax on dogs, for they are helpless creatures and most faithful friends to man. But the State needs money."

"Try to get the tax law repealed," said the wife. "There are plenty of ways to raise money to pay the expenses of a great State without killing dogs. The tax law is directly responsible for thousands of dogs being turned upon the street to starve: they become ill from hunger and thirst, are supposed to be mad, and then suffer untold misery and even death from thoughtless and excited crowds. I would have no part in enforcing such a law, and would help to wipe it from the statute books."

"But some of the farmers have their sheep killed by dogs, and they must have their losses made up to them," said the Governor.

"Let the town pay for the sheep which are killed, and not cause the death of thousands of innocent dogs because a few have done wrong," replied the wife.

The money was sent to Annie Conlon, and there was thanksgiving in the plain home. Pet wagged her short tail, and looked up into Annie's eyes, as though she understood that her life had been spared by those three dollars.

23

Dogs and Men

by Henry C. Merwin

In a change-of-pace from dramatic stories to essay, author Merwin gives us plenty to think about with the lives of dogs we love.

THERE ARE MEN AND WOMEN IN THE WORLD WHO, OF THEIR OWN FREE will, live a dogless life, not knowing what they miss; and for them this essay, securely placed in the dignified *Atlantic*, there to remain so long as libraries and books shall endure, is chiefly written. Let them not pass it by in scorn, but rather stop to consider what can be said of the animal as a fellow being entitled to their sympathy, and having, perhaps, a like destiny with themselves.

As to those few persons who are not only dogless but dog-haters, they should excite pity rather than resentment. The man who hates a good dog is abnormal, and cannot help it. I once knew such a man, a money-lender long since passed away, whose life was largely a crusade against dogs, carried on through newspapers, pamphlets, and in conversation.

He used to declare that he had often been bitten by these animals, and that, on one occasion, a terrier actually jumped on the streetcar in which he was riding, took a small piece out of his leg (a mere soupçon, no doubt), and then jumped off—all without apparent provocation, and in a moment of time. Probably this story, strange as it may sound, was substantially true. The perceptions of the dog are wonderfully acute. A recent occurrence may serve as the converse of the money-lender's story.

A lost collie, lame and nearly starved, was taken in, fed, and cared for by a household of charitable persons, who, however, did not like or understand dogs, and were anxious to get rid of this one, provided that a good home could be found for him. In the course of a week there came to call upon them in her buggy an old lady who is extremely fond of dogs, and who possesses that combination of a masterful spirit with deep affection which acts like witchcraft upon the lower animals. The collie was brought out, and the story of his arrival was related at length.

Meanwhile the old lady and the dog looked each other steadfastly in the eye. "Do you want to come with me, doggie?" she said at last, not really meaning to take him. Up jumped the dog, and sat down beside her, and could not be dislodged by any entreaties or commands—and all parties were loath to use force. She took him home, but brought him back the next day, intending to leave him behind her. Again, however, the dog refused to be parted from his new and real friend. He bestowed a perfunctory wag of the tail upon his benefactors—he was not ungrateful; but, like all dogs, he sought not chiefly meat and bones and a comfortable place by the fire, but affection and caresses. The dog does not live that would refuse to forsake his dinner for the companionship of his master.

The mission of the dog—I say it with all reverence—is the same as the mission of Christianity, namely, to teach mankind that the universe is ruled by love. Ownership of a dog tends to soften the hard hearts of men. There are two great mysteries about the lower animals: one, the suffering which they have to endure at the hands of man; the other, the wealth of affection which they possess, and which for the most part is unexpended. All animals have this capacity for loving other creatures, man included. Crows, for example, show it to a remarkable degree. As much latent affection goes to waste in every flock of crows that flies overhead as would fit a human household for heaven. A crow and a dog, if kept together, will become almost as fond of each other as of their master.

Surely this fact, this capacity of the lower animals to love, not only man, but one another, is the most significant, the most deserving to be pondered, the most important in respect to their place in the universe, of all the facts that can be learned about them. Compared with it, how trivial is anything that the zoologist or biologist or the physiologist can tell us about the nature of the lower animals!

The most beautiful sight in the world, I once heard it said (by myself, to be honest), is the expression in the eyes of an intelligent, sweet-tempered pup—a pup old enough to take an interest in things about him, and yet so young as to imagine that everybody will be good to him; so young as not to fear that any man or boy will kick him, or that any dog will take away his bone. In the eyes of such a pup there is a look of confiding innocence, a consciousness of his own weakness and inexperience, a desire to love and to be loved, which are irresistible. In older dogs one is more apt to notice an eager, anxious, inquiring look, as if they were striving to understand things which the Almighty had placed beyond their mental grasp; and the nearest approach to a really human expression is seen in dogs suffering from illness. Heine, who, as the reader well knows, served a long apprenticeship to pain, somewhere says that pain refines even the lower animals; and all who are familiar with dogs in health and in disease will see the truth of this statement. I have seen in the face of an intelligent dog, suffering acutely from distemper, a look so human as to be almost terrifying; as if I had accidentally caught a glimpse of some deep-lying trait in the animal which nature had intended to conceal from mortal gaze.

The dog, in fact, makes a continual appeal to the sympathies of his human friends, and thus tends to prevent them from becoming hard or narrow. There are certain families, especially perhaps in New England, and most of all, no doubt, in Boston, who need to be regenerated, and might be regenerated by keeping a dog, provided that they went about it in the proper spirit. A distinguished preacher and author, himself a Unitarian, remarked recently in an address to Unitarians that they were usually the most self-satisfied people that he ever met. It was a casual remark, and perhaps neither he nor those who heard it appreciated its full significance. However, the preacher was probably thinking not so much of Unitarians as of a certain kind of person often found in this neighborhood, and not necessarily professing any particular form of religion. We all know the type. When a man *invariably* has money in the bank, and is respectable and respected, was graduated at Harvard, has a decorous wife and children, has never been carried away by any passion or enthusiasm, knows the right people, and conforms strictly to the customs of good society; and when this sort of thing has been going on for, perhaps, two or three generations, then there is apt to creep into the blood a coldness that would chill the heart of a bronze statue. Such persons are really degenerates of their peculiar kind, and need to be saved, perhaps by desperate measures. Let them elope with the cook; let them get religion of a violent kind; or if they cannot get religion, let them get a dog, give him the run of the house, love him and spoil him, and so, by the blessing of Providence, their salvation may be effected.

Reformers and philanthropists should always keep dogs, in order that the spontaneous element may not wholly die out of them. Their tendency is to regard the human race as a problem, and particular persons as "cases" to be dealt with, not according to one's impulses, but according to certain rules approved by good authority, and supposed to be consistent with sound economic principles. To my old friend _____, who once liked me for myself, without asking why, I have long ceased to be an individual, and am now simply an item of humanity to whom he owes such duty as my particular wants or vices would seem to indicate. But if he had a dog he could not regard him in that impersonal way, or worry about the dog's morals: he would simply take pleasure in his society, and love him for what he was, without considering what he might have been.

I know and honor one philanthropist who, in middle life or thereabout, became for the first time the possessor of a dog; and thenceforth there was disclosed in him a genuine vein of sentiment and affection which many years of doing good and virtuous living had failed to eradicate. Often had I heard of his civic deeds and of his well-directed charities, but my heart never quite warmed toward him until I learned that, with spectacles on nose and comb in hand, he had spent three laborious hours in painfully going over his spaniel, and eliminating those parasitic guests which sometimes infest the coat of the cleanest and most aristocratic dog. I am not ashamed to say that I have a confidence in his wisdom now which I did not have before, knowing that his head will never be allowed to tyrannize over his heart. His name should be recorded here, were it not that his modesty might be offended by the act. (Three letters would suffice to print it.)

In speaking of the dog as a kind of missionary in the household, I mean, it need hardly be said, something more than mere ownership of the animal. It will not suffice to pay a large sum for a dog of fashionable breed, equip him with a costly collar, and then relegate him to the stable or the kitchen. He should be one of the family, living on equal terms with the others, and their constant companion. The dog's life is short at the best, and every moment of it will be needed for his development. It is wonderful how, year by year, the household pet grows in intelligence, how many words he learns the meaning of, how quick he becomes in interpreting the look, the tone of voice, the mood of the person whom he loves. He is old at ten or eleven, and seldom lives beyond thirteen or fourteen. If he lived to be fifty, he would know so much that we should be uneasy, perhaps terrified, in his presence.

A certain amount of discipline is necessary for a dog. If left to his own devices, he is apt to become somewhat dissipated, to spend his evenings out, to scatter among many the affection which should be reserved for a few. But, on the other hand, a dog may easily receive too much discipline; he becomes like the child of a despotic father. A dog perfectly trained, from the martinet point of view—one who never "jumps up" on you, never lays an entreating paw on your arm, never gets into a chair, or enters the drawing-room—such a dog is a sad sight to one who really knows and loves the animal. It is against his nature to be so repressed. Over-careful housewives, and persons who are burdened with costly surroundings, talk of injury to carpets and other furniture if the dog has a right of entry everywhere in the house. But what is furniture for? Is it for display, is it a guaranty of the wealth of the owners, or is it for use? Blessed are they whose furniture is so inexpensive or so shabby that children and dogs are not excluded from its sacred precincts. Perhaps the happiest household to which I ever had the honor of being admitted was one where it was sometimes a little difficult to find a comfortable vacant chair: the dogs always took the arm-chairs. Alas, where are those hospitable chairs now?

Where the dogs that used to sit up in them, and wink and yawn, and give their paws in humorous embarrassment?

"The drawing-room was made for dogs, and not dogs for the drawing-room," would be Lady Barnes's thesis, did she formulate it. It was this same Lady Barnes—Rhoda Broughton—who once said, "I have no belief in Eliza, the housemaid I leave in charge here. When last I came down from London the dogs were so unnaturally good that I felt sure she bullied them. I spoke very seriously to her, and this time, I am glad to say, they are as disobedient as ever, and have done even more mischief than when I am at home." And she laughed with a delicate relish of her own folly.

Of all writers of fiction, by the way, is there any whose dogs quite equal those of Rhoda Broughton? Even the beloved author of *Rab and His Friends*, even Sir Walter himself, with his immortal Dandie Dinmonts, has not, it seems to me, given us such life-like and home-like pictures of dogs as those which occur in her novels. They seem to be there, not of set purpose, but as if dogs were such an essential part of her own existence that they crept into her books almost without her knowing it. No room in her novels is complete without a dog or two; and every remark that she makes about them has the quality of a caress. Even in a tragic moment, the heroine cannot help observing, that "Mink is lying on his small hairy side in a sunpatch, with his little paws crossed like the hands of a dying saint." "Mr. Brown," that dear, faithful mongrel, is forever associated with the unfortunate Joan; and Brenda's "wouff" will go resounding down the halls of time so long as novels are read.

Perhaps the final test of anybody's love of dogs is willingness to permit them to make a camping-ground of the bed. There is no other place in the world that suits the dog quite so well. On the bed he is safe from being stepped upon; he is out of the way of draughts; he has a commanding position from which to survey what goes on in the world; and, above all, the surface is soft and yielding to his outstretched limbs. No mere man can ever be so comfortable as a dog looks.

Some persons object to having a dog on the bed at night; and it must be admitted that he lies a little heavily upon one's limbs; but why be so base as to prefer comfort to companionship! To wake up in the dark night, and put your hand on that warm soft body, to feel the beating of that faithful heart—is not this better than undisturbed sloth? The best night's rest I ever had was once when a cocker spaniel puppy, who had just recovered from stomach-ache (dose one to two soda-mints), and was a little frightened by the strange experience, curled up on my shoulder like a fur tippet, gently pushed his cold, soft nose into my neck, and there slept sweetly and soundly until morning.

Companionship with his master is the dog's remedy for every ill, and only an extreme case will justify sending him away or boarding him out. To put a dog in a hospital, unless there is some surgical or other like necessity for doing so, is an act of doubtful kindness. Many and many a dog has died from homesickness. If he is ill, keep him warm and quiet, give him such simple remedies as you would give to a child: pour beef tea or malted milk down his throat, or even a little whiskey, if he is weak from want of food; and let him live or die, as did our fathers and our fathers' dogs—at home.

Many dogs are sensitive to an excessive degree, so sensitive indeed that any correction of them, beyond such as can be conveyed by a word, amounts to positive cruelty. A dog of that kind may easily be thrown by harsh treatment into a state of nervous disorder, and will be really unable to do what is required of him. In that state he often presents an appearance of obstinacy, whereas in fact he is suffering from a sort of nervous atrophy or paralysis, closely resembling that of a "balky" horse.

This nervous temperament makes the dog susceptible to misery in many forms, but the worst evil that can befall is to be lost. The very words "lost dog" call up such pictures of canine misery as can never be forgotten by those who have witnessed them. I have seen a lost dog, lame, emaciated, wounded, footsore, hungry, and thirsty, yet suffering so intensely from fear, and loneliness, and despair—from the mere sense of being lost—as to be absolutely unconscious of his bodily condition. The mental agony was so much greater that it swallowed up the physical pain. A little Boston terrier, who was lost in a large city for two or three days, became so wrecked in his nervous system that no amount of care or petting could restore him to equanimity, and it was found necessary to kill him. Oh, reader, pass not by the lost dog! Succor him if you can; preserve him from what is worse than death. It is easy to recognize him by the look of nervous terror in his eye, by his drooping tail, by his uncertain movements.

There is a remorseful experience of my own, of which I should be glad to unburden myself to the reader. It once became my duty to kill a dog afflicted with some incurable disease. Instead of doing it myself, as I should have done, I took him to a place where lost dogs are received, and where those for whom no home can be found are mercifully destroyed. There, instead of myself leading him to the death-chamber, as, again, I should have done, I handed him over to the executioner. The dog was an abnormally nervous and timid one; and as he was dragged most unwillingly away, he turned around, as nearly as he could, and cast back at me a look of horror, of fear, of agonized appeal—a look that has haunted me for years.

Whether he had any inkling of what was in store for him, I do not know, but it is highly probable that he had. Dogs and other animals are wonderful mind-readers. I have known three cases in which some discussion about the necessity of killing an old dog, held in his presence, was quickly followed by the sudden, unaccountable disappearance of the animal; and no tidings of him could ever be obtained, although the greatest pains were taken to obtain them. Horses are inferior only to dogs in this capacity. Often, especially in the case of vicious or half-broken horses, an intention will flash from the mind of the horse to the mind of the rider or driver, and vice versa, without the slightest indication being given by horse or man. Men who ride race-horses have told me that a sudden conviction in their own minds, in the course of a race, that they could not win has passed immediately to the horse and caused him to slacken his speed, although they had not ceased to urge him. It is notorious in the trotting world that faint-hearted and pessimistic drivers often lose races which they ought to win.

As to remarkable stories about this or that animal, perhaps it might be said that they are probably true when they illustrate the animal's perceptive abilities, and are probably false when they depend upon his power to originate. There appeared lately an account of a race between loons in the wild state: how the loons got together and arranged the preliminaries (whether they made books on the event or adopted the pool system of betting was not stated), how the race was run, or rather flown, amid intense loon excitement, and how the victor was greeted with screams of applause!

Some power of origination animals, and dogs especially, certainly have. There is the familiar trick which dogs play when one, to get a bone away from another, rushes off a little space, gives the bark which signifies the presence of an intruder, then comes back and quietly runs away with the bone which the other dog, in his curiosity to see who is coming, has impulsively dropped. This is an example, not of reasoning only, but of origination.

In general, however, when dogs surprise us, as they frequently do, it is by the delicacy and acuteness of their perceptive powers. How unerringly do they distinguish between different classes of persons, as, for example, between the members of the family and the servants; and again, between the servants and the friends of the household! Unquestionably the dog has three sets of manners for these three classes of persons. He will take liberties in the kitchen that he would never dream of taking in the dining-room. We have known our cook to fly in terror from the kitchen because Figaro, a masterful cocker spaniel, threatened to bite her if she did not give him a piece of meat forthwith. Figaro reasoned that the cook was partly *his* cook, and that he had a right to bully her if he could.

As for the different members of the family, the dog will "size them up" with an unerring instinct. It is impossible to conceal any weakness of character from him; and if you are strong, he will know that, too. As I write these lines, the vision of "Mr. Guppy" rises before me. Mr. Guppy was a very small Boston terrier with a white head, but otherwise of a brindle color. He had a beautiful "mug," much like that of a bulldog, with a short nose, wide jaws, and plenty of loose skin hanging about his stout little neck. It must be admitted that he was somewhat self-indulgent, being continually on the watch for a chance to lie close by the fire—a situation considered by his friends to be unwholesome for him. Mr. Guppy understood me very well. He knew that I was a poor, weak, easy-going, absent-minded creature, with whom he could take liberties; accordingly, when we were alone together, the rogue would lie sleeping with his head on the hearth, while I was absorbed in my book. But hark! There is a step on the stairs, of one whom Mr. Guppy both loved and feared more than any dog ever loved or feared me; and forthwith the little impostor would rise and crawl softly back to his place on a rug in the corner; and there he would be found lying and winking, with an expression of perfect innocence, when the disciplinarian entered the room.

Dogs have the same sensitiveness that we associate with well-bred men and women. Their politeness is remarkable. Offer a dog water when he is not thirsty, and he will almost always take a lap or two, just out of civility, and to show his gratitude. I know a group of dogs that never forget to come and tell their mistress when they have had their dinner, feeling sure that she will sympathize with them; and if they have failed to get it, they will notify her immediately of the omission. If you happen to step on a dog's tail or paw, how eagerly—after one irrepressible yelp of pain—will he tell you by his caresses that he knows you did not mean to hurt him and forgives you!

In their relations with one another, also, dogs have a keen sense of etiquette. A well-known traveler makes this unexpected remark about a tribe of naked black men, living on one of the South Sea Islands: "In their everyday intercourse there is much that is stiff, formal, and precise." Almost the same remark might be made about dogs. Unless they are on very intimate terms, they take great pains never to brush against or even to touch one another. For one dog to step over another is a dangerous breach of etiquette unless they are special friends. It is no uncommon thing for two dogs to belong to the same person, and live in the same house, and yet never take the slightest notice of each other. We have a spaniel so dignified that he will never permit another member of the dog family to pillow his head on him; but, with the egotism of a true aristocrat, he does not hesitate to make use of the other dogs for that purpose.

Often canine etiquette is so subtle that one has much difficulty in following it out. In our household are two uncongenial dogs, who, in ordinary circumstances, completely ignore each other, and between whom any familiarity would be resented fiercely. And yet, when we are all out walking, if I am obliged to scold or punish one of these two, the other will run up to the offender, bark at him, and even jostle him, as if he were saying, "Well, old man, you got it that time; aren't you ashamed of yourself?" And the other dog, feeling that he is in the wrong, I suppose, submits meekly to the insult.

A family of six dogs used to pair off in couples, each couple being on terms of special intimacy and affection; and besides these relationships, there were many others among them. For example, they all deferred to the oldest dog, although he was smaller and weaker than the rest. If a fight began, he would jump in between the contestants and stop it; if a dog misbehaved, he would rush at the offender with a warning growl; and this exercise of authority was never resented. The other dogs seemed to respect his weight of years, his character, which was of the highest, and his moral courage, which was undoubted. This same dog—his name was Pedro—had many human traits. He and his companions slept together on a sofa upstairs, where, of a cold night, they would curl up together in an indistinguishable heap. Sometimes the old dog would put himself to bed before the others, and then, finding that he needed the warmth and companionship of their presence, he would go into the hall, put his head between the balusters, and whine softly until they came upstairs to join him.

That animals reason is a fact of everyday experience. That they can communicate their wants and feelings to one another and to man is equally plain. "When a cat or a dog," wrote the late Mr. Romanes, "pulls one's dress to lead one to the kittens or puppies in need of assistance, the animal is behaving in the same manner as a deaf mute might behave when invoking assistance from a friend. That is to say, the animal is translating the logic of feelings into the logic of signs; and so far as this particular action is concerned, it is psychologically indistinguishable from that which is performed by the deaf mute."

Mentally, we are not so many epochs removed from the other animals, and emotionally the connection is closer yet. I will not discuss the question whether dumb animals have any sense of right and wrong. I believe that they have this sense in a rudimentary degree; or at least that it is latent in them, and may be developed. The popular instinctive notions about animals, the result of the experience of the race, seem to justify this view. "If we say a *vicious* horse," remarked Dr. Arnold, "why not a *virtuous* horse?" And we do speak of a "kind" horse.

Moreover, it is obvious that dogs have a sense of humor; and they have also a sense of shame, perfectly distinct from the fear of punishment. Of this sense of shame let me give one example. The dog's eyesight, so far at least as stationary objects are concerned, is very poor, his real reliance being on his sense of smell; and I have often seen a dog mistake one of his own family for a strange animal, run toward him, with every sign of hostility, and then, when he came within a few feet of the other dog, suddenly drop his tail between his legs and slink away, as if he feared that somebody had noticed his absurd mistake.

Can it be that an animal should possess a sense of humor and a sense of shame, without having also some elementary sense of right and wrong? But even if it be thought that he is devoid of that sense, it is certain that he has those kindly impulses from which it has been developed. All that is best in man springs from something which is practically the same in the dog that it is in him, namely, the instinct of pity or benevolence. To that instinct, as it exists in the lower animals, Darwin attributed the origin of conscience in man; and there are now few, if any, philosophers who would give a different account of it.

I have seen a pup not six months old run to comfort another pup that cried out from pain; and the impulse that prompted this act was essentially the same as that which impels the noblest of mankind when they befriend the poor or the afflicted. We are akin to the lower animals morally, as well as physically and mentally.

But this is a modern discovery. It is astonishing and confusing to realize how little organized Christianity has done for the lower animals. The ecclesiastical conception of them was simply that they were creatures without souls, and therefore had no rights as against, or at the hands of, mankind. To this day that conception remains, although it is qualified, of course, by other and more humane considerations. Even Cardinal Newman said:

"We have no duties toward the brute creation; there is no relation of justice between them and us. Of course, we are bound not to treat them ill, for cruelty is an offense against the holy law which our Maker has written on our hearts, and it is displeasing to Him. But they can claim nothing at our hand; into our hand they are absolutely delivered. We may use them, we may destroy them at our pleasure: not our wanton pleasure, but still for our own ends, for our own benefit and satisfaction, provided that we can give a rational account of what we do."

This position, although not perhaps cruel in itself, inevitably results in immeasurable cruelties. When an English traveler remonstrated with a Spanish lady for throwing a sick kitten out of the second-story window, she justified herself by saying that the kitten had no soul; and that is the national point of view.

Protestantism has been almost as indifferent as Catholicism to the lower animals. In fact, the conscience which exists outside of the church, Catholic or Protestant, has in this matter, outstripped the conscience of the church. "Cruelty," said Du Maurier, "is the only unpardonable sin"; and the world is slowly but surely coming to that opinion. The long-deferred awakening of mankind to the sufferings of dumb animals was not due to a decline of the ecclesiastical conception of them, although it has declined; nor even to the new knowledge concerning the common origin of man and beast—indeed, it slightly preceded that knowledge; but it was due to the gradual enlightenment and moral improvement of the race, especially of the English-speaking race.

The nineteenth century, as we are often told, saw more discoveries and inventions than had been made in the preceding six thousand years; but I believe that in future ages not one of those discoveries and inventions, nor all together, will bulk so large as factors in the development and uplifting of man, as will those humane laws and societies which first came into existence in that century.

We overvalue intellectual as compared with moral and emotional gifts. The material civilization upon which we pride ourselves is almost wholly the achievement of the intellect. Fame and wealth, luxury, cultivation, and leisure—all the big prizes of the world, in fact—are obtained by the successful exercise of the intellect. The moral qualities, of themselves, can procure us nothing but a clear conscience, and the approval, perhaps mixed with contempt, of our neighbors.

And yet, when the intellectual qualities are brought to the test of reality; when one's view of them is not clouded by pride, avarice, or passion, then how amazingly does their value shrink and shrivel! When a man lies on his deathbed, for example, his intellectual achievements, though of the highest order, will seem as nothing to him—he will ask himself simply whether he has lived a good or a bad life; and after his death his family and his friends will look at the matter in precisely the same way.

Even the progress of mankind is far more moral than intellectual. Competent authorities tell us that the Anglo-Saxon of to-day is mentally inferior to the Greek who lived two thousand years ago; and if the human race has improved during that time, it is not so much because man has advanced in knowledge as because he has acquired more sympathy with his inferiors, be they brute or human, more generosity, more mercy toward them. Not Stevenson, nor Faraday, nor Morse, nor Fulton, nor Bell did so much for the human race, to say nothing of the other animals, as did that dueling Irishman who, in the year 1822, proposed in the English Parliament, amid shrieks and howls of derision, what afterward became the first law for the protection of dumb animals ever placed on the statute-book of any country. Every movement for the relief of the brute creation has originated in England; and when we damn, as we righteously may, John Bull for one thing and another, let us remember this fact to his eternal honor!

It is hard to part from an old dog-friend with no hope of ever meeting him again, hard to believe that the spirit of love which burned so steadfastly in him is quenched forever. But for those who hold what I have called the ecclesiastical conception of the lower animals, no other view is possible. That devout Catholic and exquisite poet, Dr. Parsons, has beautifully expressed this fact:

When parents die there's many a word to say—
Kind words, consoling—one can always pray.
When children die 't is natural to tell their mother,
"Certainly with them 't is well!"
But for a dog, 't was all the life he had,
Since death is end of dogs, or good or bad.
This was his world, he was contented here;
Imagined nothing better, naught more dear,
Than his young mistress; sought no higher sphere.
Having no sin, asked not to be forgiven;
Ne'er guessed at God nor ever dreamed of heaven.
Now he has passed away, so much of love
Goes from our life, without one hope above!

But is there no hope? Is there not as much—or, if the reader prefers,
as little—hope for the dog as there is for man? I remember reading years
ago in a prominent magazine the statement that doubtless a few men, the
very wickedest, will become extinct at death, whereas the rest of mankind
will be immortal. This view had some adherents then, but would now be
regarded by almost everybody as irrational. Who can believe that between
the best and the worst man there is any such gulf as would justify so diverse a fate! Moreover we have learned that there are no chasms or jumps
in nature. One thing slides into another; every creature is a link between
two other creatures; and man himself can be traced back physically, mentally, and morally, to the lower animals. Is it not then reasonable to suppose that immortality belongs to all forms of life or to none? That if man
is immortal, the dog is immortal, too? Even to speculate upon this subject
seems almost ridiculous, our knowledge is so limited; and yet it is hard
to refrain from speculation. The transmigration of souls may be a fact, or
men and dogs and all other forms of life may be simply forms, temporary
phases, proceeding from one source, and returning thereto. But alas, every
supposition that we can make is rendered almost, if not quite, untenable
by the mere fact that the human intellect has conceived it—it is so un-
likely that we should hit upon the right solution!

In this situation, what we seem bound to do is to refrain from hasty and especially from egotistic conclusions, to keep our minds open, to regard the lower animals, not only with pity, but with a certain reverence. We do not know what or whence they are; but we do know that their nature resembles ours; that they have individuality, as we have it; that they feel pain, both physical and mental; that they are capable of affection; that, although innocent, as we believe, their sufferings have been, and are, unspeakable. Is there no mystery here?

To many men, to most men, perhaps, a dog is simply an animated machine, developed or created for the convenience of the human race. It may be so; and yet again it may be that the dog has his own rightful place in the universe, irrespective and independent of man, and that an injury done to him is an insult to the Creator.

24

Show Time

by Walter A. Dyer

We haven't been hearing much about show dogs in our previous chapters. But here they come—on stage front and center.

DURING THE WINTER THE WILLOWDALE DOGS HAD AGAIN WON BENCH-show honors in New York, Boston, and elsewhere, and Mr. Hartshorn and Tom Poultice were now getting some of them in shape for the smaller outdoor shows of the summer season. Several of the boys made a pilgrimage to Thornboro one day early in June and found Tom engaged in combing the soft, puppy hair out of the coat of one of the young Airedales.

"Why do you do that?" asked Elliot Garfield.

"It does seem foolish, doesn't it?" said Tom. "Well, you see a Hairedale is supposed to 'ave a short, stiff coat, and if you put one in the ring with a lot of this soft 'air on him, the judge won't look twice at 'im."

"Are you going to show this one?" asked Ernest Whipple.

"Yep," said Tom. "'E goes to Mineola next week. It'll be his first show. I don't know what his chances are. Mineola usually has a lot of good dogs. It's near New York and it's one of the biggest of the country shows. We usually try out the youngsters and the second-string dogs on these summer shows and keep the best ones for the big winter shows. Then we 'ave a chance to see 'ow they size up. If a dog wins ribbons enough in the summer shows we figure he's qualified for the big ones next winter. Sometimes a dog can win his championship without ever seeing the inside of Madison Square Garden. He has to be shown a lot of times, that's all, and win pretty regular."

"It isn't so hard to win at the summer shows, is it?" asked Theron Hammond.

"Oh, my, no," said Tom. "Sometimes when the classes are small it's a cinch. Take a rare kind of dog and he's apt to 'ave no competition."

"I wonder if any of our dogs would have a chance at one of the summer shows," said Jack, with suppressed eagerness in his voice.

"I don't know why not," Tom responded.

That started the boys thinking and talking, and a week later they trooped out to see Mr. Hartshorn about it. Half the boys in town had decided that they wanted to show their dogs, and Mr. Hartshorn was at first inclined to discourage them all.

"It's quite a job, taking dogs to a show and caring for them there, and it costs something," said he. "You have some good dogs—in fact, they're all fine fellows—but not many of them are of the show type. You would find the competition somewhat different from that in Morton's barn. I don't believe your parents would thank me for encouraging you to enter dogs that haven't a good chance at the ribbons, and I'm sure I would hesitate to be responsible for looking after a gang of you."

"But couldn't a few of the dogs be tried?" asked Jack Whipple. Mr. Hartshorn looked into the lad's eager, bright eyes and smiled. "Perhaps," said he. "Let me think it over."

As a matter of fact it was Mr. Hartshorn's desire not to seem to show favoritism that made him speak that way. For his own part he would like nothing better than to see Remus and one or two of the other dogs have a try at the ribbons, and his wife urged him to give them a chance. The outcome of it was that most of the boys were dissuaded, with quiet friendliness, from attempting the useless venture, while five dogs were eventually entered in the show of the Massatucket Kennel Club, to be held at Welden, some fifty miles from Boytown, in July. These five were Romulus, Remus, Alert, Hamlet, and Rover. These Mr. Hartshorn thought would stand the best chance of winning something. The Old English sheepdog was entered under his original name of Darley's Launcelot of Middlesex, and for once Elliot Garfield was proud of the name.

Mr. Hartshorn knew he had quite a handful of boys and dogs to look after, but Mrs. Hartshorn said she would help, while Tom Poultice took sole charge of the half-dozen Willowdale dogs that were also entered.

The Willowdale dogs were shipped ahead in crates, as usual. So was little Alert. The masters of the other four dogs, however, objected to a form of confinement which the dogs couldn't understand, and it was arranged that the boys should take the dogs with them in the baggage car. Theron Hammond courteously offered to accompany Mrs. Hartshorn in the coach and Tom Poultice took an earlier train, so the baggage car party consisted of Romulus, Remus, Hamlet, Rover, Mr. Hartshorn, Ernest and Jack Whipple, Herbie Pierson, and Elliot Garfield. It was fortunate that only half a car-load of baggage was traveling that day, or they might not have been able to crowd in. As it was, they managed to find seats on various boxes and trunks and made themselves fairly comfortable. The dogs, with their masters for company, were content, after the first sense of strangeness had worn off.

"I understand," said Mr. Hartshorn, after the train had started, "that about five hundred dogs are entered, so it ought to be a fairly representative show. It won't be like New York, of course, but you ought to have a chance to see good dogs of most of the well-known breeds. And the dogs at an outdoor show are usually happier and less nervous than if they were cooped up for two or three days in a crowded hall and compelled to spend their nights there. There are really serious objections to the big indoor shows. More danger of spreading distemper and other diseases, too, than at the outdoor shows."

"Do you think we will see any of the famous champions there?" asked Herbie.

"Yes," said Mr. Hartshorn, "I believe some of the crack Sealyhams and wire-haired fox terriers are entered, and there's sure to be a good showing of Boston terriers. Alert will be in fast company.

"The wires are always worth seeing," said he, after a pause. "It was a white bull terrier that won best of all breeds in New York last winter, but during the last half-dozen years wire-haired fox terriers have won two-thirds of the first honors. The breeders seem to have nearly achieved perfection with this variety. Matford Vic, Wireboy of Paignton, Wycollar Boy, and several others have been almost perfect specimens. But you never can tell. Their day may be passing, and for the next few years it may be Airedales or bulldogs, or almost any other breed that will force its way to the top. That's one of the interesting features of the dog-show game. Then sometimes you find all predictions upset, and all the big dogs beaten by a greyhound or an Old English sheepdog. There's always a chance for everybody."

As the train pulled up at a station somewhere along the line, a man entered the baggage car with a brace of beagles on a leash. Nice little dogs, they were, with friendly eyes and beautiful faces.

"Is the baggage man here?" asked the man.

"I haven't seen him lately," said Mr. Hartshorn. "Is there anything we can do for you?"

"Why, yes," said the man. "I'm sending these dogs down to Welden. There'll be someone to call for them there. You look as though you might be bound for that place yourselves, and if you could keep an eye on these dogs it would be a great favor."

"We'll do so with pleasure," said Mr. Hartshorn.

"What are their names?" asked Ernest.

"Tippecanoe and Tyler Too," he answered. "I'm entering them as singles and as a brace, and I think I stand a pretty good show."

The baggage man came along, and by the time the owner of the beagles had arranged for their shipment, the train was ready to start again.

"It's lucky you were here to take them," said the man, "or I shouldn't have been able to send them this way. Good-by and good luck."

"Good-by," they shouted, and proceeded to get acquainted with the beagles.

"They're like small hounds, aren't they?" said Jack.

"Yes," said Mr. Hartshorn, "they are really hounds."

"Oh," said Ernest, "that makes me think. You never told us about the hound breeds, and you said you would sometime. Couldn't you do it now?"

"Let's see," said Mr. Hartshorn, opening his grip. "Ah, yes, here it is." He took out a small paper-covered book containing the standards of the different breeds. "I always mean to take this with me to the shows. Without my books I can't always remember the facts, but with the help of this I guess I can make out.

"Now there still remain the hound and greyhound families to be covered. They are both hounds, in a way, but they have been distinct for centuries. They are both very old types of dogs.

"We will begin with the bloodhound because he's the biggest. There are a lot of people who have got their ideas about the bloodhound from 'Uncle Tom's Cabin,' and there are places where you aren't allowed to keep a bloodhound because the breed is supposed to be so dangerous and ferocious. But that is a great injustice. The true English bloodhound is not the mongrel beast that was used in slavery days, but is a finely developed and reliable dog. Contrary to the general belief, the modern bloodhound is not ferocious, but gentle and affectionate, almost shy. He is a wonderful trailer and has often been successfully used to find both criminals and lost persons, but he does not attack them when he finds them.

"The otter hound is an English dog not common with us. He has a unique appearance, something like a bloodhound in a rough coat, with a face not unlike that of an Airedale terrier or a wire-haired pointing griffon. He is a steady and methodical hunter, sure on the trail, a strong swimmer, brave, patient, and affectionate.

"The foxhound is the most popular sporting dog of England, his history being bound up with that of British hunting. I guess you know what a foxhound looks like. The American Kennel Club recognizes two separate classes of foxhounds, the English and the American. The latter is, of course, native bred, and is somewhat smaller and lighter in bone than the English hound. The so-called American coon-hound is a dog of the fox-hound type and of foxhound origin, bred carelessly as to type, but trained to hunt the raccoon and opossum.

"The name harrier was first given somewhat indiscriminately to all English hunting hounds before the foxhound was highly developed. Later the harrier was developed as a separate breed for hunting hares. It is now rare in England and there are almost no harriers in the United States. The beagle is like a smaller, finer foxhound, and has the same ancestry. He is a good, all-round sporting dog, and a good-looking fellow, as you see, with a solid build, a rugged appearance, and a fine face.

"The dachshund (don't call it dash-hund) is a canine dwarf best known for his absurdly disproportionate appearance, but he is a most attractive, serviceable little dog. He was evolved long ago from the hounds of Germany for the special work of hunting the badger. His bent forelegs and queer proportions are really deformities scientifically bred. The dachshund has a wonderful nose and is a good worker with foxes as well as with ground animals, though his peculiar build best fits him for the latter. He is a clean, companionable house dog, affectionate and spirited. The basset is a short-legged French hound resembling the German dachshund, to which it is doubtless related. We are not familiar with the breed in this country. It looks like a large dachshund with a bloodhound head."

"Do you know any good hound stories?" asked Jack, who was fondling the long, velvety ears of the two beagles.

"Not many," said Mr. Hartshorn. "Most of the foxhound stories I have heard have illustrated the sagacity and cleverness of the fox rather than that of the hound. There are also one or two stories that show that the hound has a strong homing instinct like that of some of the other breeds. The only foxhound anecdote of an amusing nature that I recall is told of one that was owned by a strict Roman Catholic. Whenever Lent arrived, this dog always ran away and paid a round of visits on Protestant acquaintances until Easter ushered in a period of more varied menus at home. This hound was not trained with a pack but was kept as a single pet, which accounts for his marked personality, more like that of a terrier than of a hound.

"I have read a number of accounts in the newspapers describing rescues by bloodhounds. I remember one was about a Brooklyn girl who wandered away from a hotel and was lost on a mountain in Vermont. A famous bloodhound was brought over from Fairhaven and was allowed to smell of a handkerchief belonging to the girl. He took up her trail at the village store and followed it along roads where horses and automobiles had been, through two other villages, and into the woods, and he at last found the girl on the verge of exhaustion far up the mountainside.

"Another bloodhound in California found a lost child at the edge of a cliff in a dense fog and drew him back from the precipice just in time. Most of the bloodhound stories are of that nature, though there are some that have to do with the trailing of criminals.

"One of the classic stories of literature is that of the hound of Montargis. He may have been a St. Hubert hound, or one of the other French hounds, though I have always suspected that he may have been a mâtin or dog of the Great Dane type. But the breed is a matter of minor importance. The main features of the story are somewhat as follows:

"There were once two officers of the King's bodyguard in France named Macaire and Montdidier. Fast friends at first, they became bitter enemies and rivals, and one day in the Forest of Bondi, near Paris, after a violent quarrel, Macaire drew his sword and slew Montdidier and buried his body in the woods.

"Now Montdidier owned a faithful hound who came to search for him. He traced him to the grave and there he remained until he was nearly famished. The poets would have us believe that the dog reached the conclusion that his master had been slain, that he discovered the scent of the murderer, and that he set out in quest of vengeance. At any rate, he went to the home of a friend of his dead master's and was given food. He attached himself to this household but went often to the grave.

"Of course, Montdidier's comrades soon missed him and his absence was reported to Charles V, the King. Foul play was suspected and the King ordered an investigation, but no evidence was forthcoming. Meanwhile Montdidier's friend had also become suspicious and one day he followed the hound to the grave. Observing the dog's actions, he surmised what must be there. He reported the matter to the King who had the body exhumed and discovered marks of violence.

"On several occasions after that the hound attempted to attack Macaire but was prevented from doing him injury. He was entirely peaceable toward everybody else, so that these circumstances were noticed. Guardsmen remembered that Macaire and Montdidier had quarreled, and suspicion fastened itself upon Macaire. The King was told of all this, and he himself observed the actions of the hound when he was brought near his master's murderer.

"In those days it was sometimes the custom for judges to settle a dispute by ordering the contestants to fight a duel. King Charles decided to adopt this method in an effort to determine whether or not Macaire was guilty, and he ordered a trial combat to take place between the man and the dog at the Château of Montargis on the Isle of Notre Dame, Paris. The man was given a stout cudgel as his only weapon, while the dog was provided with an empty cask into which he might retreat if too hard pressed.

"The battle was a terrible one, Macaire fighting for his life and the dog to revenge his dead master. The hound paid no heed to the blows that were rained upon him, but attacked blindly. At last he got a firm grip on the man's throat and hung on. Macaire, weakening and terrified, begged to be rescued and confessed his guilt. The dog was dragged away at last and the gallows robbed him of his revenge."

"Whew!" exclaimed Herbie Pierson. "Some story! Got any more like that, Mr. Hartshorn?"

"Half a dozen of them," replied Mr. Hartshorn with a laugh, "but they'll have to wait till another time, as I believe we are nearing our destination. For the same reason I must postpone telling you about the dogs of the greyhound family. Here we are, boys."

Tom Poultice was waiting for them at the Welden station, and so was the man who had come for the two beagles. Under Tom's guidance they walked out to the fair grounds, which were only a mile away. This was to be the scene of the show, and there were already a number of dogs and crates about.

"I've arranged to stay out 'ere," said Tom. "There's an 'ouse where I can sleep, and I can look after all the dogs."

They looked around the grounds a bit. Mr. Hartshorn found the superintendent of the show and had a few words with him, and then they all returned to town, leaving the dogs in Tom's care. They were all well acquainted with him and did not feel that they were being left among total strangers.

They registered at the hotel, which they found to be overcrowded. An extra cot was placed in one of the rooms, and Ernest, Jack, and Elliot were assigned to it. They did not consider the situation to be any hardship. They enjoyed a good dinner in the dining-room and then gathered in Mr. Hartshorn's room for a talk.

After discussing dog shows some more and speculating as to the outcome of the morrow's contests. Ernest, whose thirst for dog learning was insatiable, reminded Mr. Hartshorn of his promise to tell them about the breeds of the greyhound family.

"The greyhound proper," said he, "is of course the first to be considered. It is perhaps the oldest distinct type of dog now in existence. Likenesses of greyhounds are to be seen in relics of Assyrian, Egyptian, Greek, and Roman sculpture, and the type has altered surprisingly little in seven thousand years. It was developed for great speed from the first and was used in the chase. Unlike the other hounds, the dogs of the greyhound family hunt by sight and not by scent.

"The whippet is merely a smaller greyhound, but has been bred as a separate variety for upward of a century. On a short course the whippet is faster than a racehorse, covering the usual 200 yards in about 12 seconds. Whippet racing as a sport has never taken hold in America and we have comparatively few of the breed here. You have already been told about the Italian greyhound. It belongs to the greyhound family but is classed as a toy.

"Although speed is the thing for which the greyhound is most famous, stories have been told which illustrate the breed's fidelity and sagacity when his master makes a comrade of him. I will tell you one of these tales. A French officer named St. Leger was imprisoned in Vincennes, near Paris, during the wars of St. Bartholomew. He had a female greyhound that was his dearest friend and he asked to have her brought to him in prison. This request was denied and the dog was sent back to St. Leger's home in the Rue des Lions St. Paul. She would not remain there, however, and at the first opportunity she returned to the prison and barked outside the walls. When she came under her master's window, he tossed a piece of bread out to her, and in this way she discovered where he was.

"She contrived to visit him every day, and incidentally she won the admiration and affection of one of the jailers, who smuggled her in occasionally to see her master. St. Leger was at last released, but his health was broken and in six months he died. The dog grieved for him and would not be comforted by any of the members of the household. At last she ran away and attached herself to the jailer who had befriended her and her master, and with him she lived happily till the day of her death.

"Now we come to one of the grandest breeds of all—the Irish wolfhound. It is a breed of great antiquity and of great size and power. The Latin writer Pliny speaks of it as *canis graius Hibernicus*, and in Ireland it was known as *sagh clium* or wolf dog. For in ancient Ireland there were huge wolves and also enormous elk, and the great dogs were used to hunt them. These hounds were even used in battle in the old days of the Irish kings.

"Two classic stories are told of the Irish wolfhound. One is of the hound of Aughrim. There was an Irish knight or officer who had his wolfhound with him at the battle of Aughrim, and together they slew many of the enemy. But at last the master himself was killed. He was stripped and left on the battlefield to be devoured by wolves. But his faithful dog never left him. He remained at his side day and night, feeding on other dead bodies on the battlefield, but allowing neither man nor beast to come near that of his master until nothing was left of it but a pile of whitening bones. Then he was forced to go farther away in search of food, but from July till January he never failed to return to the bones of his master every night. One evening some soldiers crossed the battlefield, and one of them came over to see what manner of beast the wolfhound was. The dog, thinking his master's bones were about to be disturbed, attacked the soldier, who called loudly for help. Another soldier came running up and shot the faithful dog.

"The other story is that of devoted Gelert which you may have heard. Robert Spencer made a poem or ballad of it."

"I've never heard it," said Jack Whipple.

"Nor I," said Elliot Garfield.

"Well," said Mr. Hartshorn, "it's a rather tragic story. Put into plain and unadorned prose, it runs something like this: Gelert was an Irish wolfhound of great strength and great intelligence that had been presented by

King John in 1205 to Llewelyn the Great, who lived near the base of Snowdon Mountain. Gelert became devoted to his master and at night 'sentinel'd his master's bed,' as the poem has it. By day he hunted with him.

"One day, however, Gelert did not appear at the chase and when Llewelyn came home he was angry with the dog for failing him. He was in that frame of mind when he met Gelert coming out of the chamber of his child. The dog was covered with blood. Llewelyn rushed into the room and discovered the bed overturned, the coverlet stained with gore, and the child missing. He called to the boy but got no response.

"Believing that there was but one interpretation for all this, Llewelyn called Gelert to him and in his wrath thrust his sword through the dog's body. Gelert gave a great cry of anguish that sounded almost human, and then, with his eyes fixed reproachfully on his slayer's face, he died. Then another cry was heard—that of the child, who had been awakened from sleep by the shriek of the dying dog. Llewelyn rushed forward and found the child safe and unscratched in a closet where he had fallen asleep. The father hurried back to the bloody bed, and beneath it he found the dead body of a huge gray wolf which told the whole story. In remorse Llewelyn erected a tomb and chapel to the memory of faithful Gelert and the place is called Beth Gelert to this day."

There was a suspicious moisture about more than one pair of eyes as Mr. Hartshorn finished this narrative, and he hurried on to less tragic matters.

"The Irish wolfhound is to-day a splendid animal," said he, "and the breed deserves to be better known in this country. It has had an interesting history. There was a time when it nearly died out in Ireland, and the modern breed was started with the remnants some fifty years ago, with the help of Great Dane and Scottish deerhound crosses. The new breed was not thoroughly established, however, until the latter part of the last century. As a made breed, so called, it is a remarkable example of what can be accomplished by patient, scientific breeding. The Irish wolfhound is a big, active, sagacious, wonderfully companionable dog, muscular and graceful, and as full of fun as a terrier.

"The Scottish deerhound is similar in most respects to the Irish wolfhound, but is lighter, speedier, and less powerful. They have a common ancestry, though the two breeds were distinct as long ago as the twelfth century. The breed was a favorite with Sir Walter Scott.

"The Russian wolfhound, known in Russia as the borzoi, is one of the most graceful and aristocratic of all the breeds, combining speed, strength, symmetry, and a beautiful coat. He has been used for centuries in Russia for hunting wolves and has been bred as the sporting dog of the aristocracy."

"It makes a dog show a lot more interesting to know something about the different breeds," said Ernest Whipple.

"Of course it does," said Mr. Hartshorn. "And if I am not mistaken, I have told you something about almost every breed that you will ever be likely to see at a dog show or anywhere else."

Soon afterward they separated for the night.

The Boytown party was at the fair grounds long before the show opened the following morning, and you may be sure the dogs were glad to see their masters, though they had been well cared for by Tom.

Though technically an outdoor show, there was room for all the dogs in the commodious cattle-show sheds in case of rain. The weather promised to be fair and warm, however, so only the smaller dogs and some of the larger short-coated ones were benched inside, where they had plenty of room and plenty of ventilation. The collies and Old English sheepdogs were tied in a row in the shade of some maple trees at one side of the grounds, and the rough-coated terriers, the setters, and some of the other breeds were also outside. The boys found the places reserved for their dogs and saw to it that they were properly and comfortably benched.

When the show opened and the spectators began to arrive, the Boytown dogs were at first nervous and excited and could not bear to have their masters leave them. After an hour or two, however, they became accustomed to their surroundings, and leaving them in charge of Tom Poultice, the boys made the rounds of the show under the guidance of Mr. Hartshorn.

It was a most interesting experience for them. Some of the breeds were of course familiar to them, and Mr. Hartshorn called attention to their points and showed how some of the dogs back home fell short of conforming to the requirements of the standard. In some instances they recognized breeds that Mr. Hartshorn had told them about but which they had never seen before. There were, for example, a Scottish deerhound, an Irish water spaniel, and some cairn terriers. As Mr. Hartshorn had predicted, there were noteworthy entries of Sealyhams, wire-haired fox terriers, and Boston terriers, and particularly interesting exhibits of bulldogs and chows. There was one dog that puzzled them—a white dog with fluffy coat and bright eyes. The catalogue stated that it was a Samoyede.

"What is a Samoyede, Mr. Hartshorn?" asked Herbie Parsons. "I don't think I ever heard of that kind."

"That's so," said Mr. Hartshorn. "I guess I never told you about the Arctic breeds. This is one of them. They're not very common."

There were individual dogs, too, that demanded special attention, friendly dogs that wanted to shake hands and be patted and that begged the boys to stay with them. This encouraged loitering and made the circuit of the benches quite a protracted affair. Mr. Hartshorn had warned them about approaching the dogs without an introduction.

"There are always some dogs that aren't to be trusted," said he, "and as the day wears on and they get more and more nervous, they may snap. It's always well to be cautious at a dog show, no matter how well you understand dogs. Never make a quick motion toward a dog or try to put your hand on the top of his head at first. Reach your hand out toward him quietly and let him sniff at the back of it. Then you can soon tell whether he invites further advances or not."

The boys became so absorbed in trying out this form of introduction that it was noon before they had finished visiting all the benches. Mrs. Hartshorn insisted on having luncheon.

"I'm hungry if no one else is," said she.

The five boys suddenly discovered that they were hungry, too. Mr. Hartshorn led them to a restaurant on the grounds and ordered the meal. It might have been better, but the boys were not critical. When they had finished eating they went out and sat for a little while in the shade of some trees, not far from the collies, and watched the people.

"Now I'll tell you about those Arctic breeds," said Mr. Hartshorn, "and get that off my mind."

It was very warm, and they were all glad of a little chance to rest. It is tiring to walk around a dog show and one becomes more weary than one realizes. The boys stretched themselves out on the grass and listened to Mr. Hartshorn's words mingled with the barking of the dogs in all keys.

"It won't take very long to tell about these northern breeds," he began. "Their natural habitat is in the Arctic and sub-Arctic regions of Asia, Europe, Greenland, and North America. They are probably related to the Arctic wolf and they are generally used in those countries as sledge dogs.

"The spitz dog found his way down from the cold countries long ago, but he still retains some of his racial characteristics. The proper name for the one occasionally seen here is the wolfspitz. He is the largest of the spitz family, of which the Pomeranian is the miniature member.

"The Samoyede or laika is the sledge dog of northern Russia and western Siberia and was used by Nansen in his explorations. Next to the wolfspitz, the Samoyede is the most attractive and domestic of the Arctic breeds and has acquired some popularity among American fanciers, especially the white ones.

"The Norwegian elkhound is used as a bird dog as well as for hunting big game in Scandinavia. It is not a hound at all, but a general utility dog of the Arctic type, dating back to the days of the Vikings. A few have been shown in this country.

"The Eskimo dog is larger than the Samoyede and is nearer to the wolf in type. He has long been known as a distinct breed, being a native of Greenland and northern Canada, and was used by Peary, the Arctic explorer. The breed has occasionally been shown in the United States.

"There are also a number of loosely bred sledge dogs in North America, including the Canadian husky and the malamutes and Siwash dogs of Alaska. The husky is a powerful dog, weighing 125 pounds or more, and is the common draught dog of Canada. He is said to be the result of a cross between the Arctic wolf and the Eskimo dog."

"He sounds rather unattractive to me," said Mrs. Hartshorn.

"Well, he is, as a pet," said her husband, "but he is a wonderfully useful animal in his own country. Is everybody rested now? I imagine we'd better be going back. I want to be on hand when they judge the Airedales."

The party rose and trooped back to the sheds. At intervals during the afternoon they visited their own dogs and before night they had finished their rounds of the show, but a good share of the time was spent in the vicinity of the judging rings. These were two roped-off enclosures on the open lawn, with camp chairs arranged about them for the ladies. At all times there was a goodly gathering about the rings of people whose interest was in the outcome of the judging. Considering the fact that there was no lively action like that of a field trial or an athletic contest, it was remarkable how much excitement could be derived from these quiet competitions. When a favorite dog was given the blue ribbon there was much hand-clapping and a little cheering, and the boys heard very little complaining or rebellion against the decisions of the judges. Dog fanciers are, for the most part, good sports.

The Airedales were judged among the first, and as usual the Willowdale dogs, skilfully exhibited by Tom Poultice, bore off their fair share of the honors. Soon the Boston terriers were called for. This was Theron Hammond's big moment, and when Alert was awarded second prize in the novice class, Theron was warmly congratulated by friends and strangers alike, for there were a lot of good dogs shown and, as Mr. Hartshorn had said, Alert was in fast company.

Rover, as Darley's Launcelot of Middlesex, had an easier time of it, for only eight Old English sheepdogs were benched and none of the famous kennels were represented here. There were only three dogs in the novice class, and as the other two were second-rate dogs, Rover won first place. He also won third in the open class, but was beaten out by better dogs in the winners contest.

Hamlet, however, didn't win anything. His forelegs weren't straight and the judge took special note of them. He had better dogs against him, and the better dogs won. It was a fair contest, but Herbie was bitterly disappointed.

"Never mind, Herbie," said Jack Whipple, consolingly. "I bet Hamlet is a better dog to own than any of them. That's what I said about Remus when they said he hadn't any nose."

And Herbie, not to be outdone by the younger boy, plucked up spirit and bore his defeat manfully.

It was a two-day show, and the judging of the bird dogs, hounds, and some of the other breeds was put over to the second day. Ernest and Jack, therefore, still had their exciting time ahead of them, but the whole party was tired with so much walking about and watching, and they were glad to turn their dogs over to Tom's care and return to the hotel, with another day of it before them.

"Have you told us about all the breeds there are?" asked Ernest that evening in Mr. Hartshorn's room.

"I believe I have," said Mr. Hartshorn, "except some little known foreign ones."

"Oh, please tell us about those," pleaded Ernest.

Mr. Hartshorn laughed. "You're bound to know it all, aren't you?" said he. "There are a number of European, Asiatic, and Australasian breeds, some of which are very interesting, but you will probably never see any of them and I haven't a list of them with me. When we get back to Boytown, if there are any of you boys that would like to look up these uncommon breeds, just to make your dog knowledge complete, I shall be very glad to lend you a book which contains them all. For instance, there's the German boxer, which has sometimes been shown in this country, and the Pyrenean sheepdog, whose blood is to be found in several of our large breeds, including the St. Bernard and the Irish wolfhound. There are other European sheepdogs and hunting dogs, Asiatic greyhounds, and some queer hairless freaks. When you've looked those all up, you'll know more about dogs than most naturalists do."

"Then if the breeds are all used up, I suppose the anecdotes have all been used up, too," said Jack.

Mr. Hartshorn looked at his watch. "Well, no, not quite all used up," said he. "I have thought of two or three more, and I guess we've got time for one of them to-night. It is about a tradesman of the Rue St. Denis in

Paris, a man named Dumont. He had a very smart dog, but I don't know what kind of dog it was. Perhaps a terrier or a poodle. This dog was great at finding hidden articles. One day Dumont was walking with a friend in the Boulevard St. Antoine and was bragging about his dog. The friend would not believe his statements, so they laid a wager, the master claiming that the dog could find and bring home a six-livre piece hidden anywhere in the dust of the road.

"So the piece of money was hidden in the dust when the dog was not looking, and they went on a mile farther. Then the dog, whose name was Caniche, was told to go back and get the coin, and he promptly started. The friend wished to wait and see how it would come out, but Dumont said, 'No, we will proceed. Caniche will bring the money home.' They accordingly went to Dumont's home and waited, but no dog appeared. The friend asserted that the dog had failed and claimed the wager, but Dumont only said, 'Be patient, *mon ami*; something unexpected has happened to delay him, but he will come.'

"Something unexpected had indeed happened. A traveler from Vincennes came driving along in a chaise soon after Dumont and his friend had passed that way, and his horse accidentally kicked the coin out of the dust. The traveler, seeing it glisten, got out and picked it up, and then drove on to his inn.

"When Caniche came up the money was, of course, not there, but he picked up the traveler's scent and followed his chaise to the inn. Arriving there and finding his man, Caniche proceeded to make friends with him. The traveler, flattered by this attention, and being fond of dogs, said he would like to adopt Caniche, and took him to his room. The dog settled down and appeared to be quite content.

"When bedtime came and the man began to undress, Caniche arose and barked at the door. The man, thinking this was quite natural, opened the door to let him out. Suddenly Caniche turned, seized the man's breeches, which he had just taken off, and bolted out with them. There was a purse full of gold pieces in the breeches, and the traveler dashed after the dog in his nightcap and *sans culottes*, as the French say. Caniche made for home with the angry man after him.

"Arriving at Dumont's house, Caniche gained admittance and deposited the breeches at his master's feet. Just then the owner of the breeches burst in, loudly demanding his property and accusing Dumont of having taught his dog to steal.

"'Softly, softly,' said Dumont. 'Caniche is no thief, and he would not have done this without a reason. You have a coin in these breeches that is not yours.'

"At first the stranger denied this, and then he remembered the coin he had picked up in the Boulevard St. Antoine. Explanations followed, the breeches and gold were restored to the traveler, and the six-livre piece was handed to Caniche, who returned it to his master with the air of one who had fulfilled his duty. Dumont's friend paid his wager and Dumont opened a bottle of wine, and they all drank to the health of the cleverest dog in France.

"Whether that is a true story or not you must judge for yourselves. I have told it as it was told to me, and I prefer not to vouch for it."

Laughing over this story, and thanking Mr. Hartshorn for telling it to them, the boys trooped off to bed.

So far as Ernest and Jack Whipple were concerned, all the interest of the second day of the Massatucket Dog Show centered about the judging of the English setters. They had been studying the entry carefully, and though there were some champions entered in the open and limit classes, and though Mr. Hartshorn pointed out to them the superior qualities of several of these dogs from the fancier's point of view, it seemed to the boys that Romulus and Remus were as good as any dogs there.

"Don't set your hopes too high," cautioned Mr. Hartshorn. "They will be pitted against some good dogs, and I don't want to see you too greatly disappointed. One has to learn to lose in the dog-show game more often than one wins."

"Anyway," said Ernest, "I haven't seen anything in the novice class that can beat them."

At last the hour arrived for the judging of the setters. The puppy class was disposed of first, and then the novices. Ernest and Jack led their own dogs into the ring, with numbers pinned to their coat-sleeves. The two dogs behaved beautifully, holding up their heads and standing at attention, as their masters had patiently taught them to do. They were both in good condition, their eyes bright and their coats soft and glossy. It was quite evident to the spectators about the ring that the other dogs in the novice class were not to be compared with them. Ernest and Jack were quite unconscious of the fact that they were being observed as much as the dogs and that there were some people present who admired their bright eyes as much as those of Romulus and Remus. But it was the judge of this class that held their fixed attention. He was a brusque, dour-looking man, without a smile for anybody, but he had a reputation for strict impartiality and for a true judgment of dog-flesh. It did not take him long to reach his decision. With no word of congratulation, he handed Jack a blue ribbon and Ernest a red one and ushered them out of the ring.

"The Remus dog has the best head and most shapely body," was all that he said.

But the spectators clapped and showered congratulations upon the boys, and they were very happy.

"I knew it, I knew it!" cried Jack in an ecstasy of triumph. "Nose doesn't count in the show ring, and Remus is, in every other way, the best dog in the world. I told you he'd have his day. Good old Remus!"

And right before all those people he leaned down and hugged his dog and kissed him on the silky ear.

But that was only the beginning. Remus also took first in the open class, which was more than Mr. Hartshorn had hoped for, and Romulus took third. And when it came to the final contest of the winners, Remus won reserve to Ch. The Marquis, a dog that had won his spurs in the biggest shows in the country. He was the only dog in this bunch that could beat Remus, and there were those who affirmed that in another year Remus would defeat him.

Ernest showed himself to be a good sport and was glad that Remus had won. Jack communicated his high spirits to the other boys, and by the time the afternoon was over they were in a hilarious mood and eager to bring their trophies back to Boytown. They forgot their weariness, and as the spectators began to leave the grounds, and it was proper to release the dogs, they started off pell-mell, across the central oval of the race track, boys and dogs together, shouting and barking in a gladsome chorus. It was a goodly sight for some of the grown-ups to see, and they paused to watch the frolic.

"I'm so glad Remus won," said Mrs. Hartshorn, smiling upon them all.

"Yes," responded her husband, "Jacky deserved it. He has stood by his dog through thick and thin."

As the boys and dogs came romping back, Mrs. Hartshorn observed, "Youth is a wonderful thing."

"Sometimes," said her husband, "I think it is a greater thing than wisdom."

Perhaps a vision of her own youth came back to her, for she leaned against her husband's arm and softly quoted:

"When all the world is young, lad,
And all the fields are green,
And every goose a swan, lad,
And every lass a queen;
Then hey, for boot and horse, lad!
Around the world away!
Young blood must have its course, lad,
And every dog his day."

25

Douglas

by Sarah Knowles Bolton

"The Story of Douglas," by Sarah Knowles Bolton, is from A Country Idyll and Other Stories, *Thomas Crowell & Co., New York, 1898.*

DOUGLAS WAS A SHAGGY BLACK PUPPY, ONE OF A FAMILY OF ELEVEN, ALL of them yellow and white but himself. His fur, when you pushed it apart, showed its yellow color near the skin, revealing what he really was—a St. Bernard.

He was the most gentle of all the puppies, and would not fight his way at the dish when the others clamored for their bread and milk, but stood apart and looked up to his mistress with a beseeching and sometimes aggrieved air. From the first he seemed to hunger for human affection, and would cry to be held in one's lap, or follow one about the house or the grounds like a petted kitten.

When quarrels took place between some members of the large family Douglas never joined, but hastened to tell it by his bark, that the disturbance might be quelled. When finally the puppies went to various homes, Douglas became the property of a lady who, not having children, loved him almost as a child.

He followed her up and down stairs and lay at her feet if she read. The house was well furnished, but not too good to be used and enjoyed. Douglas was not put out of doors at night to whine in the rain or sleet, or even into a barn, and wisely, for he saved the house once from very unwelcome intruders.

He gambolled beside his mistress if she walked in the woods, and when she was ill he was constantly at her bedside, refusing to eat, and seeming to suffer in her suffering. When she was unavoidably absent, Douglas cried and walked the floor, and if allowed to go out of doors howled and waited on the hillside for her return.

Once when at the seashore he followed her without her knowledge, and plunged into the bay after her steamer. He swam till well-nigh exhausted, his agonized owner fearing every minute that he would sink, while she besought the men to stop the boat. Finally he was rescued, and though he could scarcely move, the glad look in his eyes and the wag of his tail told as plainly as words the joy of the reunion.

No amount of money could buy the companionable creature. He never wearied one by talk; he never showed anger, perhaps because no one spoke angrily to him. Some persons like to show authority, even over a dog, and talk loud and harsh, but Douglas's owner was too wise and too good for this. Kindness begot kindness, and the puppy who longed for love appreciated it none the less when he was grown, and could protect the woman who loved him.

One autumn day, just before leaving her country home for the city, Miss Benson was obliged to return to town for a half day. "Good-by, dear Douglas," she said in her usual way. "I shall come home soon," and the unwilling creature followed her with his brown eyes, and whined that he could not go also. Later in the afternoon he was let out of doors, and soon disappeared.

When Miss Benson returned her first word was, "Douglas! Douglas!" but there was no response to her call. He had followed her, had lost the trail, and had gone too far to find his way back to his home. In vain she called for her pet. She left the door ajar, hoping at nightfall she should hear the patter of his feet, or his eager bark to come in, but he did not come. She wondered where he slept, if he slept at all; thought a dozen times in the night that she heard him crying at the door; imagined him moaning for her, or, supperless and exhausted, lying down by the roadside, to wait for the sunrise to begin his fruitless journey.

Douglas had become that sad thing, a lost dog. He belonged to nobody now, and both owner and dog were desolate. Miss Benson could scarcely go about her work. She spent days in searching, and hired others to search, but all was useless. For weeks she thought Douglas might possibly come back. If she could know that he was dead, that even would be a consolation; but to fear he was cold and hungry, to realize that the world is all too indifferent to animals, unless perchance they are our own, to imagine he might be in some medical college, the victim of the surgeon's knife—all this was bitter in the extreme. Weeping and searching did no good, and finally the inevitable had to be accepted, though the sadness in Miss Benson's heart did not fade out.

As is ever the case, those of us who have lost something precious become more tender and helpful in a world full of losses. Miss Benson welcomed and cared for every stray animal that she found, perhaps never quite giving up the hope that she would see gentle, great-hearted Douglas again.

And what of Douglas? He ran fast at first, eager to overtake the one to whom he was passionately devoted. She had been gone so long that he soon lost track of her footsteps, and then with a dazed look he began to howl, hoping that she would hear his voice. He lay down to rest, but it was growing dark and he was hungry.

He stopped at a large house and the servants drove him away. He was unused to this, but he dragged himself along to the next place. Here a kind woman gave him something to eat, and would have made him welcome for the night, but he would not stay after he had eaten. He must needs wander on, hoping to find his home and his beloved mistress. All night long he tramped, lying down now and then by the side of the road to rest a few minutes.

The next day was a hard one. He was beginning to realize that he was lost. He ran more slowly, looked eagerly at every passer-by, and seemed half demented. At night he stopped at a home where the lights had just been lighted, and some pretty children seemed flitting from room to room. He whined at the back door.

A flaxen-haired little girl opened it. "Oh, mamma," said the child, "here is a big black dog, and I know he is hungry! May I feed him?"

"No," replied the woman, "take a whip and send him off. I will have no lean stray dogs about this house."

"But he looks hungry, mother," pleaded little Emma Bascomb, "and I know he won't bite."

Mrs. Bascomb, pity it is to tell it, was a very pious person, never failing to be present at prayer-meetings, always deeply interested in the heathen, and most helpful at sewing societies of the church. She never fed stray cats or dogs, as she did not wish them to stay at her house. She did not remember that God made them, and that He lets not a sparrow fall to the ground without His notice, and she forgot that she was to emulate Him. Mrs. Bascomb varied her treatment of stray dogs and cats. Sometimes she used a long black whip, sometimes pails of water. On this occasion she threw on Douglas, already weak and hungry, a pail of cold water, and sent him frightened and hurt away from her door.

Emma protested. "When I have a home of my own, mamma," she said, "I will never turn away a dog or a cat hungry." The child knew that it was useless to say more, as a stray cat had stayed about the house for a week, and Mrs. Bascomb had refused to feed it, burning up the scraps from the table lest some starving animal might be tempted to remain. And yet the Bascombs had family prayers, and asked God to provide clothes for the needy and food for the hungry!

Douglas was beginning to learn the sorrows of the poor and homeless. He longed to see some familiar face, to hear some familiar voice. He went on and on, and it began to rain. It was almost sleet, and the dog, used to a warm fire, shivered and longed for shelter. Approaching a large rambling house with a shed attached, Douglas ran under it for cover, and crouched down at the side under a bench. A man came out with a lamp. Evidently he had been drinking, for his step was unsteady. He had come out to close the shed door, and espying the dog gave him a kick with his hard boot.

"Get out, you scoundrel! What are you doing here?" he said gruffly, and poor Douglas ran as though a gun had been fired at him.

"Oh, if there were only a home for such lost ones!" he must have thought; but there was none, and again the hungry and wet dog travelled on. A wagon soon passed with two men in it, and Douglas followed, hoping it would lead to a home for him. "Whip him off," said one of the men to the other. "We've got two dogs already, and my wife would never allow a third," and they brandished the whip in the rear and drove on. Douglas crawled under a tree, and rolling himself as nearly as he could into a round ball for warmth finally fell asleep.

In the morning he started again on his toilsome journey. He was lame now and half sick. Soon the houses were nearer together, and Douglas realized that he was coming into a city. He did not know there was little room for dogs in an overcrowded, fashionable city. There was little green grass to roam over, and the rushing world did not want the bother of animals. Perhaps, however, where there were so many people there would be some kind hearts, he thought.

He crept along and looked into the window of a restaurant. There was a boiled ham in the window, cake, pies, and other attractive things. He wagged his tail a little, and looked into a man's face as he went in, but the man paid no attention. Then a young lady passed, and she said, "Poor dog!" but went on.

Douglas walked away and lay down in front of a store, but a man came and said, "Get out! The ladies will be afraid of you."

Douglas looked no longer the petted, handsome creature of several days before. The dust had settled in his black hair, which looked rough and coarse. He was thin and dejected. An unthinking boy chased him, and threw something at him, and as he was too peaceable to resent it he hurried along an alley and tried to hide up a stairway. A big red-faced man came out of a room at the head of the stairs and kicked him down the steps.

Douglas ran into a shoe-store. Three men cornered him with a broom and a pole, and one man, braver than the others, put a cloth over his head, and then seized him by the hind legs and threw him into the street. Then somebody on the sidewalk said, "That dog acts strangely. He must be mad!"

That was enough to excite the passers-by, who had read in the papers various accounts of supposed cases of rabies. "He is weak," said one person, "and he totters." "He is frothing at the mouth," said another. A boot-black ran after him and threw his box at the thoroughly frightened animal. A crowd gathered, and ran and shouted. "Shoot him! Shoot him!" was the eager cry.

Douglas did indeed froth at the mouth from excessive running. A lady hurried along and said, "Let me have the dog. He is not mad, but has lost his owner. Frothing at the mouth is not a sign of hydrophobia, as the best physicians will tell you."

"No, madam," said a looker-on. "Don't touch the dog. We men will not allow you to be bitten."

A policeman fired his pistol, and the ball entered Douglas's shoulder. Half dead with pain as well as fright, the dog rushed on and finally escaped.

He lay in his hiding-place till midnight, and then when no human eye could see him he crept away from the city. If only Miss Benson could see him now, and dress his wounds, and say the petting words of old that he had so loved to hear!

Towards morning, exhausted, he lay down by the fence in the front yard of a house in the outskirts of the city. The owner of the home was a lawyer, a kind-hearted man, in part because he had a noble mother and wife.

"There's a poor wounded dog on our lawn, Jeannette," Mr. Goodman said to his wife. "Call him in at the back door, and we'll see if we can't help him."

Mrs. Goodman took a basin of warm water and castile soap and carefully washed the wound, the children standing about and anxiously watching the operation. "Nice dog," said Teddy, a boy of five. "He no bite."

"No," said his mother, as Douglas looked pitifully up into her face. "He is a kind dog, and must belong to a good home somewhere."

After she had finished washing the sore and tender place, Douglas licked her hand in appreciation. "Have Dr. Thayer come in"—he was the veterinary surgeon—said Mrs. Goodman to her husband. "We might as well make the care of animals a part of our missionary work in the world. The doctor will find the ball, if it is still there, and save the dog, I hope."

"All right, wife," said Mr. Goodman, as he started for the office.

"I suppose you want some breakfast, doggie," said Mrs. Goodman, and she placed before Douglas a dish of meat and of milk. Douglas was too tired and too full of pain to eat much, but he felt as though a new world had opened to him. After all, there were some good people in the land, and at last he had reached them.

Dr. Thayer came, found the ball in the patient, abused animal, and the wounded shoulder soon began to heal.

When night came Mrs. Goodman made Douglas a warm bed of blankets by the kitchen stove, for she knew that a cold kennel was not a suitable place for him. Later he was washed and dried, by rubbing with cloths, till his coat was silky and black.

Teddy and the dog became inseparable companions. Wherever the child went Douglas was always close behind him, now licking his extended hand, now lying down for the child to clamber over him, or to lay his dark curls against the darker curls of the dog. They shared their food, and they frequently went to sleep together, if it could be called sleep on the part of the dog, whose eyes were usually open that his little charge might be guarded. Douglas never showed an inclination to bite unless some one touched the boy, and then he growled and looked concerned.

One summer day Teddy and a playmate wandered off with the dog during Mrs. Goodman's absence. They sat down under a tree and all three lunched together. Then they played along the meadow till the banks of a river were reached. Two men were working near by and occasionally watched the children at their play, as they dabbled their hands in the water. Finally they heard a child scream, and before they could reach the place, Douglas was dragging Teddy, dripping and frightened, from the river. The men carried the boy home to his awe-struck but overjoyed parents, and Douglas, wet and excited, was praised for his heroic conduct.

A year later, when Teddy went to school, Douglas missed his comrade, and for days whined piteously. He never failed to go, at the regular hour for closing school, to meet his little friend, and always brought home in his teeth the dinner basket of the lad. Sometimes Douglas whined in his sleep, as though he were dreaming of other days, but love for Teddy made him, on the whole, very happy.

When Teddy was seven years old, diphtheria raged in the school and marked him for one of its victims. No love or care could save him. When conscious, he could not bear Douglas out of his sight or reach. As in the case with his former mistress, Douglas neither ate nor slept. When all was over he disappeared. Where he went nobody knew. Probably he lay upon the grave of the child, and later wandered off, thinking perchance to find again his first love.

The Goodmans had intended to leave their home in the suburbs and move to the city before their boy died, and now Mrs. Goodman was anxious to go away from the place as quickly as possible. A home was soon obtained, and the family moved thither. They deeply regretted that Douglas could not be found to go with them, because they were much attached to him for his own sake, and because he was so dear to their child.

Douglas meantime had hunted far and wide for his lost ones. He had the same bitter experience of neglect and hunger, but a dog's love is his strongest quality, and despite suffering he was seeking his own. Miss Benson he could not find; that was past hope, but Teddy, perhaps, he might see again. Probably Douglas did not know that death has no awakening in this world, and that Teddy could never come to his home, but the dog finally stole back to the porch and yard where they had played together and waited, hoping that the boy would come. The house was vacant. Some neighbors saw him on the steps, but he went away again. Finally a policeman saw him and heard him howl.

"Whose dog is that?" he said to a neighbor.

"It's a dog that came to the Goodmans and disappeared when their little boy died. I suppose he has come back to find the child," was the reply. "Ah!" said the man, "and he hasn't any collar on his neck. He is unlicensed. I will send the Society for the Prevention of Cruelty to Animals after him."

"I'll see that he doesn't starve," said the woman. "Will the Society find a home for him?"

"Oh, no, they can't find homes for so many as they take off the streets! They'll kill him."

"He isn't to blame for not being licensed. I don't see the use of the license law, because it means the death of so many thousands of animals."

"Neither do I," said the kind-hearted policeman. "Poor folks can't always pay the fee. I love my dog, and he's a great comfort to my children. But I don't make the law. I only help to enforce it."

"What is done with the license money? It makes so much heartache it ought to do great good."

"I've heard that it is given sometimes to public schools and to libraries to buy books on kindness to animals, and sometimes to the Humane Society so that they can pay men to catch and kill unlicensed dogs. You see, the licensed dogs help to kill the unlicensed and homeless," said the man.

"I should think a better way would be to provide homes for the really homeless instead of killing them. I think that we have a duty to animals, seeing that they are under our protection."

The policeman told the S. P. C. A. that a black unlicensed dog was howling on the steps of a vacant house because his little friend had died. Two officers in a big wagon hastened to the spot, caught him, and threw him in with a score of other animals which they had seized on the street.

Douglas cowered in the corner, and wondered what new sorrow had befallen him. The other poor things were as frightened as himself. Two were black-and-white puppies scarcely bigger than kittens, and two were pretty black-and-tan pets. A large mastiff looked out of her great brown eyes, trembling from head to foot. One shepherd dog was poor and thin, but most looked well cared for, only they had no collars, and their owners had not paid their license fee.

The wagon soon reached a barn-like structure, and the animals were hastily emptied into a pen with sawdust on the floor. What was in store for them they could only guess. After a time they were offered a mixture of meal and meat, but most were too frightened to eat.

All the next day they listened for footsteps, hoping that some friend would come for them. Douglas lay in the corner and expected nobody. Miss Benson did not know where he was, and Teddy had never come back when he howled for him.

There was a large pen adjoining that of Douglas, and this was filled with dogs—fox-terriers, some black like himself, and several yellow ones.

Cats, many of them large and handsome, were in cages about the room. Some animals had been brought to the pound, or refuge, by persons who did not or could not take the trouble to find homes for them. An advertisement in the paper saying that a dog had been found and would be given to a good home would in almost every case have met with responses, but this cost a little money and time.

A boy brought in two pretty creatures, one red and the other yellow, which he said he had found without collars. A woman had hired him and other children by paying each a few cents to do this work, which meant almost certain death to animals, believing, probably, that she was doing good.

Late in the afternoon Douglas witnessed a strange, sad sight. Every cat, fifty or more, was thrown into a large cage, and poisonous gas turned in upon them. The terrified creatures huddled together, as though they knew their helplessness in the hands of their destroyers, and died.

Then several men, as soon as the cats were removed, threw the shrinking, crying dogs into the cage, and they too were soon dead, piled upon each other. Douglas and the rest knew that their turn would come soon.

On the second day a lady called at the refuge because her own city contemplated establishing a home where dogs could be killed, the license fees to be used to pay the salaries of the S. P. C. A. agents. Her heart was touched by the appealing looks of the helpless animals. She went away and found homes for two fox-terriers, paid the license fees and fines, and the dogs were released, licking her hands, as though they realized from what they had been saved.

Douglas crept towards the visitor, because he had been used to a woman's voice. He was thin, but his eyes were as beautiful as when he was a puppy and responded to the petting of Miss Benson's gentle hands. "You have been a handsome dog," the lady said to Douglas, "and somebody has loved you. I know of a place for you. A noble woman who loves dogs has provided a home for the homeless, as far as her means will allow, and is devoting her life to the care of such of God's creatures as you are. Would you like to go with me?"

Douglas whined, and the other poor animals crowded around as much as to say, "Can you not take us too, and save us from death to-morrow? We cannot pay the license, but we would love and protect anybody who would pay it and take us home." The lady could not take them all—the city and State, by reason of their wealth and humaneness, instead of license or tax, should provide homes for those committed to their keeping by the Creator. Douglas was let out, and followed the lady with a thankful heart but with a downcast look, as though life had been so uncertain that he could not be sure of anything good in the future.

The lady hired a cab, and the dog lay at her feet. They were driven to an attractive-looking brick house, with several small buildings adjoining. A young girl came to the door.

"Do you wish to see the matron of the Dogs' Home?" said the girl. "Yes, I am a friend of the matron," said the lady, "and I have taken a fancy to a homeless dog and have brought him here to find a home." The matron soon appeared, and, with one wild cry, Douglas sprang into her arms. It was Miss Benson, who, since she had lost Douglas, had been moved to spend her life and her fortune for other dogs who were lost.

"Oh, Douglas! Douglas!" she exclaimed, while the visitor looked on with amazement. "Have you found me and I you at last?" And the dog whined and caressed her till she feared he would die from excess of joy unless she calmed him.

"You and I will never be parted again. You shall live here and help care for other lost and unwanted ones."

For years Douglas thankfully shared in the care and love of his mistress. She could not bear to see him grow old, but he had suffered too much to live to the usual age of St. Bernards. When he died his head was in Miss Benson's lap, and his great brown eyes looked upon her face and whitening hair as the last precious thing to be seen in life. She buried him and laid flowers upon his grave, for was he not her devoted, loyal friend? A neat headstone tells where faithful Douglas sleeps.

26

The Amazing Letter-Writing Dog

by Christopher Morley

First published by Doubleday in 1923, this tale clearly demonstrates how some writers were willing to throw off prose shackles and try something different.

WHAT KIND OF A DOG IS HE?" SAID THE SEA CLIFF VETERINARY OVER the phone.

We must confess we were stumped. All we could say was that he is— Oh, well just a kind of a dog. We didn't like to say that he is a Synthetic Hound, and that his full name is Haphazard Gissing I. We didn't like to admit, at any rate over the telephone, that one of his grandmothers may have been a dachshund and that certainly one of his brothers-in-law is an Airedale. But at any rate it was fixed that we should take our excellent Gissing over to the kennels to be boarded while we were in the city.

Gissing's behaviour was odd. He seemed, in some inscrutable way, to suspect that something was going to happen. The night before his departure he disappeared, and was away all night—saying good-by to his cronies, we suppose. When we came home early in the afternoon to convoy him to Sea Cliff, he was nowhere to be found. But about suppertime he turned up, looking more haggard and disreputable than ever. There was a fresh scar on his face, and he was very hungry. He ate his supper hurriedly, with no dignity at all. As soon as he heard the rattle of his chain, his spirits went very low.

But the admirable creature was docile. Dogs are profoundly religious at heart: they put their trust in their deities. Unlike cats, who are determined atheists and fight to the last against fate, dogs accept calmly what they see is ordered by the gods. Gissing hopped into Dame Quickly without protest and sat in silence during the ride. His nose was unusually cold, but then that may have been only the winter evening. He had somewhat the bearing of one who is going to the dentist.

Dog fanciers are always baffled and set at naught when they see Gissing. But the Sea Cliff veterinarian made the most penetrating remark when we arrived. He is accustomed, indeed, to dogs of high degree—such dogs as are favoured by the North Shore of Long Island, and Gissing was rather a shock to him. After a long look, "What is his name?" he said. "Gissing," we replied, with just a little of that embarrassment we always feel when such questions are asked; for it is generally shown in the manner of the inquirer that Gissing is an unusual name, particularly for a dog who looks as though he ought to be called Rover. So we said, perhaps a little defiantly, "Gissing." But the Doctor misunderstood it. "Guessing!" he said dubiously, and looked again at the abashed quadruped. "That's because he keeps you guessing what breed he is."

It amuses us the more to have Gissing staying there, associating with the lordly dogs of Long Islanders who are spending the snow season in Florida, because we feel that it is rather like sending a child to a fashionable boarding school. It is probably useless as far as education is concerned, but it ought to be an interesting experience, and he may pick up a little polish. Gissing may make friends with some influential dogs who will be of help to him in future life; who knows? It is expensive, we admit; but since we paid nothing for him in the first place, and have used him liberally for copy, we feel that we owe Gissing this opportunity to improve himself. At any rate, he has promised to write us a letter from time to time, and we shall see how he gets on.

A Letter from Gissing

SEA CLIFF, L. I., February 13.

DEAR FRIEND, I thought that as to-morrow is Valentine's Day I had better send you a line to report progress and to wish you my respectful greeting. This Dr. R with whom I am living is a fine man and he smells good to me. I heard him say something about a Dog Show being on in New York now and I thought I ought to tell you what the old veterans in this veterinary hotel say, they say not to go to any such show because those things there are not Regular Dogs, not Red Blooded He Dogs not Dogs as you might say with the Bark On. Of course at first it was a bit hard for me here being as I am a self-made dog so to say and not accustomed to associate with pedigree folks and I rather wish you would send me a new collar, that old strap is about wore out and to tell you the truth there is a little Airedale flapper in the next cage that I would like to make an impression on, some of the boys have those collars that are studded with brass spikes and look mighty fine don't forget my size is 16. As I was saying, at first things were a bit unpleasant, there is a big collie who looked me over the first morning I was here and said "Ye men, how do they get that way? Who let this mutt in here among cultivated animals?" Well, I wasn't going to stand for that stuff, so I talked right back to him and asked him if he had ever been in print, but I didn't get it across very big because he was so ignorant he didn't seem to realize what it means to have been written up right along in the *Evening Post*. By the way, I get kennel-sick for the old paper, out here they all read the sensational sheets and I wish you would tell the Circulation Manager to put me down for a two-months' subscription. All the other fellows here gave me the razz when I told them my name, Gissing, what kind of a name is that for a dog they said? I told them I was named after a Writer but none of the roughnecks ever heard of him. But I noticed right away that the little Airedale kid was interested, she seems to have some imagination her name is Mistress Zephine IV and I understand that the Airedales are a very fine family. I told her that it had been suggested by some that I had some Airedale in me too, and she laughed and looked a bit scandalized. Either you are an Airedale or you aren't, she said; there's no half and half measures. Live and learn, I told her. Anyway she and I go out for a walk together with one of the men every morning, and I have got her quite interested in books, she has promised to write me when she gets home and tell what kind of books her master reads. When you write, send me a cake of flea soap, I want to make myself solid with this dame. There is a whole lot I could write about, but this is just to say that You are my Valentine. These dogs here all have three-barrelled names so I will sign myself in full,

Your affectionate dog,
HAPHAZARD GISSING I.

P. S. Please write right away and tell me what is the name of your publisher, I want to give one of your books to Zephine, when I told her you were a Writer she wouldn't believe it, I am talking you up big all the time here, but it is hard work to get away with it because appearances are against us; never mind, some day we will knock them cold; and what is the name of your car, one of these fellows here says he rides around in a Rolls Royce and I told him yours was a Dame Quickly and he says there isn't any such boat, it's an imported car I told him. Yes, he says, imported from Detroit; never mind, I've got them all guessing, they're all keen to see what kind of a guy you are, I told them the story about the old trousers, I guess it was a mistake.

H. G. I.

27

Point!

by Peter B. Kyne

If you've ever seen a pointing dog doing his thing in bobwhite quail country, you'll appreciate how Peter Kyne has captured the feeling in this tale from a wonderful anthology, My Story That I Like Best. *The book, published in 1925, featured stories from some of the great writers of that time, including Edna Ferber, Irvin S. Cobb, and James Oliver Curwood, among others.*

LITTLE OLD DAN PELLY OCCUPIED A POSITION IN LIFE ANALOGOUS TO that of a tragedian who aspires to play comedy rôles. By reason of early environment, natural inclination and years of practice, he was a dog trainer; now, in the sunset of his rather futile life, he was a cross between a chicken raiser, farmer and dreamer of old dreams that had to do mostly with dogs and good quail cover. In a word, old Dan was not happy, and this morning as he sat on a fallen scrub oak tree on the highest point on his alleged ranch and gazed off into Little Antelope Valley, he almost wished that a merciful Providence would waft him out of this cold world.

"The Indians had the right idea of a hereafter," mused Dan Pelly. "To them the next world was a happy hunting ground. This world is no longer fit for a white man to live in. It's getting too civilized. Travel as far as you will for good trout-fishing and upland hunting and you'll find some scrub there ahead of you in a flivver. Get out on your own ground at dawn on the day the shooting season opens—and you'll find empty shotgun shells a week old. Tim, old pal, the more I see of some men the more I love you."

Tim—or, to accord him his registered name, Tiny Tim—ran his cool muzzle into Dan Pelly's horny palm and rested it there. Just rested it and spoke never a word, for Tiny Tim was one of those rare dogs who know when their masters are troubled of soul and forbear to weary their loved ones with unnecessary outbursts of affection or sympathy. He leaned his shoulder against Dan's knee and rested his muzzle in Dan's hand as who should say: "Well, man alone is vile. Here I am and I'll stick, depend upon it."

Tiny Tim was an English setter and the last surviving son of Keepsake, the greatest bitch Dan Pelly had ever seen or owned. Dan had wept when an envious scoundrel had poisoned her the night before a field trial up Bakersfield way. All of her puppies out of Kenwood Boy had survived, and all had made history in dogdom. Three of them had been placed—one, two, three—in the Derby. The other two had been the runners-up, and the least promising of these runners-up had been Tiny Tim.

Tim had been the runt of the litter and as if his physical deficiency had not been sufficient handicap, he had grown into a singularly unbeautiful dog. He had a butterfly nose, one black ear, a solid white coat with the exception of a black spot as big as a man's hand just over the root of his tail; and his tail was his crowning misfortune. Dog fanciers like a setter with a merry tail, but Tiny Tim carried his very low when he ran that Derby, and he had never carried it very high since. As if to offset the tragedy of his tail, however, Tiny Tim ran with a high head, for he had, tucked away in that butterfly nose, a pair of olfactory nerves that carried him unerringly to birdy ground. He could always manage to locate a bird lying close in cover that had been thoroughly prospected by other dogs.

Dan Pelly had sold Tiny Tim's litter mates at a fancy figure after that memorable Derby, but for homely Tiny Tim there were no bidders; so Dan Pelly expressed him back to the kennels. He was homely and lacked style and dash in his bird work; he appeared a bit nervous and uncertain and inclined to limit his range, and it seemed to Dan that as a field trial prospect he was so much inferior to other dogs that it was scarcely worth while spending any time or money on his education. However, he did have a grand nose; when he grew older Dan hoped he might outgrow his nervousness and be steadier to shot and wing; in view of his undoubted instinct for birds, it seemed the part of wisdom to make a "plug" shooting dog of him. Every dog trainer keeps such an animal, if not for his own use then for the use of stout old bank presidents and of retired brewers whose idea of the sport of hunting is to come home with "the limit." A grand hunting dog means little in the lives of such "sportsmen"; they want a dog that will work close to the gun, thus enabling them to proceed leisurely, as becomes a fat man. It is no pleasure to them to be forced to walk down a steep hill, clamber across a deep gully and climb the opposite hill to kill a bird their dog has been pointing for fifteen or twenty minutes. It is reserved for idealists like old Dan Pelly to thrill to the work of a dog like that. The dead bird is a secondary consideration.

So Tiny Tim had been sent back to the kennel, and now, in his fifth year, he was still on Dan Pelly's hands. But that was no fault of Tiny Tim's. And he had never again been entered in a field trial. That was no fault of his, either. Dan Pelly had merely gone out of the dog business, and Tiny Tim, his last dog and best beloved, was neither a field trial dog nor yet a potterer for fat bankers and retired brewers who came down to Dan Pelly's place for a week-end shoot in the season. No, Tiny Tim had never achieved that disgrace. Dan Pelly had given up dog training and dog boarding and dog raising and dog trading after his return from that field trial where old Keepsake's litter had brought him more money than he had ever seen at any one time before. Consequently, Tiny Tim was Dan's own shooting dog and Dan had trained him not for filthy lucre but for that love and companionship for a good dog which idealists of the Dan Pelly type can never repress.

Tiny Tim had known but one master, and but one code of sportsmanship; he responded to but one set of signals; he had never been curbed in his range or speed; he had never been scolded or shouted at or beaten, but he had received much of love and caressing and praise. He had been fed properly, housed properly, wormed regularly every three months, bathed every Saturday afternoon and brushed and combed almost every day, and as a result he was an extremely healthy dog, albeit a small dog, even among small, field type English setters. Dan Pelly loved him just a little bit more because he was a runt and because, though royally bred, his bearing was a bit ignoble.

"I'll have none of your bench type setters," Dan was wont to remark when speaking of setters. "I could weep from just lookin' at them—the poor boobs, with their domed foreheads and their sad, bloodshot eyes and dribbling chops. Too heavy and slow for anybody but a fat man. An hour's hard going of a warm day and they're done. I'll have a light, neat little setter for a long, hard, drivin' day of it."

Dan Pelly's choice of dog was an index to his character. He, too, was a light, compact little man, with something of a lost dog's wistfulness about him. Dan didn't like pointers. They were too aggressive, too head-strong, too noisy for him. The sight of a bulldog or a bull terrier or an Airedale made him angry, for such dogs could always be depended upon to pounce upon a shooting dog and worry him. Toy dogs depressed him. They seemed so unworthy of human attention and moreover they had no brains.

This morning Dan Pelly was more than ordinarily unhappy. He needed five hundred dollars worse than he needed salvation . . .

And only the day before while he and Tim had been working a patch of low cover just off the county road, a man in a very expensive automobile driven by a liveried chauffeur had paused in the road to watch them. Presently Tim had made one of those spectacular points which always give a real dog lover a thrill. In mid-air, while leaping over a small bush, he had caught the scent of a quail crouching close under that bush. He had landed with his body half turned toward the bush, his head had swung around and there he had stood, "frozen." Dan had walked up, kicked the bird out, waited until the quail was forty yards away and fired. Meanwhile Tim had broken point and, head up, was following the flushed bird with anxious eyes.

As the gun barked the bird flinched slightly but did not reduce its speed. Wings spread stiffly, it sailed away out of sight and Dan Pelly, seeing himself watched by the man in the motor car, grinned deprecatingly.

"Missed him a mile," he called.

"You let him get too far away before you fired," the stranger replied with that hearty camaraderie which always obtains between lovers of upland shooting.

"My gun is a full choke; I can kill nicely with it at fifty yards, but I like to give the birds a chance for their white alley, so I never shoot under forty yards."

"Grand point your little setter made then. Steady to flush and shot, too. Homely little rascal, but man, he's a dog! I must have a look at him, if you don't mind, my friend." And he got out of the car.

"Certainly, sir. Come, Timmy, lad. Shake hands with the gentleman."

But Tiny Tim had other and more important matters to attend to. He was racing at full speed after that departing bird. Dan whistled him to halt, but Tim paid no attention. He crossed a gentle rise of ground and disappeared on the other side. He was out of sight for about five minutes; then he appeared again on the crest and came jogging sedately back to Dan Pelly. In his mouth he held tenderly a wounded quail. Straight to Dan Pelly he came, and as he advanced he twisted his little body sinuously and arched and lowered his shoulders and flipped his tail from side to side and smiled with his eyes. In effect he said:

"Dan, you didn't think you hit that bird, but I saw him flinch ever so little. I've had a lot of experience in such matters and experience has taught me that a bird hit like that will fly a couple of hundred yards and then drop. So I kept my eye on this one and sure enough just as he reached the top of that little rise I saw him settle rather abruptly. So I went over and nosed around and picked up his trail. He had an injured wing—numbed, probably—and he was down and running to beat the band. It's sporty to chase a runner, because if we don't get him, Dan, a weasel will."

The stranger looked at the bird in Tim's mouth and then he looked at Dan Pelly. "Well, I'll be swindled!" he declared. "If I live to be a million years old I'll never see a prettier piece of bird work than that. The dog's human."

"Yes, he's a right nice little feller," Dan declared pridefully. "Timmy, boy, take the bird to the gentleman and then shake hands with him."

Timmy looked at the stranger, who smiled at him, so he walked sedately to the latter and gently dropped the frightened bird into his hand. Not a feather had been disturbed; not a tooth had marred the tender flesh.

The stranger reached down and twigged Tiny Tim's nose; then he tugged his ear a little, said "Good dog" and stroked Tim's head. Tim extended a paw to be shaken. They were friends.

"Want to sell this dog, my friend?" the newcomer demanded.

"Oh, no! Timmy's the only dog I have left. He's just my little shooting dog and I'm right fond of him. He has a disposition that sweet, sir, you've never seen the beat of it. If I sold Timmy I'd never dare come home. My wife would take the rolling pin to me."

"I'll give you two hundred and fifty dollars for him."

"Timmy isn't for sale, sir."

"Not enough money, eh? Well, I don't blame you. If Timmy was my dog five thousand dollars wouldn't touch him. It was worth that to me to see him perform. Let me see him work this cover, if you please." To Tiny Tim: "All right, boy. Root 'em out. Lots of birds in here yet."

The dog was off like a streak. Suddenly he paused, sniffing up-wind, swung slowly left and slowly right, trotted forward a few paces and halted, head up, tail swinging excitedly, every muscle aquiver.

"It's dry as tinder and the birds don't lay close. He's on to some running birds now, sir. Watch him road 'em to heavier cover and then point."

Instead, they flushed. Tim watched them interestedly, marked where they had settled, moved gingerly forward—and froze on a single that had failed to flush. Dan Pelly handed the stranger his gun. "Perhaps, sir," he said with his wistful smile, "you might enjoy killing a bird over Timmy's point."

This was the apotheosis of field courtesy. The stranger took the gun, smiling his thanks, walked over to Tiny Tim, kicked out the bird and missed him. Tim glanced once at the bird and promptly dismissed him from consideration. He made a wide cast to come up on the spot where he had seen the flushed covey settle.

"Point!" called Dan Pelly. This time the stranger killed his bird, which Tim retrieved in handsome style.

"He brought the dead bird to me!" the stranger shouted. "Did you notice that? He brought it to me!"

"Of course. It's your bird. You killed it. Timmy knows that. It wouldn't be mannerly of him to bring it to me. I see you appreciate a good shooting dog, sir. I suppose, living in the city and a busy man, you don't get much afield. There's a lot of birds scattered in this cover. Have a little shoot over Timmy. I have four birds and that's enough for our supper. I'll sit down under this oak tree and have a smoke."

"That's devilish sporting of you, my friend. Thank you very much." And the stranger hurried away after Tiny Tim. He was an incongruous figure in that patch of cover, what with his derby hat and overcoat, and he seemed to realize this, for he shed both, stuffed a dozen cartridges into his pockets—he was far too big a man to wear Dan Pelly's disreputable old hunting jacket—and hurried away after Tiny Tim. From the far corner of the field Dan presently heard a merry fusillade, and in about fifteen minutes his guest returned with half a dozen quail and Tiny Tim trotting at his heels.

"I'll give you a thousand dollars for Timmy, my friend," was his first announcement. "Why, he works for me as if I were his master."

"You're the first man except his master who has ever shot over him," Pelly replied proudly. "Sorry, but Timmy is not for sale."

"I'll bet nobody has ever offered you a thousand dollars for him. Here's my card, Mr.—er—er—"

"Dan Pelly's my name, sir."

"Mr. Pelly, and if you change your mind, wire me collect and I'll send a man down with the cash and you can send the dog back by him."

Dan took the card. The stranger thanked him and departed with his quail in his expensive car.

And this morning Dan Pelly sat at the highest point on his so-called ranch and looked down into Little Antelope Valley and was unhappy. He needed five hundred dollars to meet a mortgage; he could get a thousand dollars within twenty-four hours by sending a telegram collect to the man who had admired Tiny Tim—and he didn't have the courage to send the telegram. In fact, he hadn't had sufficient courage to tell Martha, his wife, of the stranger's offer. Martha was made of sterner stuff than her husband, and a terrible panic of fear had seized Dan at the mere thought of telling her. What if she should accept the thousand dollars?

Dan loaded his pipe and smoked ruminatively. He thought of his wasted and futile life. Twenty-five years wasted as a professional dog trainer. Faugh! And all he had to show for it was a host of memories, sweet and bitter; sweet as he remembered the dear days afield with good dogs and good fellows, the thrill of many a hard-fought field trial; bitter as he thought of dogs he had loved and which had been sold or poisoned or died of old age or disease; bitterer still as he reflected that he and Martha had come to a childless old age with naught between them and the county poor farm save a thousand acres of rough sage-covered land which, with the exception of about twenty-five acres of rich, sub-irrigated bottom land, was worthless save as a training ground for dogs. It had numerous springs on it, good cover and just enough scrub oaks to form safe roosting places for quail. It was a rather decent little game preserve and occasionally Dan made a few dollars by granting old customers the privilege of a shoot on it. He ran about a hundred head of goats on it, while in the bottom land he and Martha eked out a precarious existence with a few chickens and turkeys, a few hogs, a few stands of bees, three cows, a couple of horses and Tiny Tim. For Tim was known to a few dog fanciers as the last of the old Keepsake-Kenwood Boy strain in the state and not infrequently they sent their bitches to Tiny Tim's court.

Poor Martha! Hers had not been a very happy life with Dan Pelly. A dog trainer is—a dog trainer. He can't very well be anything else because God has made him so. And in his heart of hearts he doesn't want to be. He trains dogs ostensibly for money but in reality because he loves them and the job affords him a legitimate excuse to be afield with them, to enjoy their society and that of the jovial devotees of upland game-shooting. Dan Pelly wasn't an ambitious man. He had no desire to dip coupons or wear fine raiment; his taste in automobiles went no further than an old ruin he had picked up for two hundred dollars for the purpose of carting his dogs around in the days before Martha took over the handling of the Pelly fortunes, when Dan had had dogs to cart around.

The crux of the situation was this. Dog trainers are so busy with their dogs that they neglect to send out bills for board and training, and the men who can afford to buy expensive dogs and have them boarded and trained seldom think of their dogs until fall. Then they pay the bill and sometimes wonder why it is so large. In a word, the income of a dog trainer is never what one might term staggering, and it is more or less uncertain.

Martha had grown weary of this uncertainty and when distemper for the second time had cleaned out Dan Pelly's kennels, taking all of his own dogs with the exception of Tiny Tim and either killing or ruining the dogs of his customers, Mrs. Pelly felt that it was time to act. She knew it would be years before Dan's old customers would send dogs to him again. Friendship and a reputation as a great trainer are undoubtedly first aids to a dog trainer's success, but men who love their dogs hesitate to send them to a kennel where the germs of virulent distemper are known to exist. It was up to Dan Pelly to burn his old kennels and build new ones far removed from the location of the old. He could not afford to do this, and since Martha was desirous of seeing him engage in something more constructive, Dan Pelly had gone out of business and become a farmer in the trifling manner heretofore described.

Martha told him she was weary of dogs. She had shed too many tears over dead favorites; she had assisted at too many operations for the cure of canker of the ear, fistula, tumor and cancer, broken legs, smashed toes and cuts from barbed wire. She was already too learned in the gentle art of healing mange and exorcising tapeworms. She loved dogs, but to have thirty pointers and setters set up a furious barking whenever a stranger appeared at the Pelly farm had finally "gotten on her nerves." She understood Dan better than he understood himself and she knew how bitter was the sacrifice she demanded; yet she realized that she must be firm and lead Daniel in the way he must go, else would they come to want and misery in a day when Dan would be too old to tramp over hill and dale training dogs. Dan had readily consented to her direction—particularly after she had wept a little. Poor Martha!

From where he sat Dan Pelly could this morning see great activity on the floor of Little Antelope Valley, just below him. Half a dozen men on horseback were riding backward and forward and at least a dozen white specks that Dan Pelly knew for hunting dogs were ranging here and there among the low sage cover.

"The first arrivals for the Pacific Coast Field Trials, and they're out on the grounds, looking them over and seeing how their dogs behave. Three days from now they'll be running the Derby, and after that the All Age Stake. Ah, Timmy lad, if we two could only go to a field trial again! How like old times it would be, Timmy! We'd be down at the station to greet all the gentlemen coming in for the trials, and then we'd be crowding around the baggage car watching the dogs in their crates bein' lifted out. And we'd be peekin' through the air-holes in the crates to see whether they'd be setters or pointers, and if setters, whether they'd be English or Irish. And then the banquet up at the hotel the night before the Derby and the toastmaster rappin' for order and sayin': 'Gentlemen, we have with us tonight one of the Old Guard, Dan Pelly. Dan is going to tell us something about the field trials of other days—other days and other dogs. Gentlemen—old Dan Pelly.'

"Ah, Tim my lad, we're out of it. Think, Timmy, if we two were driving out to Antelope Valley in the morning, with you in my lap, and the entrance fee up and me wild with excitement, if you were paired say with a dog like Manitoba Rap or Fischel's Frank or Mary Montrose or Ringing Bells or Robert the Devil—any one of the big ones, eh, Timmy? No, Timmy, I wouldn't be excited. They're all great dogs. Didn't Mary Montrose win the All America three times—the only dog in the world that ever proved her championship caliber three times?

"But Timmy lad, you'd run circles around her. You might run with a low head and a dead tail—though your head is high and your tail is none so low as it was in the Derby, when you were a wee puppy and nervous and frightened—but you'd make the judges notice you, Timmy. You'd show them dash and range and speed and style and brains; steady to flush, steady to shot, steady to command, no false pointing, no roading birds to a flush if you could help it, picking up singles on ground the other dog thought he had covered, marking where the flushed coveys settle and picking them up again. Ah, Timmy dog, it's breaking my heart to hide your light under a bushel basket. I owe it to you to let men that know and can appreciate a good dog see you work. Of the hundreds of dogs I've owned, of the thousand I've trained since boyhood, you are the king of them all. God help me, Timmy, I gave Martha my word I'd never attend another field trial or handle another dog in one, either for myself or another. We're whipped, Timmy. Whipped to a frazzle."

Tiny Tim leaned a little closer and licked the palm of Dan's hand. He was an understanding little dog. Even when Dan finally heaved slowly to his feet and started down the hillside toward home, Tiny Tim followed at his heels, forbearing to follow his natural instinct, which was to frisk ahead of Dan far and wide and attend to the business for which he really had been created.

Arrived at the house, Dan encountered with a sheepish glance the searching one of his wife.

"Where have you been, Dan?" she queried.

"Oh, takin' a little walk," he replied.

She sat down beside him on the porch and put her arm around his neck. "Hard to be out of it, isn't it, dear?"

"It's hard to think that a dog like Timmy shouldn't have his chance, Martha. Why not make an exception to our agreement in this one case? I'm sure I could win the All Age Stake with him. The entrance fee is twenty-five dollars and there'll be upwards of forty dogs entered. That'll be a thousand-dollar purse, divided five hundred, three-fifty, and a hundred and fifty. Might win first prize and be able to pay the mortgage. Somehow I got a notion the bank won't renew the loan."

Martha's eyes were as wistful as her husband's, but hers was a far more resolute nature. She kept her bargains and expected others to keep theirs; she knew the weakness of Dan Pelly. If he should go down to the field trials and enter Tiny Tim, he would meet old friends and old customers. It was four years since he had quit the game—long enough for men to forget those distemper germs and take another chance on Dan, for Dan's fame as a trainer was almost national. Somebody would be certain to ask him to train a Derby or Futurity prospect for next fall, or to handle a string of dogs in the Manitoba chicken trials.

And Dan was weak. He was one of those men who could never quite say no as if he meant it. Let him go down to dogdom and he would be back in the game again as deep as ever within a year. Decidedly (thought Martha) they couldn't afford to go over that ground again.

"Yes," Dan sighed, "it's a pity Timmy can't have his chance. He never was a kennel-raised dog. He's been allowed to rove and roam and he's hunted so much on his own I don't really understand why he hasn't been spoiled. But the exercise and experience he's had in one year exceed that of most dogs in a lifetime. He's little, but he's well muscled and tough and can hold his speed long after other dogs have slowed up. I wish he could have his chance, Martha."

Martha felt herself slipping, so, to avoid that catastrophe, she left Dan and entered the house.

All day long Dan sat on the porch, glooming and grieving. Having the field trials held practically at his own door was a sore temptation. Dan dwelt in Gethsemane. All day he suffered until finally, being human, he was tempted beyond his strength and fell. About four o'clock, while Martha was busy feeding the chickens, locking them up and gathering eggs, Dan Pelly sneaked into the house, donned his Sunday suit, abstracted the sum of fifty dollars from Martha's cache in the tomato can back of the jars of preserves on the back porch, cranked his prehistoric automobile, and with Tiny Tim on the seat behind him fled to the fleshpots. He left a note on the dining-room table for Martha.

Dear Martha:

Can't stand it any longer. Timmy *must* have his chance. It's for his sake, dear. I've robbed you of your egg money, but I *know* you'll have it back tomorrow.

Your loving
DAN.

Dan Pelly felt like a criminal as he rattled down the dusty country lane. But if he could only have seen Martha's face as she read his note! She laughed at first and then her eyes grew moist. "Poor old Dan!" she murmured to the cat. "I'm so glad he defied me. It proves he's a human being. I'm so grateful to him for his weakness. He didn't force me to a decision."

Arrived in town Dan Pelly parked his car at the village square, went to the local hotel and engaged a room. He registered, "Dan Pelly and his dog, Tiny Tim." Before he could go up to the room he was seen and recognized by the secretary of the field trial club, Major Christensen.

"Hello, Dan, you old fossil. When did they dig you up?" the Major saluted him affably. "Back in the game again?"

"Oh, no," Dan replied. "Just blew in to look 'em over. Got a son of old Keepsake and Kenwood Boy here. Thought I'd start him in fast company and see if he has any class. He's just a plug shooting dog."

"Well," the Major answered, looking Tim over with a critical and disapproving glance, "it'll cost you twenty-five dollars to glean that information, Dan." He took out an entry blank; Dan filled it out and returned it together with the entrance fee. Next he visited the hotel kitchen, where he did business with the chef and procured for Tiny Tim a hearty ration of lamb stew with vegetables, after which he took the little dog up to his room. Tim sprang into bed immediately, curled up and went to sleep.

That night Dan attended the banquet. Old friends were there, fellow trainers, trainers he had never met before, with dogs from Canada to the Gulf, from Maine to California. It was an exceedingly doggy party and poor old starved Dan reveled in it. He was living again, and under the stimulus of the unusual excitement and a couple of nips of contraband Scotch whisky he made the speech of his career, ripped the Fish and Game Commission up the back and ended by going upstairs and bringing Tiny Tim down in his arms to exhibit him to those around the festal board as the only real dog he had ever owned.

"He'll win every heat in which he's entered," Dan bragged, "and he'll win in the finals. He looks like a mutt, but oh, boy, watch his smoke!"

When the drawing for the next day's events took place, Dan discovered that Tiny Tim had been paired with a famous old pointer from

Nevada, known as Colonel Dorsey. Dan knew there were better dogs than Colonel Dorsey, but they weren't very plentiful, and under the able handling of a veteran trainer, Alf Wilkes, Dan knew Tiny Tim would have to extend himself to center the attention of the judges on his performance. To have Tim paired with Colonel Dorsey pleased Dan greatly, however, for if Tim merely succeeded in running a dead heat with the Colonel, that meant that Tim and the Colonel would fight it out together in the finals; for Colonel Dorsey was, in the opinion of all present, the class of the entries; he was in excellent form and condition and as full of ginger and go as a runaway horse.

A gentleman who had arrived too late for the banquet came shouldering his way through the crowd in the hotel lobby just after the drawing. Dan recognized in him the gentleman who had offered him a thousand dollars for Tiny Tim that day in the patch of cover by the side of the road. He came smiling up to Dan Pelly and shook his hand heartily.

"I'm the owner of Colonel Dorsey," he announced. "It'll be a barrel of fun to run my dog against Tiny Tim. A sporting dog owned and handled by a sportsman. Mr. Pelly, we're going to have a race."

"I hope so, sir," said Dan simply. "I want Timmy to have a foeman worthy of his steel, as the feller says."

"He will," the other promised.

He did. They were put down in a wide flat with a little watercourse running through the center of it. The cover was low, stunted sage, affording excellent cover for the birds and opportunities for them to sneak away from a dog without being seen, for there was not much open space between the sage bushes. They were away together, headed for the watercourse, Colonel Dorsey in the lead.

Suddenly Tiny Tim stopped dead and commenced to road at right angles, coming up into the wind. The Colonel pressed eagerly on and flushed, but was steady to flush. So was Tiny Tim. A moment later the Colonel pointed and Tiny Tim, standing in the open, honored the Colonel's point beautifully, but broke point after a minute of waiting and scouted off on a wide cast. The Colonel held his point and his handler, coming up, attempted to flush. The point was barren. Undoubtedly the bird had been there but had run out.

The Colonel's owner, who had been following the judges in a buckboard with Dan Pelly in the seat beside him, looked at his guest. "I own a colonel, but you own a general, Mr. Pelly. Your dog is handling his birds better than mine."

"Point!" came a hoarse shout from the direction in which Tim had gone. He had come back on his cast and was down in the watercourse on point. Dan Pelly got out of the buckboard and flushed a double, at the same time firing over the birds. Tim was absolutely stanch to shot and flush. He looked disappointed because no dead bird rewarded his efforts, but immediately pressed on up the gully. Dan Pelly thrilled. He knew the birds would lie close in this cover and that Tim would run up a heavy score. He did. Point after point he scored and always a single was flushed. When he had made nineteen points on single birds the whistle blew and the dogs were taken up.

Colonel Dorsey, ranging wide, had shown speed, style and dash but had found no birds. Tim had made but one cast but it was sufficient to show that he, too, had speed and range, albeit his style was nothing to brag about. But he had performed the function for which bird dogs are bred. He had found game and handled it in a masterly manner. The dogs were down forty minutes and both were fresh when taken up. The judges awarded the heat to Tiny Tim.

Colonel Dorsey's owner slapped old Dan Pelly on the back. "I came a long way for a splendid thrashing," he admitted gallantly. "However, the Colonel was out of luck. He got off into barren territory and rather wasted his time. We'll meet again in the finals."

And it was even so. Three days later Tiny Tim again faced the Colonel, who in the succeeding heats had given marvelous performances and disposed of his antagonists in a most decisive manner. But likewise so had Tiny Tim.

It was a battle from start to finish. Both dogs got on birdy ground at once and worked it thoroughly, and at the finish there was little to choose between them. Tim had two more points to his credit and no flushes; the Colonel had one flush, due to eagerness at the start, and he had failed to honor one of Tim's points. These errors appeared to offset Tim's lack of style, but the latter's marvelous bird work could not be gainsaid; and remembering the decisive manner in which the little setter had disposed of the Colonel in the initial heat, the judges awarded the All Age Stake, which carried with it the Pacific Coast championship, to Tiny Tim and Dan Pelly retired to the hotel richer by five hundred dollars and a silver loving cup. That afternoon he paid two hundred and fifty dollars on the mortgage and had it renewed for another year. Then he wrote a letter to Martha, bought a neat crate for Tiny Tim and—started down the field trial circuit.

In some ways—notably dog ways—Dan Pelly was a weak vessel. He lacked the moral courage to come home and be good forever after. Timmy was so much better in big company than he had anticipated that, should it mean death to both of them, Dan Pelly simply had to try him out in Oregon on pheasant. Poor Timmy had never seen a pheasant, and it was such a shame to deny him this great adventure.

So the next Martha heard of Dan was a wire to the effect that Timmy had taken second place in the trials on pheasant at Lebanon, Oregon. A week later came another telegram, informing her that Timmy had taken first money in the Washington field trials, handling Hungarian partridge for the first time. A letter followed and Martha read:

> Dear Wife:
>
> I don't suppose you will ever believe me again now that I have broke my word to you and run away. I don't seem to be able to help myself. Timmy is wonderful. I've got to go on to try him on chicken in Manitoba and then the International and the All America. I enclose $500.
>
> With love from Timmy and
> Your devoted husband,
> DAN PELLY.

Timmy was third on prairie chicken. Everybody said his performance was marvelous in view of his total ignorance of this splendid game, so Dan Pelly did not think it worth while to advertise the fact that he had introduced Timmy to two crippled chickens the day before in order that he might know their scent when he ran on to it. The International in Montana was won by Timmy, and Dan's cup of happiness overflowed when the judges handed him his trophies and a check for a thousand dollars. Colonel Dorsey gave him a stiff run, but the best the Colonel could do was second place.

And then came the never to be forgotten day down in Kentucky when Timmy went in on bobwhite quail for the All America, the field trial classic of the Western Hemisphere. Timmy was at home again on quail. He had some bad luck before he learned about bobwhite's peculiarities, but he had enough wins to put him in the finals, and at the finish he was cast off with a little Llewellyn bitch whose performance made Dan Pelly's heart skip a beat or two. Nothing except Timmy's age and years of experience enabled him to win over her; up to the last moments of the race predictions were freely made that it would be a dead heat.

But just before the whistle blew, Timmy roaded a small cover to a stanch point—the sole find made during the heat—and Dan Pelly went home with Timmy and more money than he had ever seen before in his life except in a bank; although better to wistful little Dan was the knowledge that he had bred, raised, trained and handled the most consistent winner and the most spectacularly outstanding bird dog champion in North America. Old Keepsake and her wonderful consort, Kenwood Boy, had transmitted their great qualities to their son, and Dan knew, in view of Tiny Tim's great record over the field trial circuit, how much in demand would be the puppies from that strain. Please God, Timmy might live long enough to perpetuate his great qualities in his offspring.

Dan's return was not a triumphal one. He felt like anything except a conquering hero. Indeed, he felt mean and low and untrustworthy; he had to call on a reserve store of courage in order to face Martha and explain his dastardly conduct in appropriating her fifty dollars, breaking his promise, and running away with Timmy.

Martha was sitting on the porch in her rocking-chair as Dan and his dog came up the lane. Tiny Tim romped ahead and sprang up in Martha's lap and kissed her and whimpered his joy at the homecoming—so Martha had ample opportunity to brace herself to meet the culprit.

"Hello, Martha, old girl," Dan cried with a cheerfulness he was far from feeling. "Timmy and I are home again. Are you going to forgive me, Martha?"

Martha looked so glum and serious that Dan's heart sank.

"Oh, Martha!" he quavered and came slowly up the steps and tossed into her lap a huge roll of banknotes. "I know I done wrong, Martha," he declaimed. "I've been gamblin' on the side—you know, honey—side bets on Timmy. I'm afraid we're never going to be real poor again. We've got the mortgage paid off and three thousand in reserve, and I'm going to sell Timmy for seven thousand five hundred dollars, with a half interest in his sire fees for three years—"

Martha stood up, her eyes ablaze with scorn and anger.

"Dan Pelly," she flared at him, "how dare you?"

Dan hung his head.

"Oh, Martha," he pleaded, "can't you realize how terrible it is to keep a good dog down?"

"Who offered to buy Timmy?"

"Mr. Fletcher, the owner of Colonel Dorsey."

"Tell him to go chase himself," Martha suggested slangily. "If you expect to make your peace with me, Dan Pelly, you'll give up all idea of selling Timmy."

"But Martha—seven thousand five hundred dollars! Think what it means to you. No more worry about our old age, everything settled fine and dandy at last after twenty-five years of hard luck."

"Do you really want to sell Timmy, Dan?"

"No, Martha, I don't. It'd break my heart. Bu-bu-but—I'll do it for your sake."

"Dan, come here."

Dan came and flopped awkwardly on his old knees while Martha's arms went around him.

"Sweet old Dan," she whispered. "What a glorious holiday you two have had! I've been so happy just realizing how happy you have been. Dan!"

"Yes, Martha."

"Perhaps we can get back into the dog business again. Don't you think you'd like to buy about half a dozen really fine brood bitches? Timmy's puppies would be spoken for before they were born. The least we could get would be a hundred dollars each for them." She stroked his old head. "I'm afraid, Dan, it's too late to reform you. Once a dog man, always a dog man—"

What else she intended to say remained forever unsaid, for little, weak, foolish, sentimental old Dan commenced to sniffle, as he had the night old Keepsake was poisoned. He wasn't a worldly man or a very ambitious man; he craved but little here below, but one of the things he craved was clean sportsmanship and love and understanding and a small, neat, field type English setter that would be just a little bit better than the other fellow's. And tonight he was so filled with happiness he just naturally overflowed. Tiny Tim, observing that something was wrong, came and leaned his shoulder against Martha's knee and laid his muzzle in her hand and rested it there. It was a big moment!

28

The Hound of the Baskervilles

by Arthur Conan Doyle

If you've never read this Sherlock Holmes tale, the two chapters excerpted from the novel here might pull you into reading the complete book. The full novel is not very long and has always been considered a Holmes masterpiece. There are no cuddly and warm dogs here. The tale takes us into uncomfortable dimensions of the world of dogs, with the lead dog character roaming dark and mysterious English moors and keeping the local gentry in total fright. The analytical genius of Holmes connects him with dogs in the first chapter, then takes him into a great dog legend in the second chapter. We're betting you'll be gripped by the beginning of a legendary story and want to read the entire book.

MR. SHERLOCK HOLMES, WHO WAS USUALLY VERY LATE IN THE MORNings, save upon those not infrequent occasions when he was up all night, was seated at the breakfast table. I stood upon the hearth-rug and picked up the stick which our visitor had left behind him the night before. It was a fine, thick piece of wood, bulbous-headed, of the sort which is known as a "Penang lawyer." Just under the head was a broad silver band nearly an inch across. "To James Mortimer, M.R.C.S., from his friends of the C.C.H.," was engraved upon it, with the date "1884." It was just such a stick as the old-fashioned family practitioner used to carry—dignified, solid, and reassuring.

"Well, Watson, what do you make of it?"

Holmes was sitting with his back to me, and I had given him no sign of my occupation.

"How did you know what I was doing? I believe you have eyes in the back of your head."

"I have, at least, a well-polished, silver-plated coffee-pot in front of me," said he. "But, tell me, Watson, what do you make of our visitor's stick? Since we have been so unfortunate as to miss him and have no notion of his errand, this accidental souvenir becomes of importance. Let me hear you reconstruct the man by an examination of it."

"I think," said I, following as far as I could the methods of my companion, "that Dr. Mortimer is a successful, elderly medical man, well-esteemed since those who know him give him this mark of their appreciation."

"Good!" said Holmes. "Excellent!"

"I think also that the probability is in favour of his being a country practitioner who does a great deal of his visiting on foot."

"Why so?"

"Because this stick, though originally a very handsome one, has been so knocked about that I can hardly imagine a town practitioner carrying it. The thick-iron ferrule is worn down, so it is evident that he has done a great amount of walking with it."

"Perfectly sound!" said Holmes.

"And then again, there is the 'friends of the C.C.H.' I should guess that to be the Something Hunt, the local hunt to whose members he has possibly given some surgical assistance, and which has made him a small presentation in return."

"Really, Watson, you excel yourself," said Holmes, pushing back his chair and lighting a cigarette. "I am bound to say that in all the accounts which you have been so good as to give of my own small achievements you have habitually underrated your own abilities. It may be that you are not yourself luminous, but you are a conductor of light. Some people without possessing genius have a remarkable power of stimulating it. I confess, my dear fellow, that I am very much in your debt."

He had never said as much before, and I must admit that his words gave me keen pleasure, for I had often been piqued by his indifference to my admiration and to the attempts which I had made to give publicity to his methods. I was proud, too, to think that I had so far mastered his system as to apply it in a way which earned his approval. He now took the stick from my hands and examined it for a few minutes with his naked eyes. Then with an expression of interest he laid down his cigarette, and carrying the cane to the window, he looked over it again with a convex lens.

"Interesting, though elementary," said he as he returned to his favourite corner of the settee. "There are certainly one or two indications upon the stick. It gives us the basis for several deductions."

"Has anything escaped me?" I asked with some self-importance. "I trust that there is nothing of consequence which I have overlooked?"

"I am afraid, my dear Watson, that most of your conclusions were erroneous. When I said that you stimulated me I meant, to be frank, that in noting your fallacies I was occasionally guided towards the truth. Not that you are entirely wrong in this instance. The man is certainly a country practitioner. And he walks a good deal."

"Then I was right."

"To that extent."

"But that was all."

"No, no, my dear Watson, not all—by no means all. I would suggest, for example, that a presentation to a doctor is more likely to come from a hospital than from a hunt, and that when the initials 'C.C.' are placed before that hospital the words 'Charing Cross' very naturally suggest themselves."

"You may be right."

"The probability lies in that direction. And if we take this as a working hypothesis we have a fresh basis from which to start our construction of this unknown visitor."

"Well, then, supposing that 'C.C.H.' does stand for 'Charing Cross Hospital,' what further inferences may we draw?"

"Do none suggest themselves? You know my methods. Apply them!"

"I can only think of the obvious conclusion that the man has practised in town before going to the country."

"I think that we might venture a little farther than this. Look at it in this light. On what occasion would it be most probable that such a presentation would be made? When would his friends unite to give him a pledge of their good will? Obviously at the moment when Dr. Mortimer withdrew from the service of the hospital in order to start a practice for himself. We know there has been a presentation. We believe there has been a change from a town hospital to a country practice. Is it, then, stretching our inference too far to say that the presentation was on the occasion of the change?"

"It certainly seems probable."

"Now, you will observe that he could not have been on the *staff* of the hospital, since only a man well-established in a London practice could hold such a position, and such a one would not drift into the country. What was he, then? If he was in the hospital and yet not on the staff he could only have been a house-surgeon or a house-physician—little more than a senior student. And he left five years ago—the date is on the stick. So your grave, middle-aged family practitioner vanishes into thin air, my dear Watson, and there emerges a young fellow under thirty, amiable, unambitious, absent-minded, and the possessor of a favourite dog, which I should describe roughly as being larger than a terrier and smaller than a mastiff."

I laughed incredulously as Sherlock Holmes leaned back in his settee and blew little wavering rings of smoke up to the ceiling.

"As to the latter part, I have no means of checking you," said I, "but at least it is not difficult to find out a few particulars about the man's age and professional career." From my small medical shelf I took down the Medical Directory and turned up the name. There were several Mortimers, but only one who could be our visitor. I read his record aloud.

"Mortimer, James, M.R.C.S., 1882, Grimpen, Dartmoor, Devon. House-surgeon, from 1882 to 1884, at Charing Cross Hospital. Winner of the Jackson prize for Comparative Pathology, with essay entitled 'Is

Disease a Reversion?' Corresponding member of the Swedish Pathological Society. Author of 'Some Freaks of Atavism' (*Lancet* 1882). 'Do We Progress?' (*Journal of Psychology*, March, 1883). Medical Officer for the parishes of Grimpen, Thorsley, and High Barrow."

"No mention of that local hunt, Watson," said Holmes with a mischievous smile, "but a country doctor, as you very astutely observed. I think that I am fairly justified in my inferences. As to the adjectives, I said, if I remember right, amiable, unambitious, and absent-minded. It is my experience that it is only an amiable man in this world who receives testimonials, only an unambitious one who abandons a London career for the country, and only an absent-minded one who leaves his stick and not his visiting-card after waiting an hour in your room."

"And the dog?"

"Has been in the habit of carrying this stick behind his master. Being a heavy stick the dog has held it tightly by the middle, and the marks of his teeth are very plainly visible. The dog's jaw, as shown in the space between these marks, is too broad in my opinion for a terrier and not broad enough for a mastiff. It may have been—yes, by Jove, it is a curly-haired spaniel."

He had risen and paced the room as he spoke. Now he halted in the recess of the window. There was such a ring of conviction in his voice that I glanced up in surprise.

"My dear fellow, how can you possibly be so sure of that?"

"For the very simple reason that I see the dog himself on our very door-step, and there is the ring of its owner. Don't move, I beg you, Watson. He is a professional brother of yours, and your presence may be of assistance to me. Now is the dramatic moment of fate, Watson, when you hear a step upon the stair which is walking into your life, and you know not whether for good or ill. What does Dr. James Mortimer, the man of science, ask of Sherlock Holmes, the specialist in crime? Come in!"

The appearance of our visitor was a surprise to me, since I had expected a typical country practitioner. He was a very tall, thin man, with a long nose like a beak, which jutted out between two keen, grey eyes, set closely together and sparkling brightly from behind a pair of gold-rimmed glasses. He was clad in a professional but rather slovenly fashion, for his frock-coat was dingy and his trousers frayed. Though young, his long back was already bowed, and he walked with a forward thrust of his head and a general air of peering benevolence. As he entered his eyes fell upon the stick in Holmes's hand, and he ran towards it with an exclamation of joy. "I am so very glad," said he. "I was not sure whether I had left it here or in the Shipping Office. I would not lose that stick for the world."

"A presentation, I see," said Holmes.

"Yes, sir."

"From Charing Cross Hospital?"

"From one or two friends there on the occasion of my marriage."

"Dear, dear, that's bad!" said Holmes, shaking his head.

Dr. Mortimer blinked through his glasses in mild astonishment. "Why was it bad?"

"Only that you have disarranged our little deductions. Your marriage, you say?"

"Yes, sir. I married, and so left the hospital, and with it all hopes of a consulting practice. It was necessary to make a home of my own."

"Come, come, we are not so far wrong, after all," said Holmes. "And now, Dr. James Mortimer—"

"Mister, sir, Mister—a humble M.R.C.S."

"And a man of precise mind, evidently."

"A dabbler in science, Mr. Holmes, a picker up of shells on the shores of the great unknown ocean. I presume that it is Mr. Sherlock Holmes whom I am addressing and not—"

"No, this is my friend Dr. Watson."

"Glad to meet you, sir. I have heard your name mentioned in connection with that of your friend. You interest me very much, Mr. Holmes. I had hardly expected so dolichocephalic a skull or such well-marked supra-orbital development. Would you have any objection to my running my finger along your parietal fissure? A cast of your skull, sir, until the original is available, would be an ornament to any anthropological museum. It is not my intention to be fulsome, but I confess that I covet your skull."

Sherlock Holmes waved our strange visitor into a chair. "You are an enthusiast in your line of thought, I perceive, sir, as I am in mine," said he. "I observe from your forefinger that you make your own cigarettes. Have no hesitation in lighting one."

The man drew out paper and tobacco and twirled the one up in the other with surprising dexterity. He had long, quivering fingers as agile and restless as the antennæ of an insect.

Holmes was silent, but his little darting glances showed me the interest which he took in our curious companion. "I presume, sir," said he at last, "that it was not merely for the purpose of examining my skull that you have done me the honour to call here last night and again today?"

"No, sir, no; though I am happy to have had the opportunity of doing that as well. I came to you, Mr. Holmes, because I recognized that I am myself an unpractical man and because I am suddenly confronted with a most serious and extraordinary problem. Recognizing, as I do, that you are the second highest expert in Europe—"

"Indeed, sir! May I inquire who has the honour to be the first?" asked Holmes with some asperity.

"To the man of precisely scientific mind the work of Monsieur Bertillon must always appeal strongly."

"Then had you not better consult him?"

"I said, sir, to the precisely scientific mind. But as a practical man of affairs it is acknowledged that you stand alone. I trust, sir, that I have not inadvertently—"

"Just a little," said Holmes. "I think, Dr. Mortimer, you would do wisely if without more ado you would kindly tell me plainly what the exact nature of the problem is in which you demand my assistance."

"I have in my pocket a manuscript," said Dr. James Mortimer.

"I observed it as you entered the room," said Holmes.

"It is an old manuscript."

"Early eighteenth century, unless it is a forgery."

"How can you say that, sir?"

"You have presented an inch or two of it to my examination all the time that you have been talking. It would be a poor expert who could not give the date of a document within a decade or so. You may possibly have read my little monograph upon the subject. I put that at 1730."

"The exact date is 1742." Dr. Mortimer drew it from his breast-pocket. "This family paper was committed to my care by Sir Charles Baskerville, whose sudden and tragic death some three months ago created so much excitement in Devonshire. I may say that I was his personal friend as well as his medical attendant. He was a strong-minded man, sir, shrewd, practical, and as unimaginative as I am myself. Yet he took this document very seriously, and his mind was prepared for just such an end as did eventually overtake him."

Holmes stretched out his hand for the manuscript and flattened it upon his knee. "You will observe, Watson, the alternative use of the long *s* and the short. It is one of several indications which enabled me to fix the date."

I looked over his shoulder at the yellow paper and the faded script. At the head was written: "Baskerville Hall," and below in large, scrawling figures: "1742."

"It appears to be a statement of some sort."

"Yes, it is a statement of a certain legend which runs in the Baskerville family."

"But I understand that it is something more modern and practical upon which you wish to consult me?"

"Most modern. A most practical, pressing matter, which must be decided within twenty-four hours. But the manuscript is short and is intimately connected with the affair. With your permission I will read it to you."

Holmes leaned back in his chair, placed his finger-tips together, and closed his eyes with an air of resignation. Dr. Mortimer turned the manuscript to the light and read in a high, cracking voice the following curious, old-world narrative:

"Of the origin of the Hound of the Baskervilles there have been many statements, yet as I come in a direct line from Hugo Baskerville, and as I had the story from my father, who also had it from his, I have set it down with all belief that it occurred even as is here set forth. And I would have you believe, my sons, that the same Justice which punishes sin may also most graciously forgive it, and that no ban is so heavy but that by prayer and repentance it may be removed. Learn then from this story not to fear the fruits of the past, but rather to be circumspect in the future, that those foul passions whereby our family has suffered so grievously may not again be loosed to our undoing.

"Know then that in the time of the Great Rebellion (the history of which by the learned Lord Clarendon I most earnestly commend to your attention) this Manor of Baskerville was held by Hugo of that name, nor can it be gainsaid that he was a most wild, profane, and godless man. This, in truth, his neighbours might have pardoned, seeing that saints have never flourished in those parts, but there was in him a certain wanton and cruel humour which made his name a by-word through the West. It chanced that this Hugo came to love (if, indeed, so dark a passion may be known under so bright a name) the daughter of a yeoman who held lands near the Baskerville estate. But the young maiden, being discreet and of good repute, would ever avoid him, for she feared his evil name. So it came to pass that one Michaelmas this Hugo, with five or six of his idle and wicked companions, stole down upon the farm and carried off the maiden, her father and brothers being from home, as he well knew. When they had brought her to the Hall the maiden was placed in an upper chamber, while Hugo and his friends sat down to a long carouse, as was their nightly custom. Now, the poor lass upstairs was like to have her wits turned at the singing and shouting and terrible oaths which came up to her from below, for they say that the words used by Hugo Baskerville, when he was in wine, were such as might blast the man who said them. At last in the stress of her fear she did that which might have daunted the bravest or most active man, for by the aid of the growth of ivy which cov-ered (and still covers) the south wall she came down from under the eaves, and so homeward across the moor, there being three leagues betwixt the Hall and her father's farm.

"It chanced that some little time later Hugo left his guests to carry food and drink—with other worse things, perchance—to his captive, and so found the cage empty and the bird escaped. Then, as it would seem, he became as one that hath a devil, for, rushing down the stairs into the dining-hall, he sprang upon the great table, flagons and trenchers flying before him, and he cried aloud before all the company that he would that very night render his body and soul to the Powers of Evil if he might but overtake the wench. And while the revellers stood aghast at the fury of the man, one more wicked or, it may be, more drunken than the rest, cried out that they should put the hounds upon her. Whereat Hugo ran from the house, crying to his grooms that they should saddle his mare and unkennel the pack, and giving the hounds a kerchief of the maid's, he swung them to the line, and so off full cry in the moonlight over the moor.

"Now, for some space the revellers stood agape, unable to understand all that had been done in such haste. But anon their bemused wits awoke to the nature of the deed which was like to be done upon the moorlands. Everything was now in an uproar, some calling for their pistols, some for their horses, and some for another flask of wine. But at length some sense came back to their crazed minds, and the whole of them, thirteen in number, took horse and started in pursuit. The moon shone clear above them, and they rode swiftly abreast, taking that course which the maid must needs have taken if she were to reach her own home.

"They had gone a mile or two when they passed one of the night shepherds upon the moorlands, and they cried to him to know if he had seen the hunt. And the man, as the story goes, was so crazed with fear that he could scarce speak, but at last he said that he had indeed seen the unhappy maiden, with the hounds upon her track. 'But I have seen more than that,' said he, 'for Hugo Baskerville passed me upon his black mare, and there ran mute behind him such a hound of hell as God forbid should ever be at my heels.' So the drunken squires cursed the shepherd and rode onward. But soon their skins turned cold, for there came a galloping across the moor, and the black mare, dabbled with white froth, went past with trailing bridle and empty saddle. Then the revellers rode close together, for a great fear was on them, but they still followed over the moor, though each, had he been alone, would have been right glad to have turned his horse's head. Riding slowly in this fashion they came at last upon the hounds. These, though known for their valour and their breed, were whimpering in a cluster at the head of a deep dip or goyal, as we call it, upon the moor, some slinking away and some, with starting hackles and staring eyes, gazing down the narrow valley before them.

"The company had come to a halt, more sober men, as you may guess, than when they started. The most of them would by no means advance, but three of them, the boldest, or it may be the most drunken, rode forward down the goyal. Now, it opened into a broad space in which stood two of those great stones, still to be seen there, which were set by certain forgotten peoples in the days of old. The moon was shining bright upon the clearing, and there in the centre lay the unhappy maid where she had fallen, dead of fear and of fatigue. But it was not the sight of her body, nor yet was it that of the body of Hugo Baskerville lying near her, which raised the hair upon the heads of these three dare-devil roysterers, but it was that, standing over Hugo, and plucking at his throat, there stood a foul thing, a great, black beast, shaped like a hound, yet larger than any hound that ever mortal eye has rested upon. And even as they looked the thing tore the throat out of Hugo Baskerville, on which, as it turned its blazing eyes and dripping jaws upon them, the three shrieked with fear and rode for dear life, still screaming, across the moor. One, it is said, died that very night of what he had seen, and the other twain were but broken men for the rest of their days.

"Such is the tale, my sons, of the coming of the hound which is said to have plagued the family so sorely ever since. If I have set it down it is because that which is clearly known hath less terror than that which is but hinted at and guessed. Nor can it be denied that many of the family have been unhappy in their deaths, which have been sudden, bloody, and mysterious. Yet may we shelter ourselves in the infinite goodness of Providence, which would not forever punish the innocent beyond that third or fourth generation which is threatened in Holy Writ. To that Providence, my sons, I hereby commend you, and I counsel you by way of caution to forbear from crossing the moor in those dark hours when the powers of evil are exalted.

"[This from Hugo Baskerville to his sons Rodger and John, with instructions that they say nothing thereof to their sister Elizabeth.]"

When Dr. Mortimer had finished reading this singular narrative he pushed his spectacles up on his forehead and stared across at Mr. Sherlock Holmes. The latter yawned and tossed the end of his cigarette into the fire.

"Well?" said he.

"Do you not find it interesting?"

"To a collector of fairy tales."

Dr. Mortimer drew a folded newspaper out of his pocket.

"Now, Mr. Holmes, we will give you something a little more recent. This is the *Devon County Chronicle* of May 14th of this year. It is a short account of the facts elicited at the death of Sir Charles Baskerville which occurred a few days before that date."

My friend leaned a little forward and his expression became intent. Our visitor readjusted his glasses and began:

"The recent sudden death of Sir Charles Baskerville, whose name has been mentioned as the probable Liberal candidate for Mid-Devon at the next election, has cast a gloom over the county. Though Sir Charles had resided at Baskerville Hall for a comparatively short period, his amiability of character and extreme generosity had won the affection and respect of all who had been brought into contact with him. In these days of *nouveaux riches* it is refreshing to find a case where the scion of an old county family which has fallen upon evil days is able to make his own fortune and to bring it back with him to restore the fallen grandeur of his line. Sir Charles, as is well known, made large sums of money in South African speculation. More wise than those who go on until the wheel turns against them, he realised his gains and returned to England with them. It is only two years since he took up his residence at Baskerville Hall, and it is common talk how large were those schemes of reconstruction and improvement which have been interrupted by his death. Being himself childless, it was his openly expressed desire that the whole countryside should, within his own lifetime, profit by his good fortune, and many will have personal reasons for bewailing his untimely end. His generous donations to local and county charities have been frequently chronicled in these columns.

"The circumstances connected with the death of Sir Charles cannot be said to have been entirely cleared up by the inquest, but at least enough has been done to dispose of those rumours to which local superstition has given rise. There is no reason whatever to suspect foul play, or to imagine that death could be from any but natural causes. Sir Charles was a widower, and a man who may be said to have been in some ways of an eccentric habit of mind. In spite of his considerable wealth he was simple in his personal tastes, and his indoor servants at Baskerville Hall consisted of a married couple named Barrymore, the husband acting as butler and the wife as housekeeper. Their evidence, corroborated by that of several friends, tends to show that Sir Charles's health has for some time been impaired, and points especially to some affection of the heart, manifesting itself in changes of colour, breathlessness, and acute attacks of nervous depression. Dr. James Mortimer, the friend and medical attendant of the deceased, has given evidence to the same effect.

"The facts of the case are simple. Sir Charles Baskerville was in the habit every night before going to bed of walking down the famous yew alley of Baskerville Hall. The evidence of the Barrymores shows that this had been his custom. On the fourth of May Sir Charles had declared his intention of starting next day for London, and had ordered Barrymore to prepare his luggage. That night he went out as usual for his nocturnal walk, in the course of which he was in the habit of smoking a cigar. He never returned. At twelve o'clock Barrymore, finding the hall door still open, became alarmed, and, lighting a lantern, went in search of his master. The day had been wet, and Sir Charles's footmarks were easily traced down the alley. Halfway down this walk there is a gate which leads out on to the moor. There were indications that Sir Charles had stood for some little time here. He then proceeded down the alley, and it was at the far end of it that his body was discovered. One fact which has not been explained is the statement of Barrymore that his master's footprints altered their character from the time that he passed the moor-gate, and that he appeared from thence onward to have been walking upon his toes. One Murphy, a Romani horse-dealer, was on the moor at no great distance at the time, but he appears by his own confession to have been the worse for drink. He declares that he heard cries but is unable to state from what direction they came. No signs of violence were to be discovered upon Sir Charles's person, and though the doctor's evidence pointed to an almost incredible facial distortion—so great that Dr. Mortimer refused at first to believe that it was indeed his friend and patient who lay before him—it was explained that that is a symptom which is not unusual in cases of dyspnœa and death from cardiac exhaustion. This explanation was borne out by the post-mortem examination, which showed long-standing organic disease, and the coroner's jury returned a verdict in accordance with the medical evidence. It is well that this is so, for it is obviously of the utmost importance that Sir Charles's heir should settle at the Hall and continue the good work which has been so sadly interrupted. Had the prosaic finding of the coroner not finally put an end to the romantic stories which have been whispered in connection with the affair, it might have been difficult to find a tenant for Baskerville Hall. It is understood that the next of kin is Mr. Henry Baskerville, if he be still alive, the son of Sir Charles Baskerville's younger brother. The young man when last heard of was in America, and inquiries are being instituted with a view to informing him of his good fortune."

Dr. Mortimer refolded his paper and replaced it in his pocket. "Those are the public facts, Mr. Holmes, in connection with the death of Sir Charles Baskerville."

"I must thank you," said Sherlock Holmes, "for calling my attention to a case which certainly presents some features of interest. I had observed some newspaper comment at the time, but I was exceedingly preoccupied by that little affair of the Vatican cameos, and in my anxiety to oblige the Pope I lost touch with several interesting English cases. This article, you say, contains all the public facts?"

"It does."

"Then let me have the private ones." He leaned back, put his finger-tips together, and assumed his most impassive and judicial expression.

"In doing so," said Dr. Mortimer, who had begun to show signs of some strong emotion, "I am telling that which I have not confided to anyone. My motive for withholding it from the coroner's inquiry is that a man of science shrinks from placing himself in the public position of seeming to indorse a popular superstition. I had the further motive that Baskerville Hall, as the paper says, would certainly remain untenanted if anything were done to increase its already rather grim reputation. For both these reasons I thought that I was justified in telling rather less than I knew, since no practical good could result from it, but with you there is no reason why I should not be perfectly frank.

"The moor is very sparsely inhabited, and those who live near each other are thrown very much together. For this reason I saw a good deal of Sir Charles Baskerville. With the exception of Mr. Frankland, of Lafter Hall, and Mr. Stapleton, the naturalist, there are no other men of education within many miles. Sir Charles was a retiring man, but the chance of his illness brought us together, and a community of interests in science kept us so. He had brought back much scientific information from South Africa, and many a charming evening we have spent together discussing the comparative anatomy of the Bushman and the Hottentot.

"Within the last few months it became increasingly plain to me that Sir Charles's nervous system was strained to the breaking point. He had taken this legend which I have read you exceedingly to heart—so much so that, although he would walk in his own grounds, nothing would induce him to go out upon the moor at night. Incredible as it may appear to you, Mr. Holmes, he was honestly convinced that a dreadful fate overhung his family, and certainly the records which he was able to give of his ancestors were not encouraging. The idea of some ghastly presence constantly haunted him, and on more than one occasion he has asked me whether I had on my medical journeys at night ever seen any strange creature or heard the baying of a hound. The latter question he put to me several times, and always with a voice which vibrated with excitement.

"I can well remember driving up to his house in the evening some three weeks before the fatal event. He chanced to be at his hall door. I had descended from my gig and was standing in front of him, when I saw his eyes fix themselves over my shoulder and stare past me with an expression of the most dreadful horror. I whisked round and had just time to catch a glimpse of something which I took to be a large black calf passing at the head of the drive. So excited and alarmed was he that I was compelled to go down to the spot where the animal had been and look around for it. It was gone, however, and the incident appeared to make the worst impression upon his mind. I stayed with him all the evening, and it was on that occasion, to explain the emotion which he had shown, that he confided to my keeping that narrative which I read to you when first I came. I mention this small episode because it assumes some importance in view of the tragedy which followed, but I was convinced at the time that the matter was entirely trivial and that his excitement had no justification.

"It was at my advice that Sir Charles was about to go to London. His heart was, I knew, affected, and the constant anxiety in which he lived, however chimerical the cause of it might be, was evidently having a serious effect upon his health. I thought that a few months among the distractions of town would send him back a new man. Mr. Stapleton, a mutual friend who was much concerned at his state of health, was of the same opinion. At the last instant came this terrible catastrophe.

"On the night of Sir Charles's death Barrymore the butler, who made the discovery, sent Perkins the groom on horseback to me, and as I was sitting up late I was able to reach Baskerville Hall within an hour of the event. I checked and corroborated all the facts which were mentioned at the inquest. I followed the footsteps down the yew alley, I saw the spot at the moor-gate where he seemed to have waited, I remarked the change in the shape of the prints after that point, I noted that there were no other footsteps save those of Barrymore on the soft gravel, and finally I carefully examined the body, which had not been touched until my arrival. Sir Charles lay on his face, his arms out, his fingers dug into the ground, and his features convulsed with some strong emotion to such an extent that I could hardly have sworn to his identity. There was certainly no physical injury of any kind. But one false statement was made by Barrymore at the inquest. He said that there were no traces upon the ground round the body. He did not observe any. But I did—some little distance off, but fresh and clear."

"Footprints?"

"Footprints."

"A man's or a woman's?"

Dr. Mortimer looked strangely at us for an instant, and his voice sank almost to a whisper as he answered.

"Mr. Holmes, they were the footprints of a gigantic hound!"

29

My Doggie and I

by R. M. Ballantyne

*When forgotten dogs and elderly forgotten people come together, the
stage is set for drama and great sympathy.*

I POSSESS A DOGGIE—NOT A DOG, OBSERVE, BUT A DOGGIE. IF HE HAD
been a dog I would not have presumed to intrude him on your notice.
A dog is all very well in his way—one of the noblest of animals, I admit,
and pre-eminently fitted to be the companion of man, for he has an affectionate nature, which man demands, and a forgiving disposition, which
man needs—but a dog, with all his noble qualities, is not to be compared
to a doggie.

My doggie is unquestionably the most charming, and, in every way,
delightful doggie that ever was born. My sister has a baby, about which
she raves in somewhat similar terms, but of course that is ridiculous, for
her baby differs in no particular from ordinary babies, except, perhaps, in
the matter of violent weeping, of which it is fond; whereas my doggie is
unique, a perfectly beautiful and singular specimen of—of well, I won't
say what, because my friends usually laugh at me when I say it, and I don't
like to be laughed at.

Freely admit that you don't at once perceive the finer qualities, either
mental or physical, of my doggie, partly owing to the circumstance that
he is shapeless and hairy. The former quality is not prepossessing, while
the latter tends to veil the amiable expression of his countenance and the
lustre of his speaking eyes. But as you come to know him he grows upon

you; your feelings are touched, your affections stirred, and your love is finally evoked. As he resembles a door-mat, or rather a scrap of very ragged door-mat, and has an amiable spirit, I have called him "Dumps." I should not be surprised if you did not perceive any connection here. You are not the first who has failed to see it; I never saw it myself.

When I first met Dumps he was scurrying towards me along a sequestered country lane. It was in the Dog Days. Dust lay thick on the road; the creature's legs were remarkably short though active, and his hair being long he swept up the dust in clouds as he ran. He was yelping, and I observed that one or two stones appeared to be racing with, or after, him. The voice of an angry man also seemed to chase him, but the owner of the voice was at the moment concealed by a turn in the lane, which was bordered by high stone-walls.

Hydrophobia, of course, flashed into my mind. I grasped my stick and drew close to the wall. The hairy whirlwind, if I may so call it, came wildly on, but instead of passing me, or snapping at my legs as I had expected, it stopped and crawled towards me in a piteous, supplicating manner that at once disarmed me. If the creature had lain still, I should have been unable to distinguish its head from its tail; but as one end of him whined and the other wagged, I had no difficulty.

Stooping down with caution, I patted the end that whined, whereupon the end that wagged became violently demonstrative. Just then the owner of the voice came round the corner. He was a big, rough fellow, in ragged garments, and armed with a thick stick, which he seemed about to fling at the little dog, when I checked him with a shout—

"You'd better not, my man, unless you want your own head broken!"

You see I am a pretty well-sized man myself, and, as I felt confidence in my strength, my stick, and the goodness of my cause, I was bold.

"What d'you mean by ill-treating the little dog?" I demanded sternly, as I stepped up to the man.

"A cove may do as he likes with his own, mayn't he?" answered the man, with a sulky scowl.

"A 'cove' may do nothing of the sort," said I indignantly, for cruelty to dumb animals always has the effect of inclining me to fight, though I am naturally of a peaceable disposition. "There is an Act of Parliament," I continued, "which goes by the honoured name of Martin, and if you venture to infringe that Act I'll have you taken up and prosecuted."

While I was speaking I observed a peculiar leer on the man's face, which I could not account for. He appeared, however, to have been affected by my threats, for he ceased to scowl, and assumed a deferential air as he replied, "Vell, sir, it do seem raither 'ard that a cove should be blowed up for kindness."

"Kindness!" I exclaimed, in surprise.

"Ay, kindness, sir. That there hanimal loves me, it do, like a brother, an the love is mootooal. Ve've lived together now—off an' on—for the matter o' six months. Vell, I gits employment in a factory about fifteen miles from here, in which no dogs is allowed. In coorse, I can't throw up my sitivation, sir, can I? Neither can my doggie give up his master wot he's so fond of, so I'm obleeged to leave 'im in charge of a friend, with stric' orders to keep 'im locked up till I'm fairly gone. Vell, off I goes, but he manages to escape, an' runs arter me.

Now, wot can a feller do but drive 'im 'ome with sticks an' stones, though it do go to my 'eart to do it? But if he goes to the factory he's sure to be shot, or scragged, or drownded, or somethink; so you see, sir, it's out o' pure kindness I'm a peltin' of 'im."

Confess that I felt somewhat doubtful of the truth of this story; but, in order to prevent any expression of my face betraying me, I stooped and patted the dog while the man spoke. It received my attentions with evident delight. A thought suddenly flashed on me:—

"Will you sell your little dog?" I asked.

"Vy, sir," he replied, with some hesitation, "I don't quite like to do that. He's such a pure breed, and—and he's *so* fond o' me."

"But have you not told me that you are obliged to part with him?"

I thought the man looked puzzled for a moment, but only for a moment. Turning to me with a bland smile, he said, "Ah, sir, I that's just where it is. I am obleeged to part with him, but I ain't obleeged to sell him. If I on'y part with 'im, my friend keeps 'im for me, and we may meet again, but if I sell 'im, he's gone for ever! Don't you see? Hows'ever, if you wants 'im wery bad, I'll do it on one consideration."

"And that is?"

"That you'll be good to 'im."

I began to think I had misjudged the man.

"What's his name?" I asked.

Again for one moment there was that strange, puzzled look in the man's face, but it passed, and he turned with another of his bland smiles.

"His name, sir? Ah, his name? He ain't got no name, sir!"

"No name!" I exclaimed, in surprise.

"No, sir; I object to givin' dogs names on principle. It's too much like treatin' them as if they wos Christians; and, you know, they couldn't be Christians if they wanted to ever so much. Besides, wotever name you gives 'em, there must be so many other dogs with the same name, that you stand a chance o' the wrong dog comin' to 'e ven you calls."

"That's a strange reason. How then do you call him to you?"

"Vy, w'en I wants 'im I shouts 'Hi,' or 'Hallo,' or I vistles."

"Indeed," said I, somewhat amused by the humour of the fellow; "and what do you ask for him?"

"Fi' pun ten, an' he's dirt cheap at that," was the quick reply.

"Come, come, my man, you know the dog is not worth that."

"Not worth it, sir!" he replied, with an injured look; "I tell you he's cheap at that. Look at his breedin', and then think of his affectionate natur'. Is the affections to count for nuffin'?"

Admitted that the affections were worth money, though it was generally understood that they could not be purchased, but still objected to the price, until the man said in a confidential tone—

"Vell, come, sir, since you do express such a deal o' love for 'im, and promise to be so good to 'im, I'll make a sacrifice and let you 'ave 'im for three pun ten—come!"

I gave in, and walked off, with my purchase leaping joyfully at my heels.

The man chuckled a good deal after receiving the money, but I took no notice of that at the time, though I thought a good deal about it afterwards.

Ah! Little did I think, as Dumps and I walked home that day, of the depth of the attachment that was to spring up between us, the varied experiences of life we were destined to have together, and the important influence he was to exercise on my career.

Forgot to mention that my name is Mellon—John Mellon. Dumps knows my name as well as he knows his own.

On reaching home, Dumps displayed an evidence of good breeding, which convinced me that he could not have spent all his puppyhood in company with the man from whom I had bought him. He wiped his feet on the door-mat with great vigour before entering my house, and also refused to pass in until I led the way.

"Now, Dumps," said I, seating myself on the sofa in my solitary room (I was a bachelor at the time—a medical student, just on the point of completing my course), "come here, and let us have a talk."

To my surprise, the doggie came promptly forward, sat down on his hind-legs, and looked up into my face. I was touched by this display of ready confidence. A confiding nature has always been to me powerfully attractive, whether in child, cat, or dog. I brushed the shaggy hair from his face in order to see his eyes. They were moist, and intensely black. So was the point of his nose.

"You seem to be an affectionate doggie, Dumps."

A portion of hair—scarce worthy the name of tail—wagged as I spoke, and he attempted to lick my fingers, but I prevented this by patting his head. I have an unconquerable aversion to licking. Perhaps having received more than an average allowance, in another sense, at school, may account for my dislike to it—even from a dog!

"Now, Dumps," I continued, "you and I are to be good friends. I've bought you—for a pretty large sum too, let me tell you—from a man who, I am quite sure, treated you ill, and I intend to show you what good treatment is; but there are two things I mean to insist on, and it is well that we should understand each other at the outset of our united career. You must never bark at my friends—not even at my enemies—when they come to see me, and you must not beg at meals. D'you understand?"

The way in which that shaggy creature cocked its ears and turned its head from side to side slowly, and gazed with its lustrous eyes while I was speaking, went far to convince me it really did understand what I said. Of course it only wagged its rear tuft of hair in reply, and whimpered slightly.

I refer to its rear tuft advisedly, because, at a short distance, my doggie, when in repose, resembled an elongated and shapeless mass; but, when roused by a call or otherwise, three tufts of hair instantly sprang up—two at one end, and one at the other end—indicating his ears and tail. It was only by these signs that I could ascertain at any time his exact position.

I was about to continue my remarks to Dumps when the door opened and my landlady appeared bearing the dinner tray.

"Oh! I beg parding, sir," she said, drawing back, "I didn't 'ear your voice, sir, till the door was open, an' I thought you was alone, but I can come back a—"

"Come in, Mrs. Miff. There is nobody here but my little dog—one that I have just bought, a rather shaggy terrier—what do you think of him?"

"Do 'e bite, sir?" inquired Mrs. Miff, in some anxiety, as she passed round the table at a respectful distance from Dumps.

"I think not. He seems an amiable creature," said I, patting his head. "Do you ever bite, Dumps?"

"Well, sir, I never feel quite easy," rejoined Mrs. Miff in a doubtful tone, as she laid my cloth, with, as it were, one eye ever on the alert: "you never knows w'en these 'airy creatures is goin' to fly at you. If you could see their heyes you might 'ave a guess what they was a thinkin' of; an' then it is so orkard not knowin' w'ich end of the 'airy bundle is the bitin' end, you can't help bein' nervish a little."

Having finished laying the cloth, Mrs. Miff backed out of the room after the manner of attendants on royalty, overturning two chairs with her skirts as she went, and showing her full front to the enemy. But the enemy gave no sign, good or bad. All the tufts were down flat, and he stood motionless while Mrs. Miff retreated.

"Dumps, what do you think of Mrs. Miff?"

The doggie ran to me at once, and we engaged in a little further conversation until my landlady returned with the viands. To my surprise Dumps at once walked sedately to the hearth-rug, and lay down thereon, with his chin on his paws—at least I judged so from the attitude, for I could see neither chin nor paws.

This act I regarded as another evidence of good breeding. He was not a beggar, and, therefore, could not have spent his childhood with the man from whom I had bought him.

"I wish you could speak, Dumps," said I, laying down my knife and fork, when about half finished, and looking towards the hearth-rug.

One end of him rose a little, the other end wagged gently, but as I made no further remark, both ends subsided.

"Now, Dumps," said I, finishing my meal with a draught of water, which is my favourite beverage, "you must not suppose that you have got a greedy master; though I don't allow begging. There, sir, is your corner, where you shall always have the remnants of my dinner—come."

The dog did not move until I said "come." Then, with a quick rush he made for the plate, and very soon cleared it.

"Well, you *have* been well trained," said I, regarding him with interest; "such conduct is neither the result of instinct nor accident, and sure am I, the more I think of it, that the sulky fellow who sold you to me was not your tutor; but, as you can't speak, I shall never find out your history, so, Dumps, I'll dismiss the subject."

Saying this, I sat down to the newspaper with which I invariably solaced myself for half an hour after dinner, before going out on my afternoon rounds.

This was the manner in which my doggie and I began our acquaintance, and I have been thus particular in recounting the details, because they bear in a special manner on some of the most important events of my life.

Being, as already mentioned, a medical student, and having almost completed my course of study, I had undertaken to visit in one of the poorest districts in London—in the neighbourhood of Whitechapel; partly for the purpose of gaining experience in my profession, and partly for the sake of carrying the Word of Life—the knowledge of the Saviour—into some of the many homes where moral as well as physical disease is rife.

Leanings and inclinations are inherited not less than bodily peculiarities. My father had a particular tenderness for poor old women of the lowest class. So have I. When I see a bowed, aged, wrinkled, white-haired, feeble woman in rags and dirt, a gush of tender pity almost irresistibly inclines me to go and pat her head, sit down beside her, comfort her, and give her money. It matters not what her antecedents may have been. Worthy or unworthy, there she stands now, with age, helplessness, and a hopeless temporal future, pleading more eloquently in her behalf than could the tongue of man or angel. True, the same plea is equally applicable to poor old men, but, reader, I write not at present of principles so much as of feelings. *My* weakness is old women!

Accordingly, on my professional visiting list I had at that time a considerable number of these. One of them, who was uncommonly small, unusually miserable, and pathetically feeble, lay heavy on my spirit just then. She had a remarkably bad cold at the time, which betrayed itself chiefly in a frequent, but feeble, sneeze.

As I rose to go out, and looked at my doggie—who was, or seemed to be, asleep on the rug—a sudden thought occurred to me.

"That poor old creature," I muttered, "is very lonely in her garret; a little dog might comfort her. Perhaps—but no. Dumps, you are too lively for her, too bouncing. She would require something feeble and affectionate, like herself. Come, I'll think of that. So, my doggie, you shall keep watch here until I return."

Sources

"The Power of the Dog," by Rudyard Kipling, from *Actions and Reactions*, Doubleday, Page & Company, 1909.

"Lad—A Dog," by Albert Payson Terhune, from book of the same title, E. P. Dutton & Company, 1919.

"The Road to Tinkhamtown," by Corey Ford, from *Field & Stream* magazine, November 1970. Reprinted by permission of Dartmouth College Library.

"The Call of the Wild," by Jack London, from book of the same title, Macmillan Company, 1903.

"A Dark-Brown Dog," by Stephen Crane, from *Men, Women, and Boats*, 1920.

"Bingo," by Ernest Thompson Seton, from *Wild Animals I Have Known*, Charles Scribner's Sons, 1900.

"A Dog's Tale," by Mark Twain, from *Harper's Magazine*, December 1903.

"Beautiful Joe," by Marshall Saunders, from book of the same title, 1903.

"Stickeen," by John Muir, Atlantic Monthly Press, Inc., 1918.

"Homebodies," by Tom Hennessey, from *Feathers 'n Fins*, Amwell Press, 1989. Reprinted by permission of Nancy Hennessey.

"A Yellow Dog," by Bret Harte, from *Barker's Luck and Other Stories*, Houghton Mifflin, 1896.

"My Most Memorable Dog," by Archibald Rutledge, from *Bird Dog Days, Wingshooting Ways*, edited by Jim Casada, University of South Carolina Press, 2016. Reprinted by permission of Jim Casada.

"That Spot," by Jack London, from *Lost Face*, Mills & Boon Ltd., London, 1916.

"The Sunnybank Collies," by Albert Payson Terhune, from *Buff: A Collie and Other Dog Stories*, Grosset & Dunlap, 1921.

"The Lead Dog," by William Francis Butler, from *The Wild North Land*, Macmillan Co. of Canada, 1910.

"Uncle Dick's Rolf," by Georgiana Marion Craik, from *The Junior Classics*, Volume 8, edited by William Patten, P. F. Collier and Son, 1912.

"Ulysses and the Dogman," by O. Henry, from *Sixes and Sevens*, Doubleday, Page & Company, 1914.

"Brown Wolf," by Jack London, from *Brown Wolf and Other Jack London Stories*, Macmillan Company, 1920.

"Tito: The Story of the Coyote That Learned How," by Ernest Thompson Seton, from *Wild Animals I Have Known*, Charles Scribner's Sons, 1900.

"Scrap," by Lucia Chamberlain, from *The Junior Classics*, Volume 8, edited by William Patten, P. F. Collier and Son, 1912.

"Bruce," by Albert Payson Terhune, from book of the same title, E. P. Dutton & Company, 1920.

"How the Dog Tax Was Paid," by Sarah Knowles Bolton, from *A Country Idyll and Other Stories*, Thomas Crowell & Co., 1898.

"Dogs and Men," by Henry C. Merwin, from *Atlantic Classics*, Second Series, Atlantic Monthly Press, 1918.

"Show Time," by Walter A. Dyer, from *The Dogs of Boytown*, Henry Holt & Co., 1918.

"Douglas," by Sarah Knowles Bolton, from *A Country Idyll and Other Stories*, Thomas Crowell & Co., New York, 1898.

"The Amazing Letter-Writing Dog," by Christopher Morley, from *The Powder of Sympathy*, Doubleday, Page & Company, 1923.

"Point!" by Peter B. Kyne, from *My Story I Liked Best*, edited by Ray Long, International Magazine Co., 1925.

"The Hound of the Baskervilles," by Arthur Conan Doyle, from book of the same title, originally serialized in *Strand Magazine*, August 1901–April 1902.

"My Doggie and I," by R. M. Ballantyne, from book of the same title, 1881.